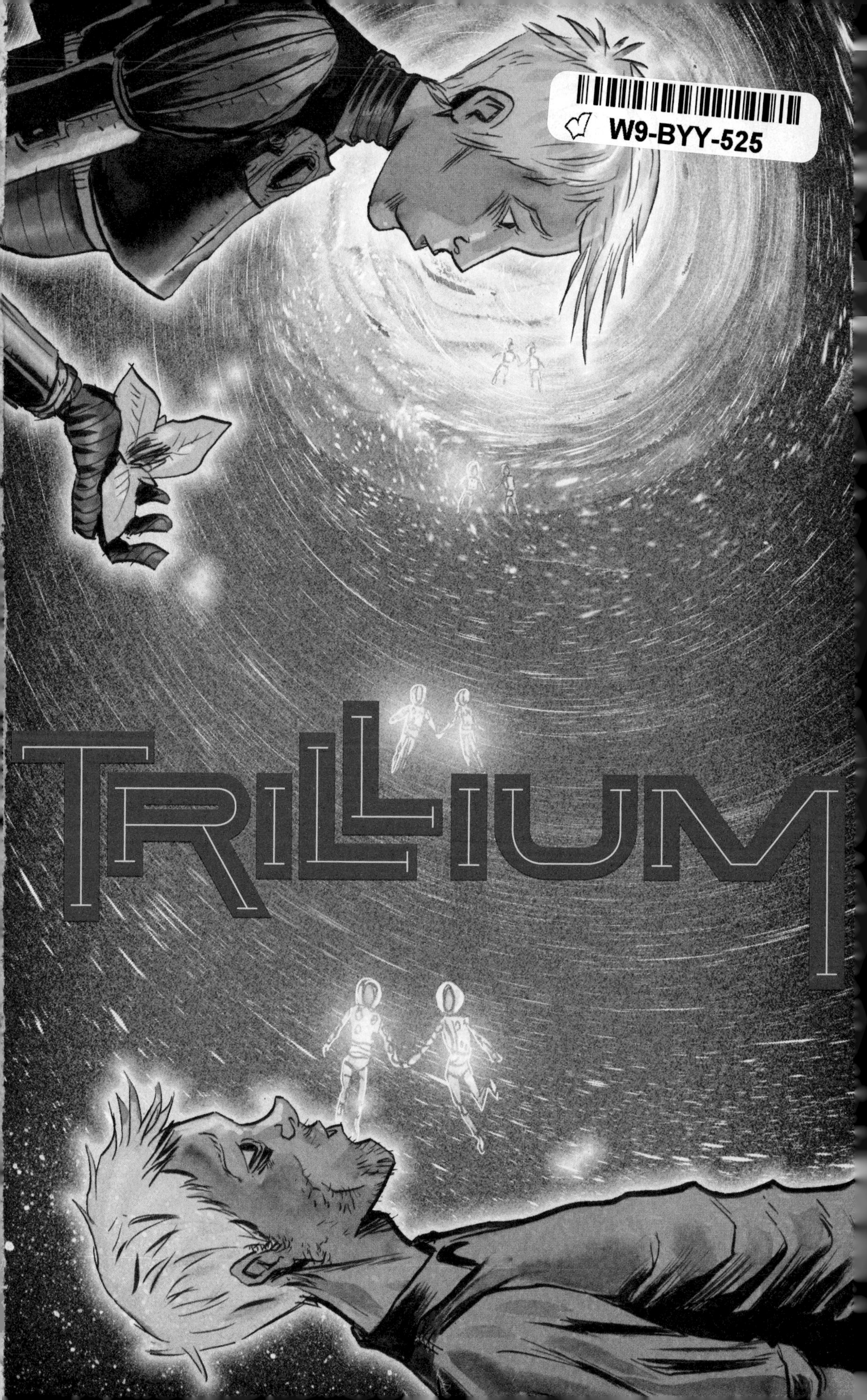
TRILLIUM

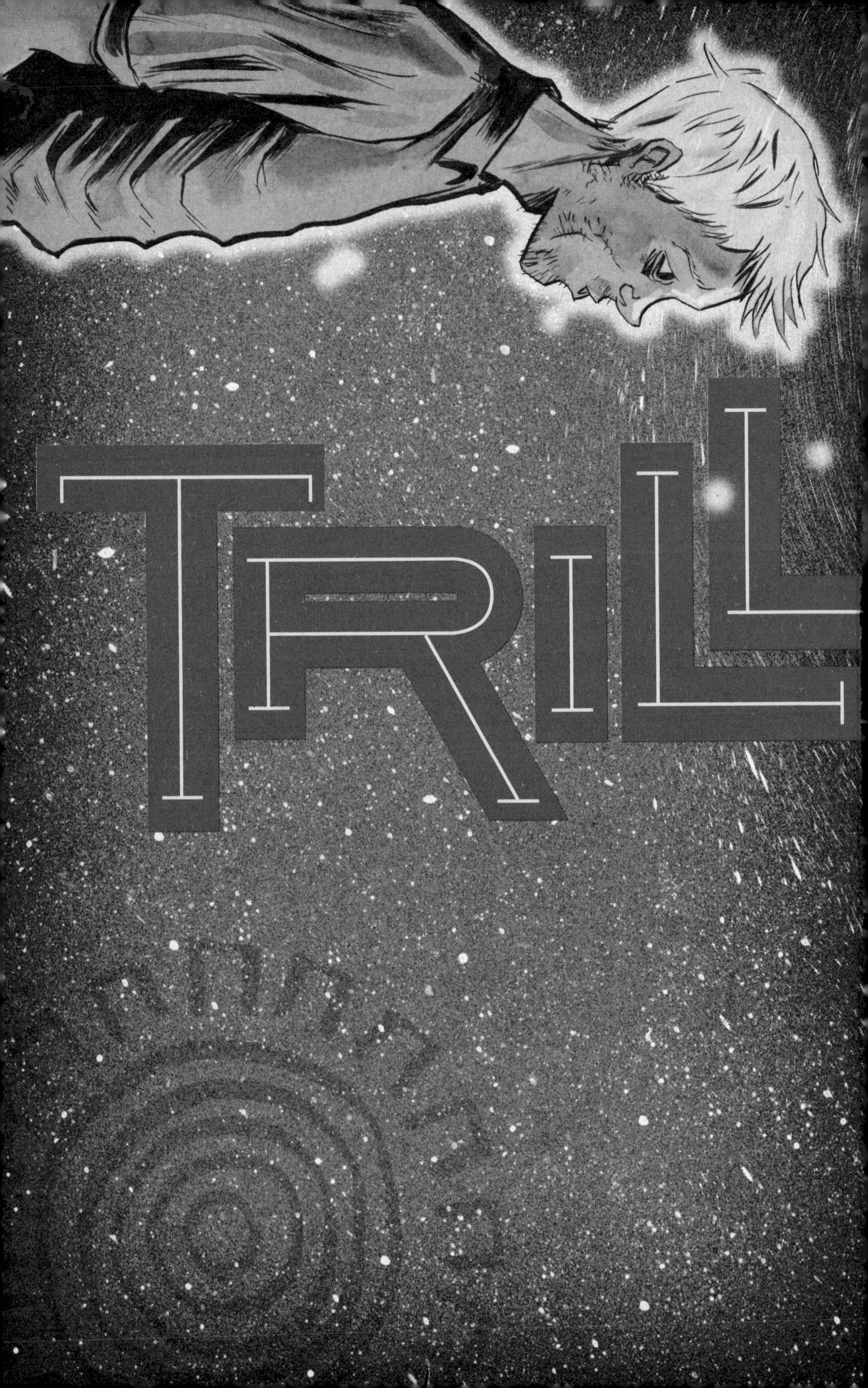
TRILL

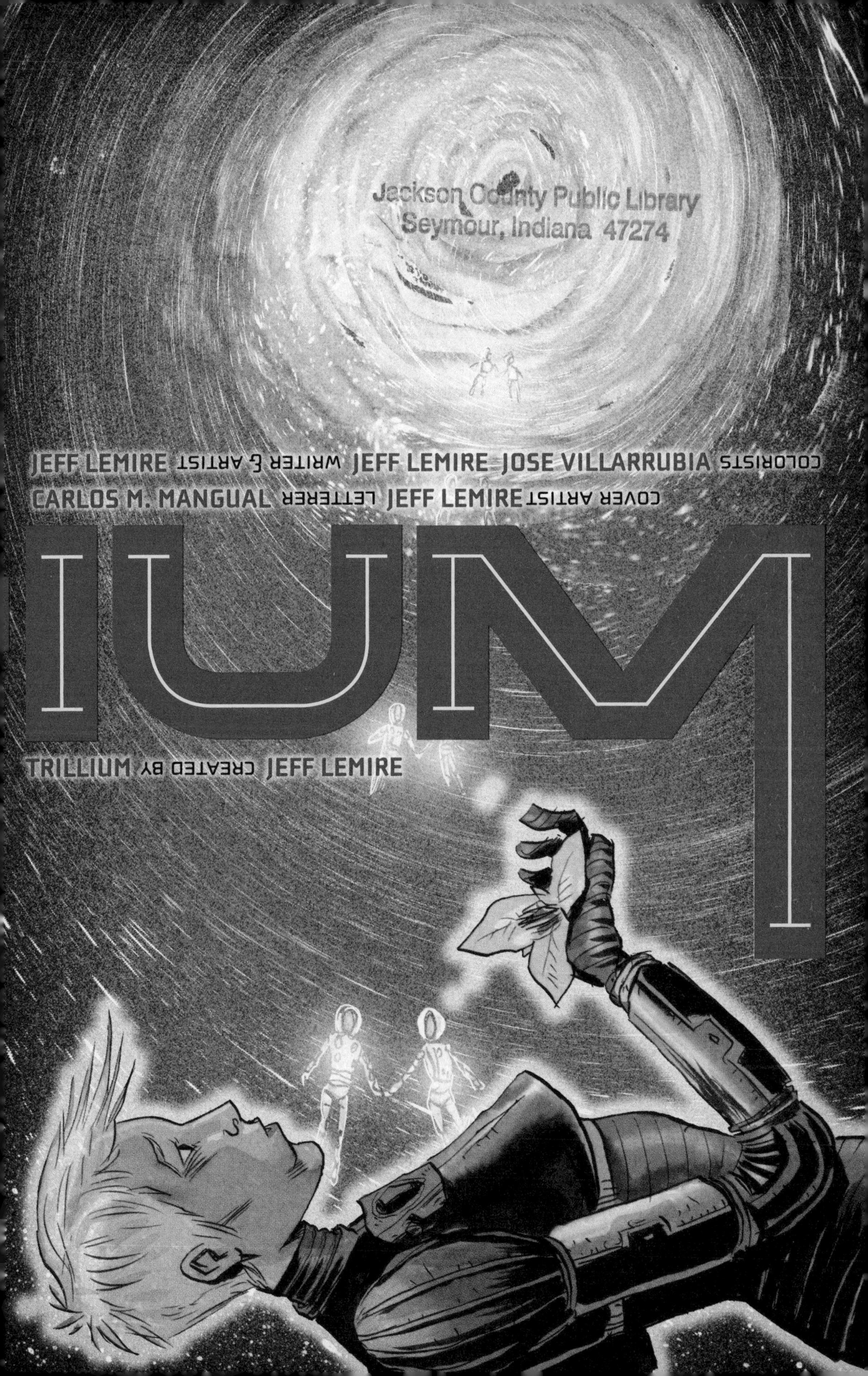

JEFF LEMIRE WRITER & ARTIST JEFF LEMIRE JOSE VILLARRUBIA COLORISTS
CARLOS M. MANGUAL LETTERER JEFF LEMIRE COVER ARTIST
IUM
TRILLIUM CREATED BY JEFF LEMIRE

Mark Doyle	Editor – Original Series
Sara Miller	Assistant Editor – Original Series
Rowena Yow	Editor
Robbin Brosterman	Design Director – Books
Damian Ryland	Publication Design

| Shelly Bond | Executive Editor – Vertigo |
| Hank Kanalz | Senior VP – Vertigo & Integrated Publishing |

Diane Nelson	President
Dan DiDio and Jim Lee	Co-Publishers
Geoff Johns	Chief Creative Officer
Amit Desai	Senior VP – Marketing & Franchise Management
Amy Genkins	Senior VP – Business & Legal Affairs
Nairi Gardiner	Senior VP – Finance
Jeff Boison	VP – Publishing Planning
Mark Chiarello	VP – Art Direction & Design
John Cunningham	VP – Marketing
Terri Cunningham	VP – Editorial Administration
Larry Ganem	VP – Talent Relations & Services
Alison Gill	Senior VP – Manufacturing & Operations
Jay Kogan	VP – Business & Legal Affairs, Publishing
Jack Mahan	VP – Business Affairs, Talent
Nick Napolitano	VP – Manufacturing Administration
Sue Pohja	VP – Book Sales
Fred Ruiz	VP – Manufacturing Operations
Courtney Simmons	Senior VP – Publicity
Bob Wayne	Senior VP – Sales

TRILLIUM

DC Comics
1700 Broadway, New York, NY 10019
A Warner Bros. Entertainment Company.
Printed in the USA. 7/4/14. First Printing.
ISBN: 978-1-4012-4900-7

Library of Congress Cataloging-in-Publication Data

Lemire, Jeff.
 Trillium / Jeff Lemire.
    pages cm
  ISBN 978-1-4012-4900-7 (paperback)
  1. Graphic novels. I. Title.
PN6733.L45T75 2014
741.5'973—dc23
                                    2014011939

SUSTAINABLE
FORESTRY
INITIATIVE

Certified Chain of Custody
Promoting Sustainable Forestry
www.sfiprogram.org
SFI-01042
APPLIES TO TEXT STOCK ONLY

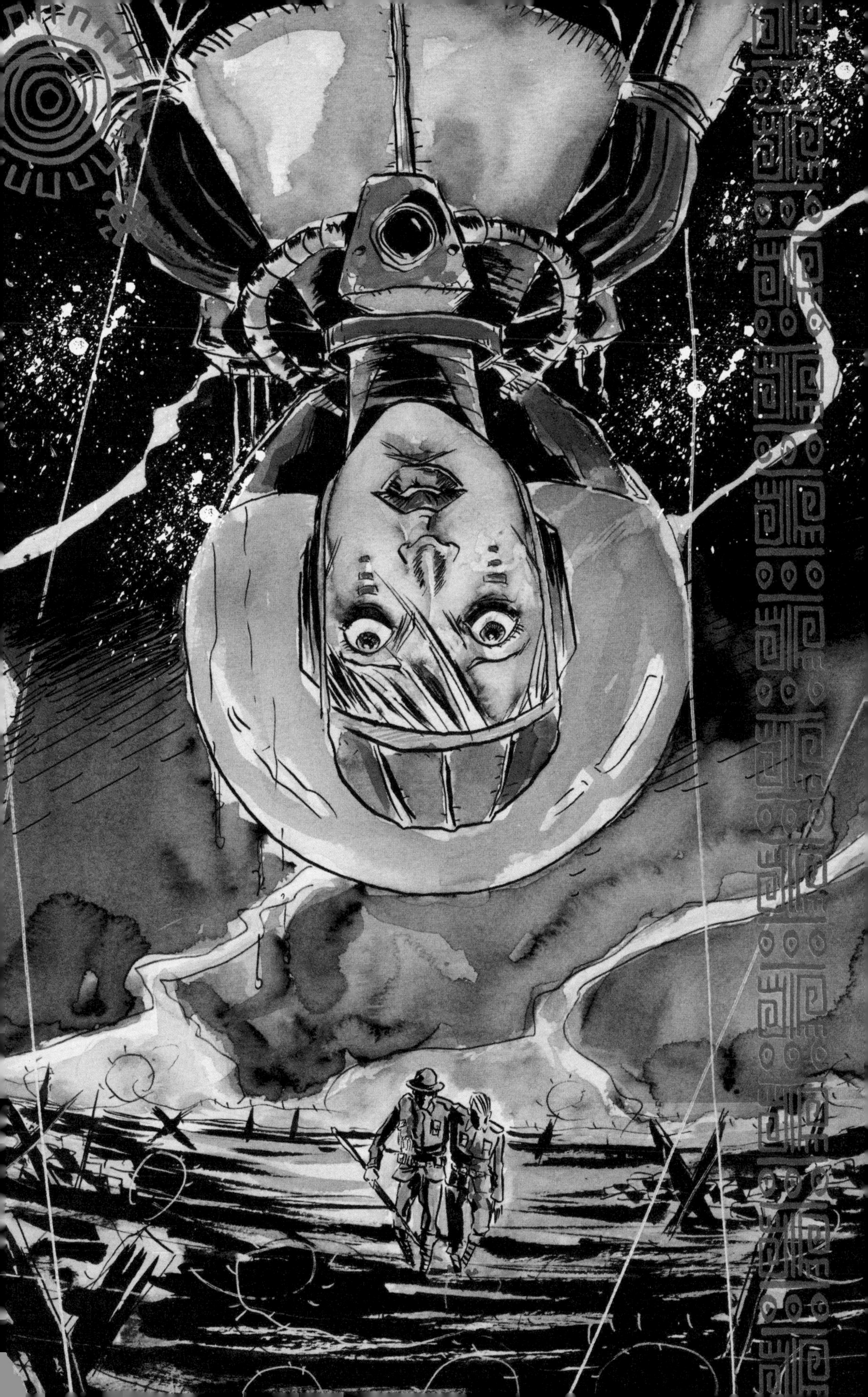

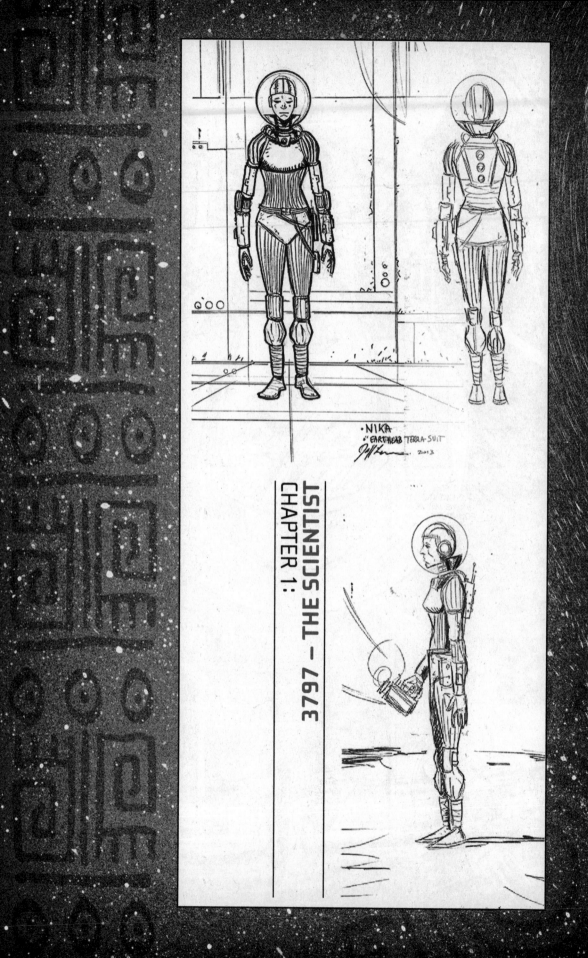

CHAPTER 1:
3797 — THE SCIENTIST

NIKA
"EARTHLAB" TERRA-SUIT

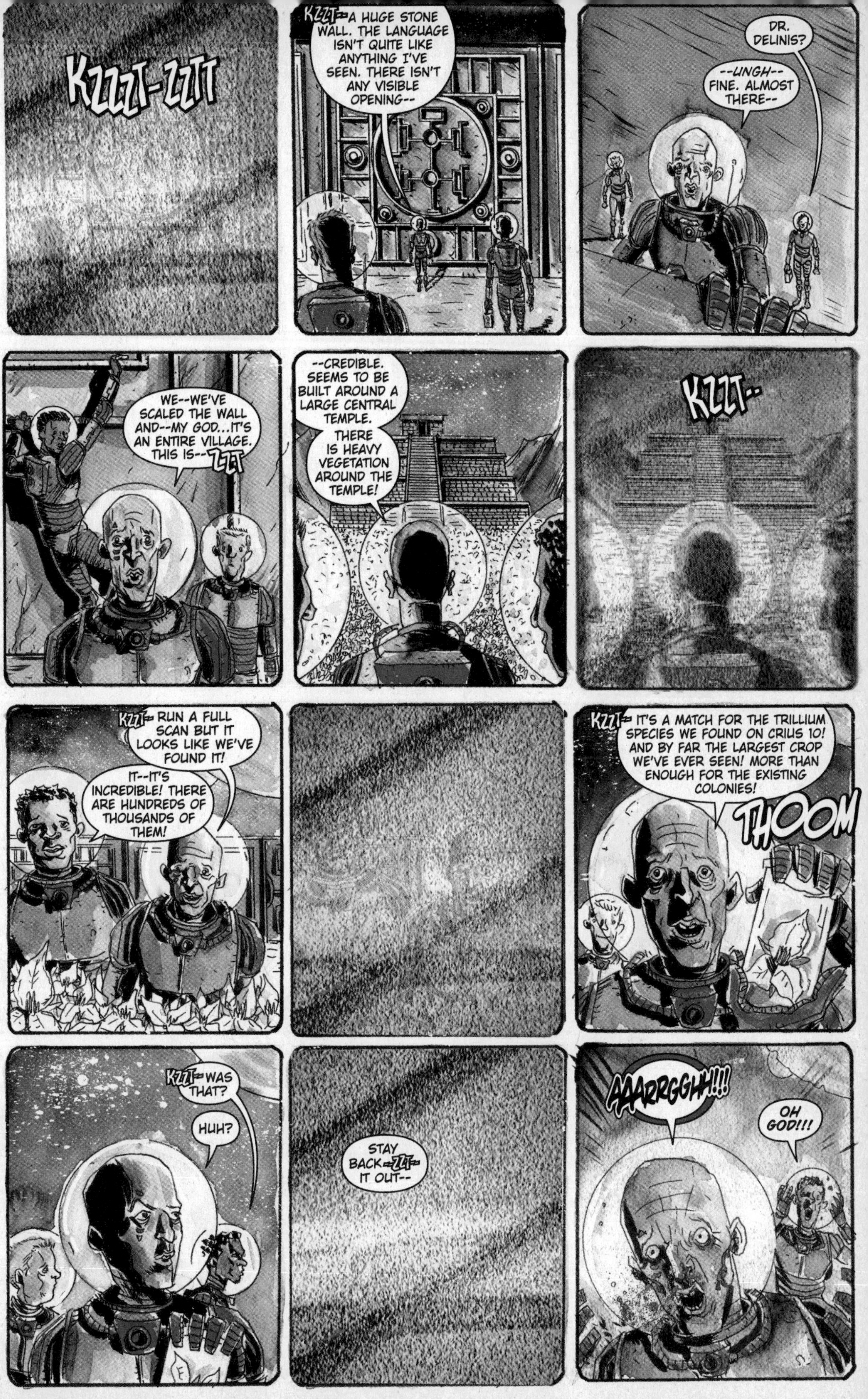
KZZZZT-ZZTT
KZZZT--A HUGE STONE WALL. THE LANGUAGE ISN'T QUITE LIKE ANYTHING I'VE SEEN. THERE ISN'T ANY VISIBLE OPENING--
DR. DELINIS?
--UNGH-- FINE. ALMOST THERE--
WE--WE'VE SCALED THE WALL AND--MY GOD...IT'S AN ENTIRE VILLAGE. THIS IS--ZZZT
--CREDIBLE. SEEMS TO BE BUILT AROUND A LARGE CENTRAL TEMPLE.
THERE IS HEAVY VEGETATION AROUND THE TEMPLE!
KZZZT--
KZZZT--RUN A FULL SCAN BUT IT LOOKS LIKE WE'VE FOUND IT!
IT--IT'S INCREDIBLE! THERE ARE HUNDREDS OF THOUSANDS OF THEM!
KZZZT--IT'S A MATCH FOR THE TRILLIUM SPECIES WE FOUND ON CRIUS 10! AND BY FAR THE LARGEST CROP WE'VE EVER SEEN! MORE THAN ENOUGH FOR THE EXISTING COLONIES!
THOOM
KZZZT--WAS THAT?
HUH?
STAY BACK--ZZZT--IT OUT--
AAARRGGHH!!!
OH GOD!!!

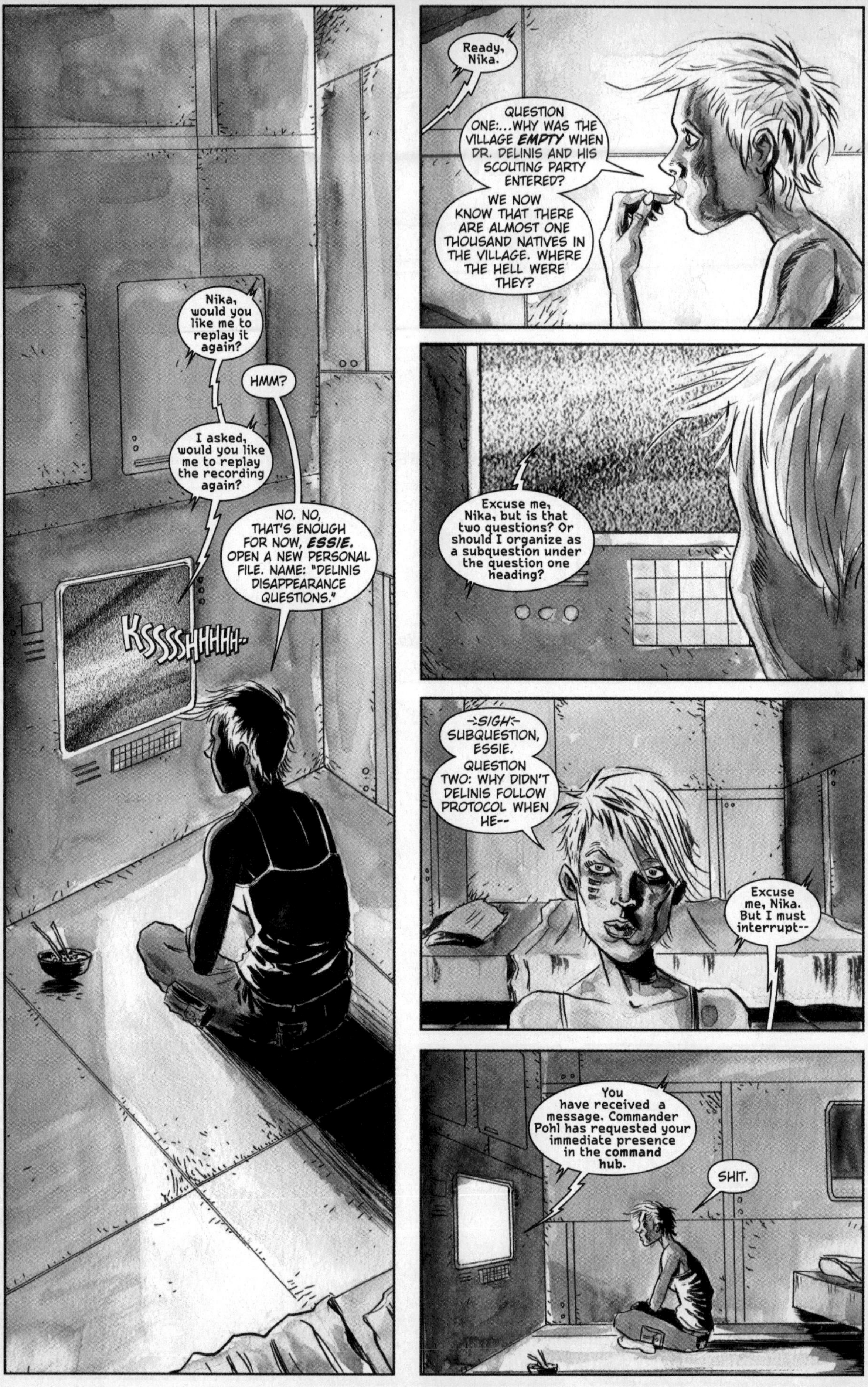
Nika, would you like me to replay it again?
HMM?
I asked, would you like me to replay the recording again?
NO. NO, THAT'S ENOUGH FOR NOW, ESSIE. OPEN A NEW PERSONAL FILE. NAME: "DELINIS DISAPPEARANCE QUESTIONS."
KSSSSHHHHH-
Ready, Nika.
QUESTION ONE:...WHY WAS THE VILLAGE EMPTY WHEN DR. DELINIS AND HIS SCOUTING PARTY ENTERED?
WE NOW KNOW THAT THERE ARE ALMOST ONE THOUSAND NATIVES IN THE VILLAGE. WHERE THE HELL WERE THEY?
Excuse me, Nika, but is that two questions? Or should I organize as a subquestion under the question one heading?
-SIGH- SUBQUESTION, ESSIE.
QUESTION TWO: WHY DIDN'T DELINIS FOLLOW PROTOCOL WHEN HE--
Excuse me, Nika. But I must interrupt--
You have received a message. Commander Pohl has requested your immediate presence in the command hub.
SHIT.

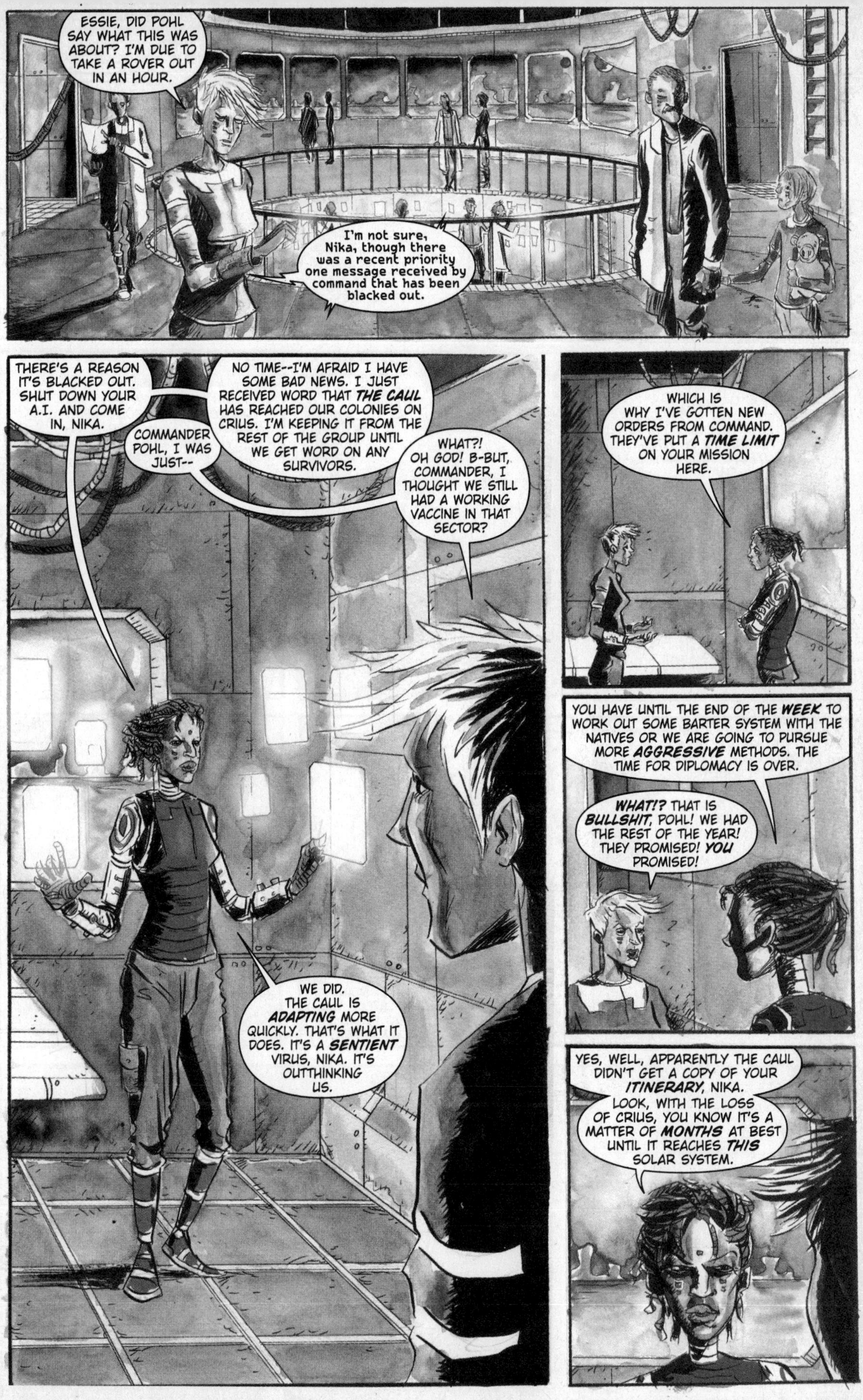
ESSIE, DID POHL SAY WHAT THIS WAS ABOUT? I'M DUE TO TAKE A ROVER OUT IN AN HOUR.
I'm not sure, Nika, though there was a recent priority one message received by command that has been blacked out.
THERE'S A REASON IT'S BLACKED OUT. SHUT DOWN YOUR A.I. AND COME IN, NIKA.
COMMANDER POHL, I WAS JUST--
NO TIME--I'M AFRAID I HAVE SOME BAD NEWS. I JUST RECEIVED WORD THAT THE CAUL HAS REACHED OUR COLONIES ON CRIUS. I'M KEEPING IT FROM THE REST OF THE GROUP UNTIL WE GET WORD ON ANY SURVIVORS.
WHAT?! OH GOD! B-BUT, COMMANDER, I THOUGHT WE STILL HAD A WORKING VACCINE IN THAT SECTOR?
WE DID. THE CAUL IS ADAPTING MORE QUICKLY. THAT'S WHAT IT DOES. IT'S A SENTIENT VIRUS, NIKA. IT'S OUTTHINKING US.
WHICH IS WHY I'VE GOTTEN NEW ORDERS FROM COMMAND. THEY'VE PUT A TIME LIMIT ON YOUR MISSION HERE.
YOU HAVE UNTIL THE END OF THE WEEK TO WORK OUT SOME BARTER SYSTEM WITH THE NATIVES OR WE ARE GOING TO PURSUE MORE AGGRESSIVE METHODS. THE TIME FOR DIPLOMACY IS OVER.
WHAT!? THAT IS BULLSHIT, POHL! WE HAD THE REST OF THE YEAR! THEY PROMISED! YOU PROMISED!
YES, WELL, APPARENTLY THE CAUL DIDN'T GET A COPY OF YOUR ITINERARY, NIKA. LOOK, WITH THE LOSS OF CRIUS, YOU KNOW IT'S A MATTER OF MONTHS AT BEST UNTIL IT REACHES THIS SOLAR SYSTEM.

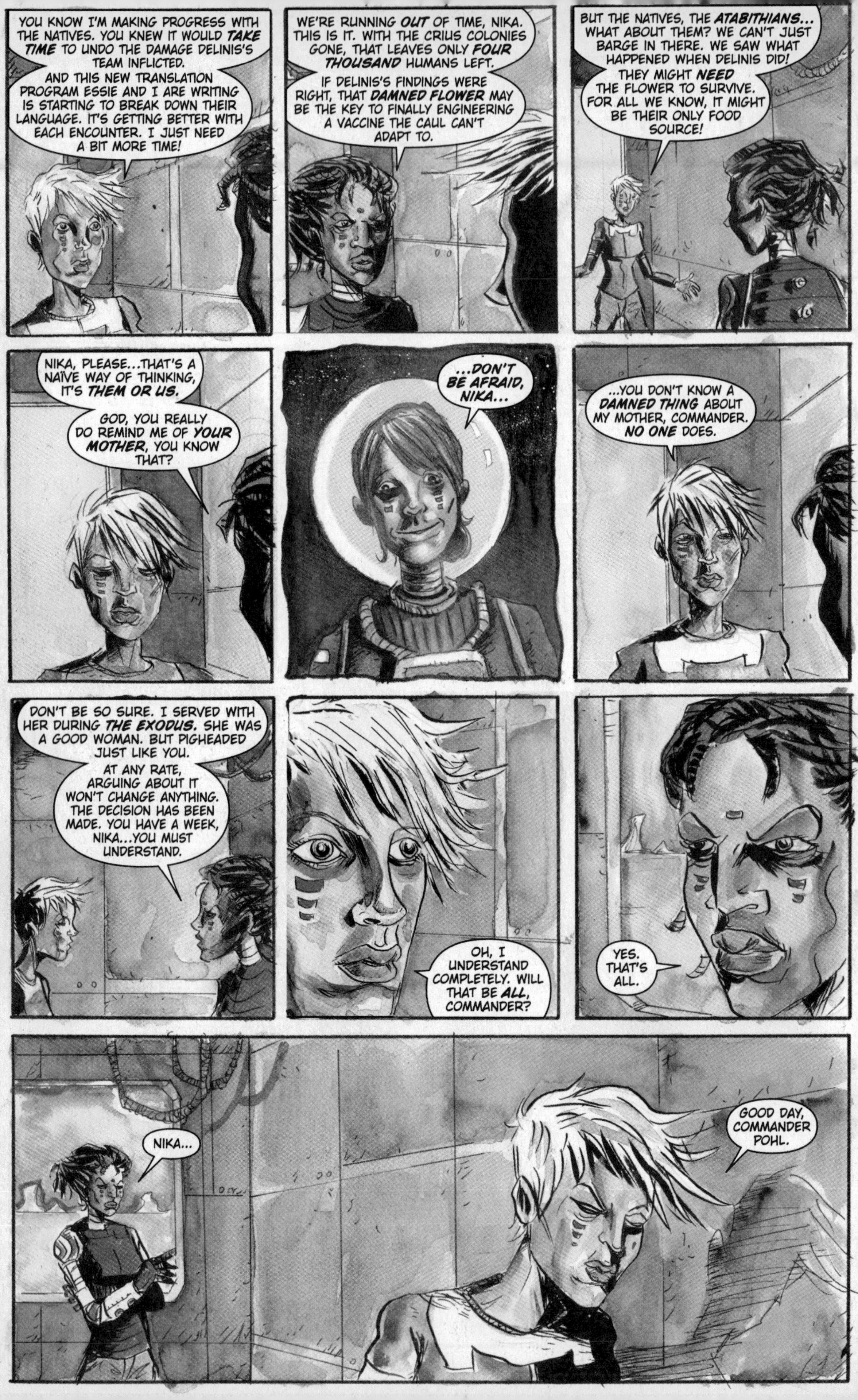
YOU KNOW I'M MAKING PROGRESS WITH THE NATIVES. YOU KNEW IT WOULD TAKE TIME TO UNDO THE DAMAGE DELINIS'S TEAM INFLICTED.
AND THIS NEW TRANSLATION PROGRAM ESSIE AND I ARE WRITING IS STARTING TO BREAK DOWN THEIR LANGUAGE. IT'S GETTING BETTER WITH EACH ENCOUNTER. I JUST NEED A BIT MORE TIME!
WE'RE RUNNING OUT OF TIME, NIKA. THIS IS IT. WITH THE CRIUS COLONIES GONE, THAT LEAVES ONLY FOUR THOUSAND HUMANS LEFT.
IF DELINIS'S FINDINGS WERE RIGHT, THAT DAMNED FLOWER MAY BE THE KEY TO FINALLY ENGINEERING A VACCINE THE CAUL CAN'T ADAPT TO.
BUT THE NATIVES, THE ATABITHIANS... WHAT ABOUT THEM? WE CAN'T JUST BARGE IN THERE. WE SAW WHAT HAPPENED WHEN DELINIS DID!
THEY MIGHT NEED THE FLOWER TO SURVIVE. FOR ALL WE KNOW, IT MIGHT BE THEIR ONLY FOOD SOURCE!
NIKA, PLEASE...THAT'S A NAÏVE WAY OF THINKING, IT'S THEM OR US.
GOD, YOU REALLY DO REMIND ME OF YOUR MOTHER, YOU KNOW THAT?
...DON'T BE AFRAID, NIKA...
...YOU DON'T KNOW A DAMNED THING ABOUT MY MOTHER, COMMANDER. NO ONE DOES.
DON'T BE SO SURE. I SERVED WITH HER DURING THE EXODUS. SHE WAS A GOOD WOMAN. BUT PIGHEADED JUST LIKE YOU.
AT ANY RATE, ARGUING ABOUT IT WON'T CHANGE ANYTHING. THE DECISION HAS BEEN MADE. YOU HAVE A WEEK, NIKA...YOU MUST UNDERSTAND.
OH, I UNDERSTAND COMPLETELY. WILL THAT BE ALL, COMMANDER?
YES. THAT'S ALL.
NIKA...
GOOD DAY, COMMANDER POHL.

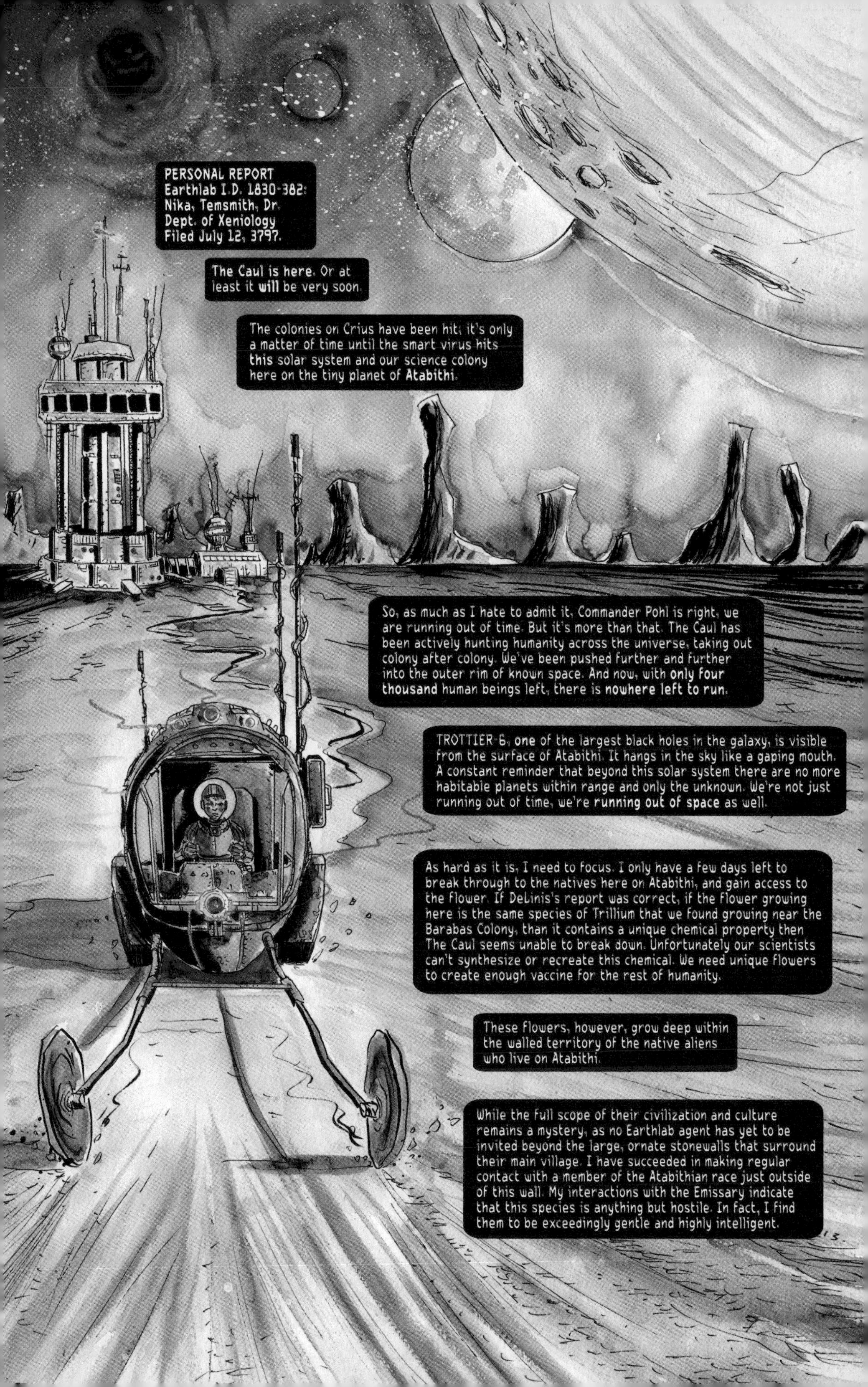
PERSONAL REPORT Earthlab I.D. 1830-382: Nika, Temsmith, Dr. Dept. of Xeniology Filed July 12, 3797.
The Caul is here. Or at least it will be very soon.
The colonies on Crius have been hit; it's only a matter of time until the smart virus hits this solar system and our science colony here on the tiny planet of Atabithi.
So, as much as I hate to admit it, Commander Pohl is right, we are running out of time. But it's more than that. The Caul has been actively hunting humanity across the universe, taking out colony after colony. We've been pushed further and further into the outer rim of known space. And now, with only four thousand human beings left, there is nowhere left to run.
TROTTIER-6, one of the largest black holes in the galaxy, is visible from the surface of Atabithi. It hangs in the sky like a gaping mouth. A constant reminder that beyond this solar system there are no more habitable planets within range and only the unknown. We're not just running out of time, we're running out of space as well.
As hard as it is, I need to focus. I only have a few days left to break through to the natives here on Atabithi, and gain access to the flower. If DeLinis's report was correct, if the flower growing here is the same species of Trillium that we found growing near the Barabas Colony, than it contains a unique chemical property then The Caul seems unable to break down. Unfortunately our scientists can't synthesize or recreate this chemical. We need unique flowers to create enough vaccine for the rest of humanity.
These flowers, however, grow deep within the walled territory of the native aliens who live on Atabithi.
While the full scope of their civilization and culture remains a mystery, as no Earthlab agent has yet to be invited beyond the large, ornate stonewalls that surround their main village. I have succeeded in making regular contact with a member of the Atabithian race just outside of this wall. My interactions with the Emissary indicate that this species is anything but hostile. In fact, I find them to be exceedingly gentle and highly intelligent.

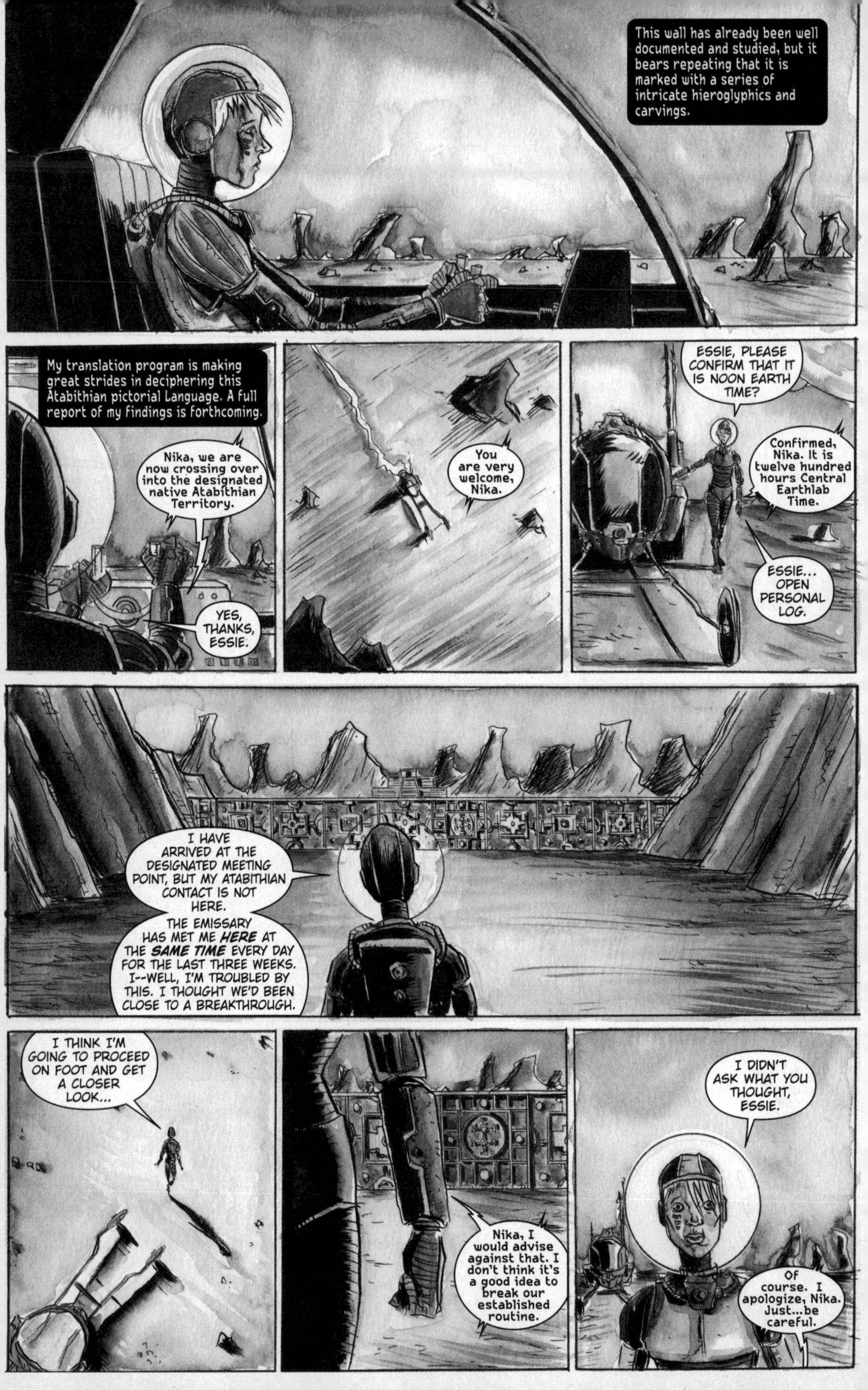
This wall has already been well documented and studied, but it bears repeating that it is marked with a series of intricate hieroglyphics and carvings.
My translation program is making great strides in deciphering this Atabithian pictorial Language. A full report of my findings is forthcoming.
Nika, we are now crossing over into the designated native Atabithian Territory.
YES, THANKS, ESSIE.
You are very welcome, Nika.
ESSIE, PLEASE CONFIRM THAT IT IS NOON EARTH TIME?
Confirmed, Nika. It is twelve hundred hours Central Earthlab Time.
ESSIE... OPEN PERSONAL LOG.
I HAVE ARRIVED AT THE DESIGNATED MEETING POINT, BUT MY ATABITHIAN CONTACT IS NOT HERE.
THE EMISSARY HAS MET ME *HERE* AT THE ***SAME TIME*** EVERY DAY FOR THE LAST THREE WEEKS. I--WELL, I'M TROUBLED BY THIS. I THOUGHT WE'D BEEN CLOSE TO A BREAKTHROUGH.
I THINK I'M GOING TO PROCEED ON FOOT AND GET A CLOSER LOOK...
Nika, I would advise against that. I don't think it's a good idea to break our established routine.
I DIDN'T ASK WHAT YOU THOUGHT, ESSIE.
Of course. I apologize, Nika. Just...be careful.

ESSIE...CAN YOU CONFIRM WITH EARTHLAB SATELLITES WHAT I'M SEEING HERE...

I THINK... I THINK THERE IS AN OPENING IN THE WALL!

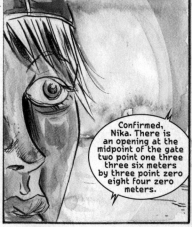

Confirmed, Nika. There is an opening at the midpoint of the gate two point one three three six meters by three point zero eight four zero meters.

AND...CAN SATELLITES CONFIRM THE PRESENCE OF THE ATABITHIANS IN THE VILLAGE?

Yes. There are nine hundred and eighty seven unique heat signatures within the village perimeters that match the recorded Atabithians' imprint.

I'M PROCEEDING INSIDE.

Nika, I recommend you wait for an Earthlab security team before proceeding.

THIS IS MY CALL, ESSIE. LAUNCH RECORDER DRONES. I WANT EVERYTHING CATALOGUED.

Very well, Nika... launching.

BLEEP

I AM ENTERING THE WALL AND I--

OH!

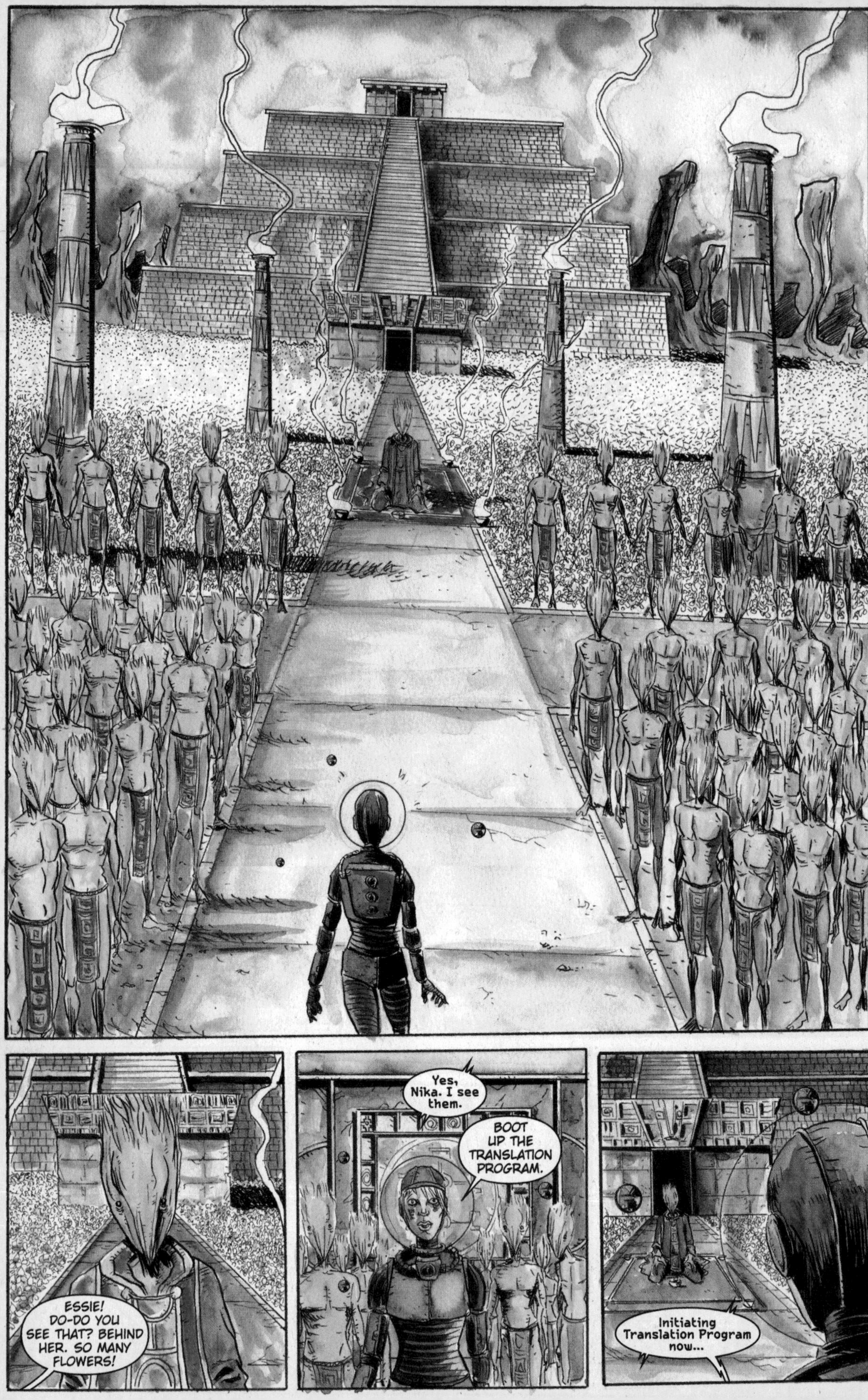
ESSIE! DO-DO YOU SEE THAT? BEHIND HER. SO MANY FLOWERS!
Yes, Nika. I see them.
BOOT UP THE TRANSLATION PROGRAM.
Initiating Translation Program now...

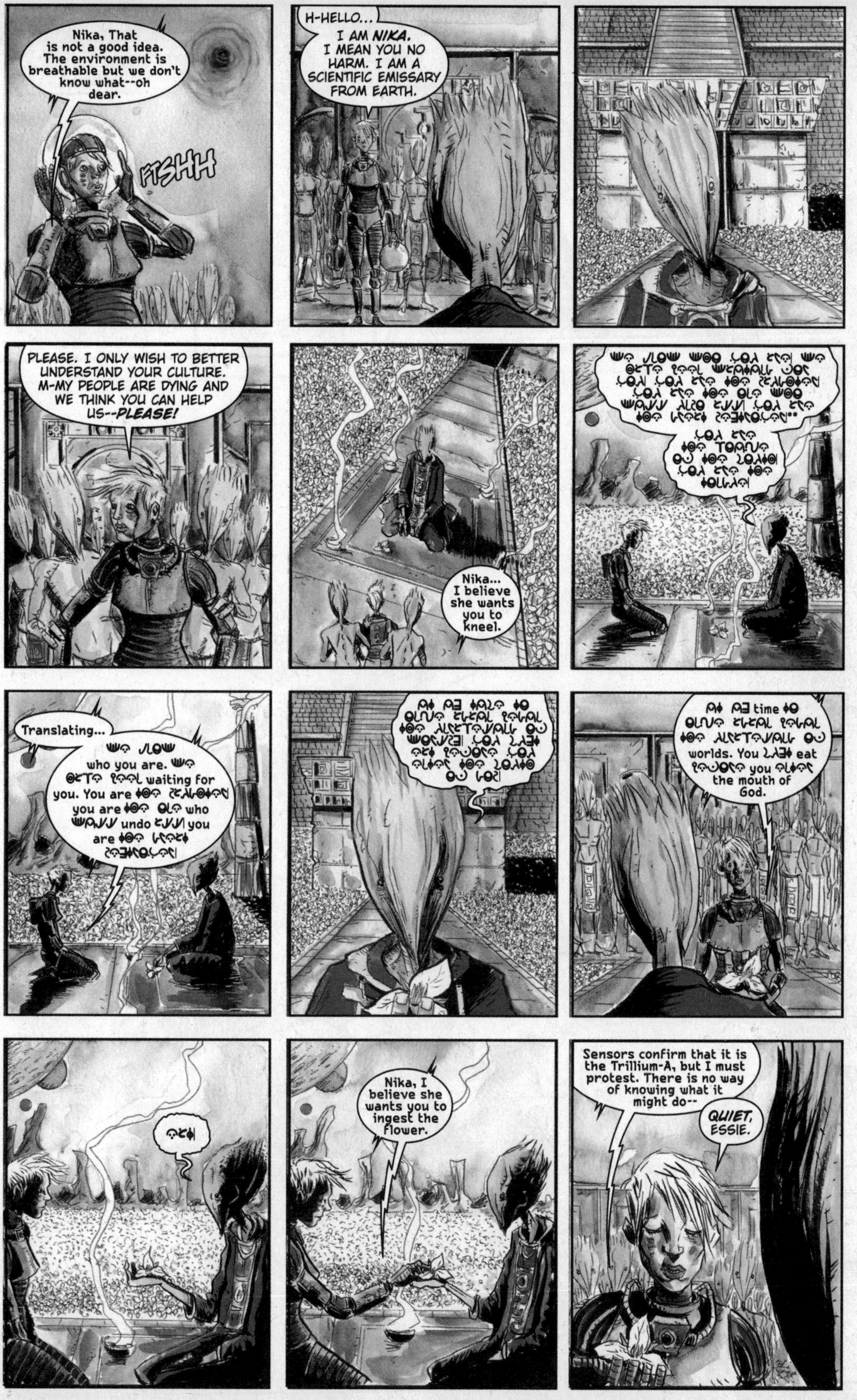

Nika, That is not a good idea. The environment is breathable but we don't know what--oh dear.
FTSHH
H-HELLO...
I AM NIKA. I MEAN YOU NO HARM. I AM A SCIENTIFIC EMISSARY FROM EARTH.
PLEASE. I ONLY WISH TO BETTER UNDERSTAND YOUR CULTURE. M-MY PEOPLE ARE DYING AND WE THINK YOU CAN HELP US--PLEASE!
Nika... I believe she wants you to kneel.
Translating...
who you are. waiting for you. You are you are who undo you are
time worlds. You eat you the mouth of God.
Nika, I believe she wants you to ingest the flower.
Sensors confirm that it is the Trillium-A, but I must protest. There is no way of knowing what it might do--
QUIET, ESSIE.

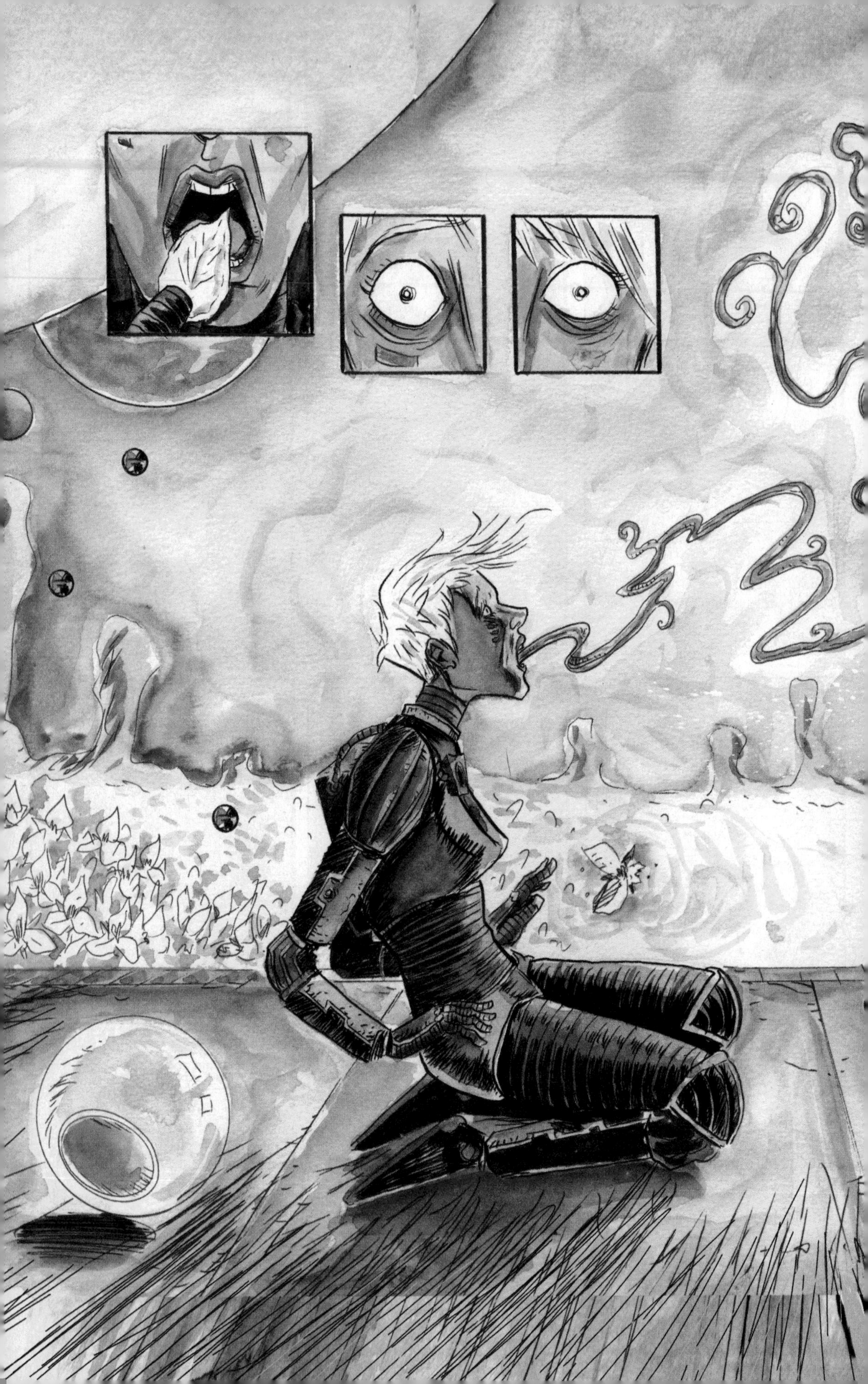

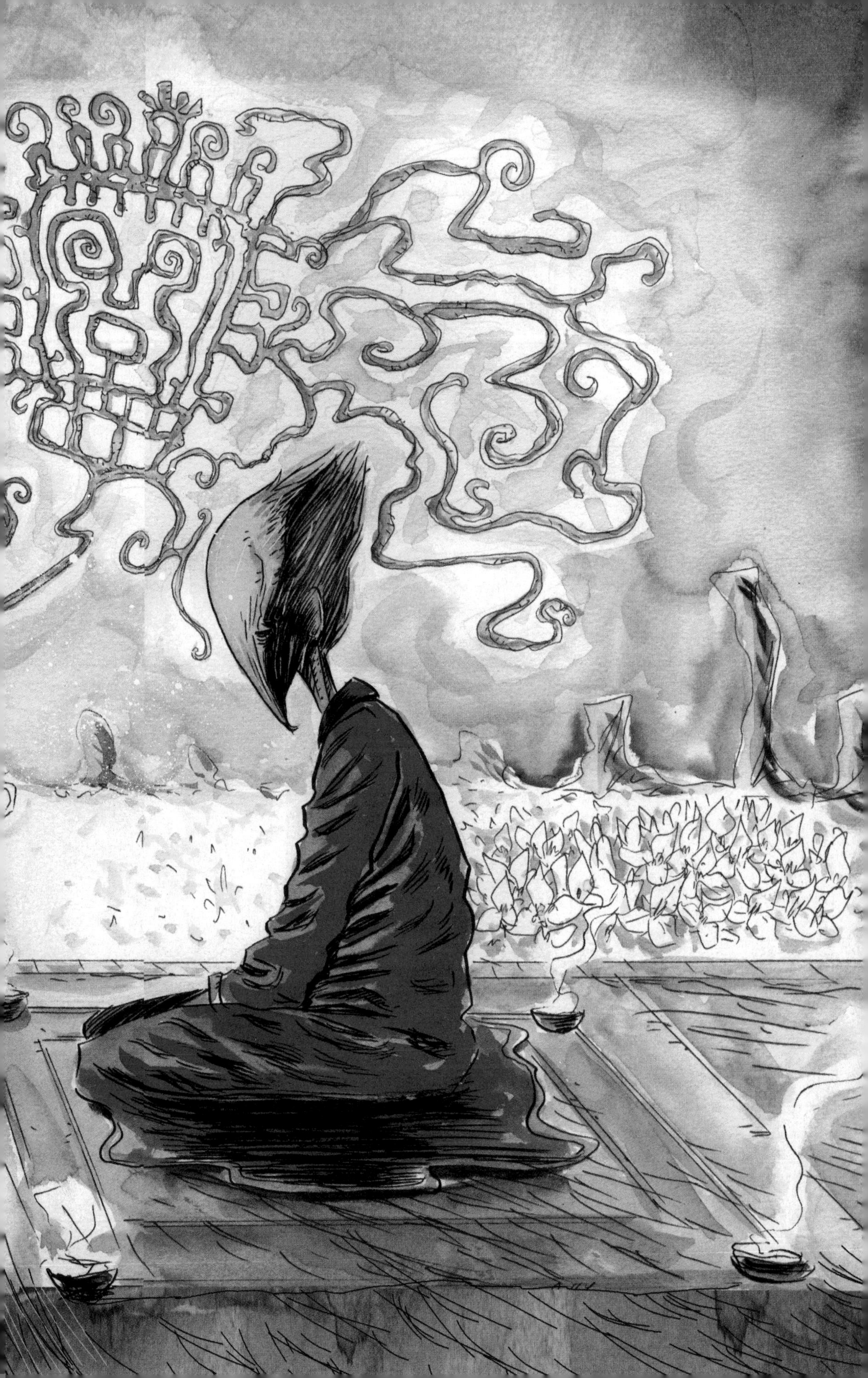

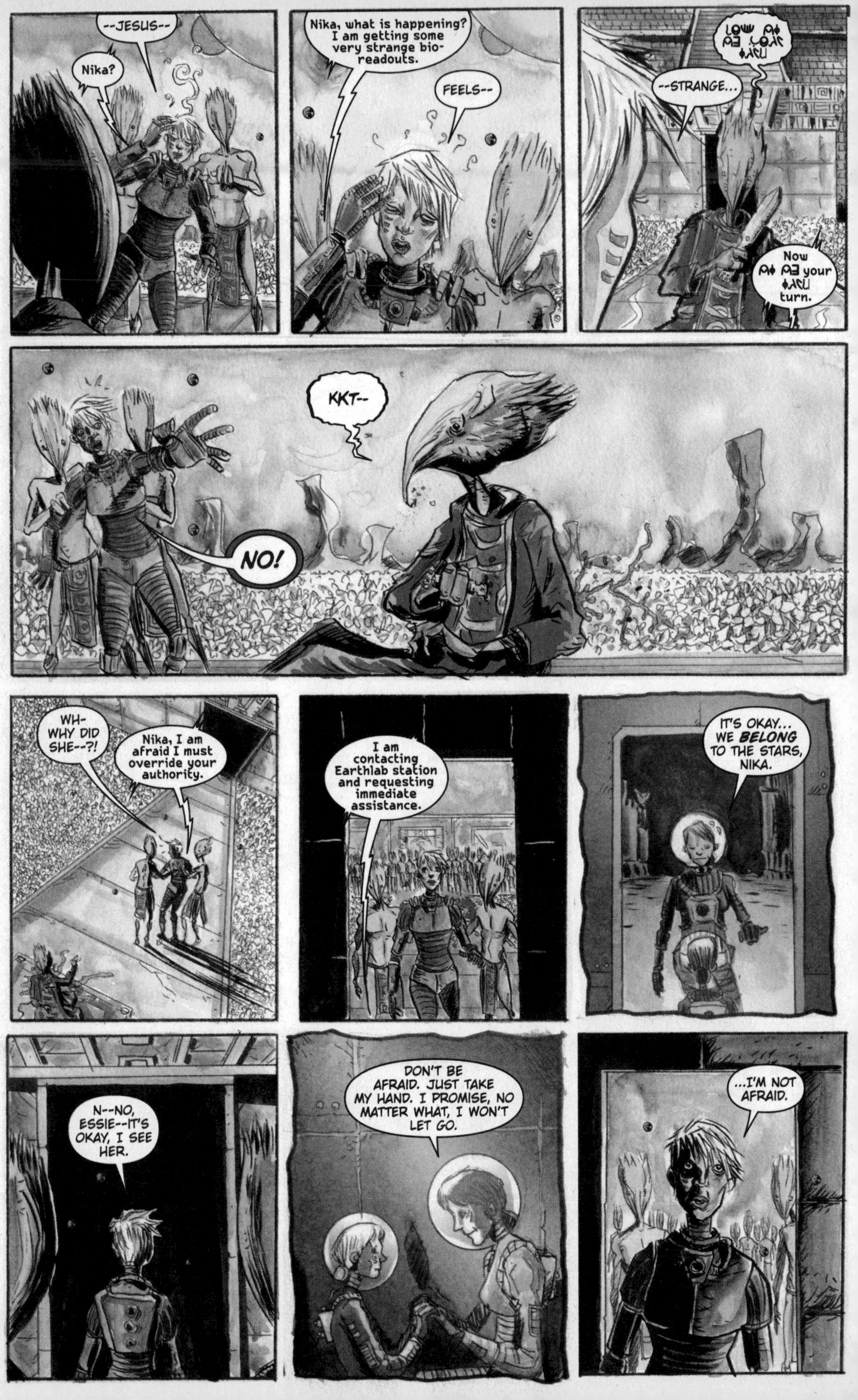
--JESUS--
Nika?
Nika, what is happening? I am getting some very strange bio-readouts.
FEELS--
--STRANGE...
Now
your
turn.
KKT--
NO!
WH-WHY DID SHE--?!
Nika, I am afraid I must override your authority.
I am contacting Earthlab station and requesting immediate assistance.
IT'S OKAY... WE *BELONG* TO THE STARS, NIKA.
N--NO, ESSIE--IT'S OKAY, I SEE HER.
DON'T BE AFRAID. JUST TAKE MY HAND. I PROMISE, NO MATTER WHAT, I WON'T LET GO.
...I'M NOT AFRAID.

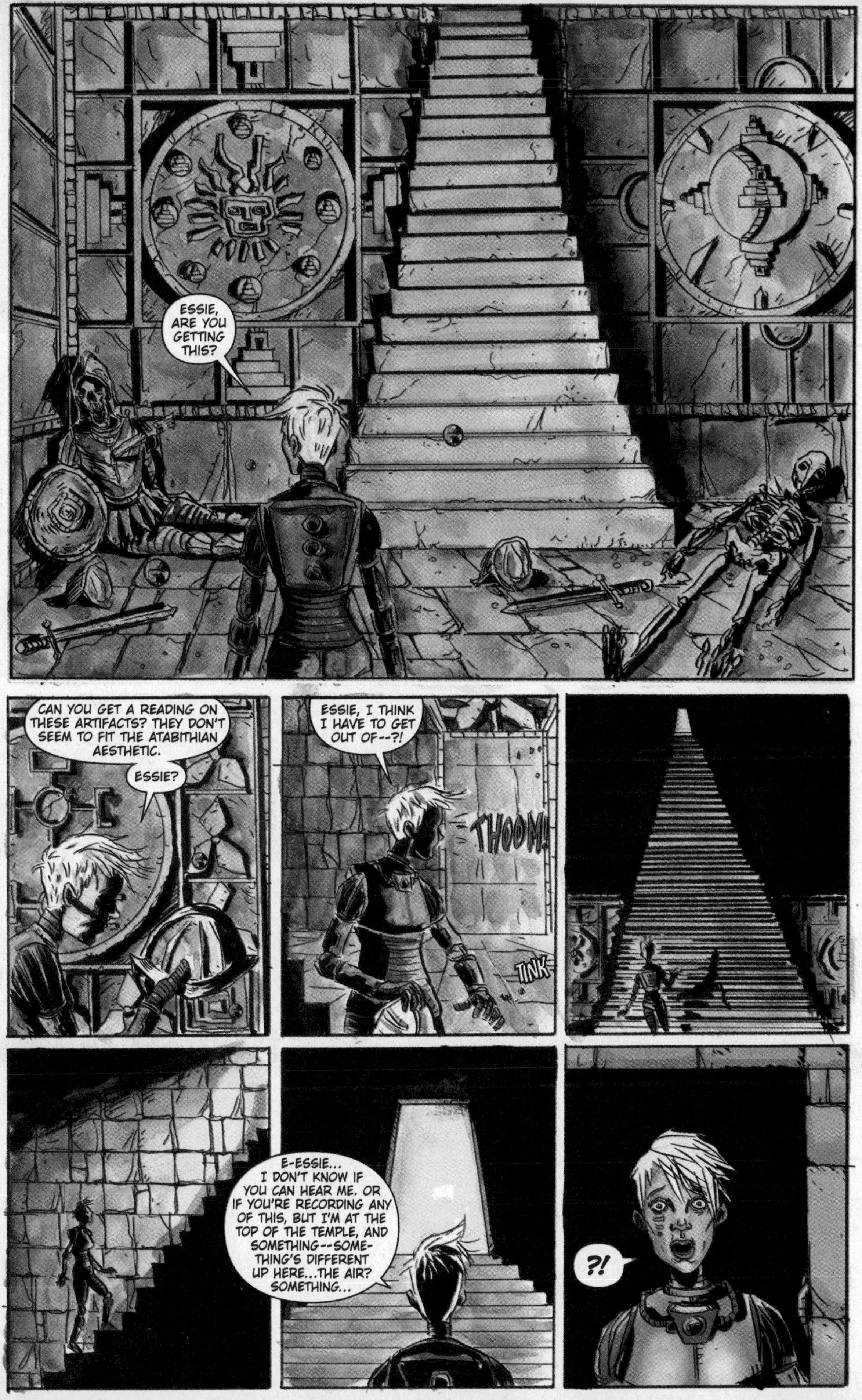
ESSIE, ARE YOU GETTING THIS?
CAN YOU GET A READING ON THESE ARTIFACTS? THEY DON'T SEEM TO FIT THE ATABITHIAN AESTHETIC.
ESSIE?
ESSIE, I THINK I HAVE TO GET OUT OF--?!
THOOM!
TINK
E-ESSIE... I DON'T KNOW IF YOU CAN HEAR ME. OR IF YOU'RE RECORDING ANY OF THIS, BUT I'M AT THE TOP OF THE TEMPLE, AND SOMETHING--SOMETHING'S DIFFERENT UP HERE...THE AIR? SOMETHING...
?!

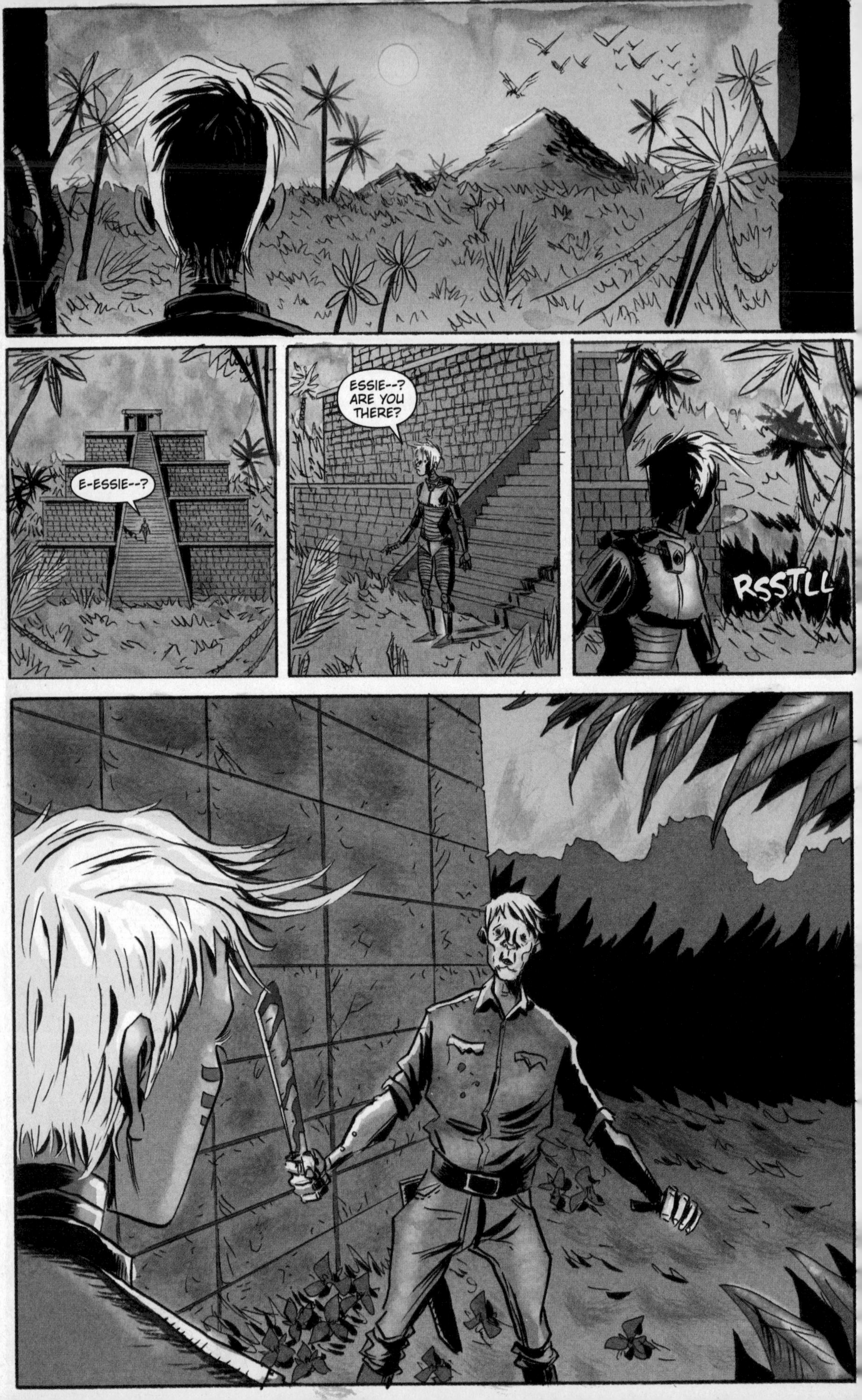
E-ESSIE--?
ESSIE--? ARE YOU THERE?
RSSTLL

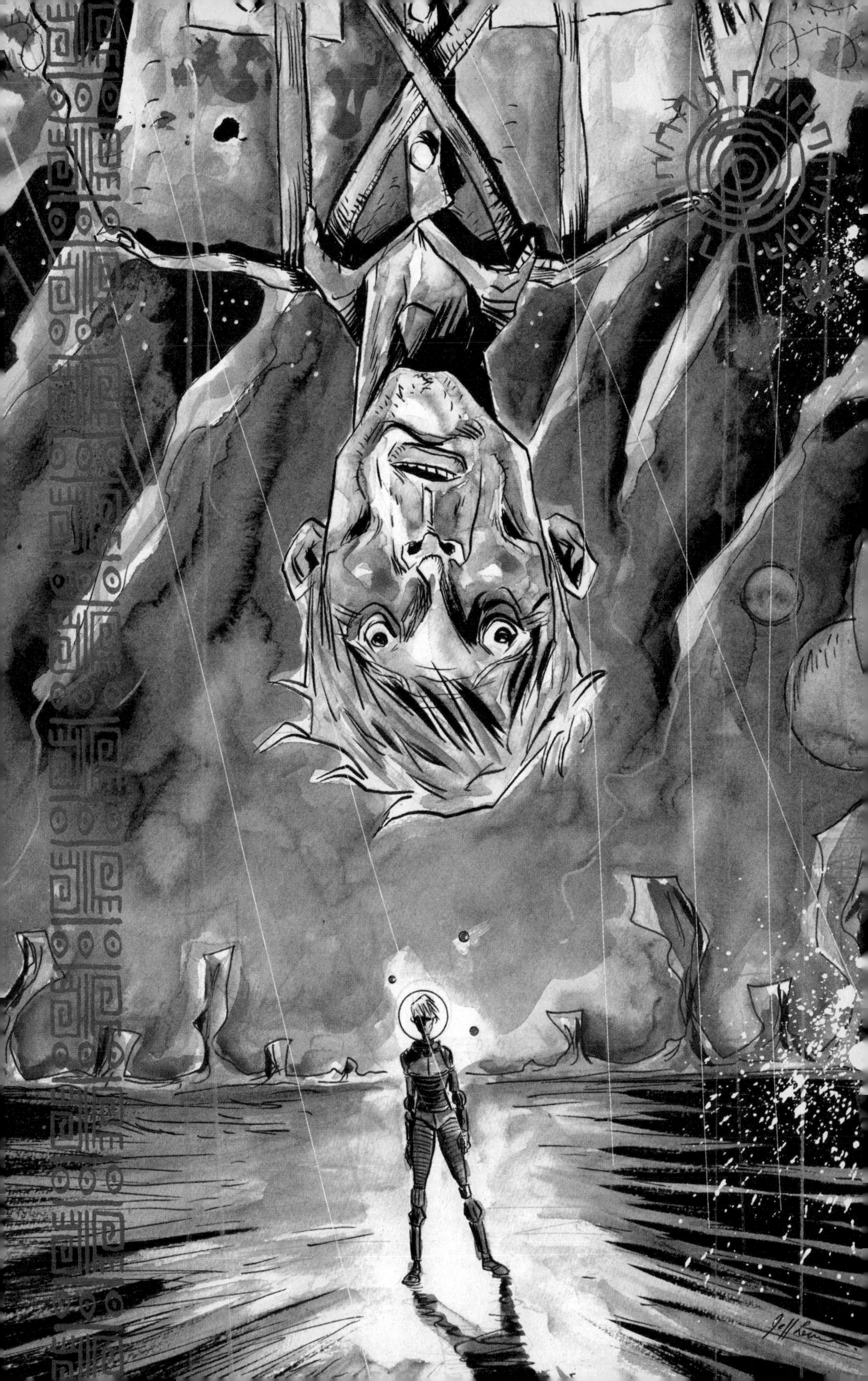

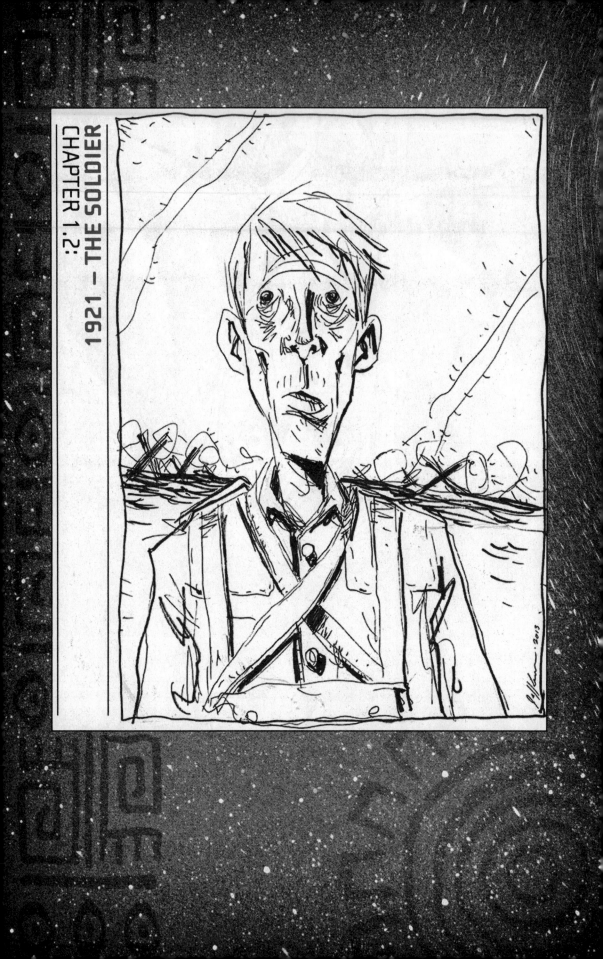

CHAPTER 1.2:
1971 — THE SOLDIER

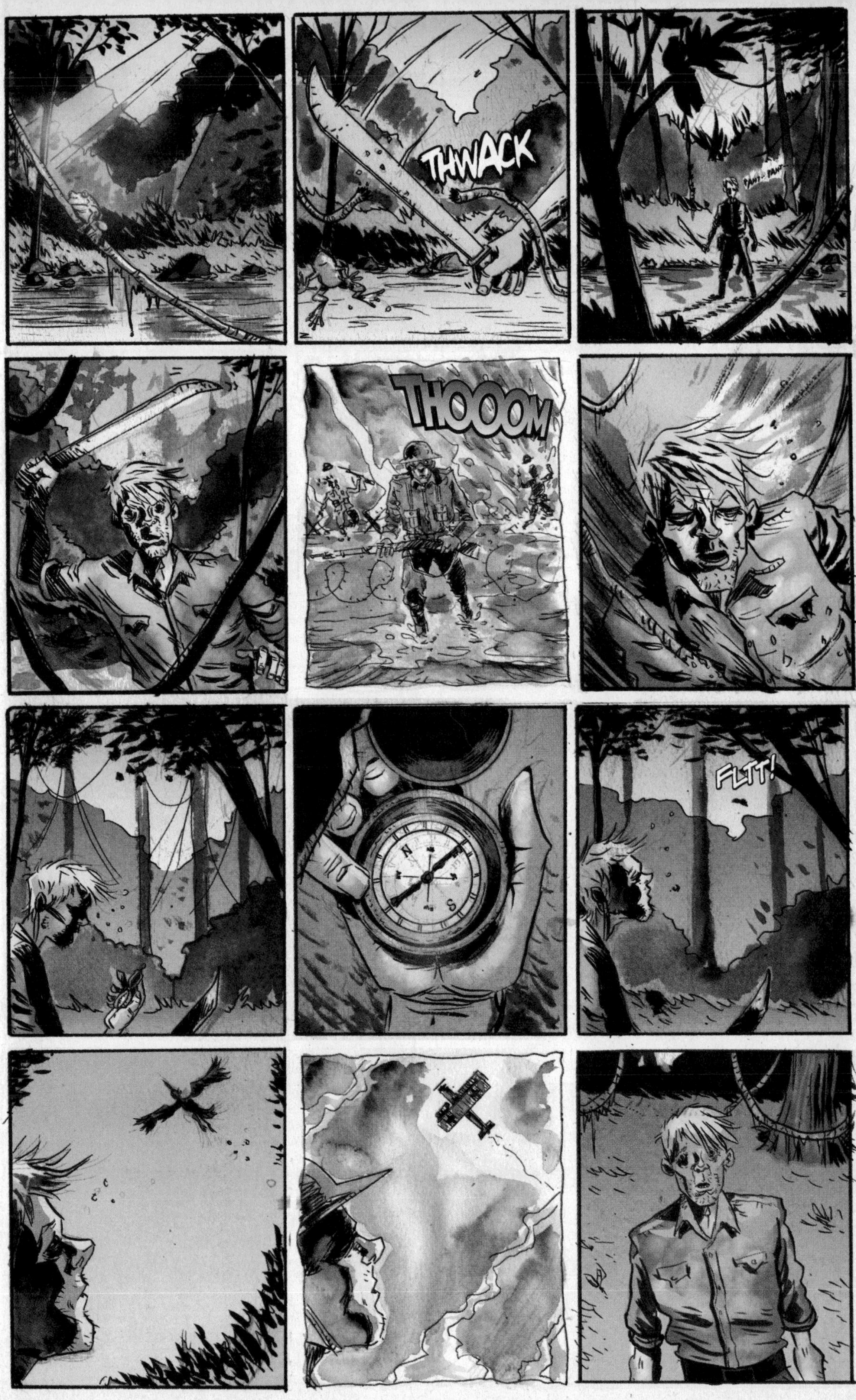
THWACK
PANT... PANT...
THOOOM
FLTT!

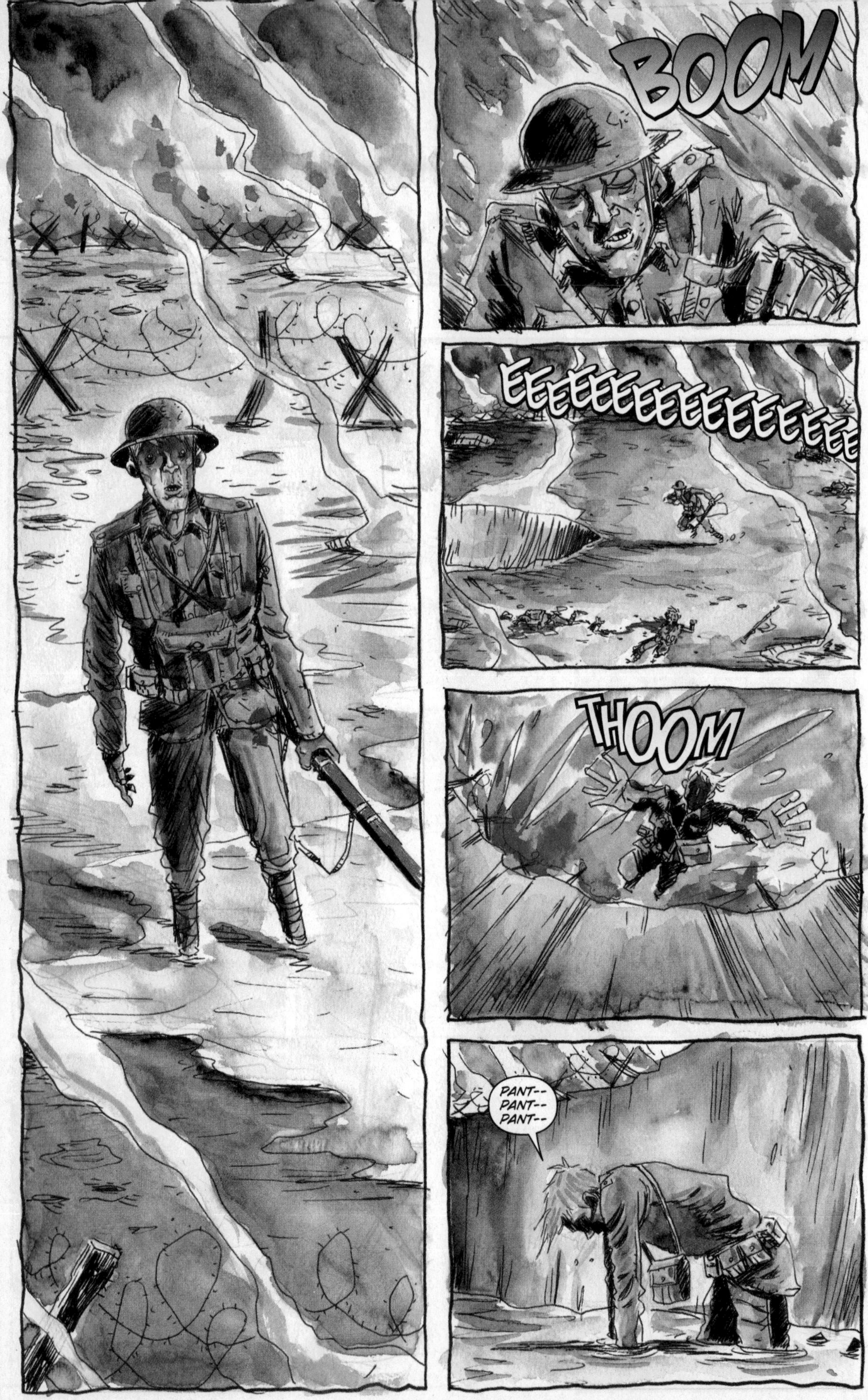
BOOM
EEEEEEEEEEEEEEEEEE
THOOM
PANT-- PANT-- PANT--

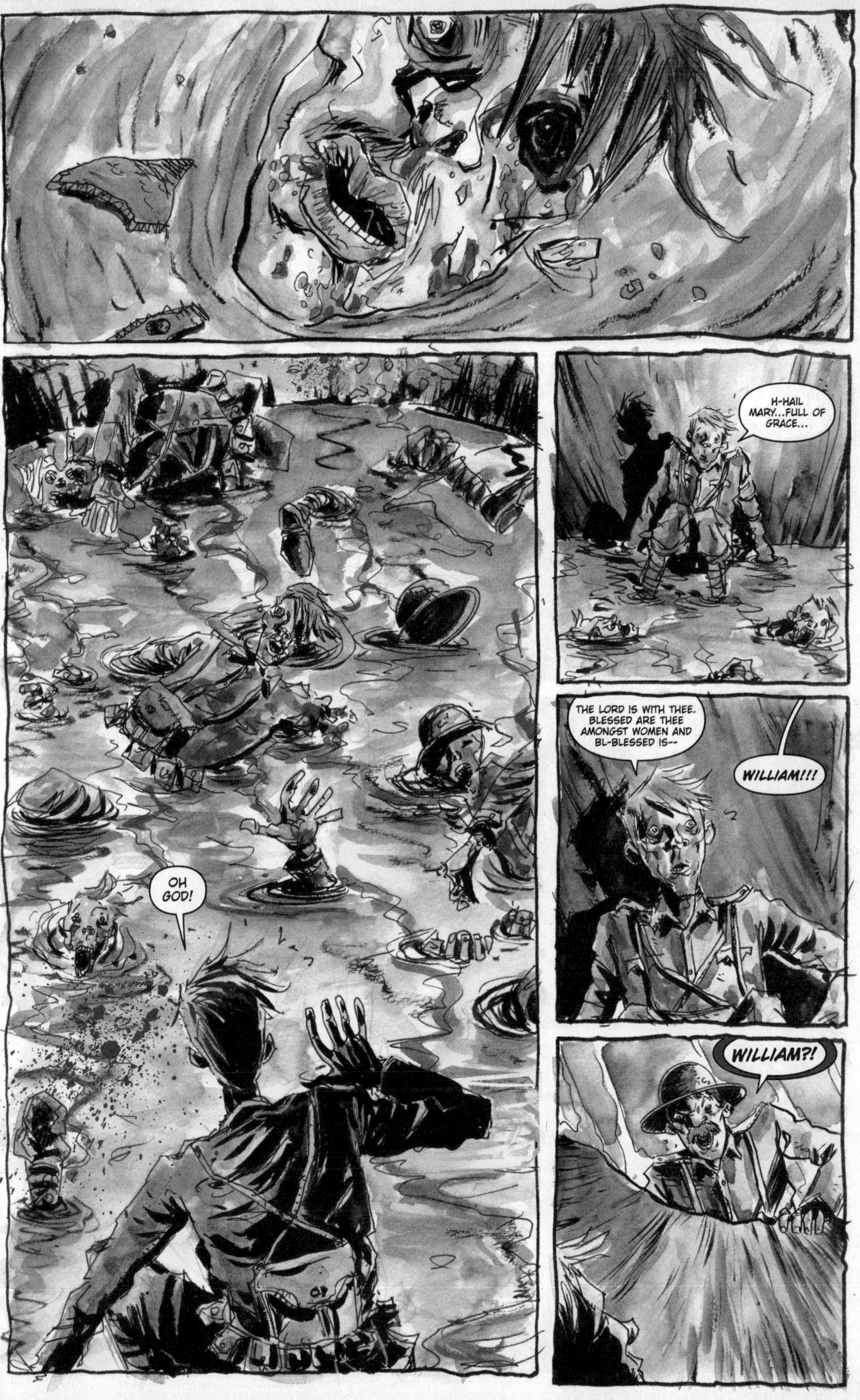

H-HAIL MARY...FULL OF GRACE...
OH GOD!
THE LORD IS WITH THEE. BLESSED ARE THEE AMONGST WOMEN AND BL-BLESSED IS--
WILLIAM!!!
WILLIAM?!

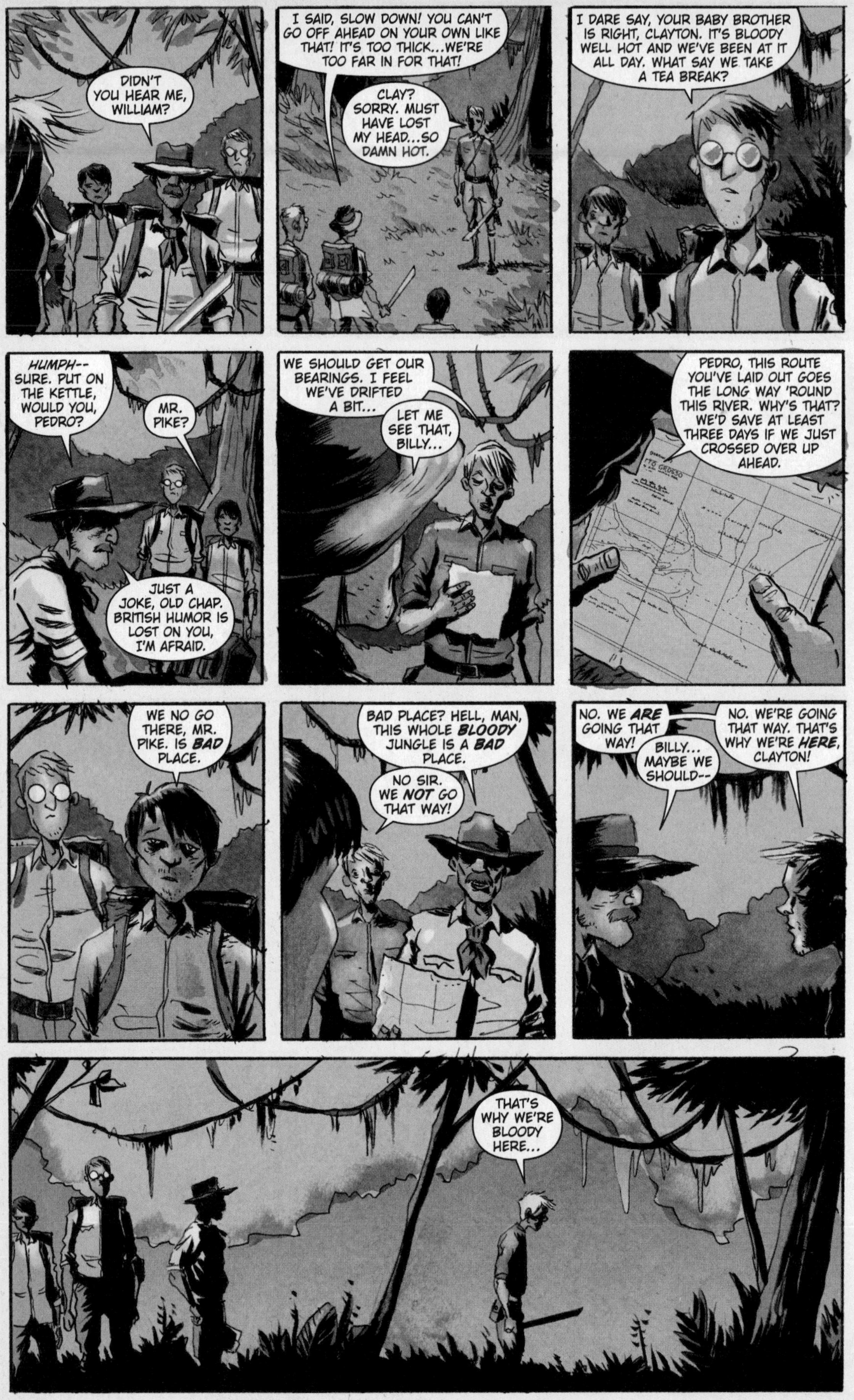
DIDN'T YOU HEAR ME, WILLIAM?
I SAID, SLOW DOWN! YOU CAN'T GO OFF AHEAD ON YOUR OWN LIKE THAT! IT'S TOO THICK...WE'RE TOO FAR IN FOR THAT!
CLAY? SORRY. MUST HAVE LOST MY HEAD...SO DAMN HOT.
I DARE SAY, YOUR BABY BROTHER IS RIGHT, CLAYTON. IT'S BLOODY WELL HOT AND WE'VE BEEN AT IT ALL DAY. WHAT SAY WE TAKE A TEA BREAK?
HUMPH-- SURE. PUT ON THE KETTLE, WOULD YOU, PEDRO?
MR. PIKE?
JUST A JOKE, OLD CHAP. BRITISH HUMOR IS LOST ON YOU, I'M AFRAID.
WE SHOULD GET OUR BEARINGS. I FEEL WE'VE DRIFTED A BIT...
LET ME SEE THAT, BILLY...
PEDRO, THIS ROUTE YOU'VE LAID OUT GOES THE LONG WAY 'ROUND THIS RIVER. WHY'S THAT? WE'D SAVE AT LEAST THREE DAYS IF WE JUST CROSSED OVER UP AHEAD.
WE NO GO THERE, MR. PIKE. IS BAD PLACE.
BAD PLACE? HELL, MAN, THIS WHOLE BLOODY JUNGLE IS A BAD PLACE.
NO SIR. WE NOT GO THAT WAY!
NO. WE ARE GOING THAT WAY!
BILLY... MAYBE WE SHOULD--
NO. WE'RE GOING THAT WAY. THAT'S WHY WE'RE HERE, CLAYTON!
THAT'S WHY WE'RE BLOODY HERE...

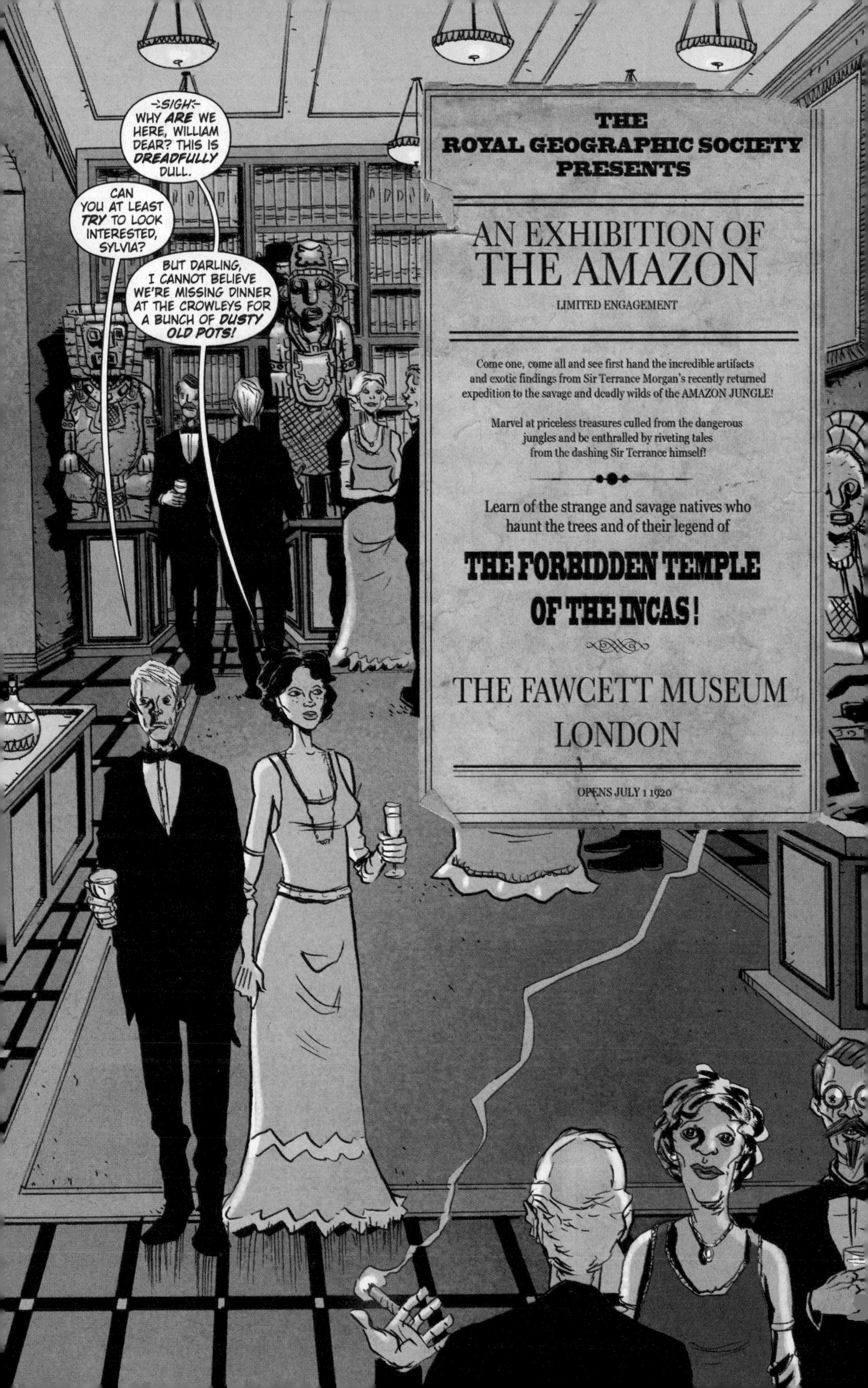

-SIGH- WHY ARE WE HERE, WILLIAM DEAR? THIS IS DREADFULLY DULL.
CAN YOU AT LEAST TRY TO LOOK INTERESTED, SYLVIA?
BUT DARLING, I CANNOT BELIEVE WE'RE MISSING DINNER AT THE CROWLEYS FOR A BUNCH OF DUSTY OLD POTS!
THE ROYAL GEOGRAPHIC SOCIETY PRESENTS
AN EXHIBITION OF THE AMAZON
LIMITED ENGAGEMENT
Come one, come all and see first hand the incredible artifacts and exotic findings from Sir Terrance Morgan's recently returned expedition to the savage and deadly wilds of the AMAZON JUNGLE!
Marvel at priceless treasures culled from the dangerous jungles and be enthralled by riveting tales from the dashing Sir Terrance himself!
Learn of the strange and savage natives who haunt the trees and of their legend of
THE FORBIDDEN TEMPLE OF THE INCAS!
THE FAWCETT MUSEUM LONDON
OPENS JULY 1 1920

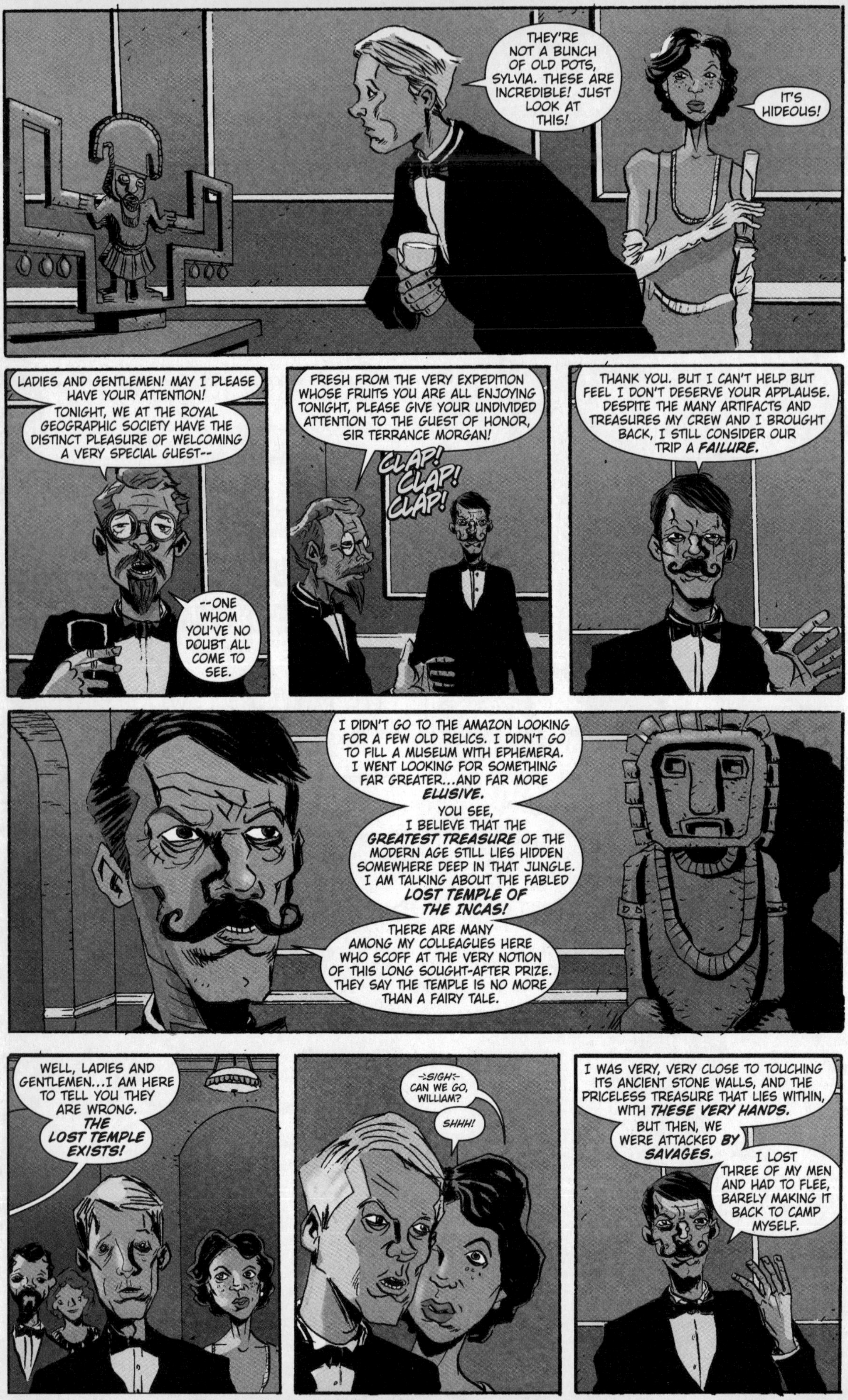
THEY'RE NOT A BUNCH OF OLD POTS, SYLVIA. THESE ARE INCREDIBLE! JUST LOOK AT THIS!
IT'S HIDEOUS!
LADIES AND GENTLEMEN! MAY I PLEASE HAVE YOUR ATTENTION!
TONIGHT, WE AT THE ROYAL GEOGRAPHIC SOCIETY HAVE THE DISTINCT PLEASURE OF WELCOMING A VERY SPECIAL GUEST--
--ONE WHOM YOU'VE NO DOUBT ALL COME TO SEE.
FRESH FROM THE VERY EXPEDITION WHOSE FRUITS YOU ARE ALL ENJOYING TONIGHT, PLEASE GIVE YOUR UNDIVIDED ATTENTION TO THE GUEST OF HONOR, SIR TERRANCE MORGAN!
CLAP! CLAP! CLAP!
THANK YOU. BUT I CAN'T HELP BUT FEEL I DON'T DESERVE YOUR APPLAUSE. DESPITE THE MANY ARTIFACTS AND TREASURES MY CREW AND I BROUGHT BACK, I STILL CONSIDER OUR TRIP A **FAILURE.**
I DIDN'T GO TO THE AMAZON LOOKING FOR A FEW OLD RELICS. I DIDN'T GO TO FILL A MUSEUM WITH EPHEMERA. I WENT LOOKING FOR SOMETHING FAR GREATER...AND FAR MORE **ELUSIVE.**
YOU SEE, I BELIEVE THAT THE **GREATEST TREASURE** OF THE MODERN AGE STILL LIES HIDDEN SOMEWHERE DEEP IN THAT JUNGLE. I AM TALKING ABOUT THE FABLED **LOST TEMPLE OF THE INCAS!**
THERE ARE MANY AMONG MY COLLEAGUES HERE WHO SCOFF AT THE VERY NOTION OF THIS LONG SOUGHT-AFTER PRIZE. THEY SAY THE TEMPLE IS NO MORE THAN A FAIRY TALE.
WELL, LADIES AND GENTLEMEN...I AM HERE TO TELL YOU THEY ARE WRONG. **THE LOST TEMPLE EXISTS!**
-SIGH- CAN WE GO, WILLIAM?
SHHH!
I WAS VERY, VERY CLOSE TO TOUCHING ITS ANCIENT STONE WALLS, AND THE PRICELESS TREASURE THAT LIES WITHIN, WITH **THESE VERY HANDS.**
BUT THEN, WE WERE ATTACKED **BY SAVAGES.**
I LOST THREE OF MY MEN AND HAD TO FLEE, BARELY MAKING IT BACK TO CAMP MYSELF.

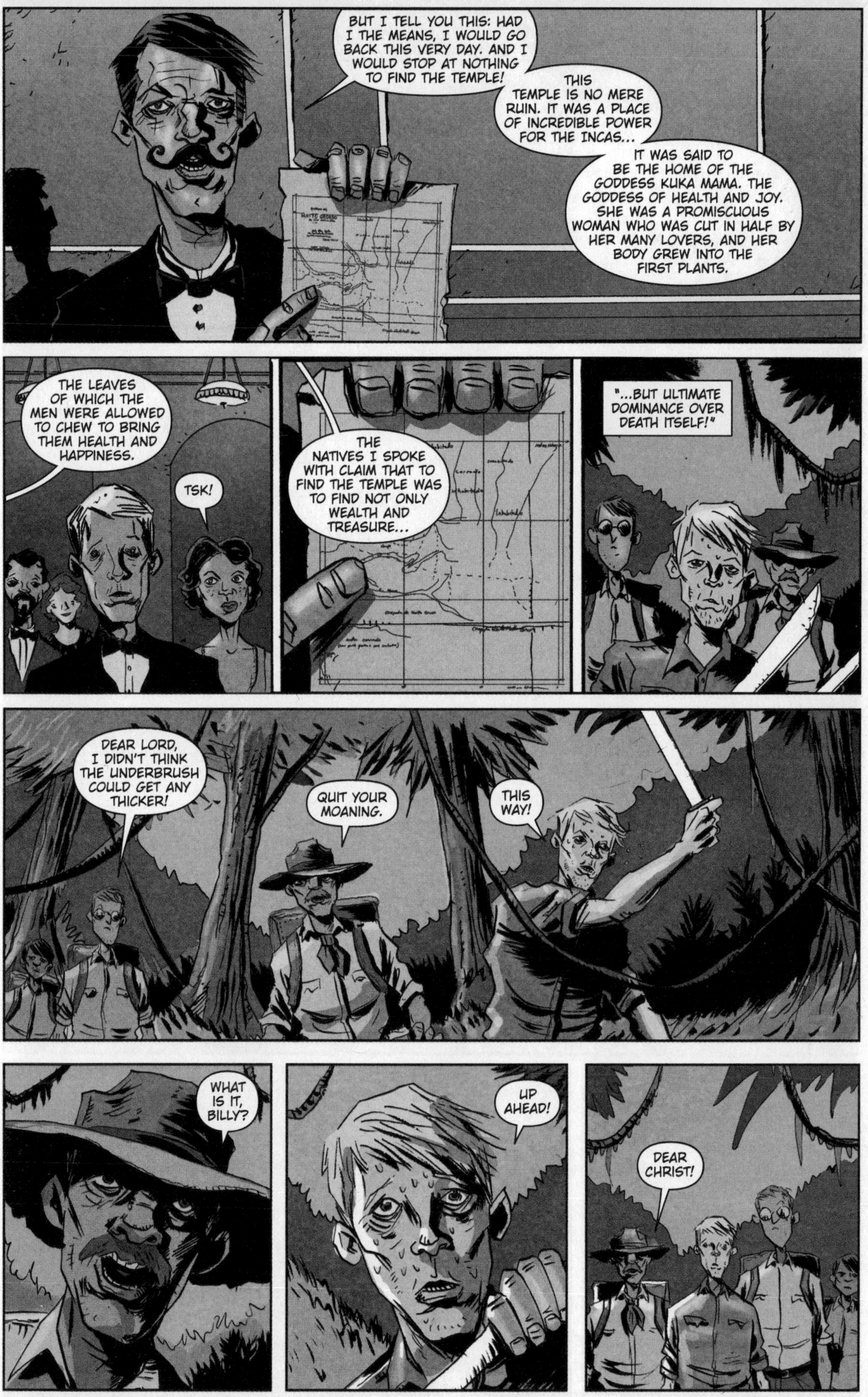
BUT I TELL YOU THIS: HAD I THE MEANS, I WOULD GO BACK THIS VERY DAY. AND I WOULD STOP AT NOTHING TO FIND THE TEMPLE!
THIS TEMPLE IS NO MERE RUIN. IT WAS A PLACE OF INCREDIBLE POWER FOR THE INCAS...
IT WAS SAID TO BE THE HOME OF THE GODDESS KUKA MAMA. THE GODDESS OF HEALTH AND JOY. SHE WAS A PROMISCUOUS WOMAN WHO WAS CUT IN HALF BY HER MANY LOVERS, AND HER BODY GREW INTO THE FIRST PLANTS.
THE LEAVES OF WHICH THE MEN WERE ALLOWED TO CHEW TO BRING THEM HEALTH AND HAPPINESS.
TSK!
THE NATIVES I SPOKE WITH CLAIM THAT TO FIND THE TEMPLE WAS TO FIND NOT ONLY WEALTH AND TREASURE...
"...BUT ULTIMATE DOMINANCE OVER DEATH ITSELF!"
DEAR LORD, I DIDN'T THINK THE UNDERBRUSH COULD GET ANY THICKER!
QUIT YOUR MOANING.
THIS WAY!
WHAT IS IT, BILLY?
UP AHEAD!
DEAR CHRIST!

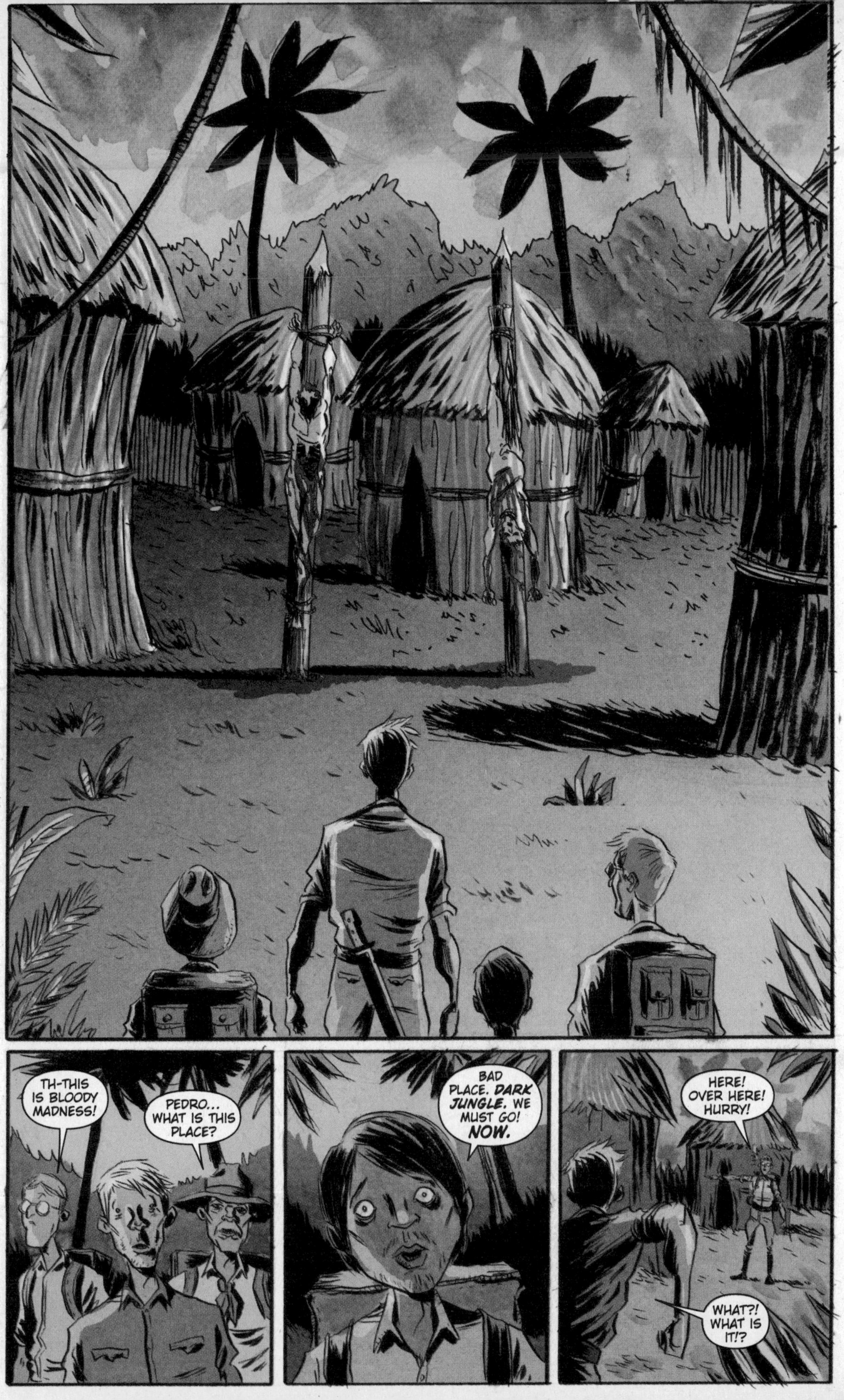
TH-THIS IS BLOODY MADNESS!
PEDRO... WHAT IS THIS PLACE?
BAD PLACE. DARK JUNGLE. WE MUST GO! NOW.
HERE! OVER HERE! HURRY!
WHAT?! WHAT IS IT!?

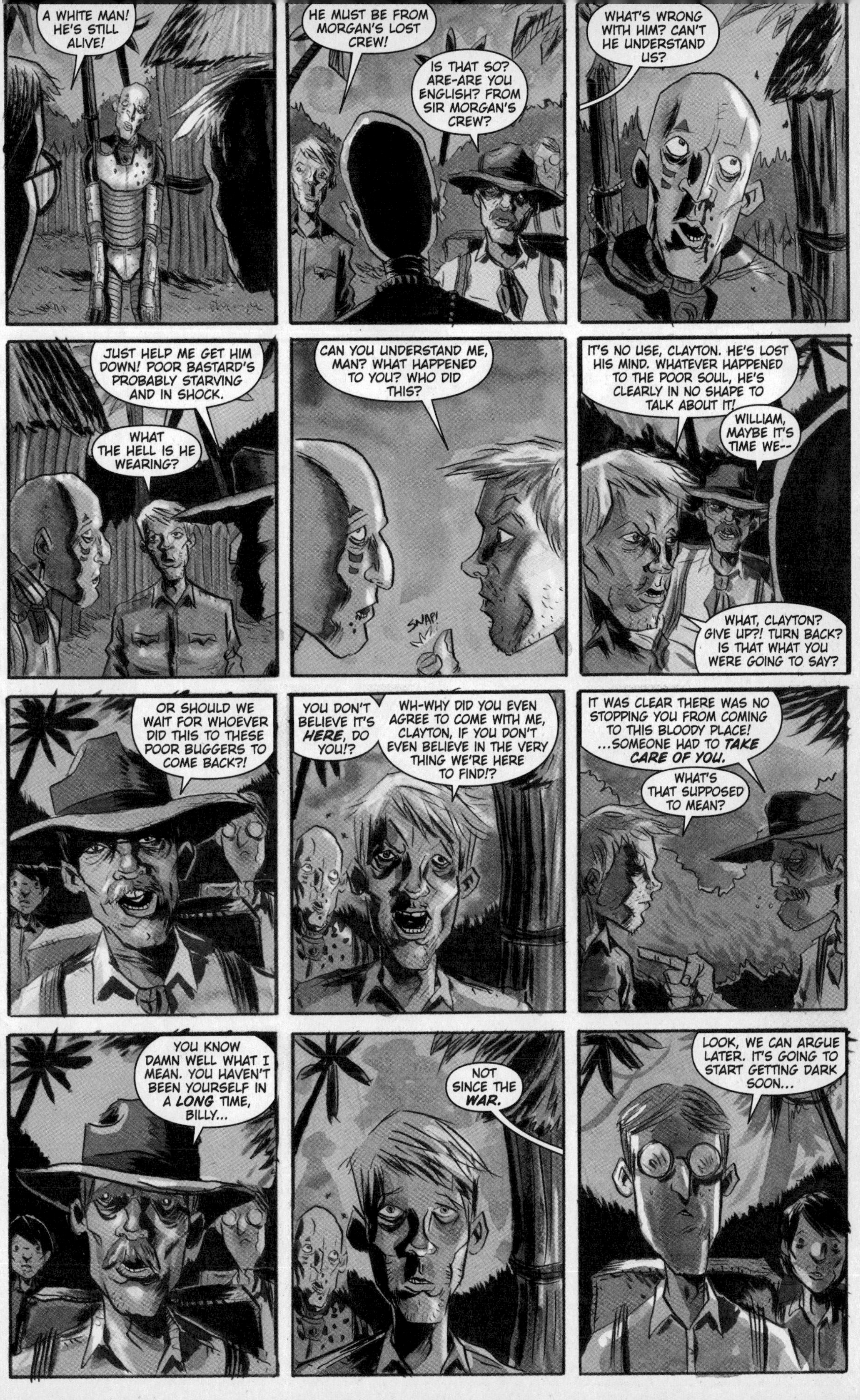
A WHITE MAN! HE'S STILL ALIVE!
HE MUST BE FROM MORGAN'S LOST CREW!
IS THAT SO? ARE-ARE YOU ENGLISH? FROM SIR MORGAN'S CREW?
WHAT'S WRONG WITH HIM? CAN'T HE UNDERSTAND US?
JUST HELP ME GET HIM DOWN! POOR BASTARD'S PROBABLY STARVING AND IN SHOCK.
WHAT THE HELL IS HE WEARING?
CAN YOU UNDERSTAND ME, MAN? WHAT HAPPENED TO YOU? WHO DID THIS?
SNAP!
IT'S NO USE, CLAYTON. HE'S LOST HIS MIND. WHATEVER HAPPENED TO THE POOR SOUL, HE'S CLEARLY IN NO SHAPE TO TALK ABOUT IT!
WILLIAM, MAYBE IT'S TIME WE--
WHAT, CLAYTON? GIVE UP?! TURN BACK? IS THAT WHAT YOU WERE GOING TO SAY?
OR SHOULD WE WAIT FOR WHOEVER DID THIS TO THESE POOR BUGGERS TO COME BACK?!
YOU DON'T BELIEVE IT'S HERE, DO YOU!?
WH-WHY DID YOU EVEN AGREE TO COME WITH ME, CLAYTON, IF YOU DON'T EVEN BELIEVE IN THE VERY THING WE'RE HERE TO FIND!?
IT WAS CLEAR THERE WAS NO STOPPING YOU FROM COMING TO THIS BLOODY PLACE! ...SOMEONE HAD TO TAKE CARE OF YOU.
WHAT'S THAT SUPPOSED TO MEAN?
YOU KNOW DAMN WELL WHAT I MEAN. YOU HAVEN'T BEEN YOURSELF IN A LONG TIME, BILLY...
NOT SINCE THE WAR.
LOOK, WE CAN ARGUE LATER. IT'S GOING TO START GETTING DARK SOON...

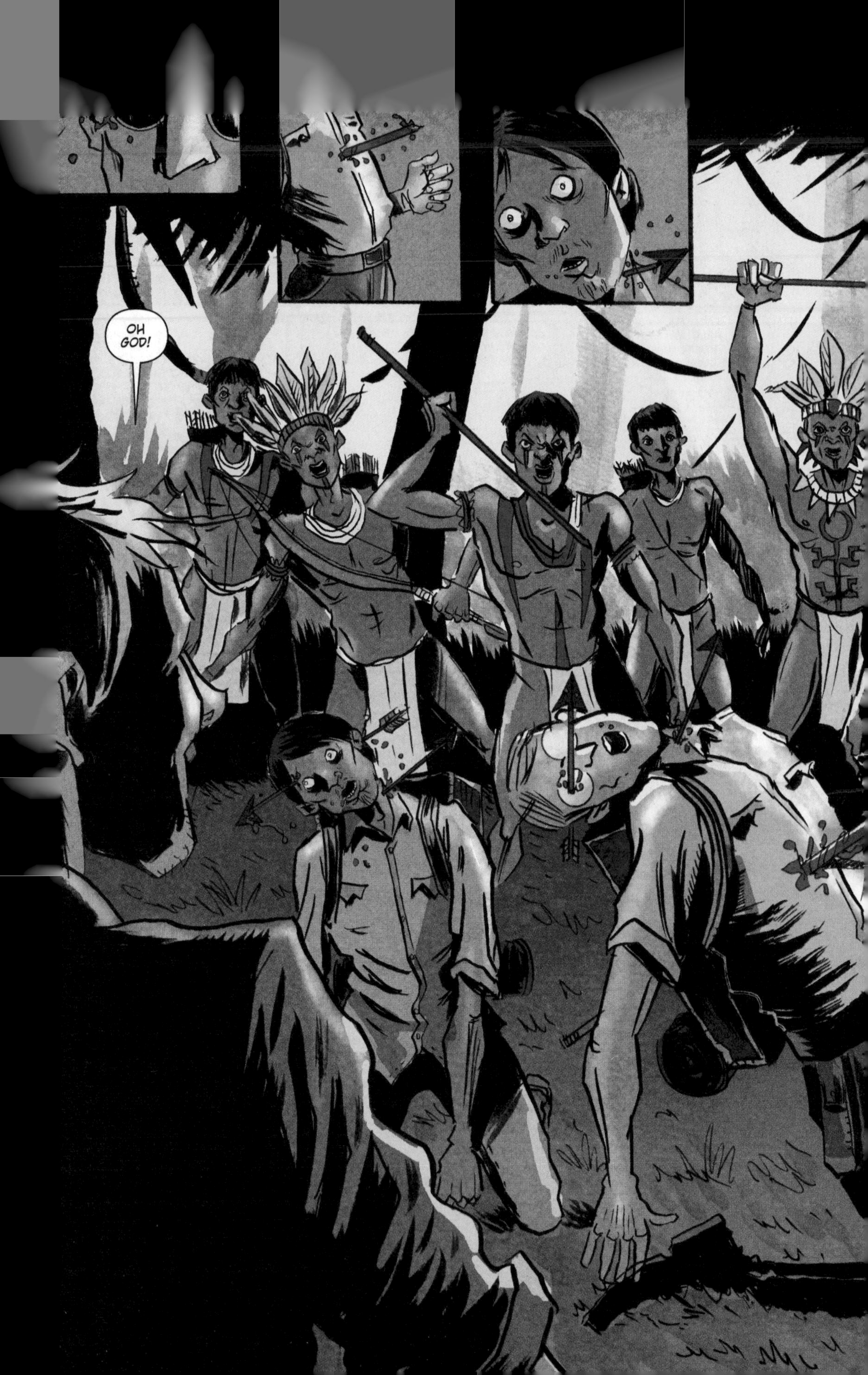
OH GOD!

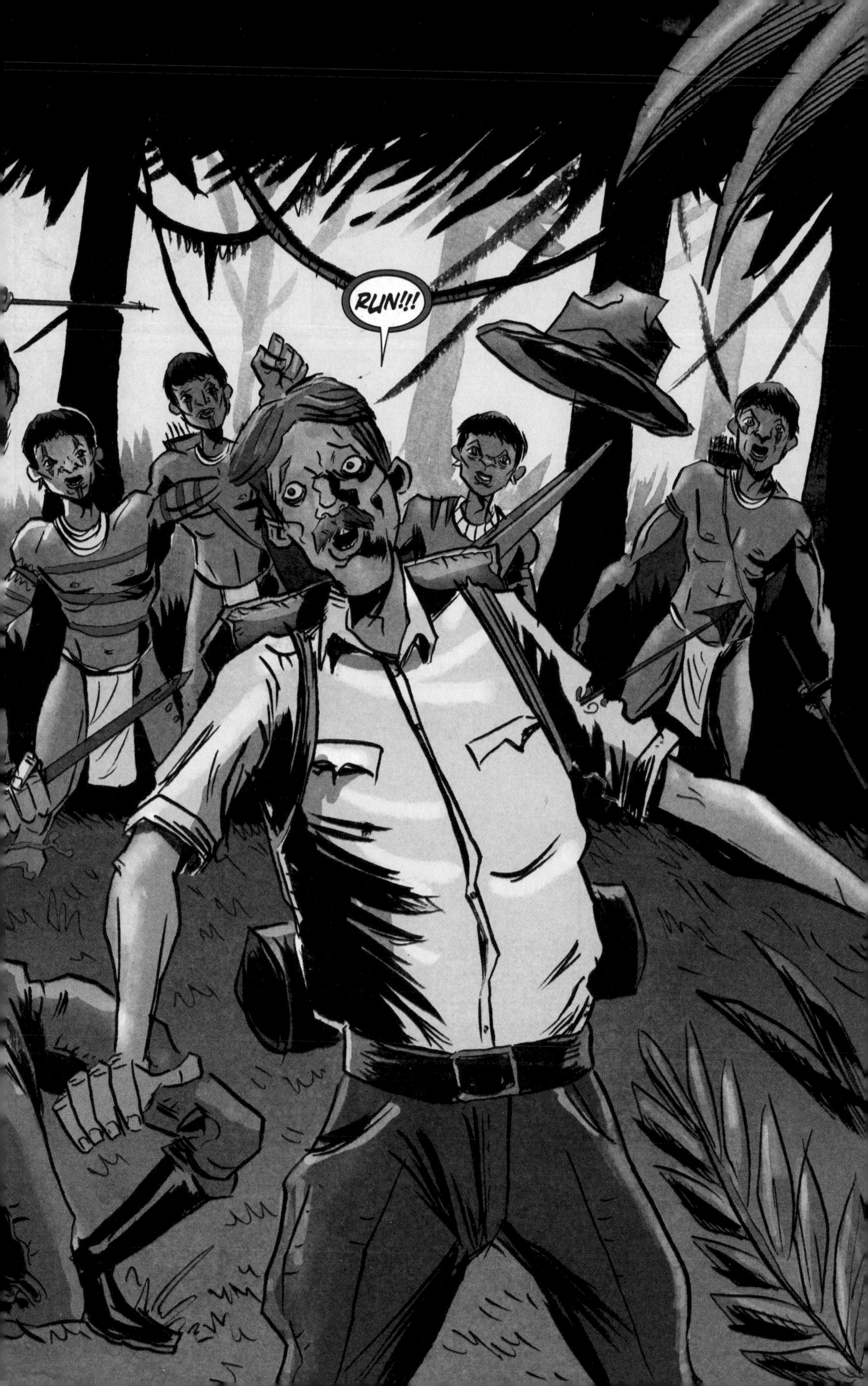
RUN!!!

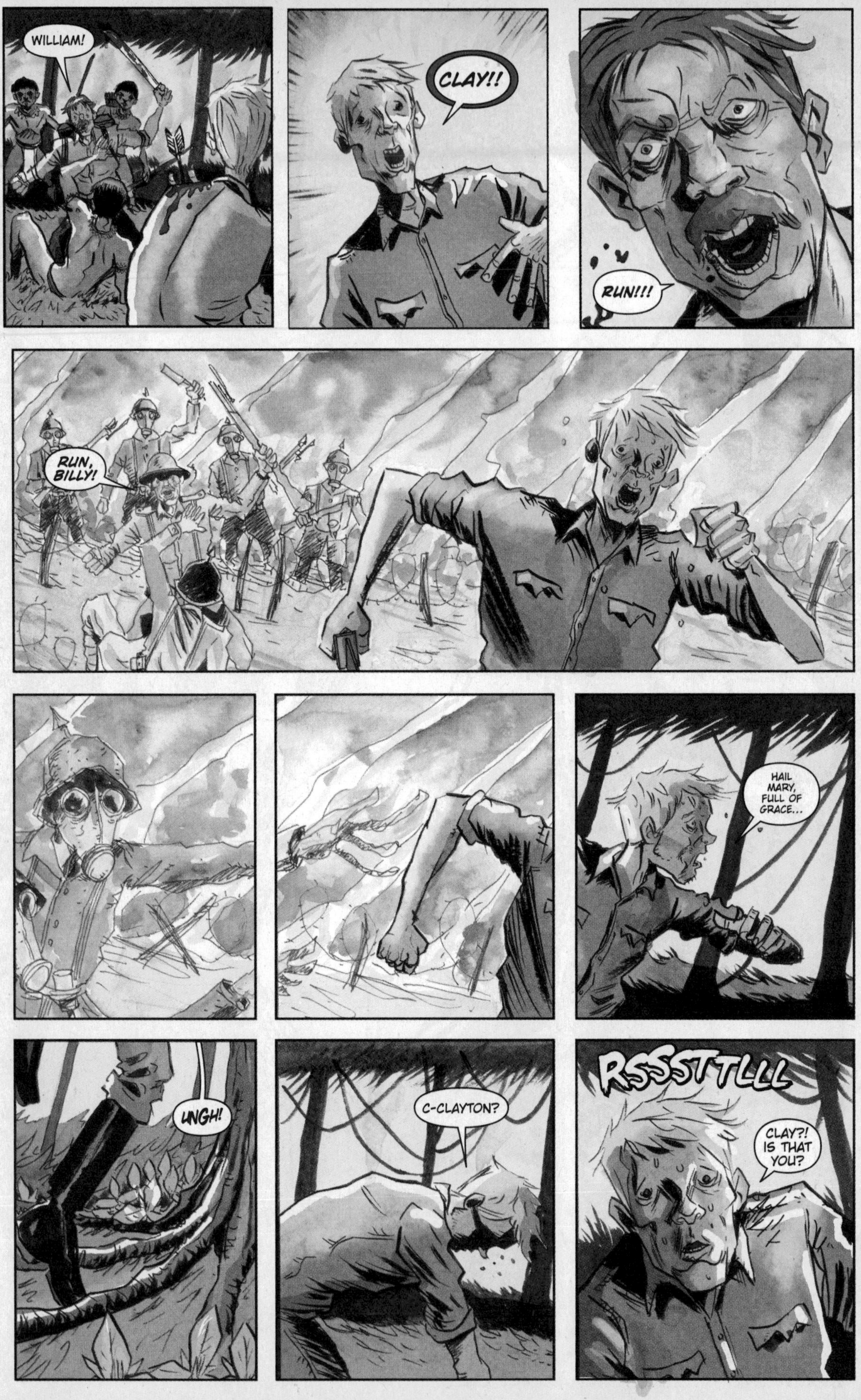
WILLIAM!
CLAY!!
RUN!!!
RUN, BILLY!
HAIL MARY, FULL OF GRACE...
UNGH!
C-CLAYTON?
RSSSTTLLL
CLAY?! IS THAT YOU?

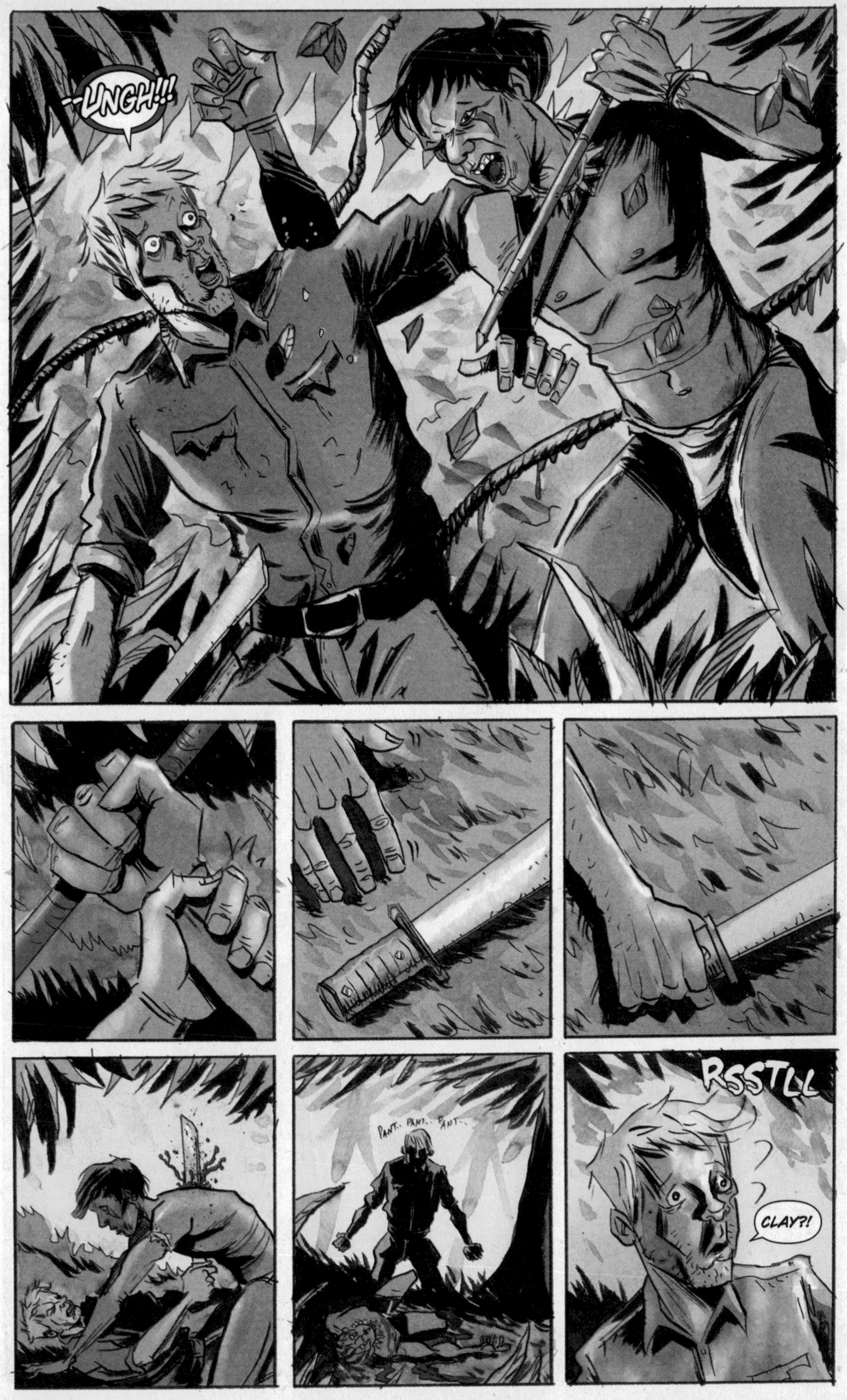
--UNGH!!!
PANT.. PANT.. PANT..
RSSTLL
CLAY?!

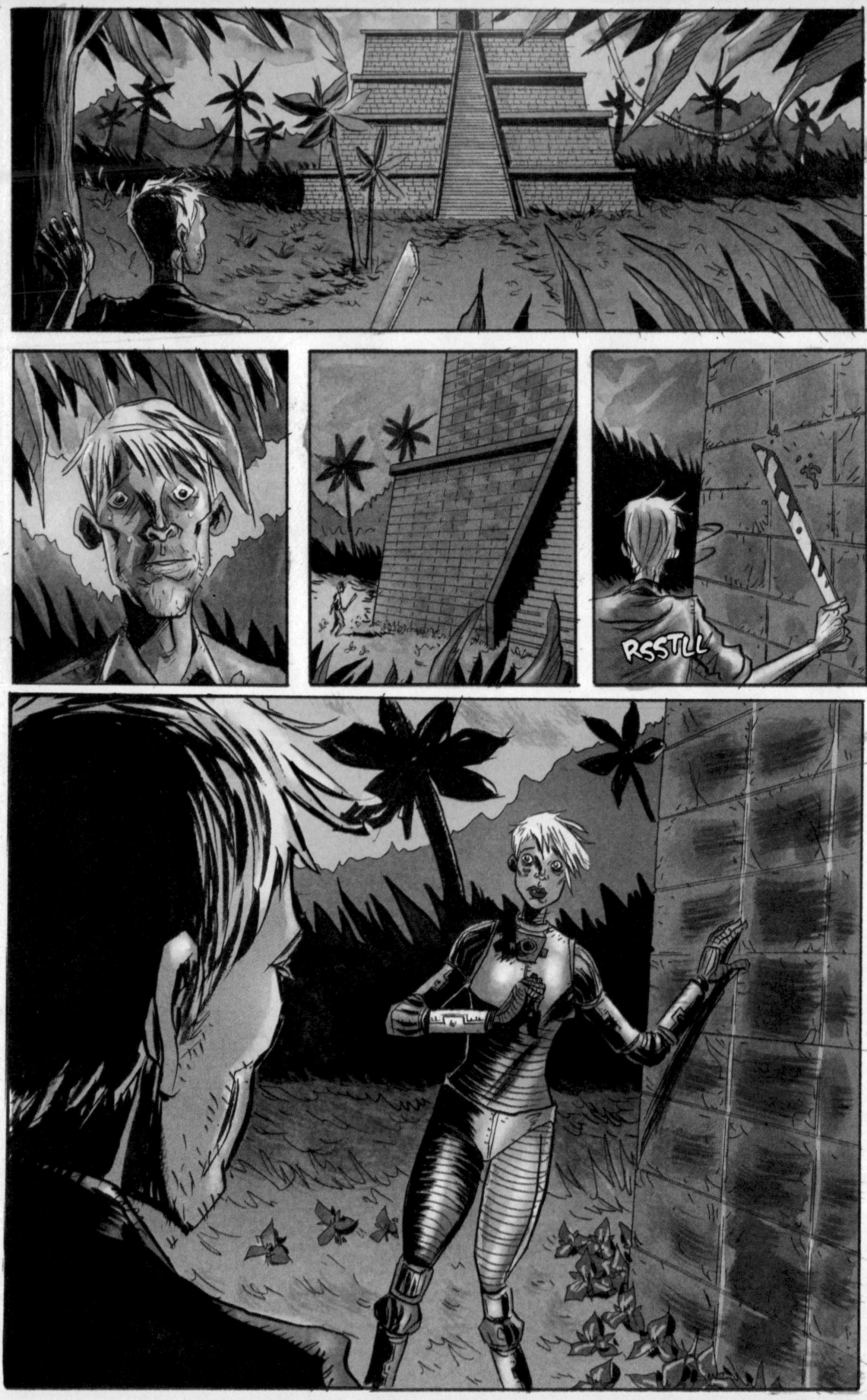
RSSTLL

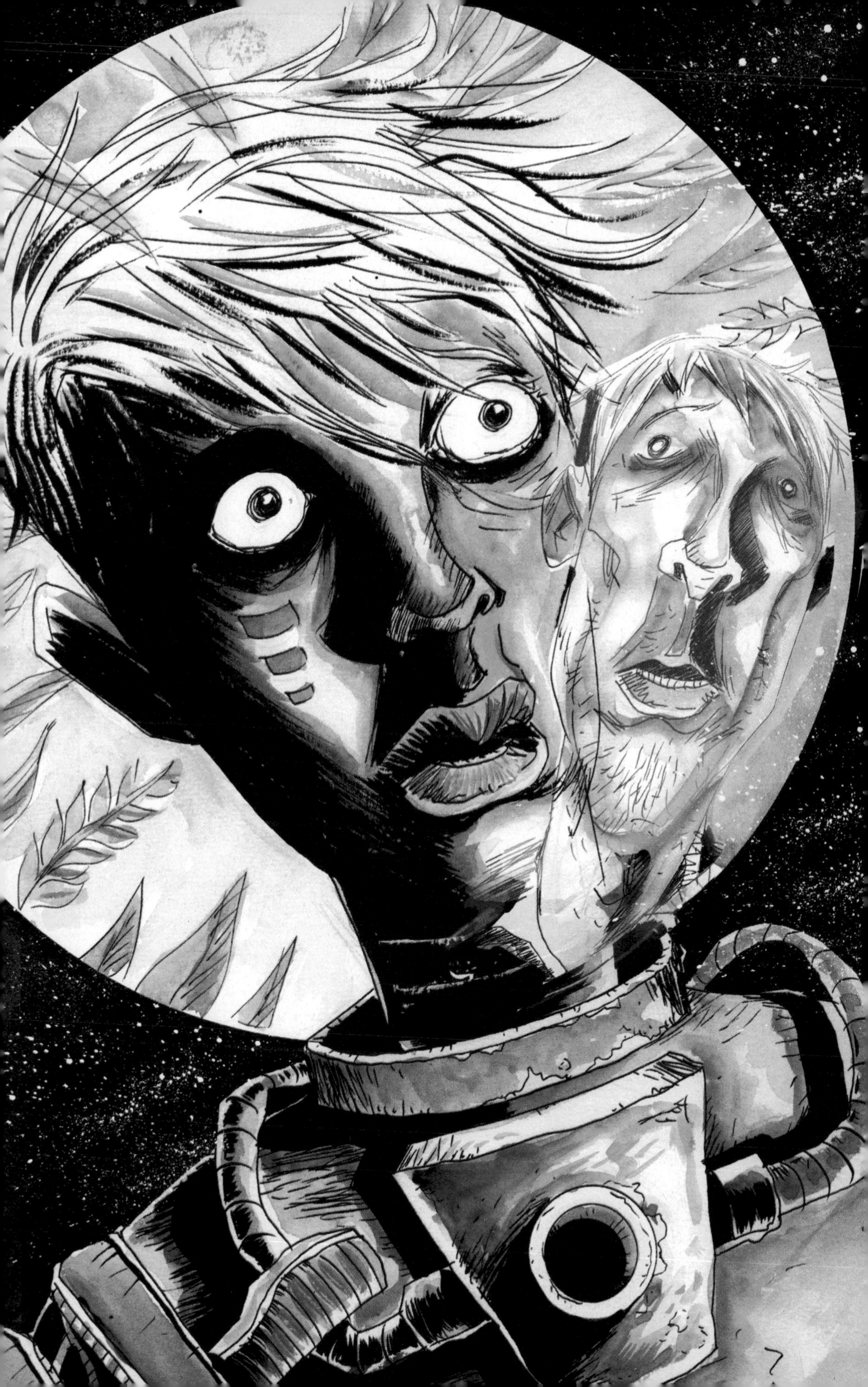

CHAPTER 2:
BINARY SYSTEMS

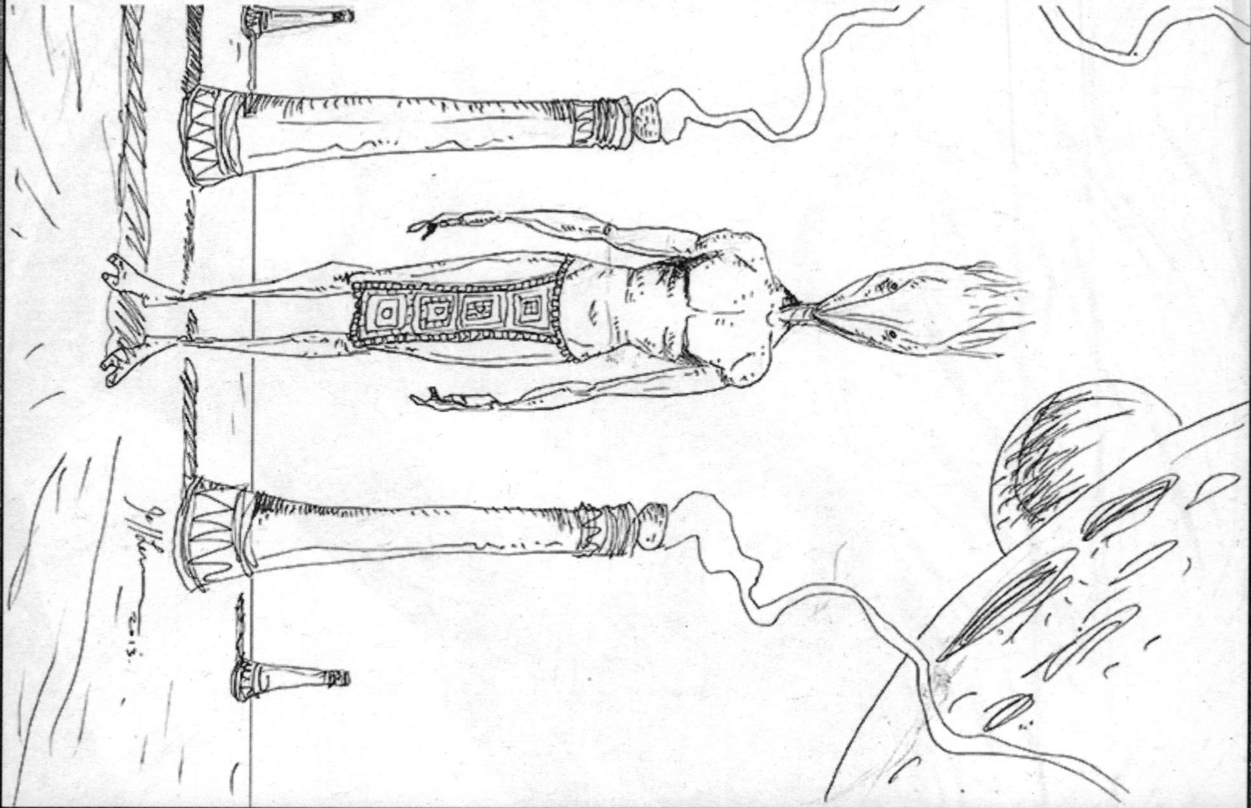

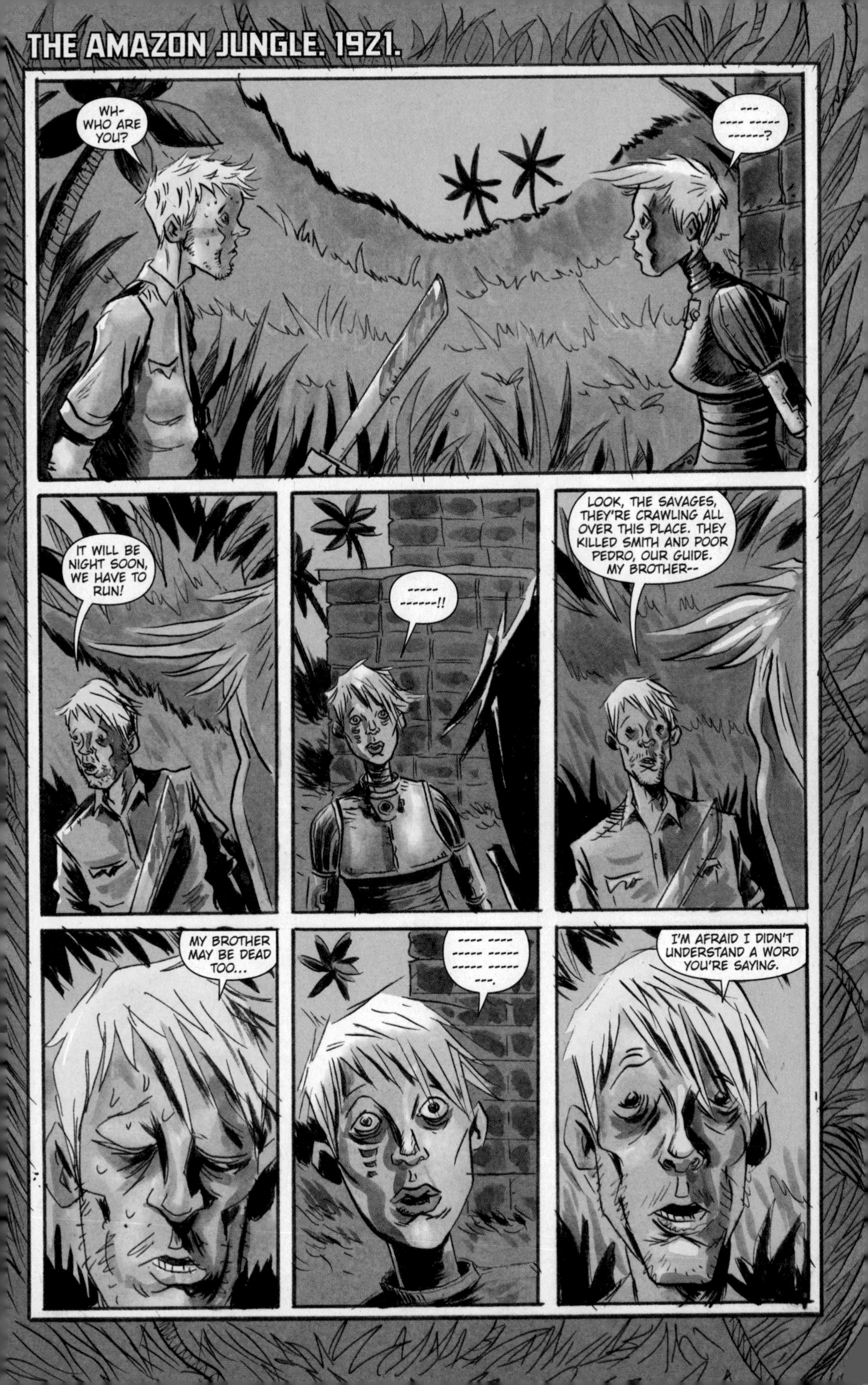
THE AMAZON JUNGLE. 1921.
WH- WHO ARE YOU?
--- ---- ----- ------?
IT WILL BE NIGHT SOON, WE HAVE TO RUN!
----- ------!!
LOOK, THE SAVAGES, THEY'RE CRAWLING ALL OVER THIS PLACE. THEY KILLED SMITH AND POOR PEDRO, OUR GUIDE. MY BROTHER--
MY BROTHER MAY BE DEAD TOO...
---- ---- ----- ----- ----- ----- ---.
I'M AFRAID I DIDN'T UNDERSTAND A WORD YOU'RE SAYING.

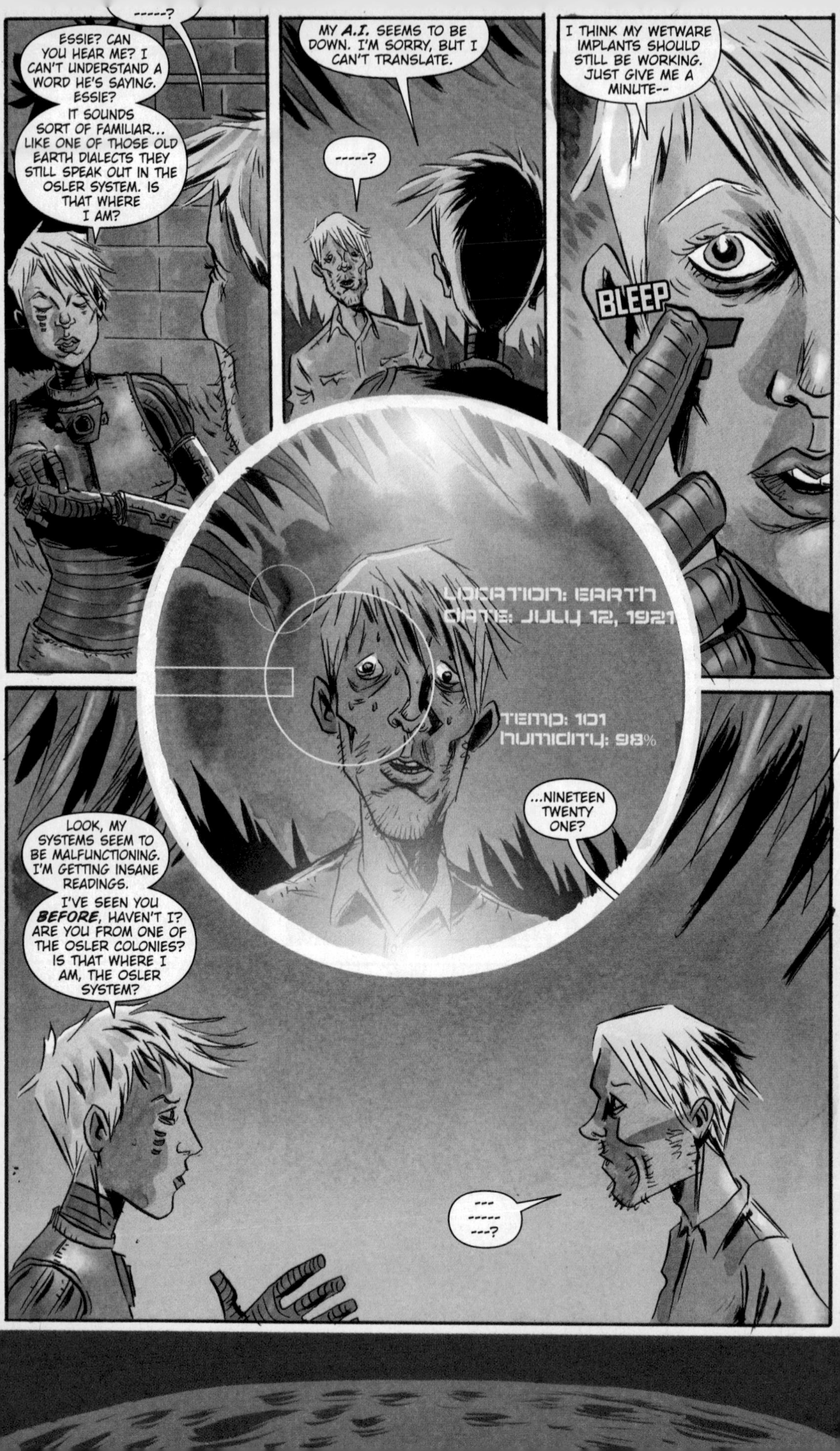

-----?
ESSIE? CAN YOU HEAR ME? I CAN'T UNDERSTAND A WORD HE'S SAYING. ESSIE?
IT SOUNDS SORT OF FAMILIAR... LIKE ONE OF THOSE OLD EARTH DIALECTS THEY STILL SPEAK OUT IN THE OSLER SYSTEM. IS THAT WHERE I AM?
MY A.I. SEEMS TO BE DOWN. I'M SORRY, BUT I CAN'T TRANSLATE.
-----?
I THINK MY WETWARE IMPLANTS SHOULD STILL BE WORKING. JUST GIVE ME A MINUTE--
BLEEP
LOCATION: EARTH
DATE: JULY 12, 1921
TEMP: 101
HUMIDITY: 98%
...NINETEEN TWENTY ONE?
LOOK, MY SYSTEMS SEEM TO BE MALFUNCTIONING. I'M GETTING INSANE READINGS.
I'VE SEEN YOU BEFORE, HAVEN'T I? ARE YOU FROM ONE OF THE OSLER COLONIES? IS THAT WHERE I AM, THE OSLER SYSTEM?
--- ----- ---?

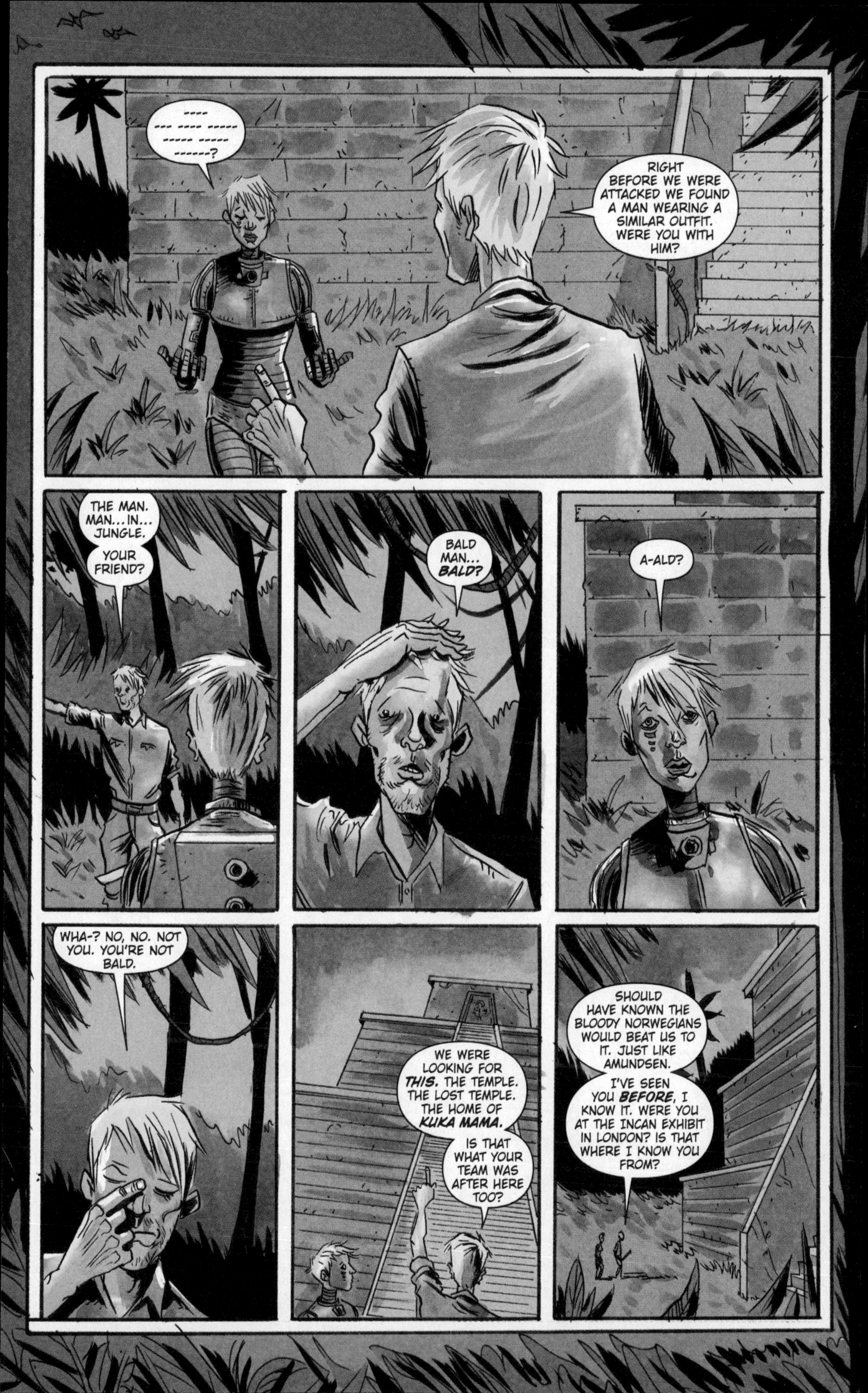

--- ---- -----
----- -----
------?
RIGHT BEFORE WE WERE ATTACKED WE FOUND A MAN WEARING A SIMILAR OUTFIT. WERE YOU WITH HIM?
THE MAN. MAN... IN... JUNGLE.
YOUR FRIEND?
BALD MAN... BALD?
A-ALD?
WHA-? NO, NO. NOT YOU. YOU'RE NOT BALD.
WE WERE LOOKING FOR THIS. THE TEMPLE. THE LOST TEMPLE. THE HOME OF KUKA MAMA.
IS THAT WHAT YOUR TEAM WAS AFTER HERE TOO?
SHOULD HAVE KNOWN THE BLOODY NORWEGIANS WOULD BEAT US TO IT. JUST LIKE AMUNDSEN.
I'VE SEEN YOU BEFORE, I KNOW IT. WERE YOU AT THE INCAN EXHIBIT IN LONDON? IS THAT WHERE I KNOW YOU FROM?

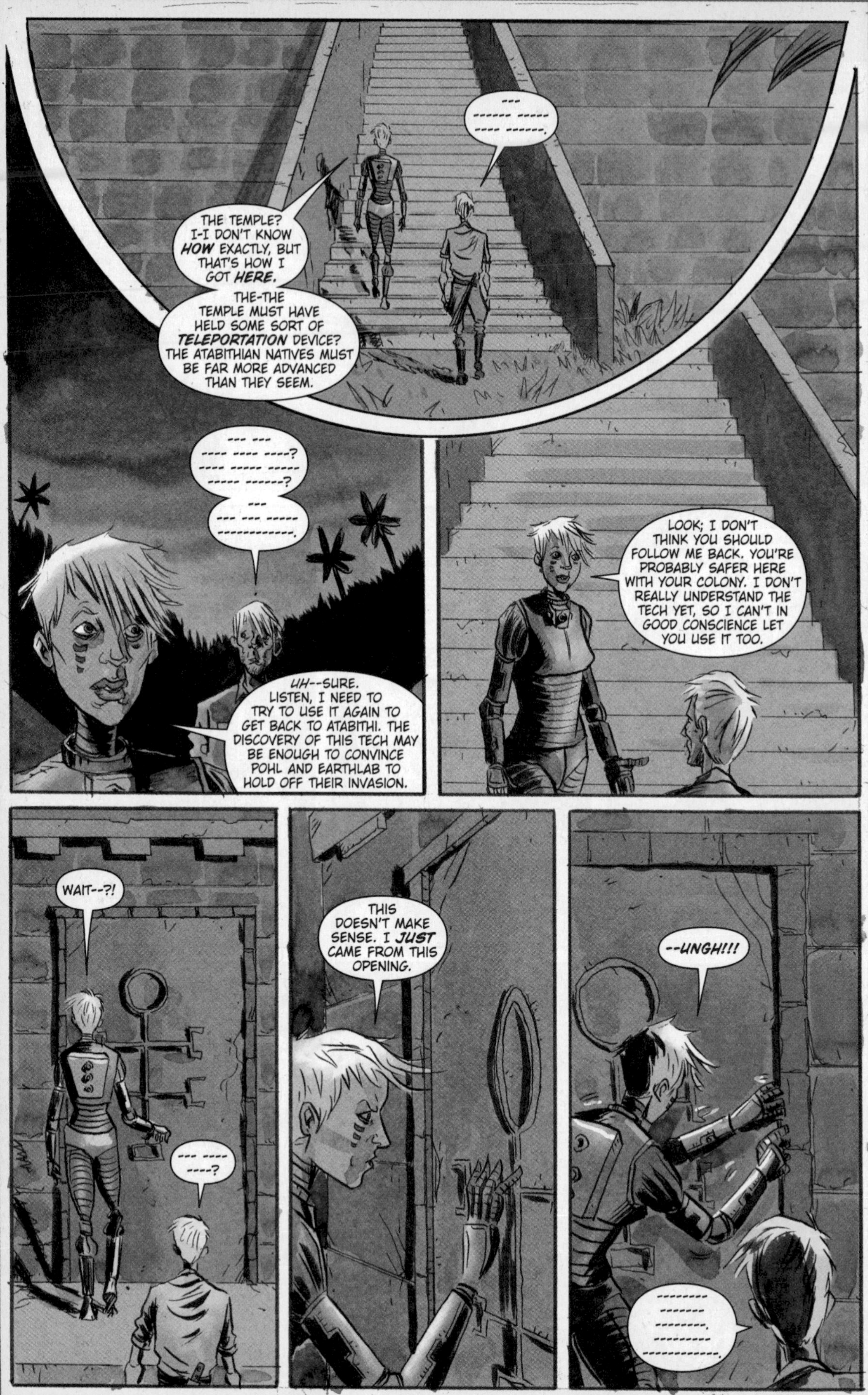
THE TEMPLE? I-I DON'T KNOW HOW EXACTLY, BUT THAT'S HOW I GOT HERE.
THE-THE TEMPLE MUST HAVE HELD SOME SORT OF TELEPORTATION DEVICE? THE ATABITHIAN NATIVES MUST BE FAR MORE ADVANCED THAN THEY SEEM.
UH--SURE. LISTEN, I NEED TO TRY TO USE IT AGAIN TO GET BACK TO ATABITHI. THE DISCOVERY OF THIS TECH MAY BE ENOUGH TO CONVINCE POHL AND EARTHLAB TO HOLD OFF THEIR INVASION.
LOOK; I DON'T THINK YOU SHOULD FOLLOW ME BACK. YOU'RE PROBABLY SAFER HERE WITH YOUR COLONY. I DON'T REALLY UNDERSTAND THE TECH YET, SO I CAN'T IN GOOD CONSCIENCE LET YOU USE IT TOO.
WAIT--?!
THIS DOESN'T MAKE SENSE. I JUST CAME FROM THIS OPENING.
--UNGH!!!

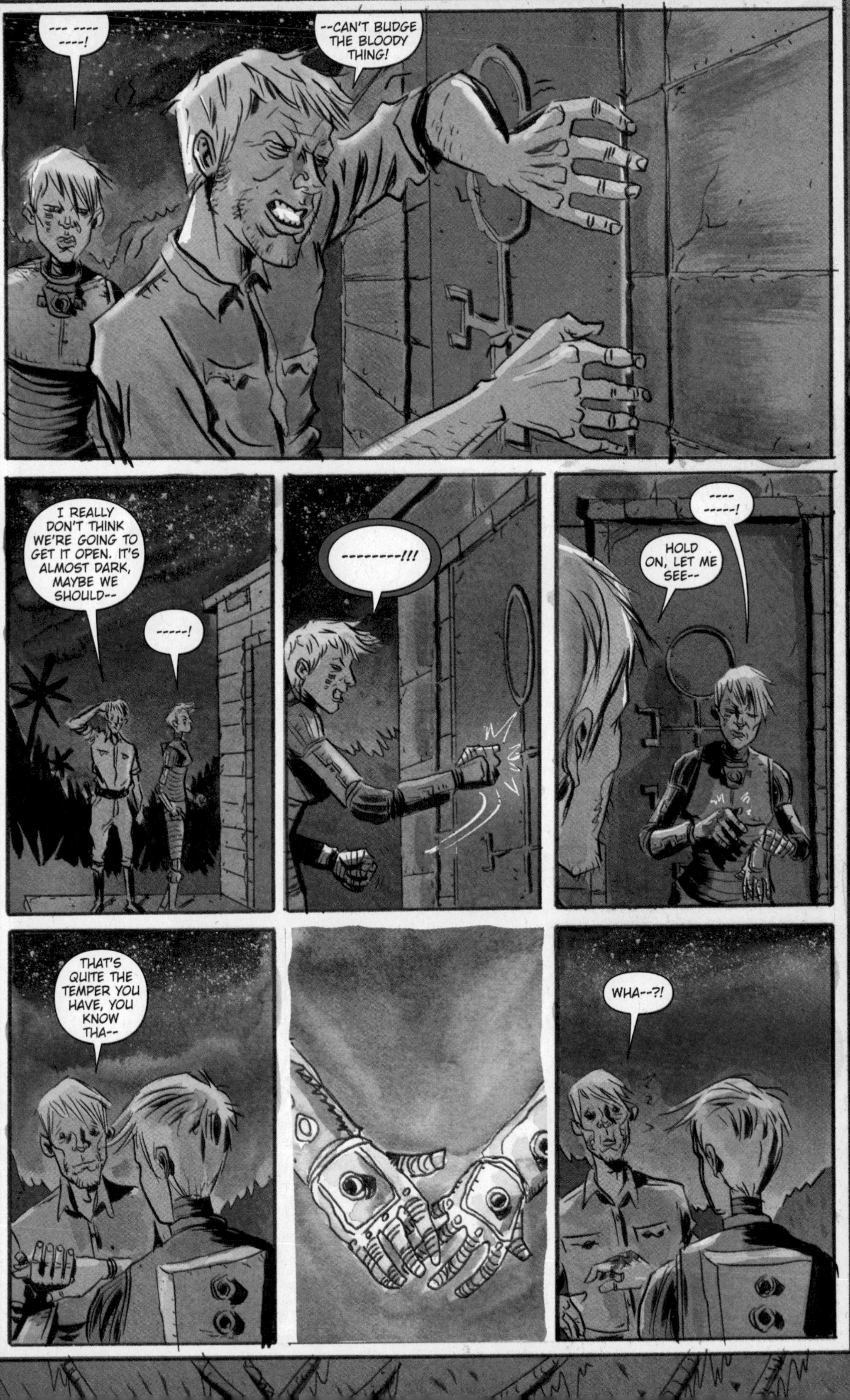
--- ----
----!
--CAN'T BUDGE THE BLOODY THING!
I REALLY DON'T THINK WE'RE GOING TO GET IT OPEN. IT'S ALMOST DARK, MAYBE WE SHOULD--
-----!
---------!!!

-----!
HOLD ON, LET ME SEE--
THAT'S QUITE THE TEMPER YOU HAVE, YOU KNOW THA--
WHA--?!

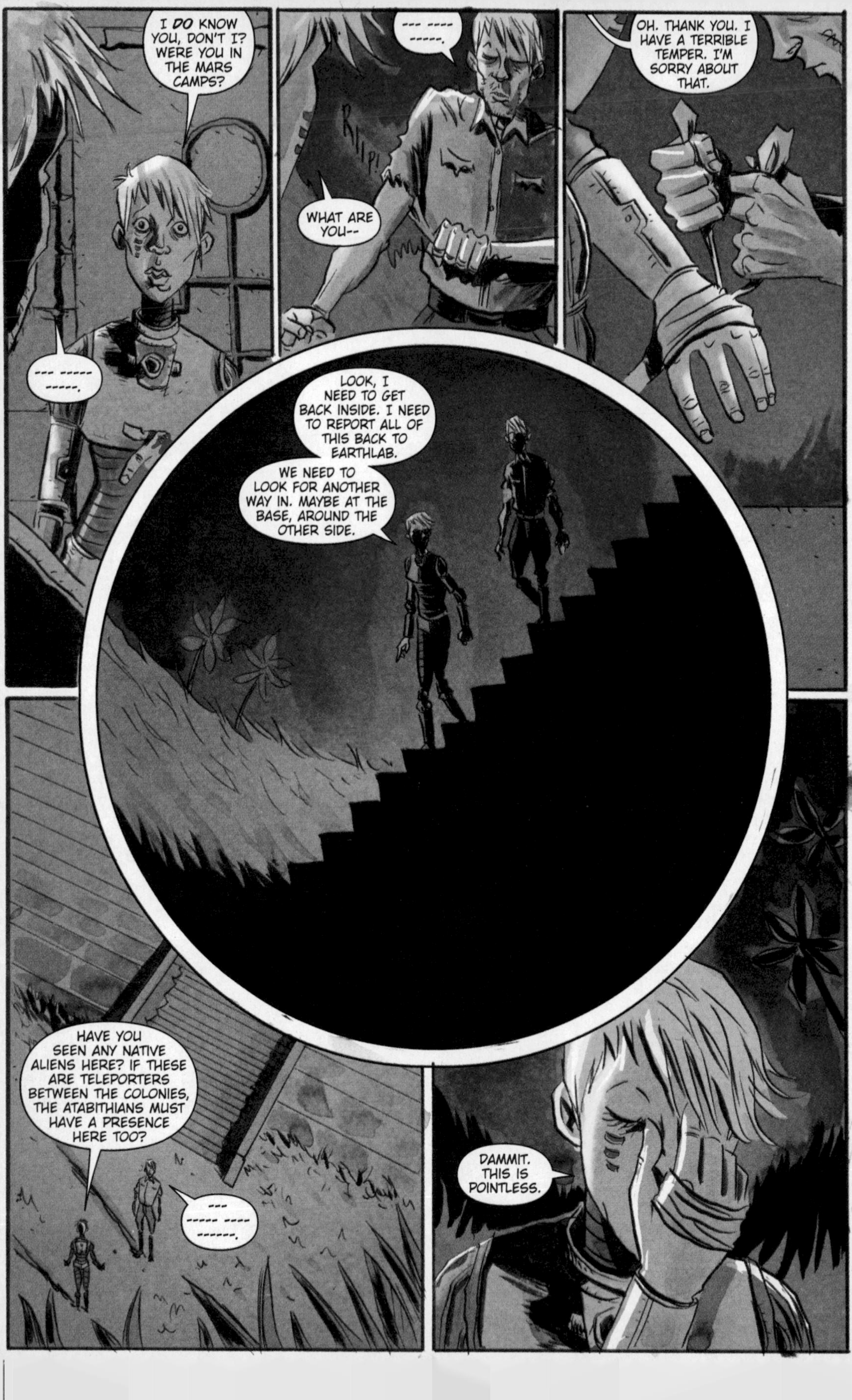
I DO KNOW YOU, DON'T I? WERE YOU IN THE MARS CAMPS?
--- ----- -----.
--- ---- -----.
WHAT ARE YOU--
OH. THANK YOU. I HAVE A TERRIBLE TEMPER. I'M SORRY ABOUT THAT.
LOOK, I NEED TO GET BACK INSIDE. I NEED TO REPORT ALL OF THIS BACK TO EARTHLAB.
WE NEED TO LOOK FOR ANOTHER WAY IN. MAYBE AT THE BASE, AROUND THE OTHER SIDE.
HAVE YOU SEEN ANY NATIVE ALIENS HERE? IF THESE ARE TELEPORTERS BETWEEN THE COLONIES, THE ATABITHIANS MUST HAVE A PRESENCE HERE TOO?
--- ----- ---- ------.
DAMMIT. THIS IS POINTLESS.

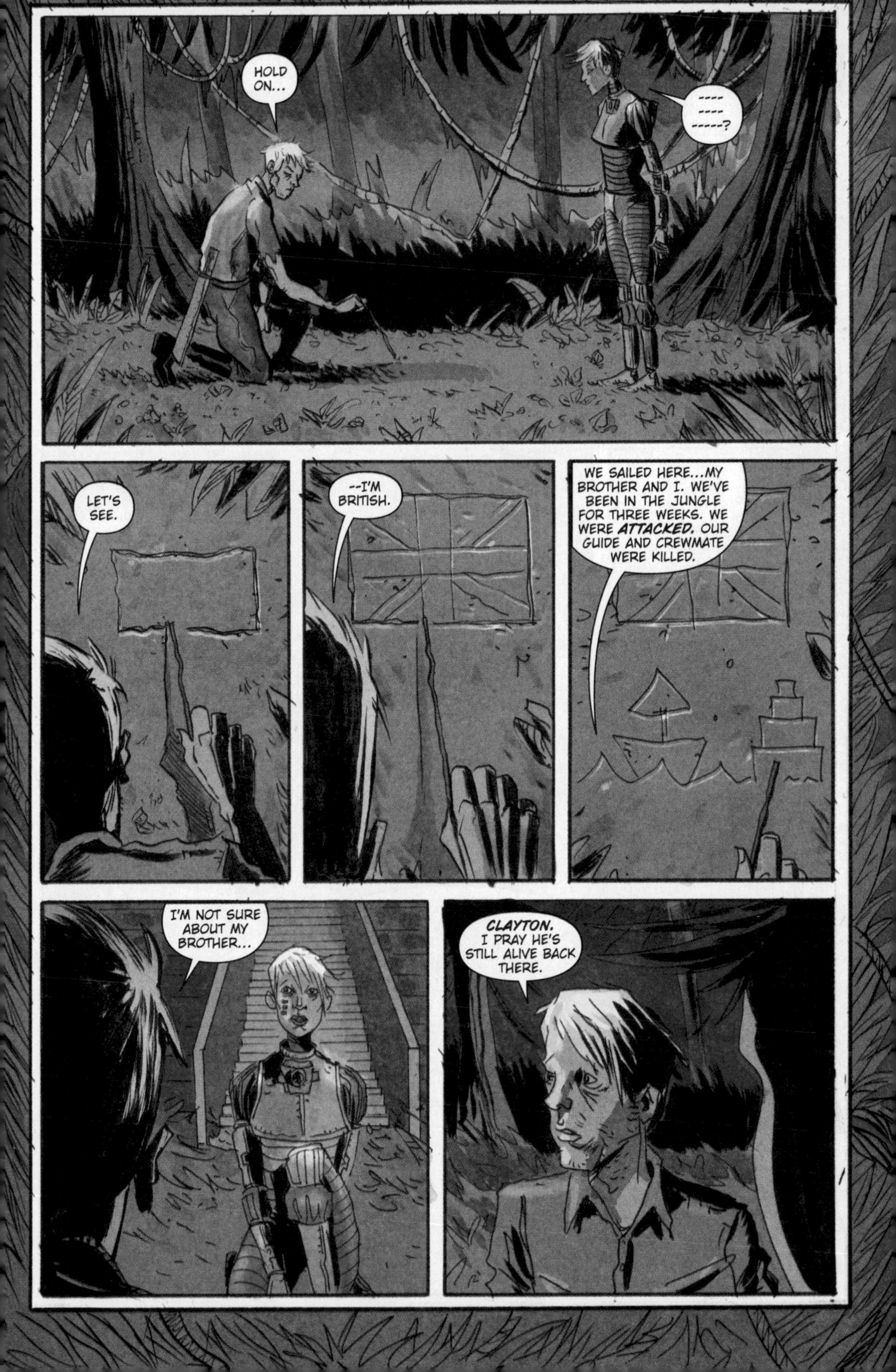
HOLD ON...

-----?
LET'S SEE.
--I'M BRITISH.
WE SAILED HERE...MY BROTHER AND I. WE'VE BEEN IN THE JUNGLE FOR THREE WEEKS. WE WERE ATTACKED. OUR GUIDE AND CREWMATE WERE KILLED.
I'M NOT SURE ABOUT MY BROTHER...
CLAYTON. I PRAY HE'S STILL ALIVE BACK THERE.

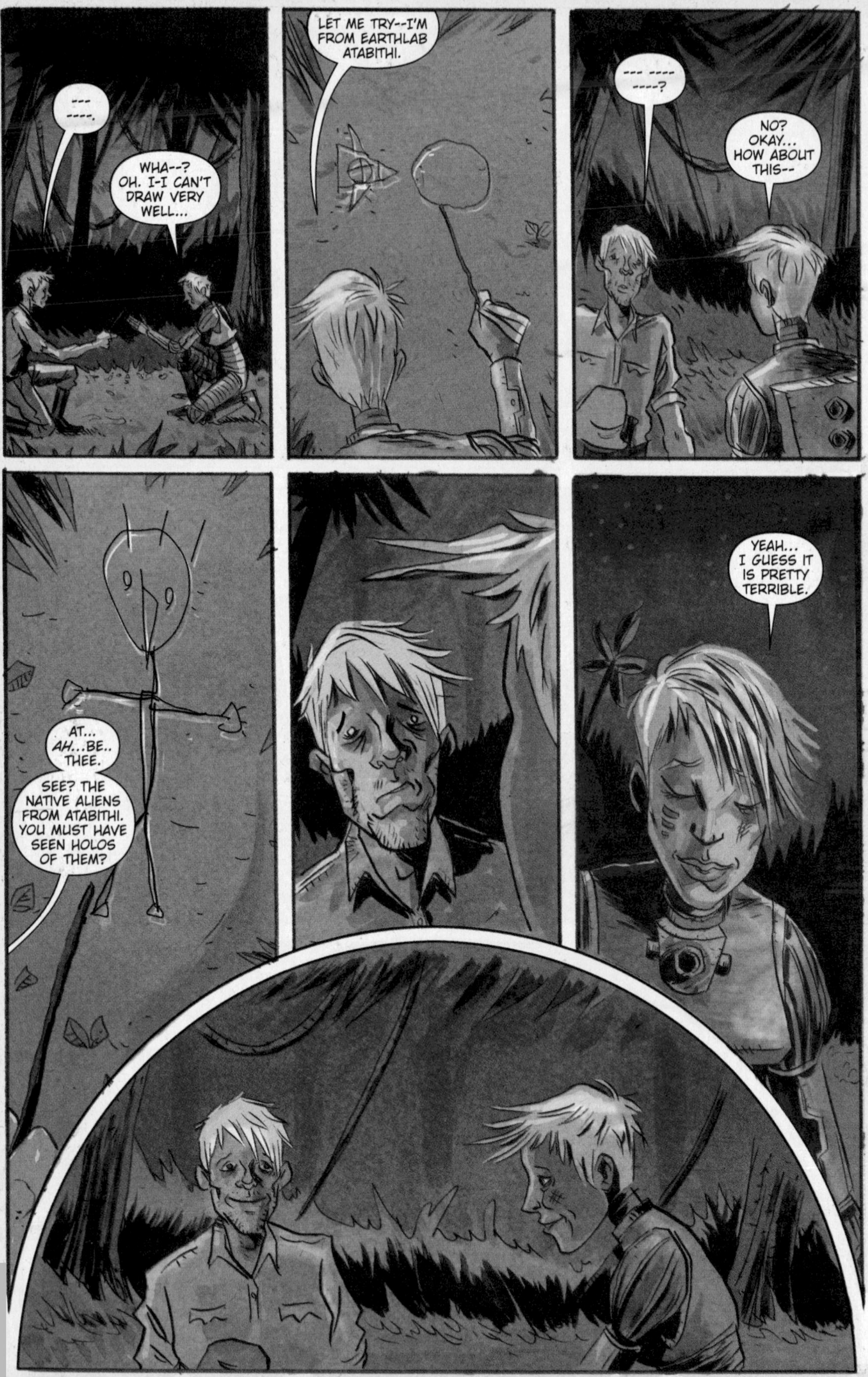
--- ----.
WHA--? OH. I-I CAN'T DRAW VERY WELL...
LET ME TRY--I'M FROM EARTHLAB ATABITHI.
--- ---- ----?
NO? OKAY... HOW ABOUT THIS--
AT... AH...BE.. THEE.
SEE? THE NATIVE ALIENS FROM ATABITHI. YOU MUST HAVE SEEN HOLOS OF THEM?
YEAH... I GUESS IT IS PRETTY TERRIBLE.

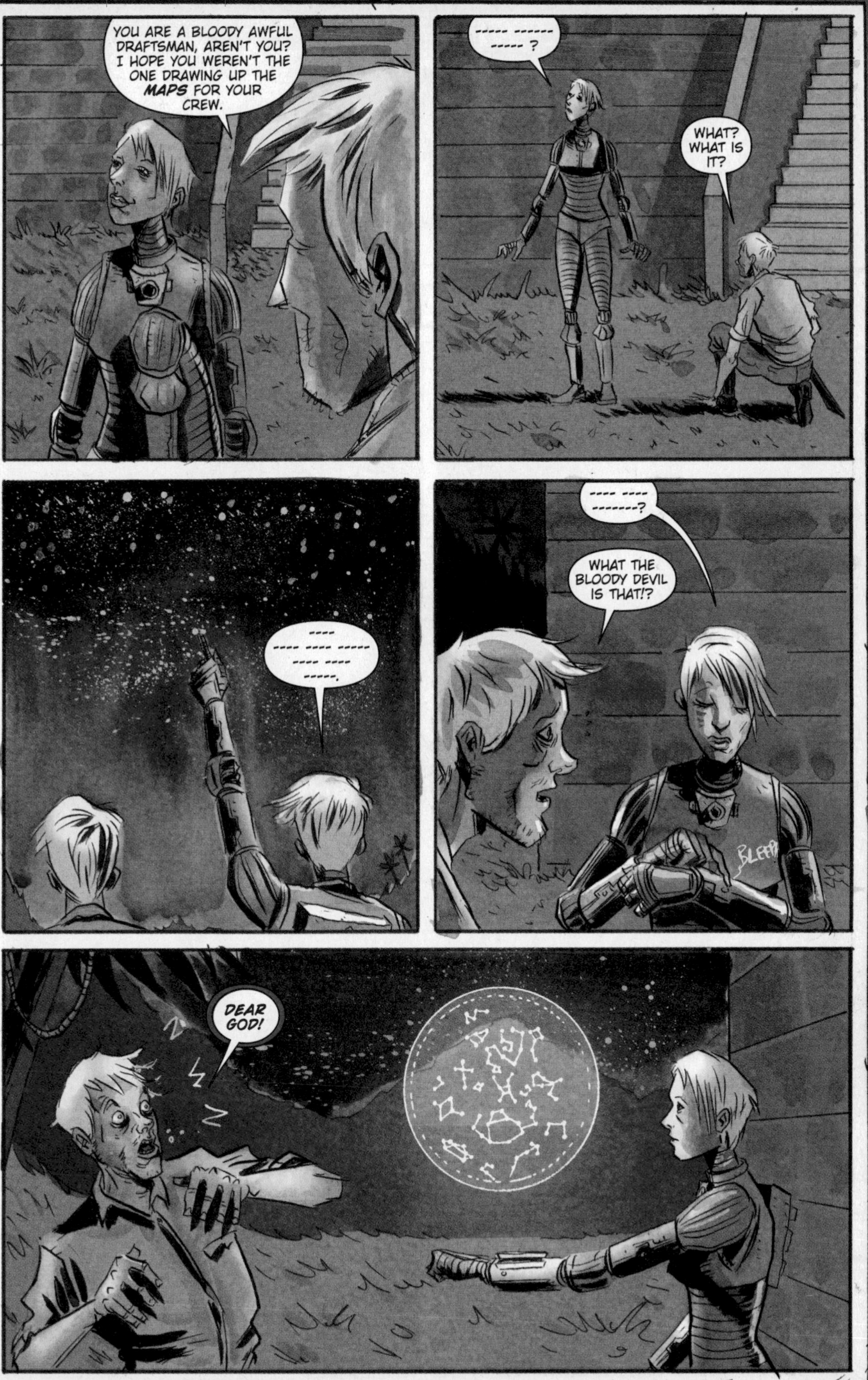
YOU ARE A BLOODY AWFUL DRAFTSMAN, AREN'T YOU? I HOPE YOU WEREN'T THE ONE DRAWING UP THE **MAPS** FOR YOUR CREW.
----- ------ ----- ?
WHAT? WHAT IS IT?
---- ---- ---- ----- ---- ---- -----.
---- ---- -------?
WHAT THE BLOODY DEVIL IS THAT!?
BLEEP
DEAR GOD!

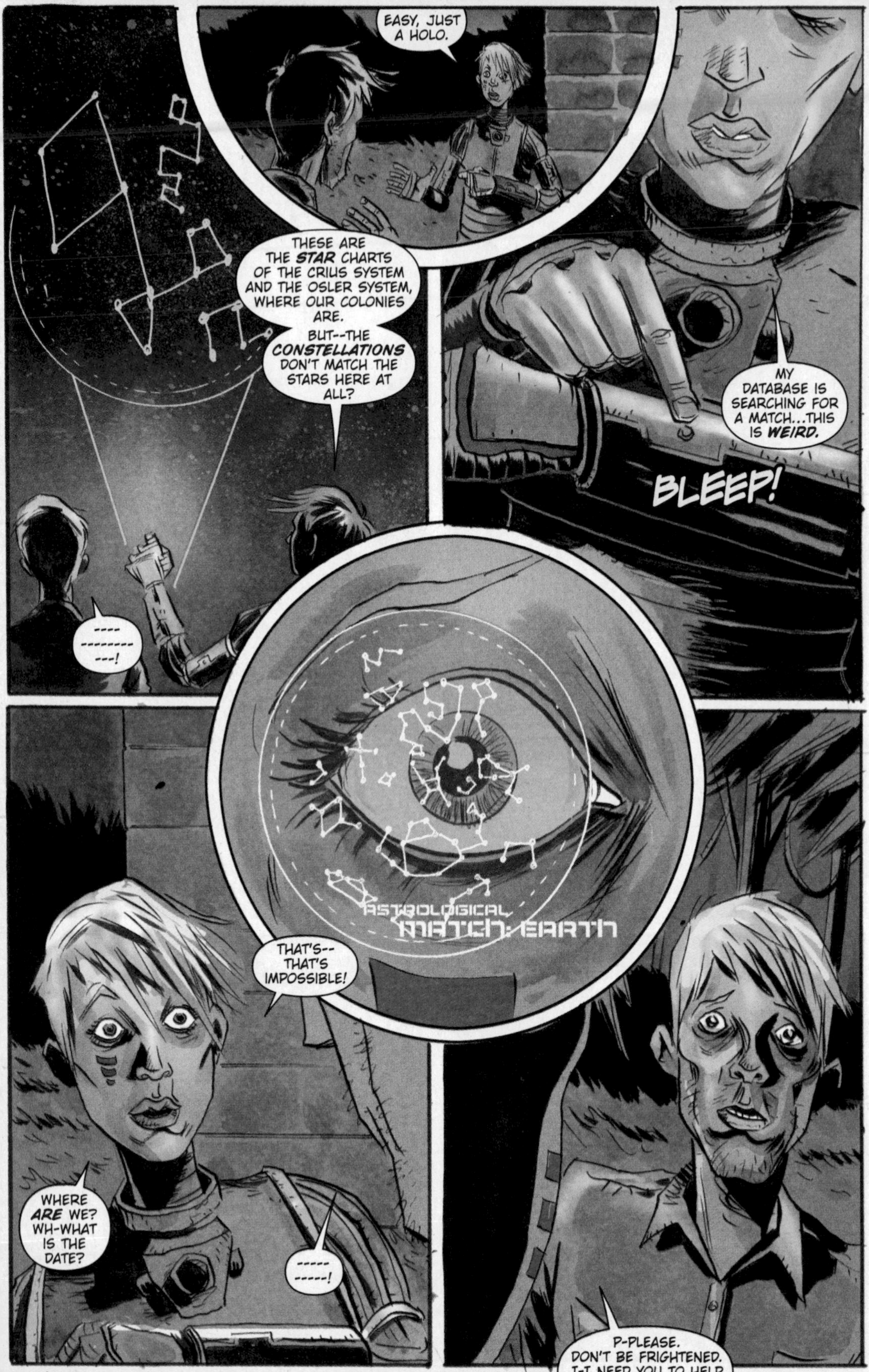

EASY, JUST A HOLO.
THESE ARE THE STAR CHARTS OF THE CRIUS SYSTEM AND THE OSLER SYSTEM, WHERE OUR COLONIES ARE.
BUT--THE CONSTELLATIONS DON'T MATCH THE STARS HERE AT ALL?

---!
MY DATABASE IS SEARCHING FOR A MATCH...THIS IS WEIRD.
BLEEP!
ASTROLOGICAL
MATCH: EARTH
THAT'S--THAT'S IMPOSSIBLE!
WHERE ARE WE? WH-WHAT IS THE DATE?

-----!
P-PLEASE. DON'T BE FRIGHTENED. I-I NEED YOU TO HELP

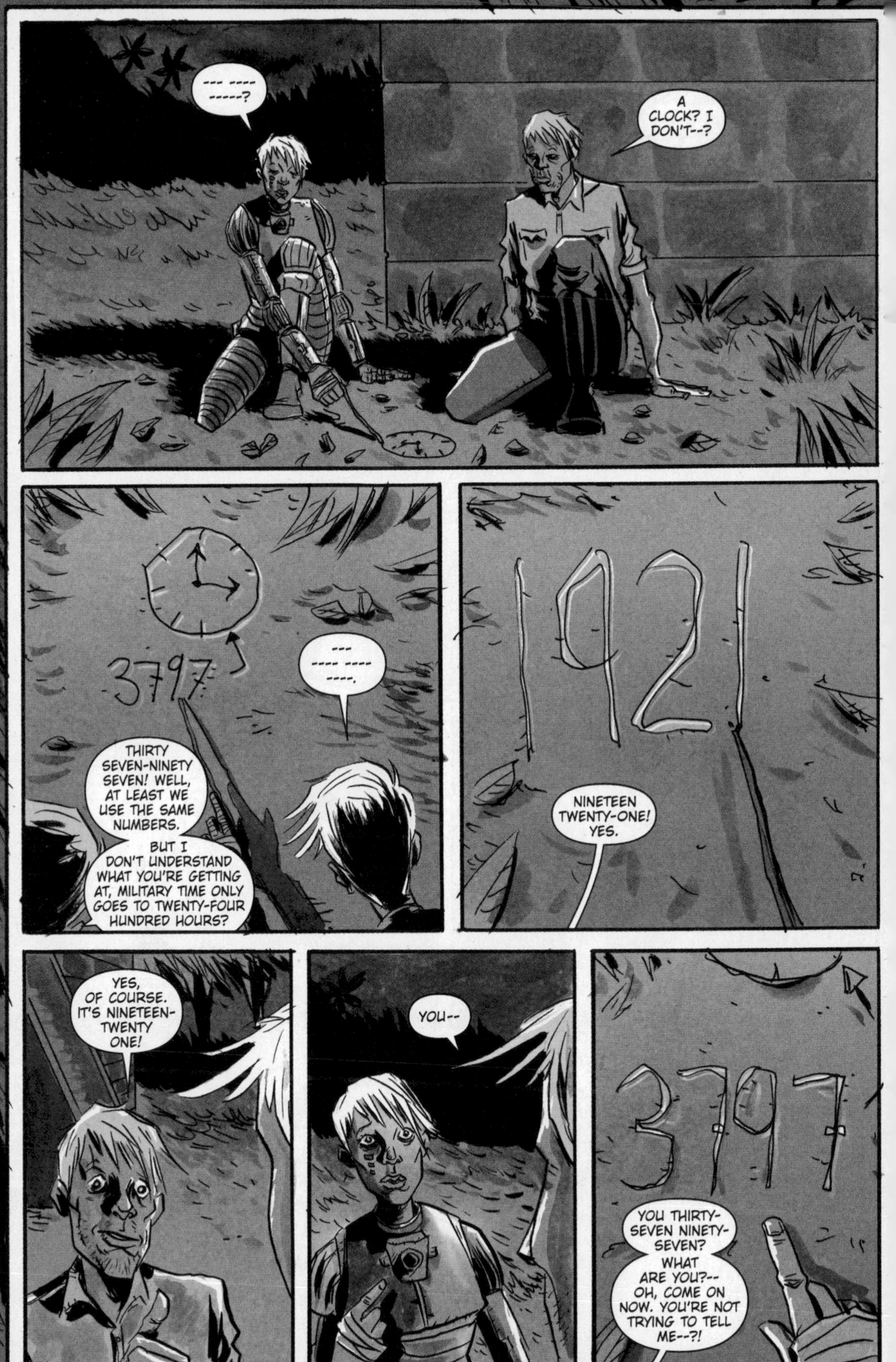
--- ----
-----?
A CLOCK? I DON'T--?

---- ----
----.
3797
THIRTY SEVEN-NINETY SEVEN! WELL, AT LEAST WE USE THE SAME NUMBERS.
BUT I DON'T UNDERSTAND WHAT YOU'RE GETTING AT, MILITARY TIME ONLY GOES TO TWENTY-FOUR HUNDRED HOURS?
1921
NINETEEN TWENTY-ONE! YES.
YES, OF COURSE. IT'S NINETEEN-TWENTY ONE!
YOU--
3797
YOU THIRTY-SEVEN NINETY-SEVEN? WHAT ARE YOU?--OH, COME ON NOW. YOU'RE NOT TRYING TO TELL ME--?!

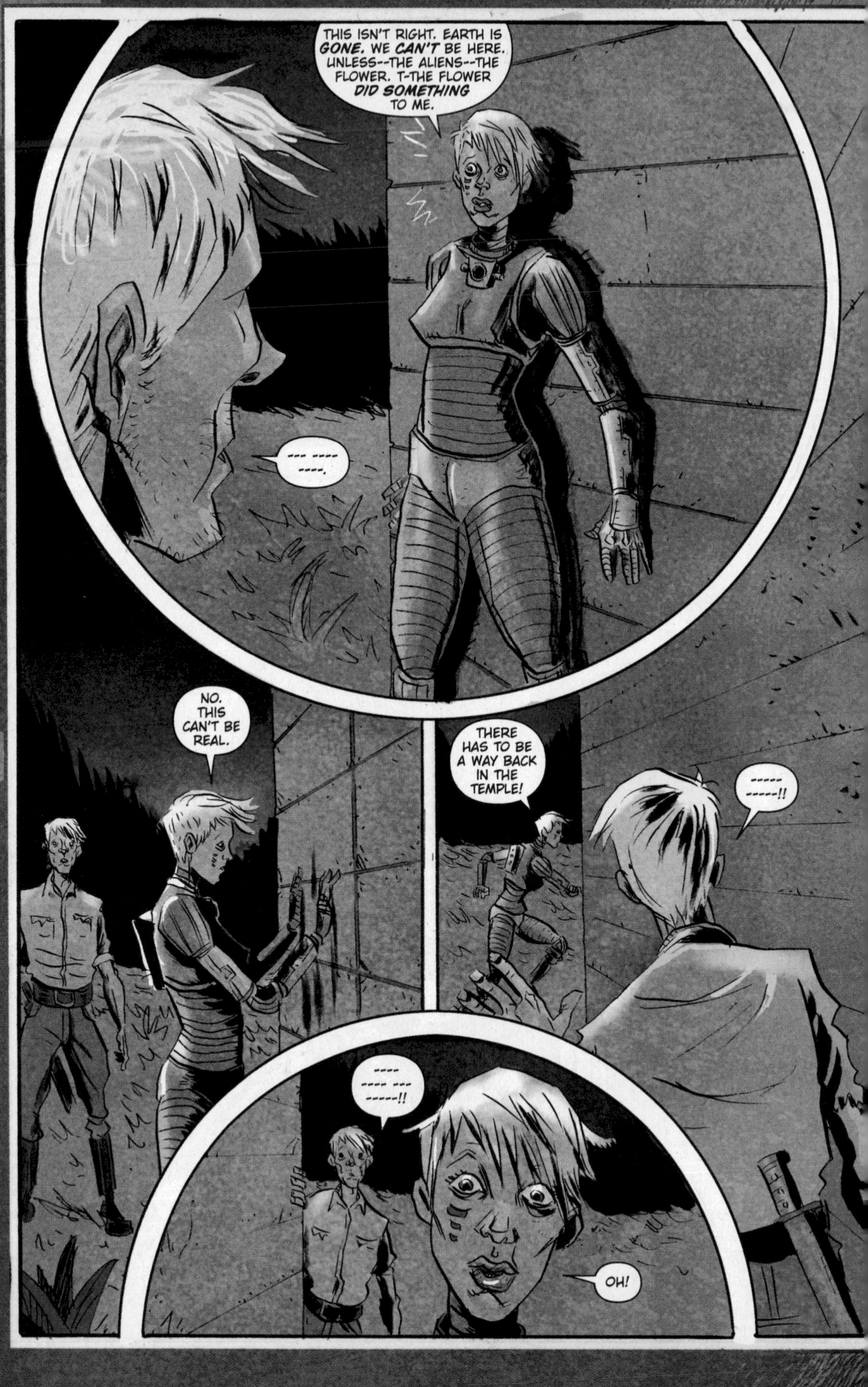
THIS ISN'T RIGHT. EARTH IS GONE. WE CAN'T BE HERE. UNLESS--THE ALIENS--THE FLOWER. T-THE FLOWER DID SOMETHING TO ME.
--- ---- ----.
NO. THIS CAN'T BE REAL.
THERE HAS TO BE A WAY BACK IN THE TEMPLE!
----- -----!!
---- ---- --- -----!!
OH!

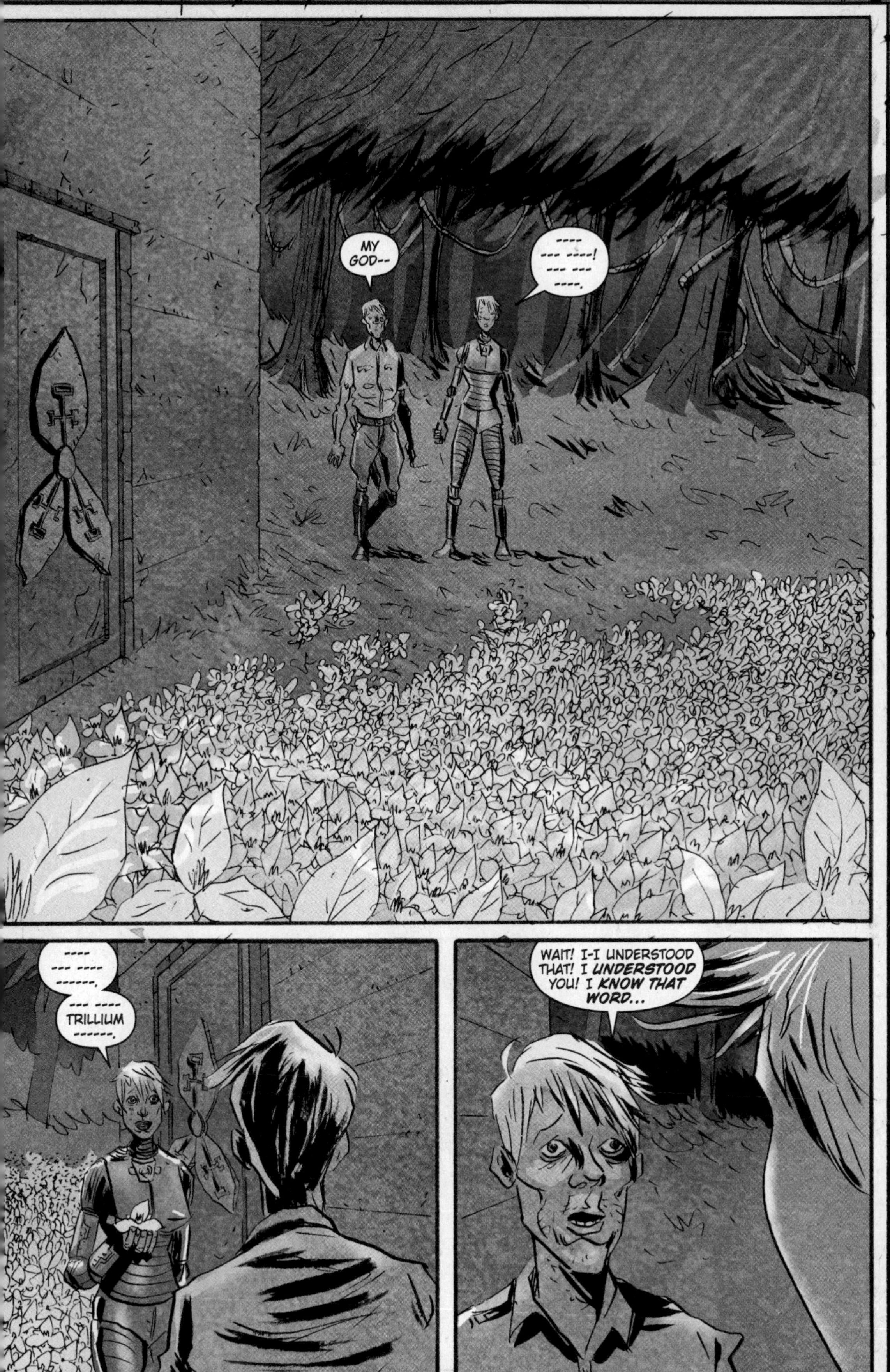
MY GOD--
---- --- ----! --- --- ----.
---- --- ---- ------.
--- ---- TRILLIUM ------.
WAIT! I-I UNDERSTOOD THAT! I *UNDERSTOOD* YOU! I *KNOW THAT WORD*...

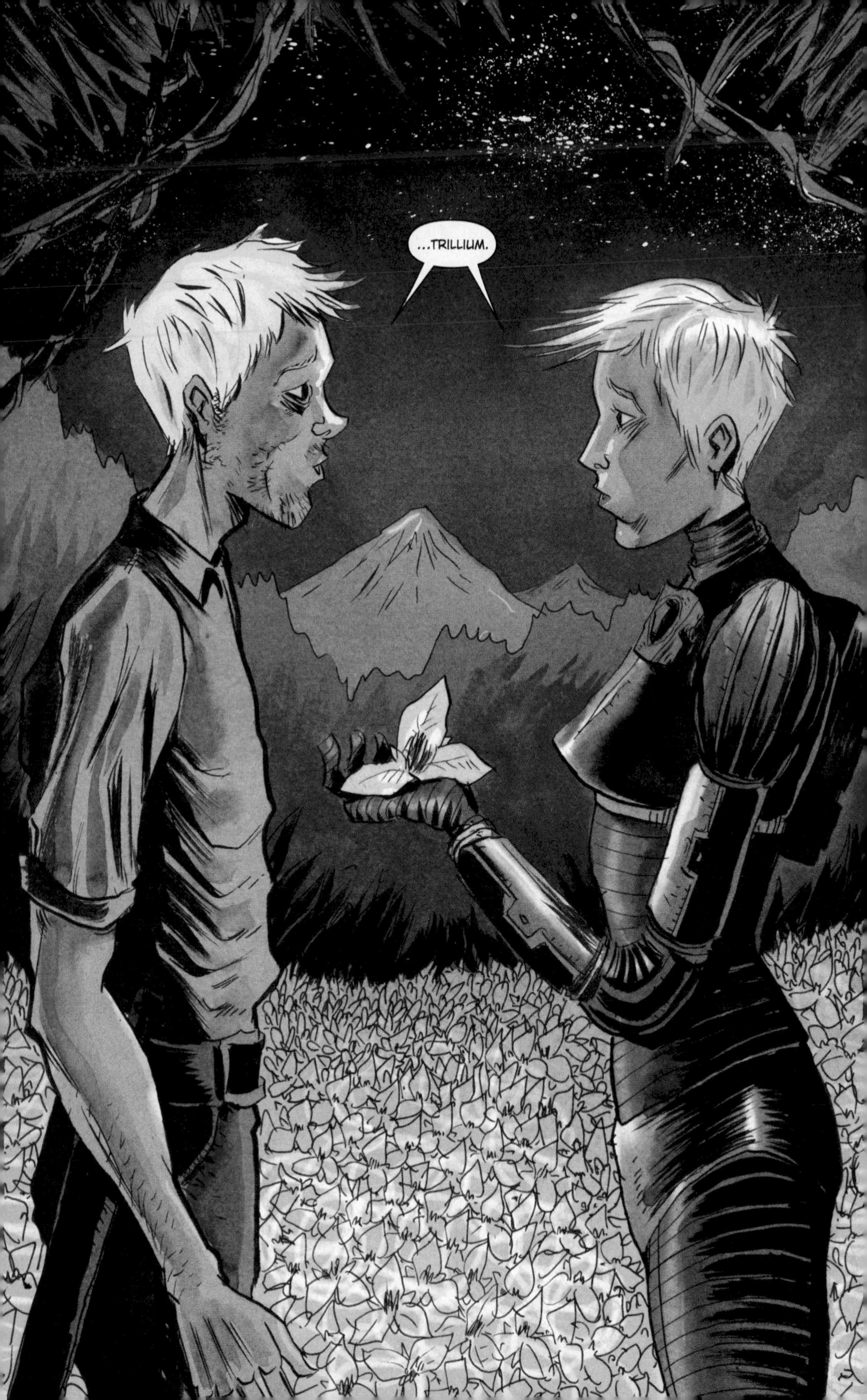
...TRILLIUM.

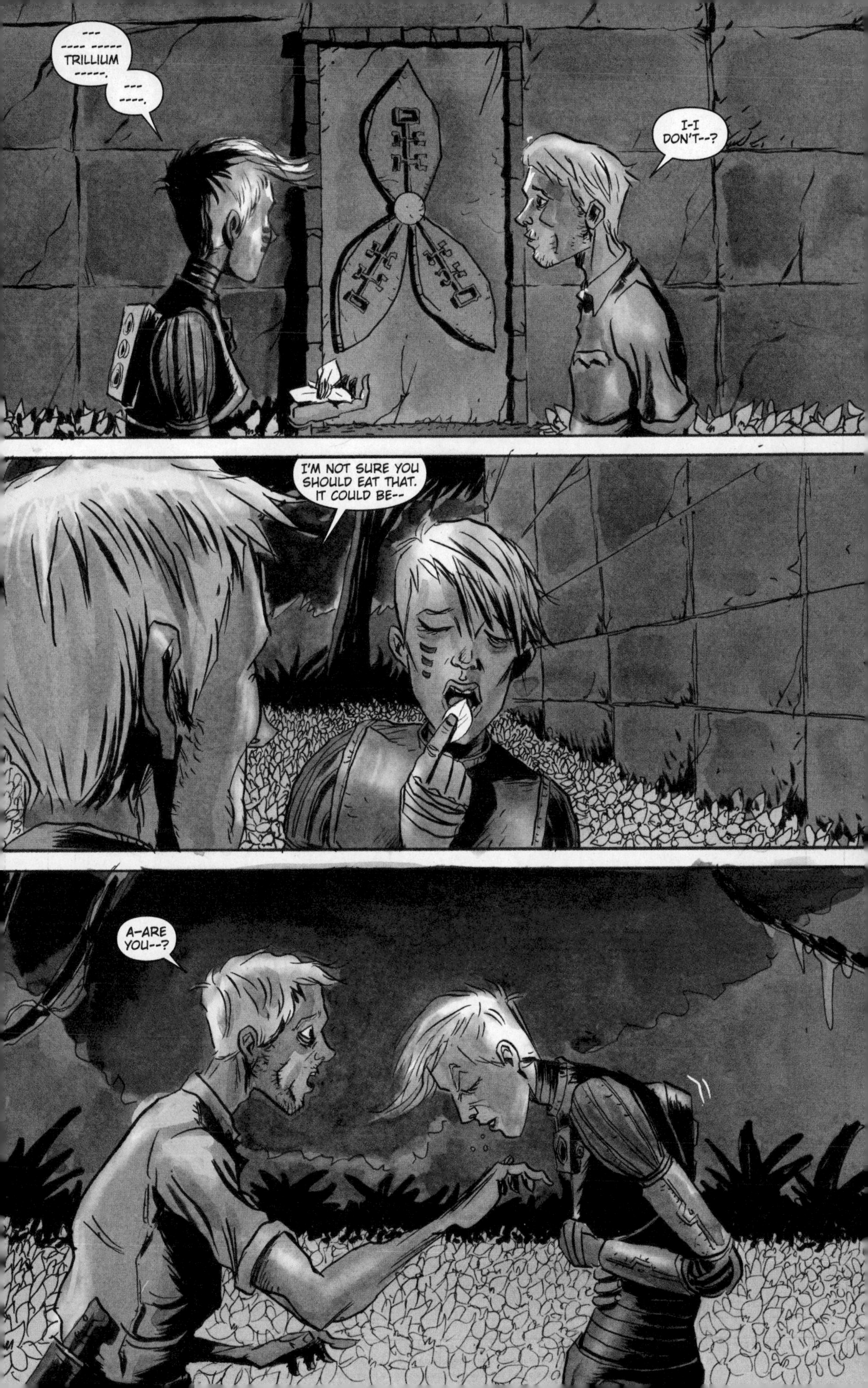

---- -----
TRILLIUM
-----.

----.
I-I DON'T--?
I'M NOT SURE YOU SHOULD EAT THAT. IT COULD BE--
A-ARE YOU--?

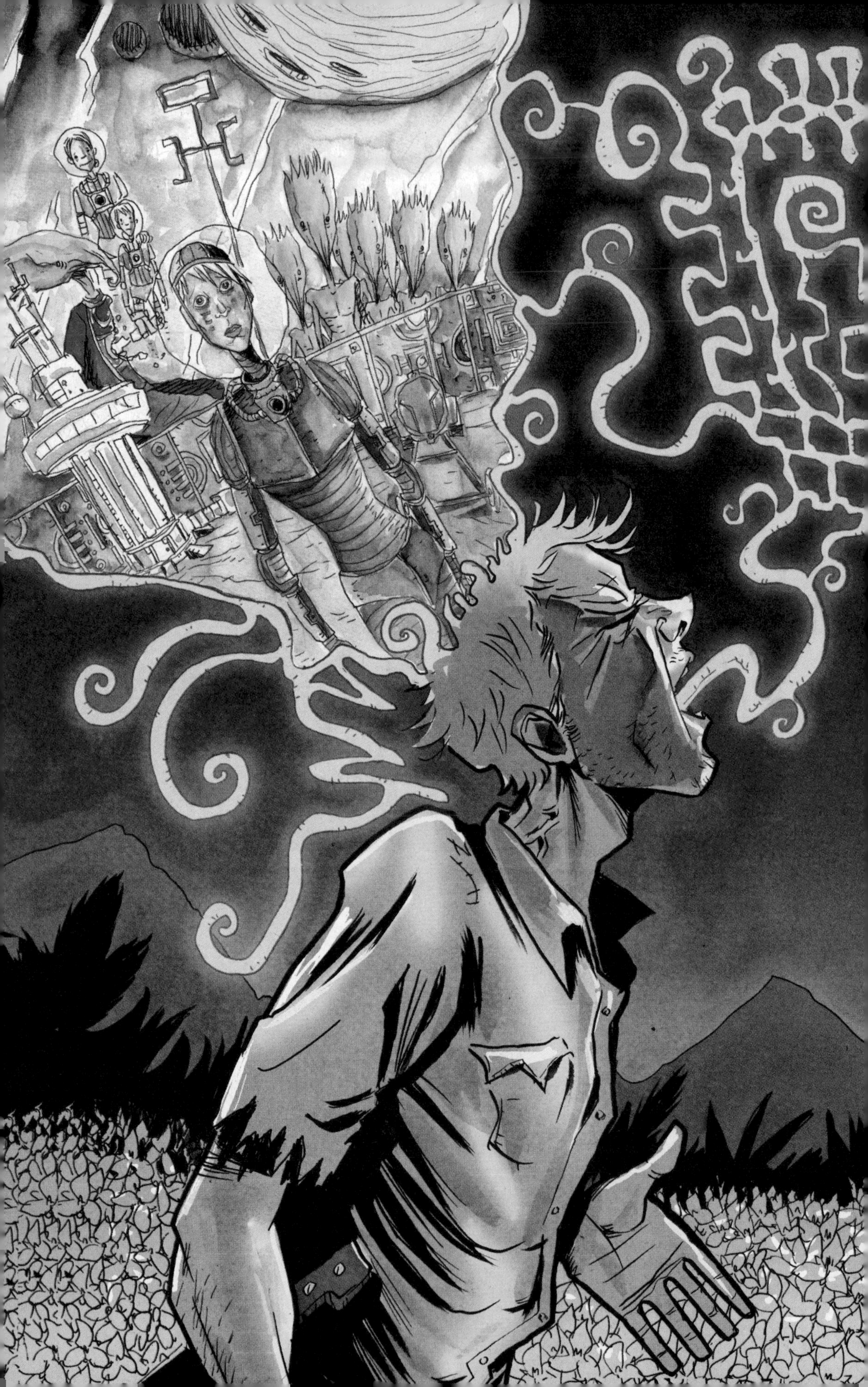

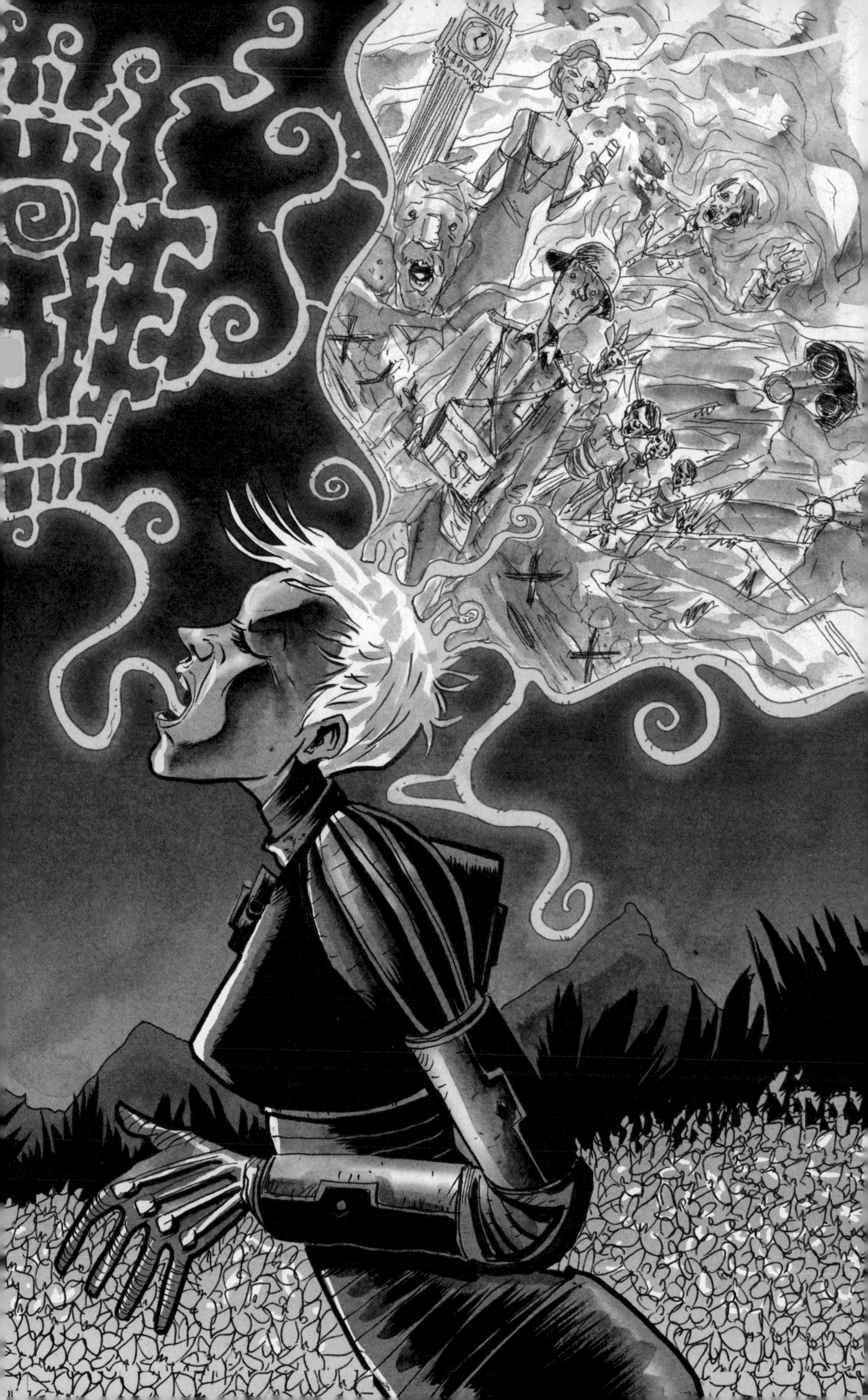

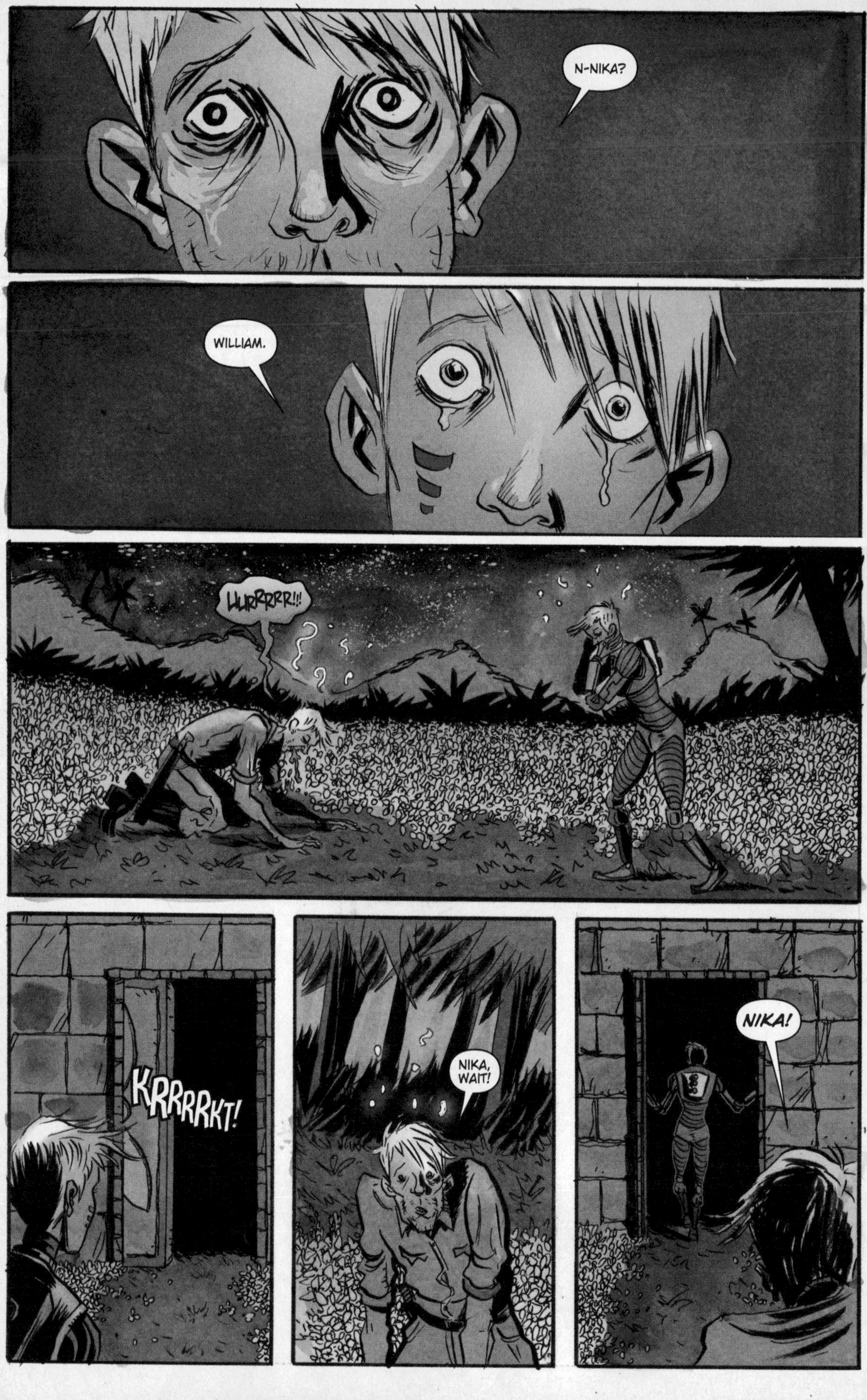
N-NIKA?
WILLIAM.
UHRRRR!!!
KRRRRKT!
NIKA, WAIT!
NIKA!

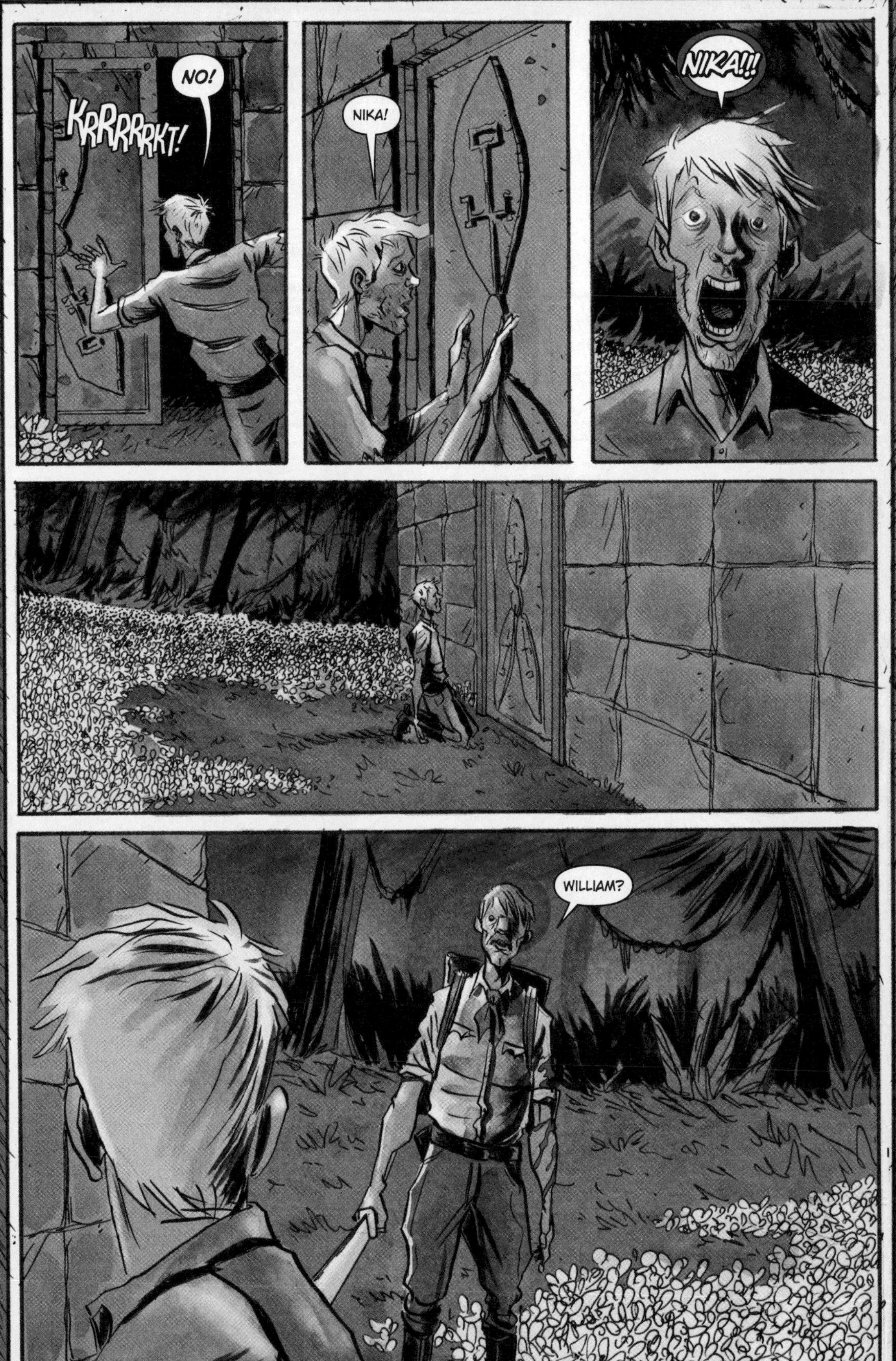
NO!
KRRRRRKT!
NIKA!
NIKA!!!
WILLIAM?

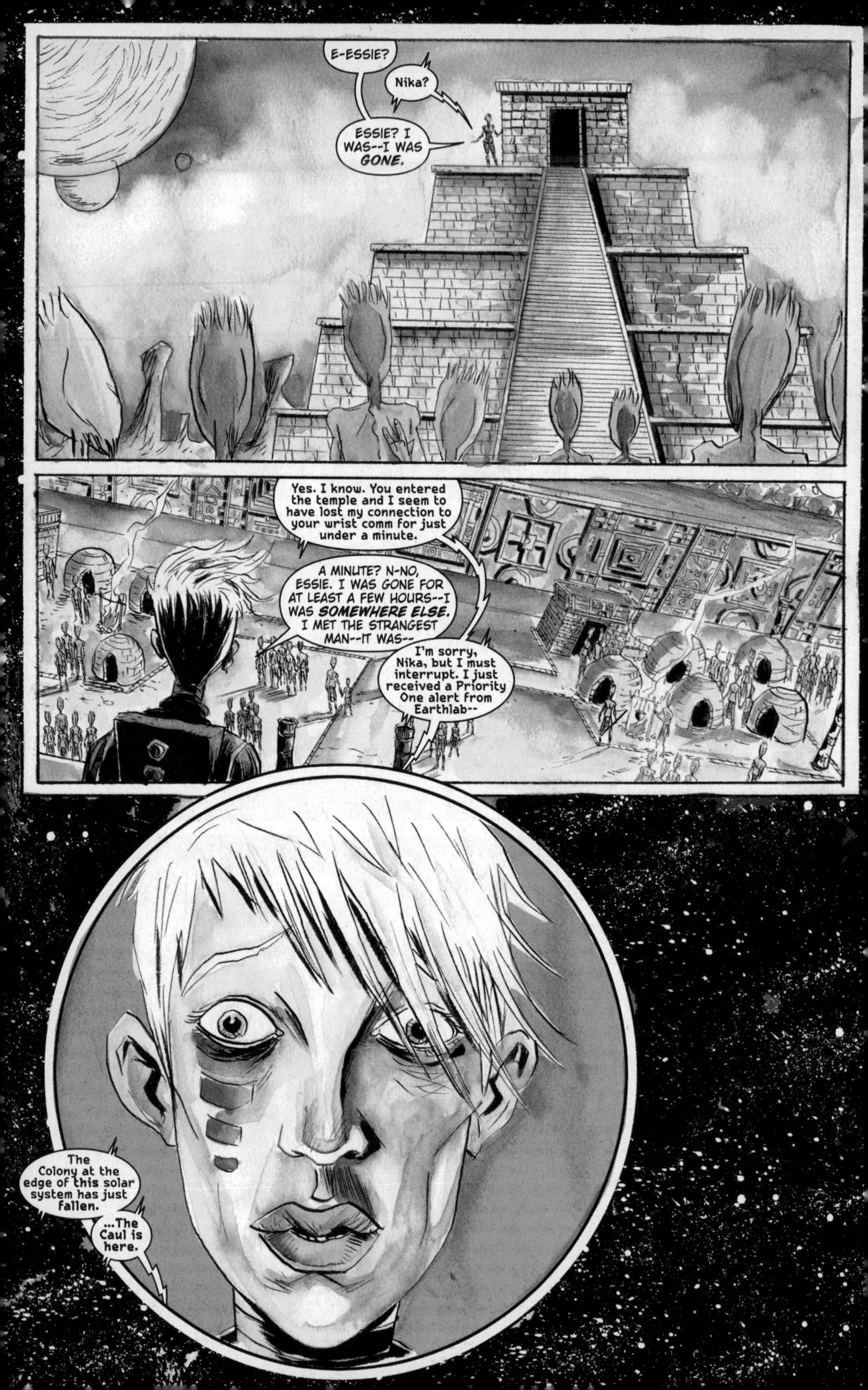
E-ESSIE?
Nika?
ESSIE? I WAS--I WAS GONE.
Yes. I know. You entered the temple and I seem to have lost my connection to your wrist comm for just under a minute.
A MINUTE? N-NO, ESSIE. I WAS GONE FOR AT LEAST A FEW HOURS--I WAS SOMEWHERE ELSE. I MET THE STRANGEST MAN--IT WAS--
I'm sorry, Nika, but I must interrupt. I just received a Priority One alert from Earthlab--
The Colony at the edge of this solar system has just fallen.
...The Caul is here.

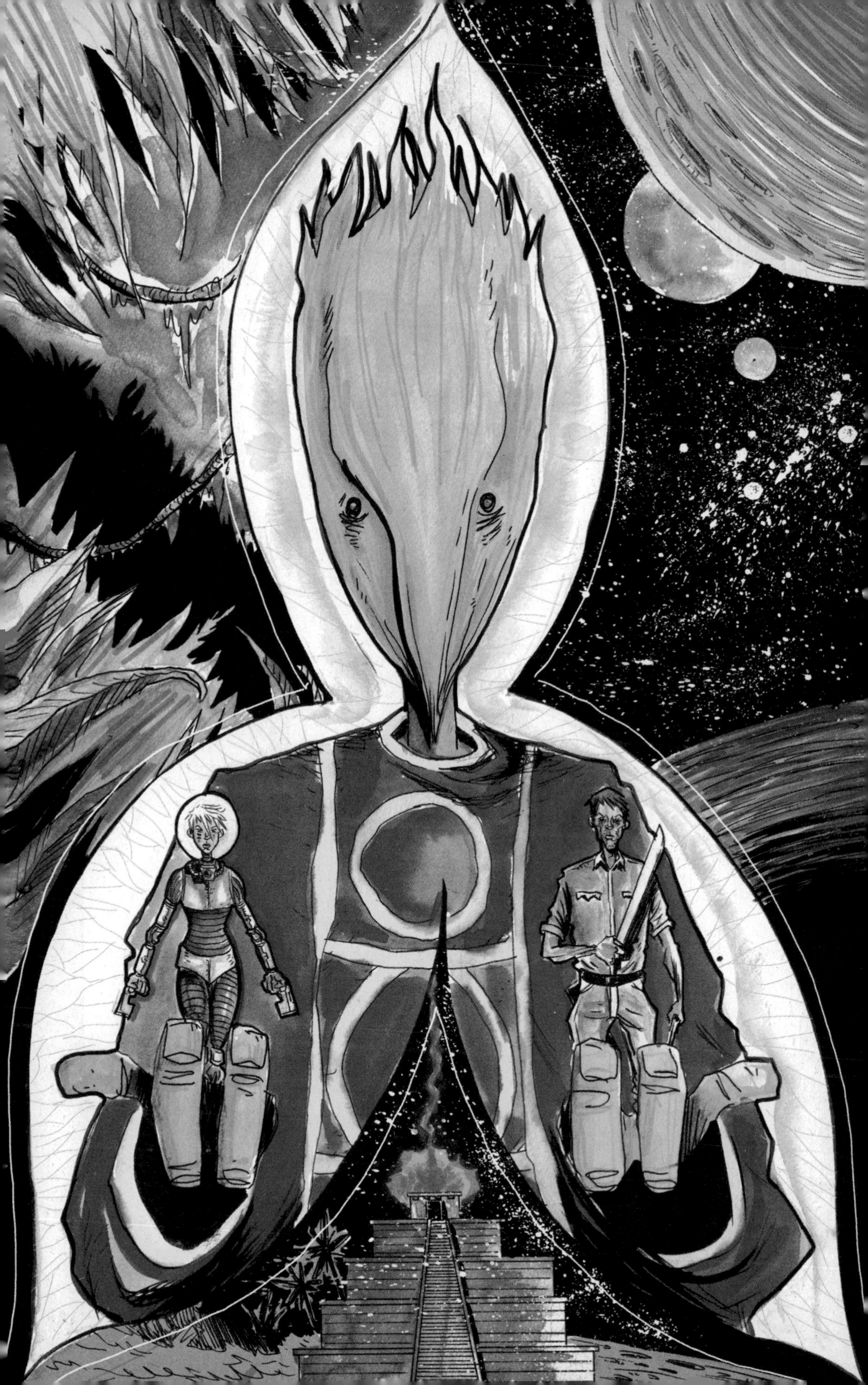

CHAPTER 3:
TELEMETRY

EARTHLAB Rover.

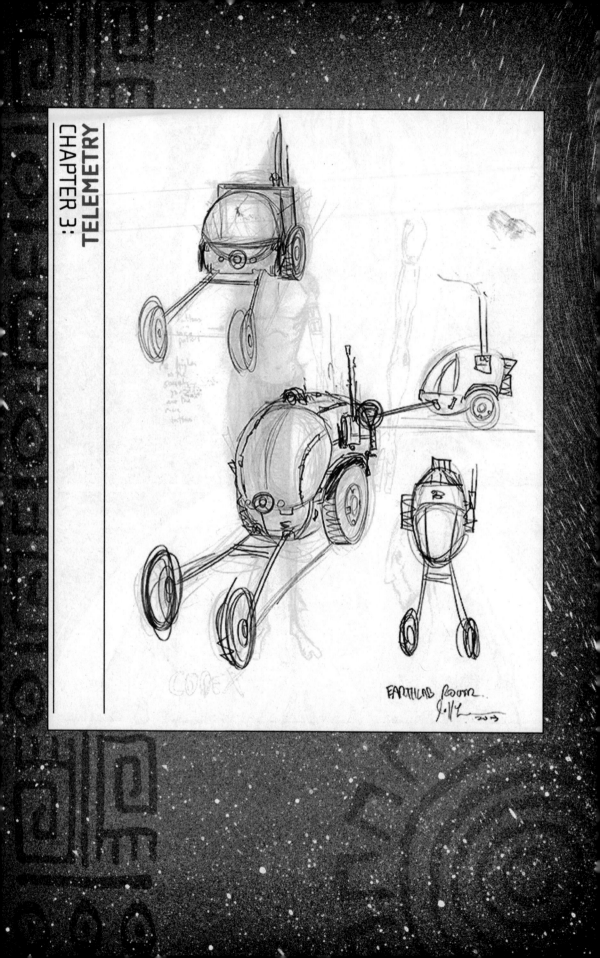

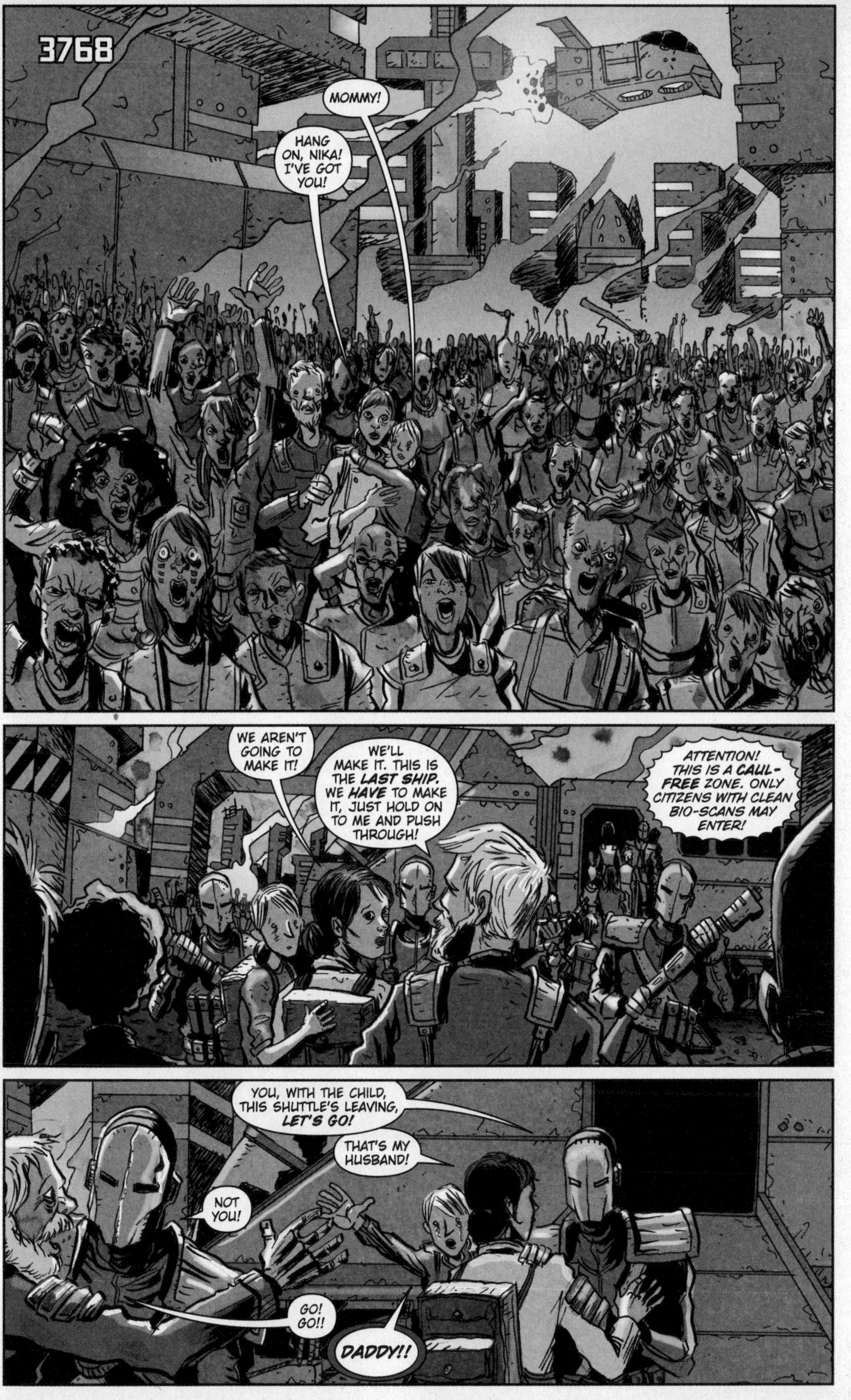
3768
MOMMY!
HANG ON, NIKA! I'VE GOT YOU!
WE AREN'T GOING TO MAKE IT!
WE'LL MAKE IT. THIS IS THE LAST SHIP. WE HAVE TO MAKE IT, JUST HOLD ON TO ME AND PUSH THROUGH!
ATTENTION! THIS IS A CAUL-FREE ZONE. ONLY CITIZENS WITH CLEAN BIO-SCANS MAY ENTER!
YOU, WITH THE CHILD, THIS SHUTTLE'S LEAVING, LET'S GO!
THAT'S MY HUSBAND!
NOT YOU!
GO! GO!!
DADDY!!

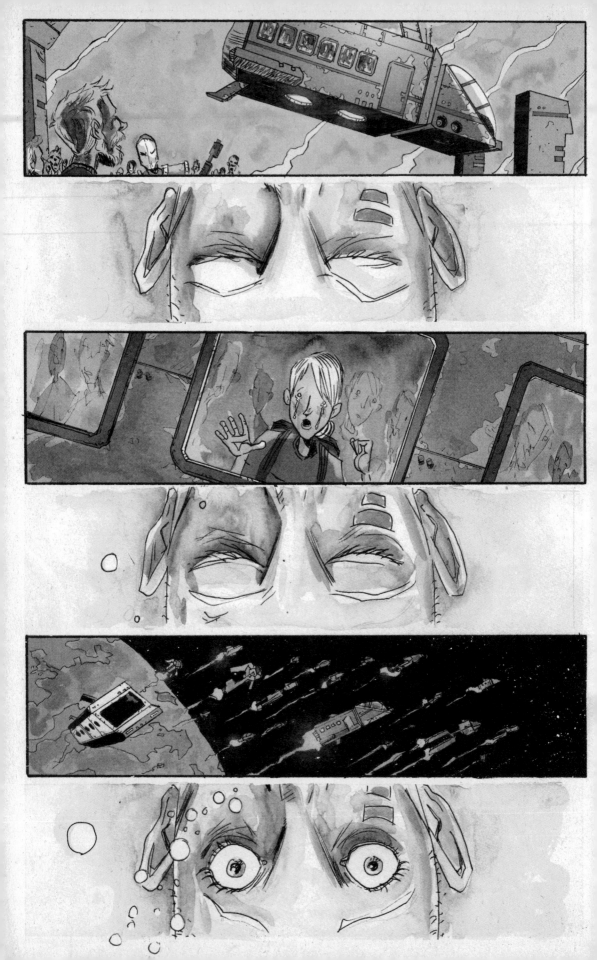

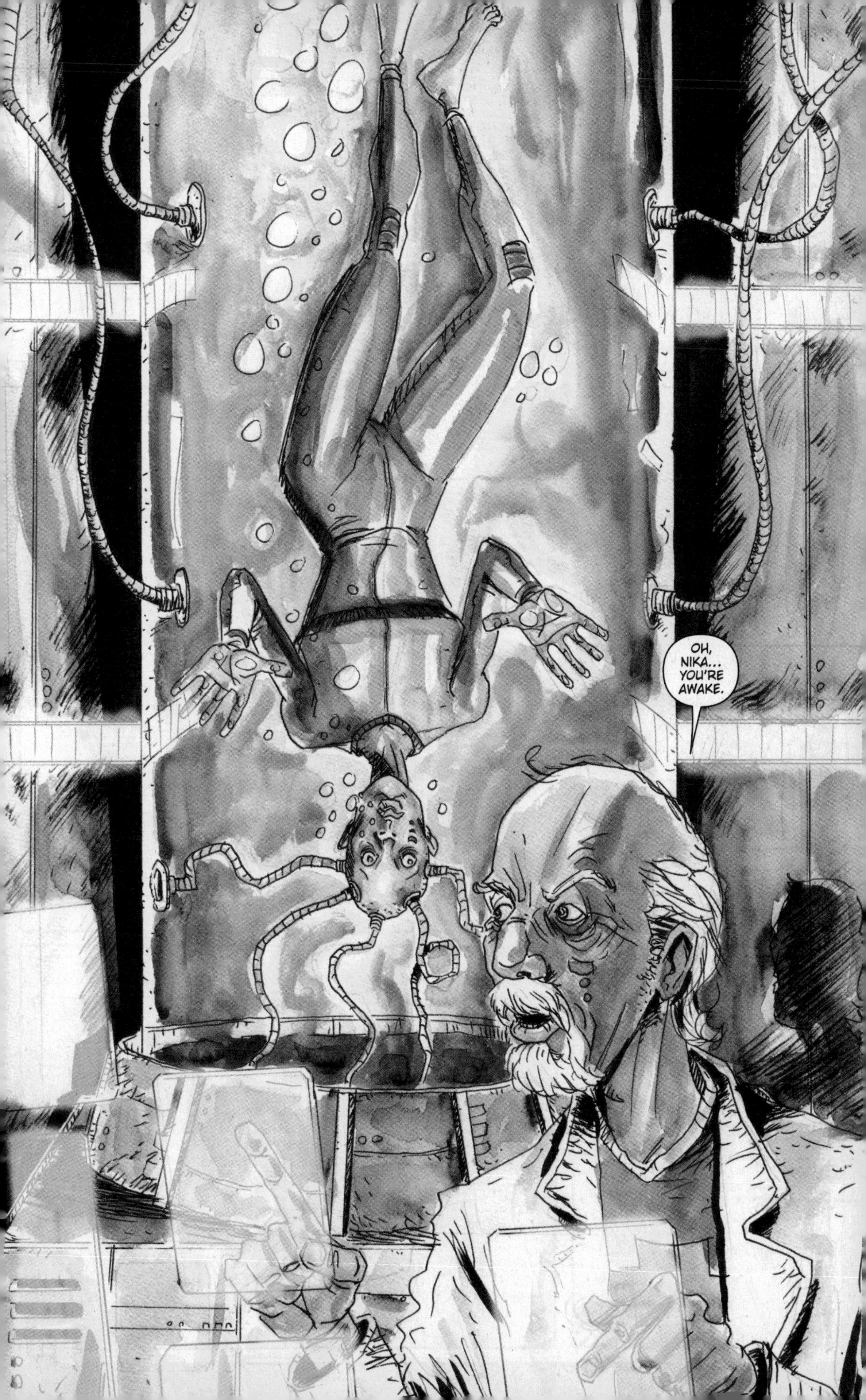
OH, NIKA... YOU'RE AWAKE.

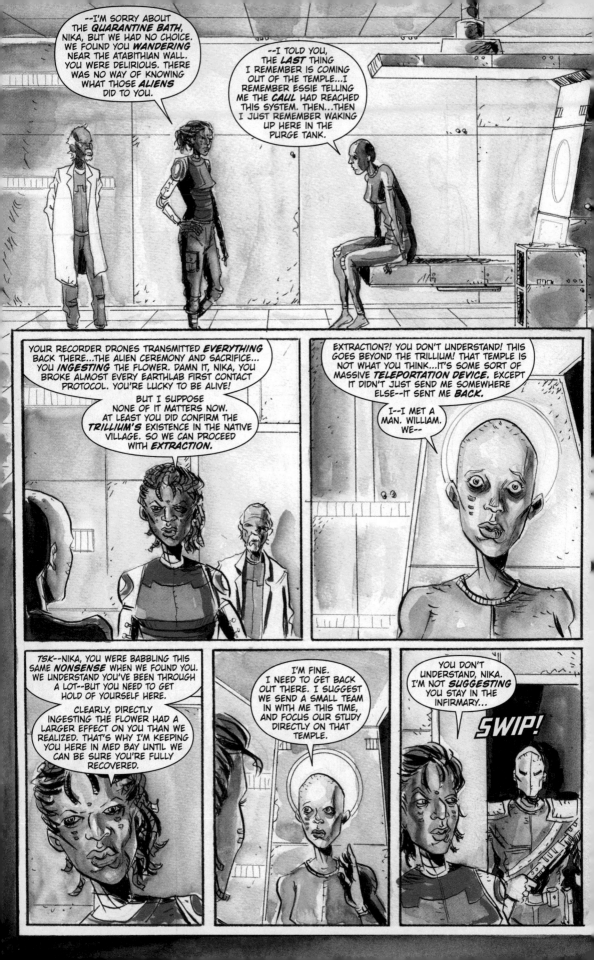

--I'M SORRY ABOUT THE *QUARANTINE BATH*, NIKA, BUT WE HAD NO CHOICE. WE FOUND YOU *WANDERING* NEAR THE ATABITHIAN WALL. YOU WERE DELIRIOUS. THERE WAS NO WAY OF KNOWING WHAT THOSE *ALIENS* DID TO YOU.

--I TOLD YOU, THE *LAST* THING I REMEMBER IS COMING OUT OF THE TEMPLE...I REMEMBER ESSIE TELLING ME THE *CAUL* HAD REACHED THIS SYSTEM. THEN...THEN I JUST REMEMBER WAKING UP HERE IN THE PURGE TANK.

YOUR RECORDER DRONES TRANSMITTED *EVERYTHING* BACK THERE...THE ALIEN CEREMONY AND SACRIFICE... YOU *INGESTING* THE FLOWER. DAMN IT, NIKA, YOU BROKE ALMOST EVERY EARTHLAB FIRST CONTACT PROTOCOL. YOU'RE LUCKY TO BE ALIVE!

BUT I SUPPOSE NONE OF IT MATTERS NOW. AT LEAST YOU DID CONFIRM THE *TRILLIUM'S* EXISTENCE IN THE NATIVE VILLAGE. SO WE CAN PROCEED WITH *EXTRACTION.*

EXTRACTION?! YOU DON'T UNDERSTAND! THIS GOES BEYOND THE *TRILLIUM*! THAT TEMPLE IS NOT WHAT YOU THINK...IT'S SOME SORT OF MASSIVE *TELEPORTATION DEVICE.* EXCEPT IT DIDN'T JUST SEND ME SOMEWHERE ELSE--IT SENT ME *BACK.*

I--I MET A MAN. WILLIAM. WE--

TSK--NIKA, YOU WERE BABBLING THIS SAME *NONSENSE* WHEN WE FOUND YOU. WE UNDERSTAND YOU'VE BEEN THROUGH A LOT--BUT YOU NEED TO GET HOLD OF YOURSELF HERE.

CLEARLY, DIRECTLY INGESTING THE FLOWER HAD A LARGER EFFECT ON YOU THAN WE REALIZED. THAT'S WHY I'M KEEPING YOU HERE IN MED BAY UNTIL WE CAN BE SURE YOU'RE FULLY RECOVERED.

I'M FINE. I NEED TO GET BACK OUT THERE. I SUGGEST WE SEND A SMALL TEAM IN WITH ME THIS TIME, AND FOCUS OUR STUDY DIRECTLY ON THAT TEMPLE.

YOU DON'T UNDERSTAND, NIKA. I'M NOT *SUGGESTING* YOU STAY IN THE INFIRMARY...

SWIP!

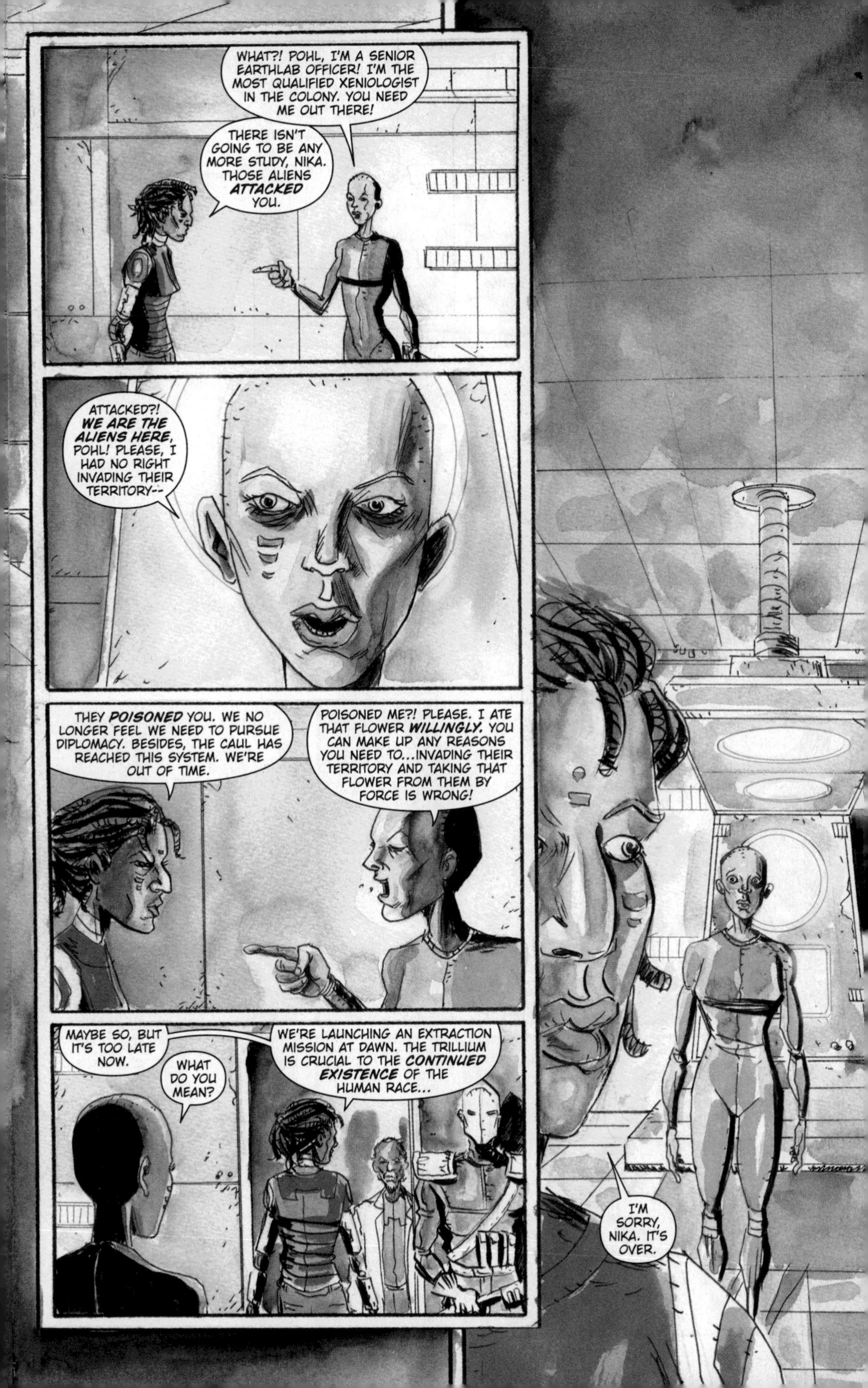
WHAT?! POHL, I'M A SENIOR EARTHLAB OFFICER! I'M THE MOST QUALIFIED XENIOLOGIST IN THE COLONY. YOU NEED ME OUT THERE!
THERE ISN'T GOING TO BE ANY MORE STUDY, NIKA. THOSE ALIENS *ATTACKED* YOU.
ATTACKED?! *WE ARE THE ALIENS HERE*, POHL! PLEASE, I HAD NO RIGHT INVADING THEIR TERRITORY--
THEY *POISONED* YOU. WE NO LONGER FEEL WE NEED TO PURSUE DIPLOMACY. BESIDES, THE CAUL HAS REACHED THIS SYSTEM. WE'RE OUT OF TIME.
POISONED ME?! PLEASE. I ATE THAT FLOWER *WILLINGLY*. YOU CAN MAKE UP ANY REASONS YOU NEED TO...INVADING THEIR TERRITORY AND TAKING THAT FLOWER FROM THEM BY FORCE IS WRONG!
MAYBE SO, BUT IT'S TOO LATE NOW.
WHAT DO YOU MEAN?
WE'RE LAUNCHING AN EXTRACTION MISSION AT DAWN. THE TRILLIUM IS CRUCIAL TO THE *CONTINUED EXISTENCE* OF THE HUMAN RACE...
I'M SORRY, NIKA. IT'S OVER.

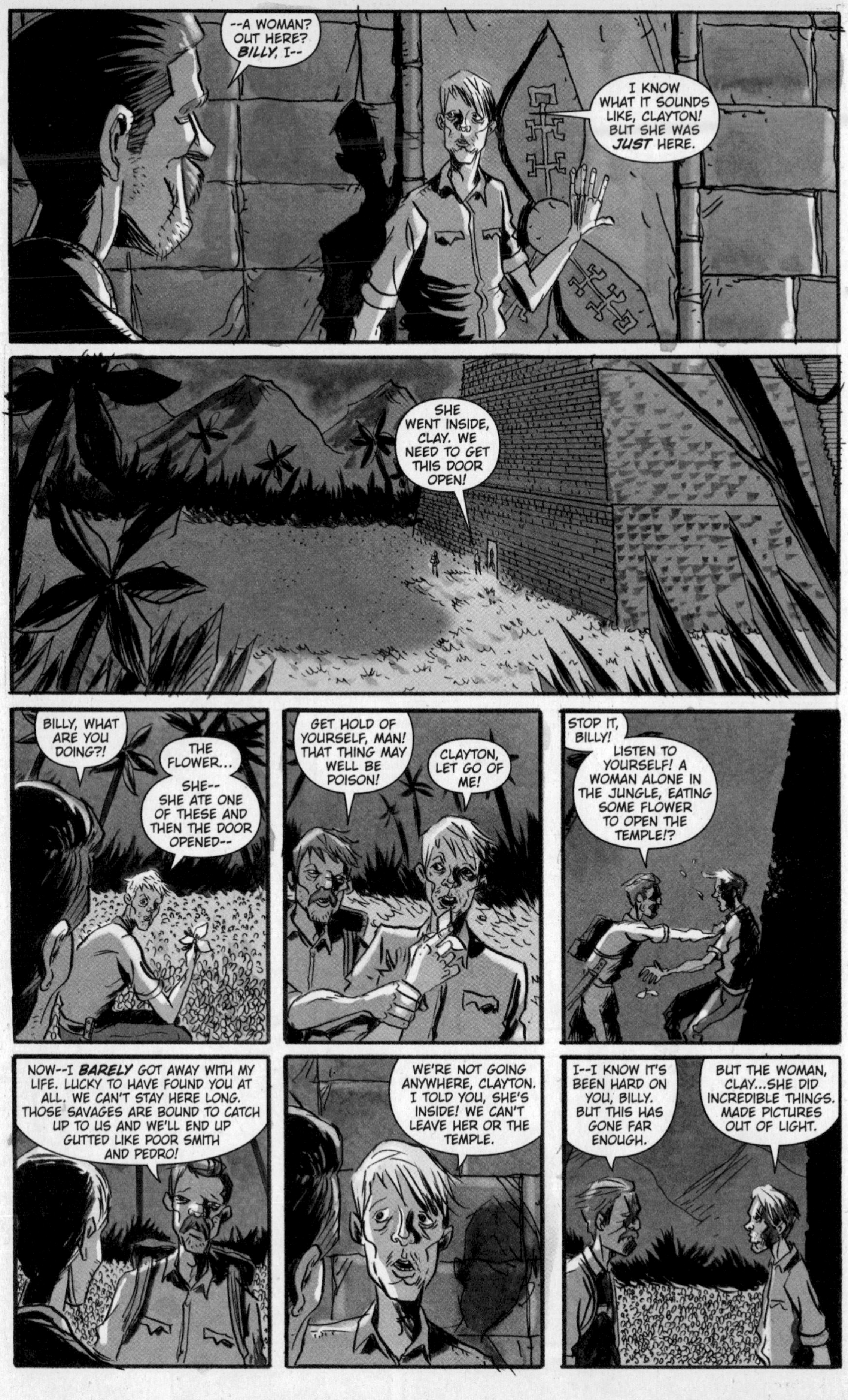
--A WOMAN? OUT HERE? BILLY, I--
I KNOW WHAT IT SOUNDS LIKE, CLAYTON! BUT SHE WAS JUST HERE.
SHE WENT INSIDE, CLAY. WE NEED TO GET THIS DOOR OPEN!
BILLY, WHAT ARE YOU DOING?!
THE FLOWER...
SHE-- SHE ATE ONE OF THESE AND THEN THE DOOR OPENED--
GET HOLD OF YOURSELF, MAN! THAT THING MAY WELL BE POISON!
CLAYTON, LET GO OF ME!
STOP IT, BILLY!
LISTEN TO YOURSELF! A WOMAN ALONE IN THE JUNGLE, EATING SOME FLOWER TO OPEN THE TEMPLE!?
NOW--I BARELY GOT AWAY WITH MY LIFE. LUCKY TO HAVE FOUND YOU AT ALL. WE CAN'T STAY HERE LONG. THOSE SAVAGES ARE BOUND TO CATCH UP TO US AND WE'LL END UP GUTTED LIKE POOR SMITH AND PEDRO!
WE'RE NOT GOING ANYWHERE, CLAYTON. I TOLD YOU, SHE'S INSIDE! WE CAN'T LEAVE HER OR THE TEMPLE.
I--I KNOW IT'S BEEN HARD ON YOU, BILLY. BUT THIS HAS GONE FAR ENOUGH.
BUT THE WOMAN, CLAY...SHE DID INCREDIBLE THINGS. MADE PICTURES OUT OF LIGHT.

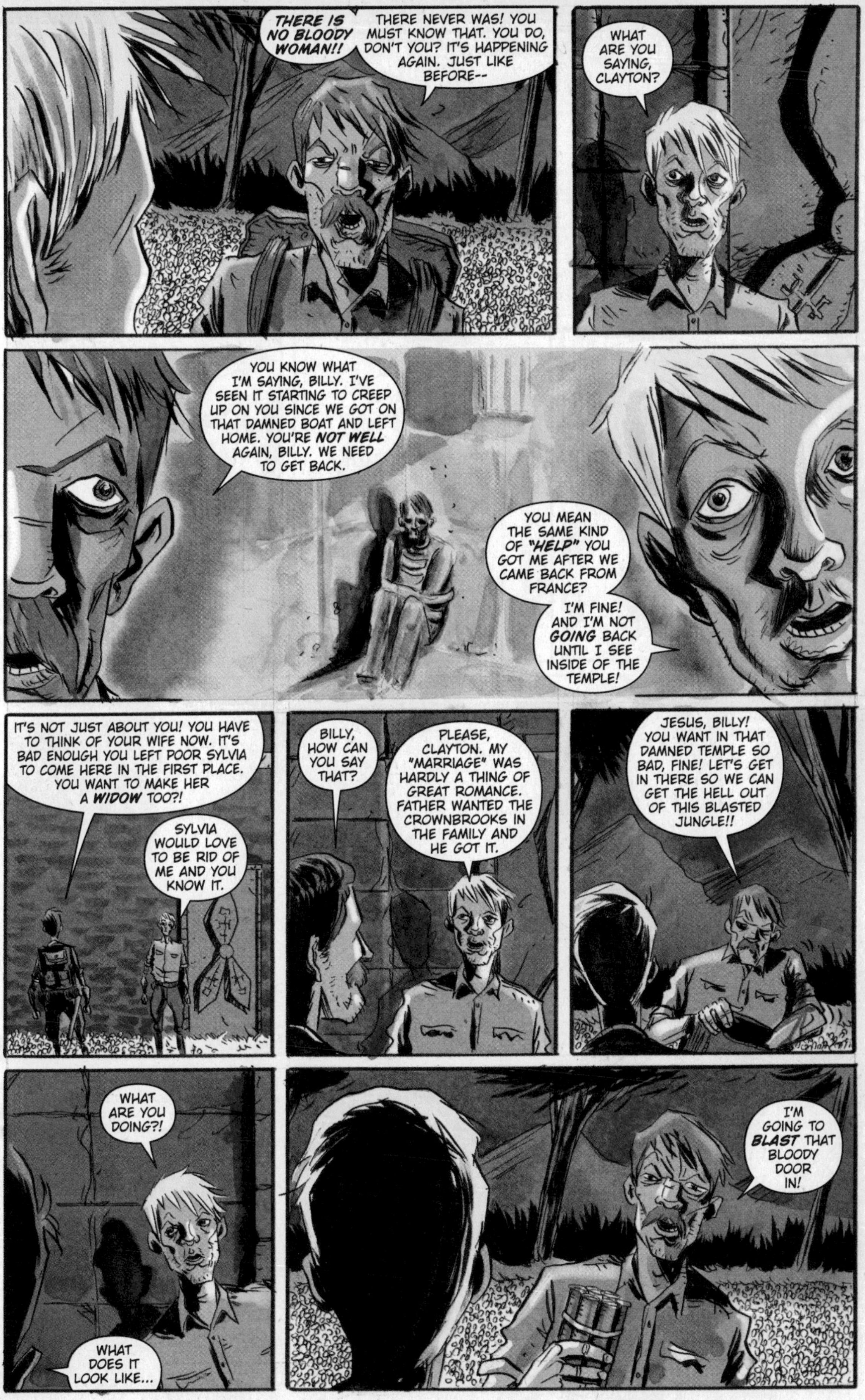
THERE IS NO BLOODY WOMAN!!
THERE NEVER WAS! YOU MUST KNOW THAT. YOU DO, DON'T YOU? IT'S HAPPENING AGAIN. JUST LIKE BEFORE--
WHAT ARE YOU SAYING, CLAYTON?
YOU KNOW WHAT I'M SAYING, BILLY. I'VE SEEN IT STARTING TO CREEP UP ON YOU SINCE WE GOT ON THAT DAMNED BOAT AND LEFT HOME. YOU'RE NOT WELL AGAIN, BILLY. WE NEED TO GET BACK.
YOU MEAN THE SAME KIND OF "HELP" YOU GOT ME AFTER WE CAME BACK FROM FRANCE?
I'M FINE! AND I'M NOT GOING BACK UNTIL I SEE INSIDE OF THE TEMPLE!
IT'S NOT JUST ABOUT YOU! YOU HAVE TO THINK OF YOUR WIFE NOW. IT'S BAD ENOUGH YOU LEFT POOR SYLVIA TO COME HERE IN THE FIRST PLACE. YOU WANT TO MAKE HER A WIDOW TOO?!
SYLVIA WOULD LOVE TO BE RID OF ME AND YOU KNOW IT.
BILLY, HOW CAN YOU SAY THAT?
PLEASE, CLAYTON. MY "MARRIAGE" WAS HARDLY A THING OF GREAT ROMANCE. FATHER WANTED THE CROWNBROOKS IN THE FAMILY AND HE GOT IT.
JESUS, BILLY! YOU WANT IN THAT DAMNED TEMPLE SO BAD, FINE! LET'S GET IN THERE SO WE CAN GET THE HELL OUT OF THIS BLASTED JUNGLE!!
WHAT ARE YOU DOING?!
WHAT DOES IT LOOK LIKE...
I'M GOING TO BLAST THAT BLOODY DOOR IN!

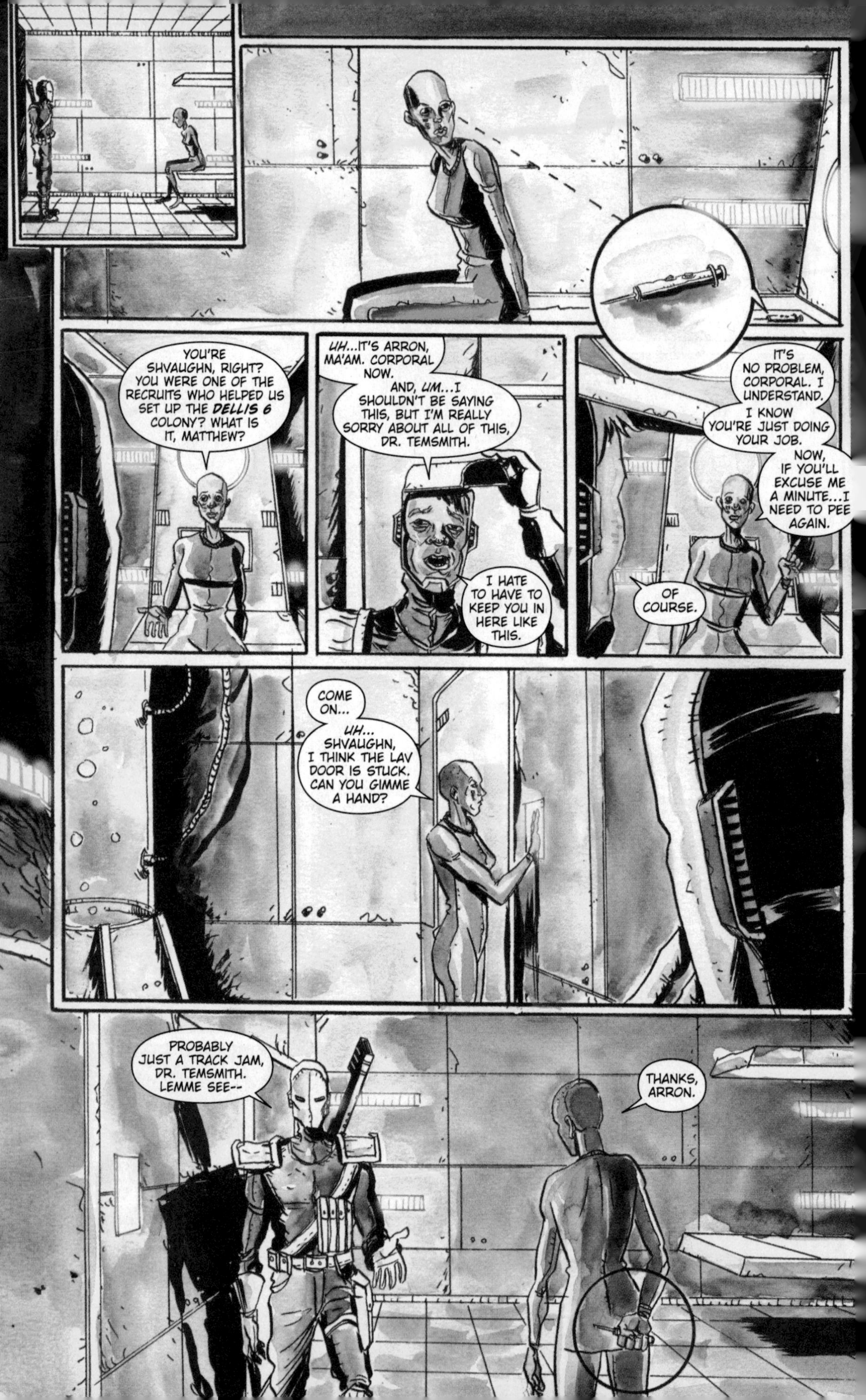
YOU'RE SHVAUGHN, RIGHT? YOU WERE ONE OF THE RECRUITS WHO HELPED US SET UP THE DELLIS 6 COLONY? WHAT IS IT, MATTHEW?
UH...IT'S ARRON, MA'AM. CORPORAL NOW.
AND, UM...I SHOULDN'T BE SAYING THIS, BUT I'M REALLY SORRY ABOUT ALL OF THIS, DR. TEMSMITH.
I HATE TO HAVE TO KEEP YOU IN HERE LIKE THIS.
IT'S NO PROBLEM, CORPORAL. I UNDERSTAND.
I KNOW YOU'RE JUST DOING YOUR JOB.
NOW, IF YOU'LL EXCUSE ME A MINUTE...I NEED TO PEE AGAIN.
OF COURSE.
COME ON...
UH... SHVAUGHN, I THINK THE LAV DOOR IS STUCK. CAN YOU GIMME A HAND?
PROBABLY JUST A TRACK JAM, DR. TEMSMITH. LEMME SEE--
THANKS, ARRON.

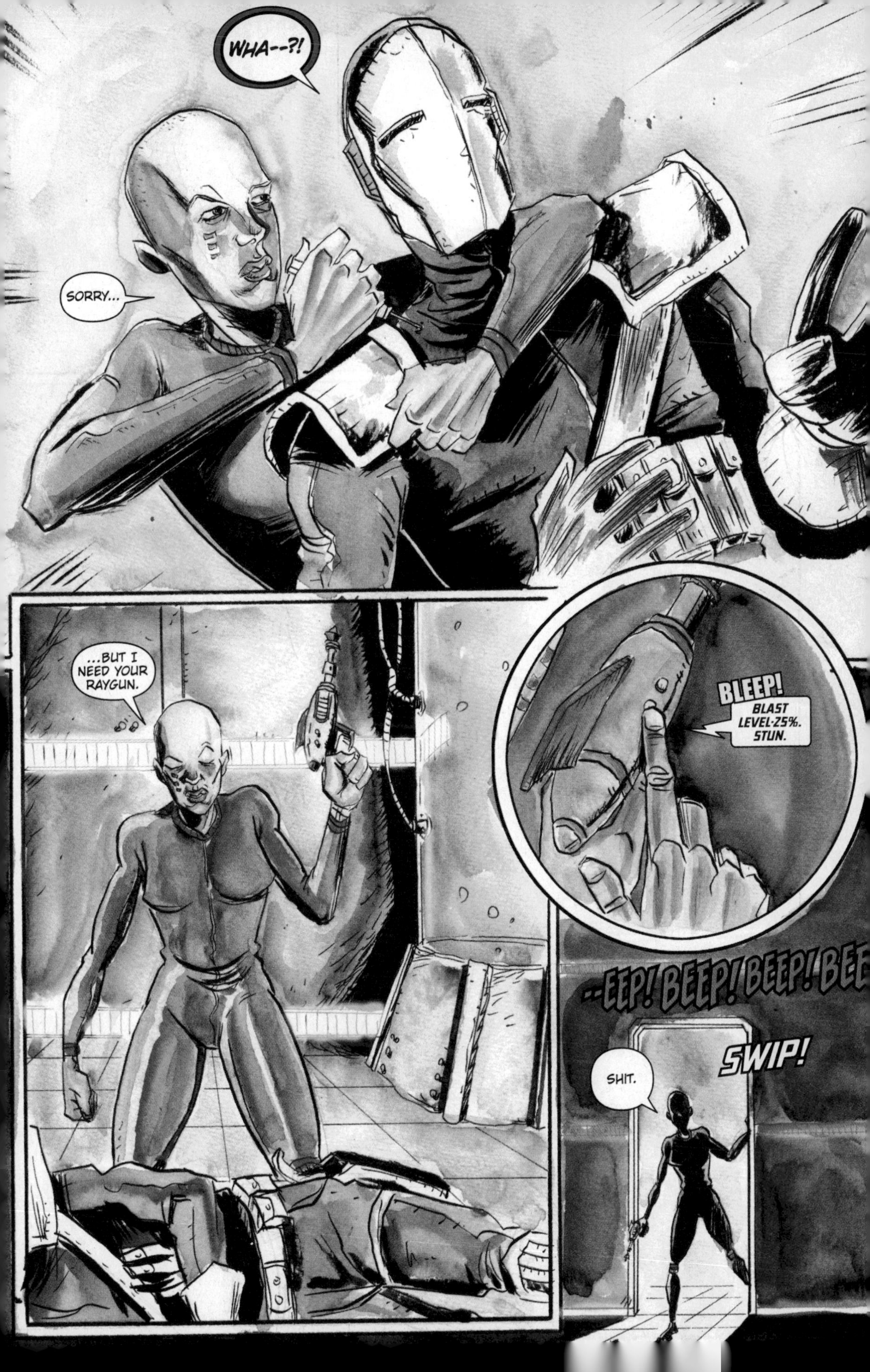
WHA--?!
SORRY...
...BUT I NEED YOUR RAYGUN.
BLEEP!
BLAST LEVEL-25%. STUN.
--EEP! BEEP! BEEP! BEE
SWIP!
SHIT.

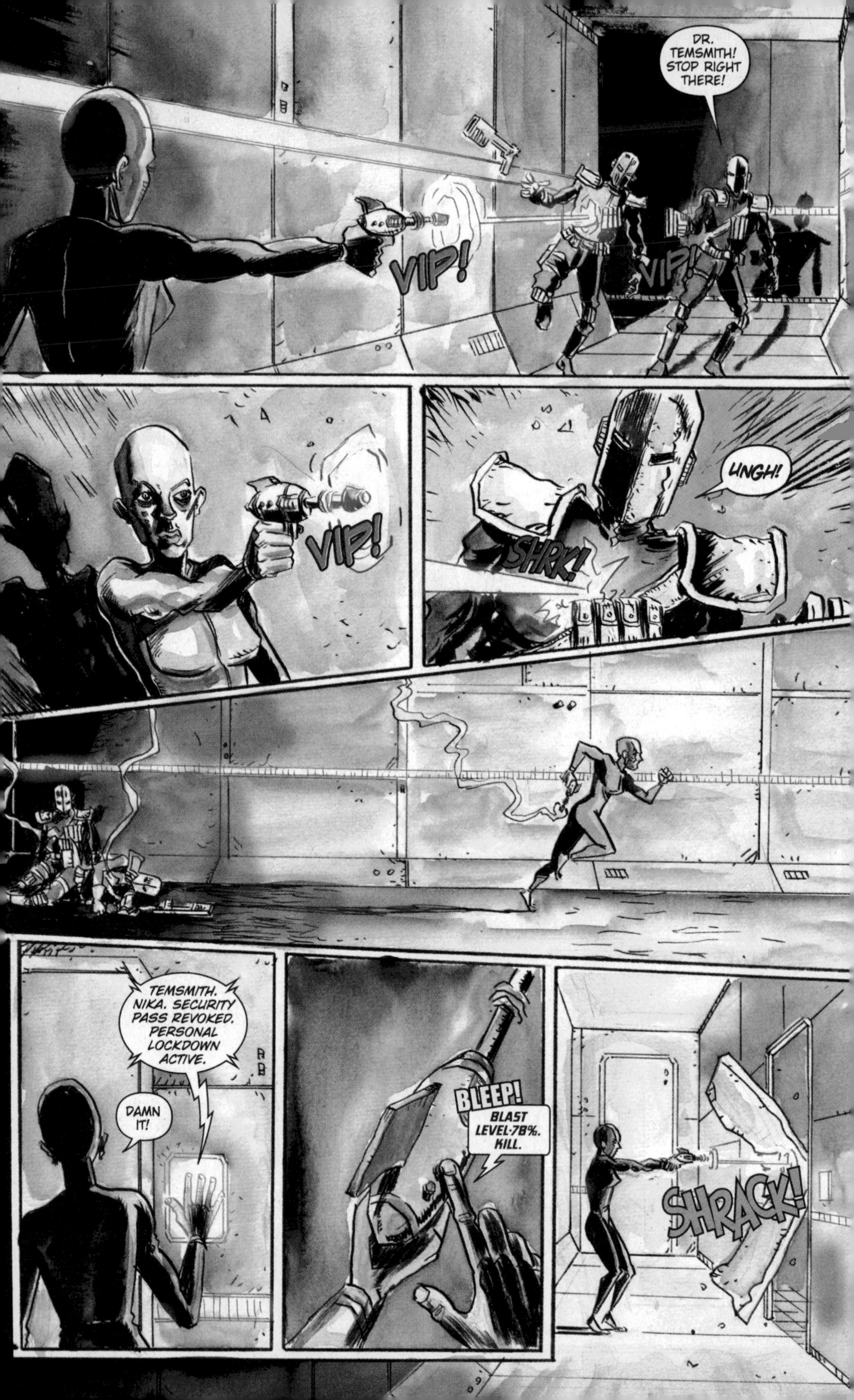
DR. TEMSMITH! STOP RIGHT THERE!
VIP!
VIP!
VIP!
UNGH!
SHRK!
TEMSMITH. NIKA. SECURITY PASS REVOKED. PERSONAL LOCKDOWN ACTIVE.
DAMN IT!
BLEEP!
BLAST LEVEL-78%. KILL.
SHRACK!

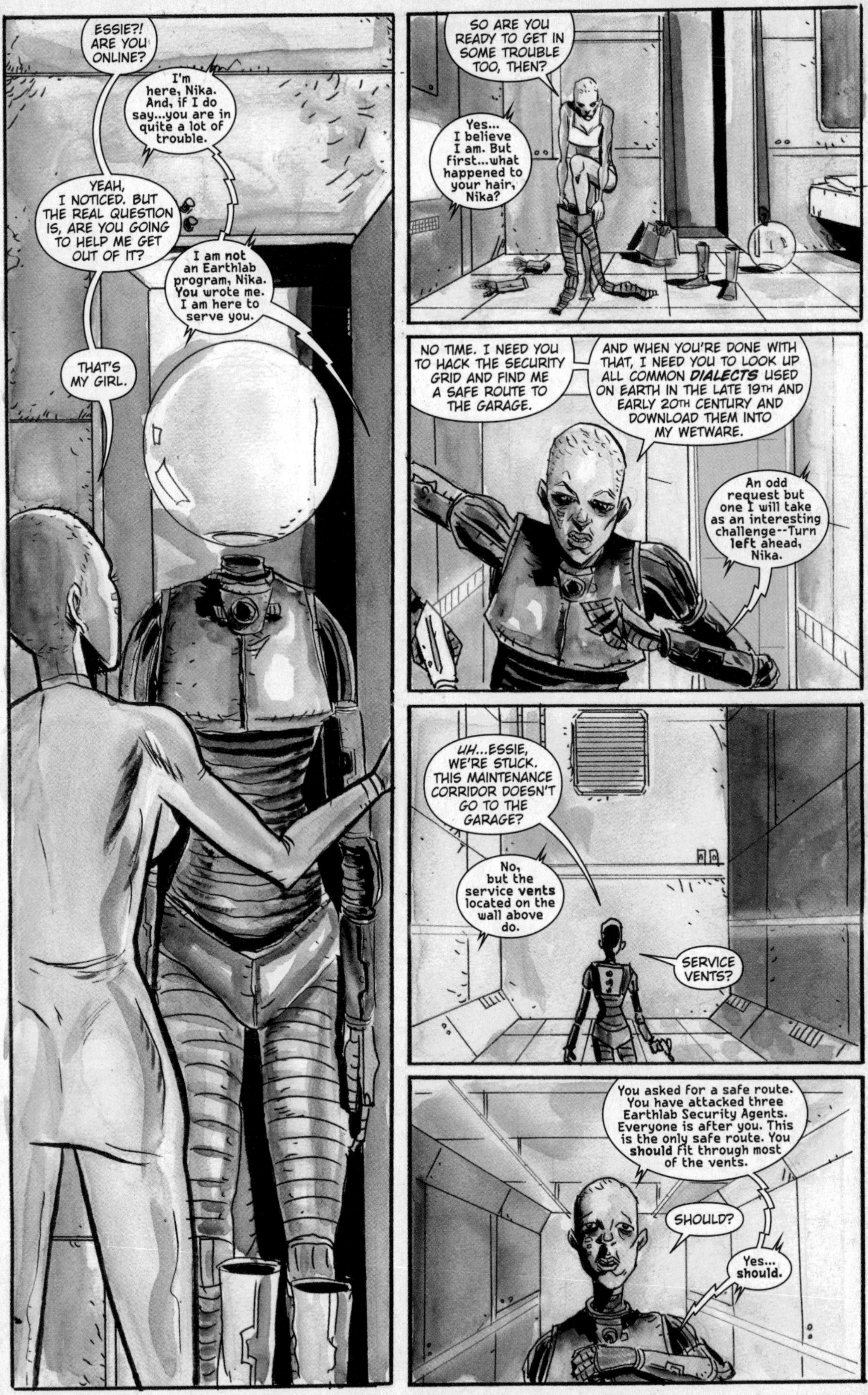

ESSIE?! ARE YOU ONLINE?
I'm here, Nika. And, if I do say...you are in quite a lot of trouble.
YEAH, I NOTICED. BUT THE REAL QUESTION IS, ARE YOU GOING TO HELP ME GET OUT OF IT?
I am not an Earthlab program, Nika. You wrote me. I am here to serve you.
THAT'S MY GIRL.
SO ARE YOU READY TO GET IN SOME TROUBLE TOO, THEN?
Yes... I believe I am. But first...what happened to your hair, Nika?
NO TIME. I NEED YOU TO HACK THE SECURITY GRID AND FIND ME A SAFE ROUTE TO THE GARAGE.
AND WHEN YOU'RE DONE WITH THAT, I NEED YOU TO LOOK UP ALL COMMON DIALECTS USED ON EARTH IN THE LATE 19TH AND EARLY 20TH CENTURY AND DOWNLOAD THEM INTO MY WETWARE.
An odd request but one I will take as an interesting challenge--Turn left ahead, Nika.
UH...ESSIE, WE'RE STUCK. THIS MAINTENANCE CORRIDOR DOESN'T GO TO THE GARAGE?
No, but the service vents located on the wall above do.
SERVICE VENTS?
You asked for a safe route. You have attacked three Earthlab Security Agents. Everyone is after you. This is the only safe route. You should fit through most of the vents.
SHOULD?
Yes... should.

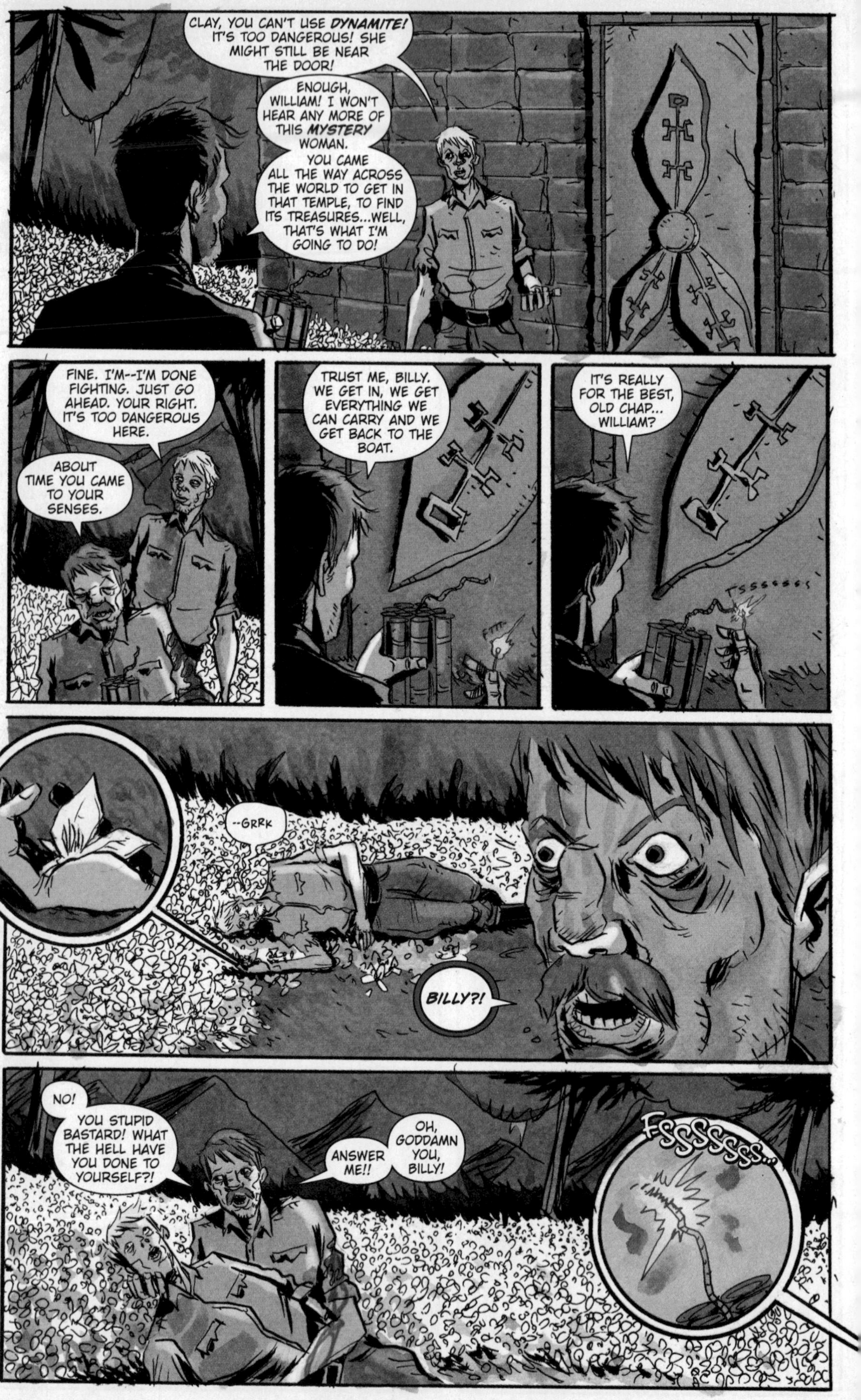
CLAY, YOU CAN'T USE DYNAMITE! IT'S TOO DANGEROUS! SHE MIGHT STILL BE NEAR THE DOOR!
ENOUGH, WILLIAM! I WON'T HEAR ANY MORE OF THIS MYSTERY WOMAN.
YOU CAME ALL THE WAY ACROSS THE WORLD TO GET IN THAT TEMPLE, TO FIND ITS TREASURES...WELL, THAT'S WHAT I'M GOING TO DO!
FINE. I'M--I'M DONE FIGHTING. JUST GO AHEAD. YOUR RIGHT. IT'S TOO DANGEROUS HERE.
ABOUT TIME YOU CAME TO YOUR SENSES.
TRUST ME, BILLY. WE GET IN, WE GET EVERYTHING WE CAN CARRY AND WE GET BACK TO THE BOAT.
IT'S REALLY FOR THE BEST, OLD CHAP... WILLIAM?
TSSSSSS
--GRRK
BILLY?!
NO!
YOU STUPID BASTARD! WHAT THE HELL HAVE YOU DONE TO YOURSELF?!
ANSWER ME!!
OH, GODDAMN YOU, BILLY!
FSSSSSS...

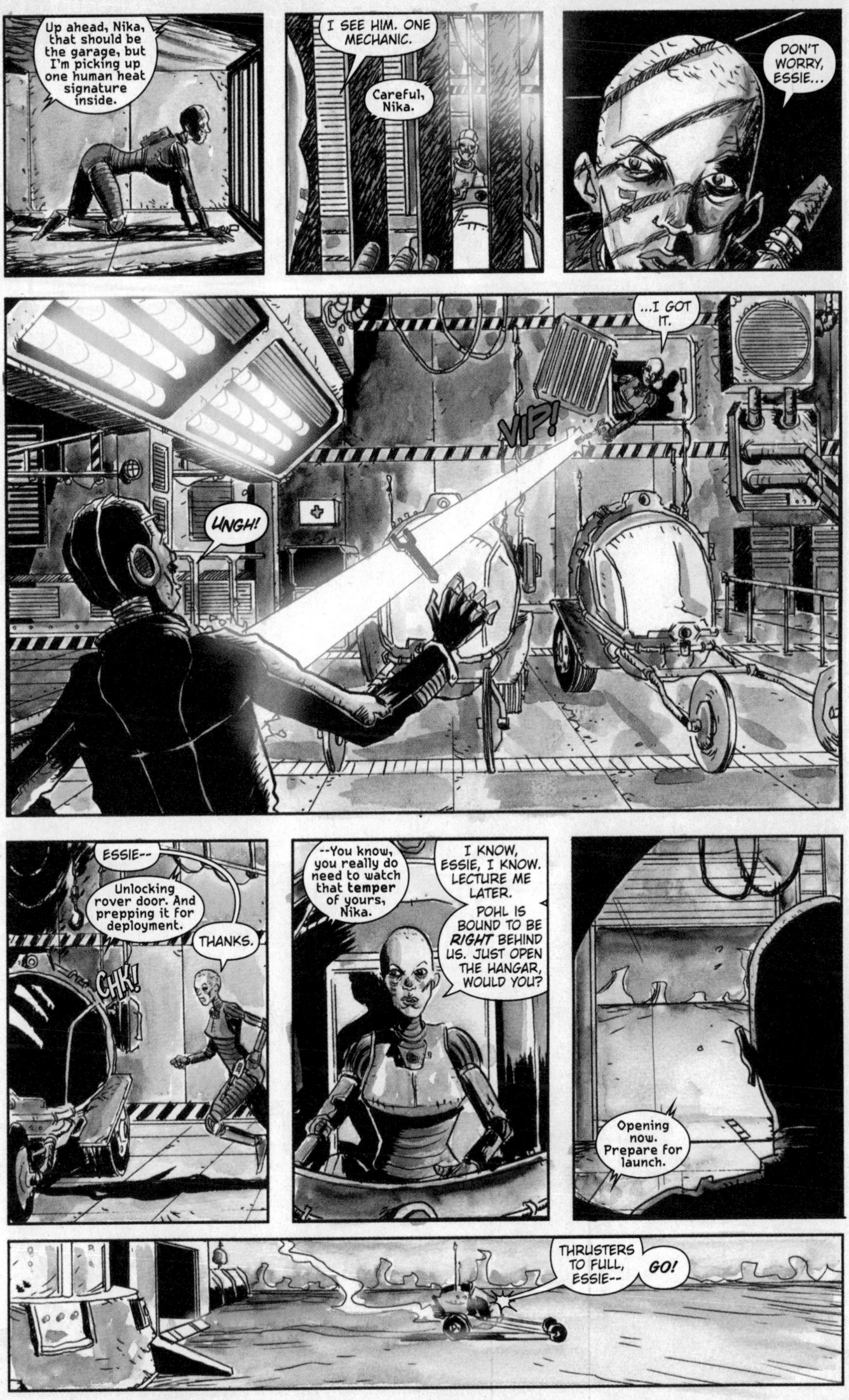

Up ahead, Nika, that should be the garage, but I'm picking up one human heat signature inside.
I SEE HIM. ONE MECHANIC.
Careful, Nika.
DON'T WORRY, ESSIE...
...I GOT IT.
VIP!
UNGH!
ESSIE--
Unlocking rover door. And prepping it for deployment.
THANKS.
CHK!
--You know, you really do need to watch that temper of yours, Nika.
I KNOW, ESSIE, I KNOW. LECTURE ME LATER.
POHL IS BOUND TO BE RIGHT BEHIND US. JUST OPEN THE HANGAR, WOULD YOU?
Opening now. Prepare for launch.
THRUSTERS TO FULL, ESSIE--
GO!

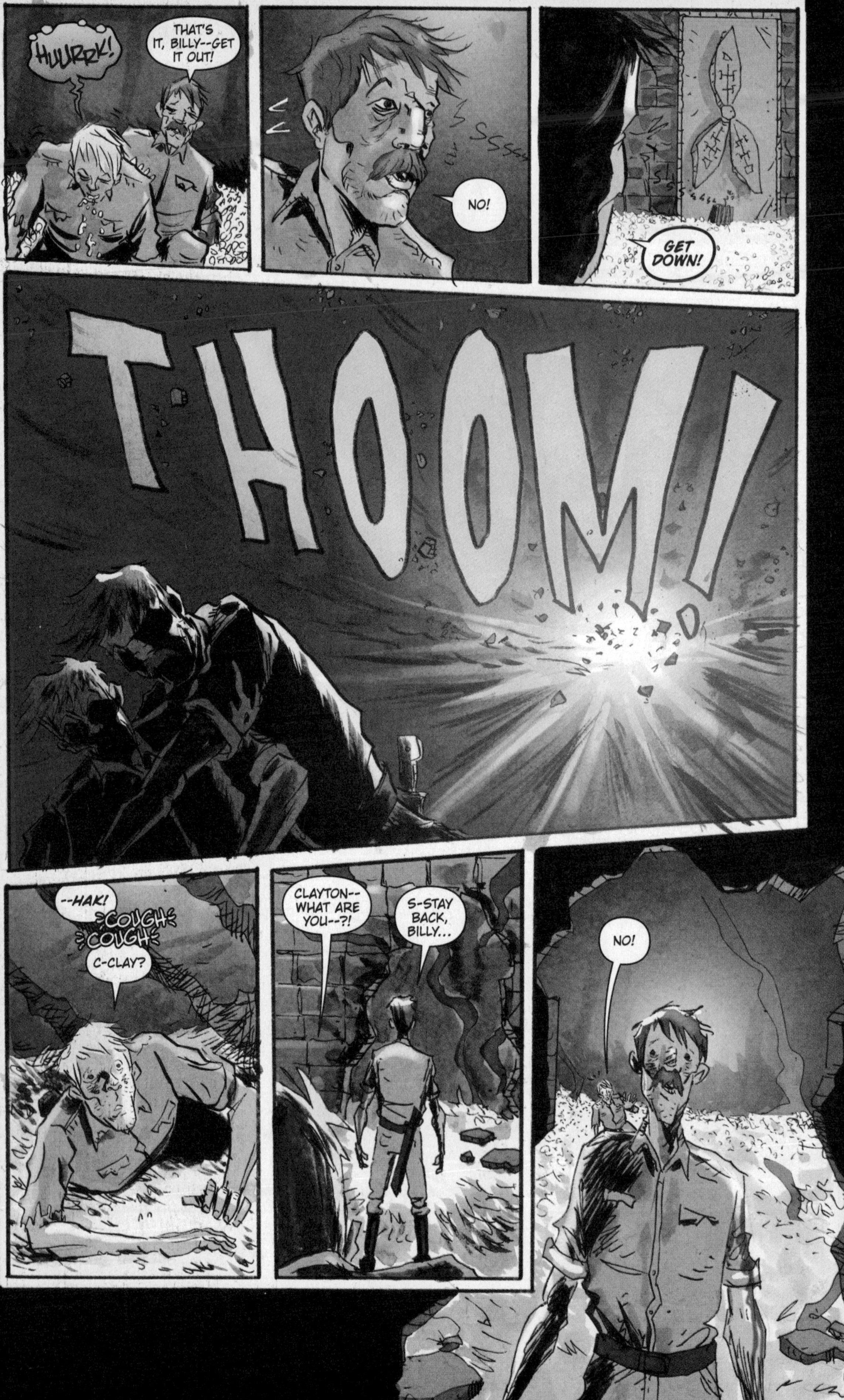
HUURRK!
THAT'S IT, BILLY--GET IT OUT!
NO!
GET DOWN!
THOOM!
--HAK!
COUGH
COUGH
C-CLAY?
CLAYTON--WHAT ARE YOU--?!
S-STAY BACK, BILLY...
NO!

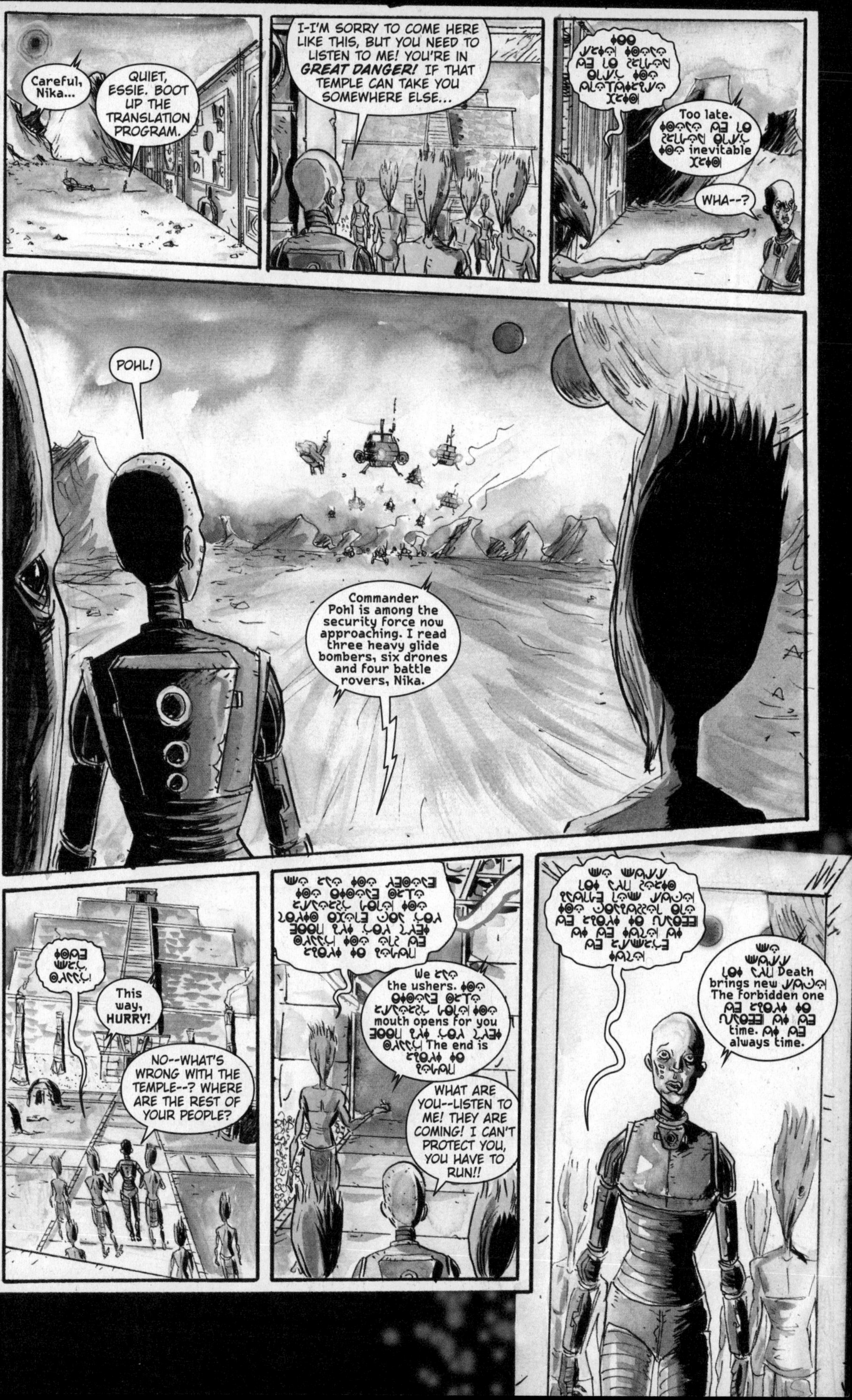
Careful, Nika...
QUIET, ESSIE. BOOT UP THE TRANSLATION PROGRAM.
I-I'M SORRY TO COME HERE LIKE THIS, BUT YOU NEED TO LISTEN TO ME! YOU'RE IN GREAT DANGER! IF THAT TEMPLE CAN TAKE YOU SOMEWHERE ELSE...
Too late.
inevitable
WHA--?
POHL!
Commander Pohl is among the security force now approaching. I read three heavy glide bombers, six drones and four battle rovers, Nika.
This way, HURRY!
NO--WHAT'S WRONG WITH THE TEMPLE--? WHERE ARE THE REST OF YOUR PEOPLE?
We
the ushers.
mouth opens for you
The end is
WHAT ARE YOU--LISTEN TO ME! THEY ARE COMING! I CAN'T PROTECT YOU, YOU HAVE TO RUN!!
Death brings new
The forbidden one
time.
always time.

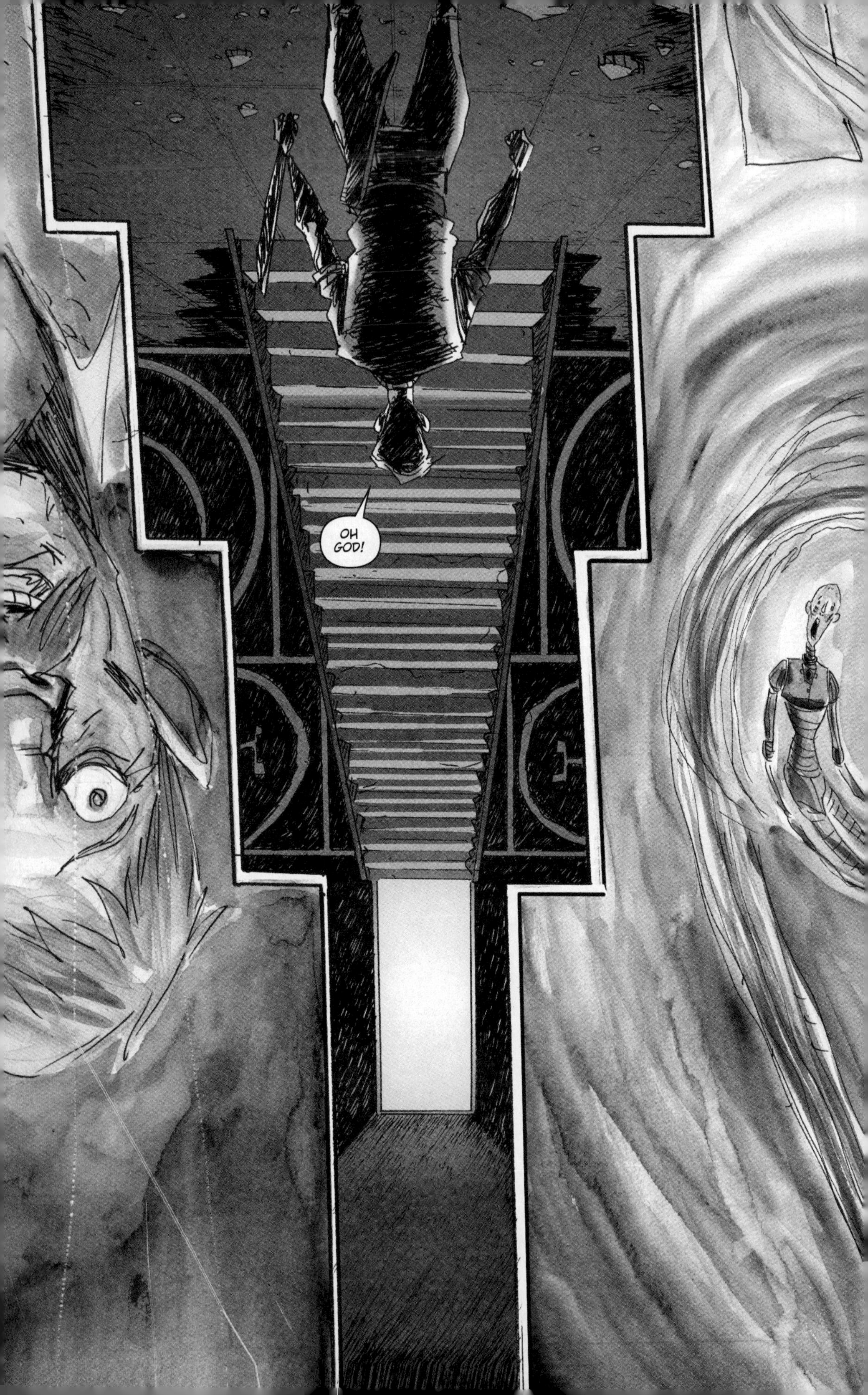
OH GOD!

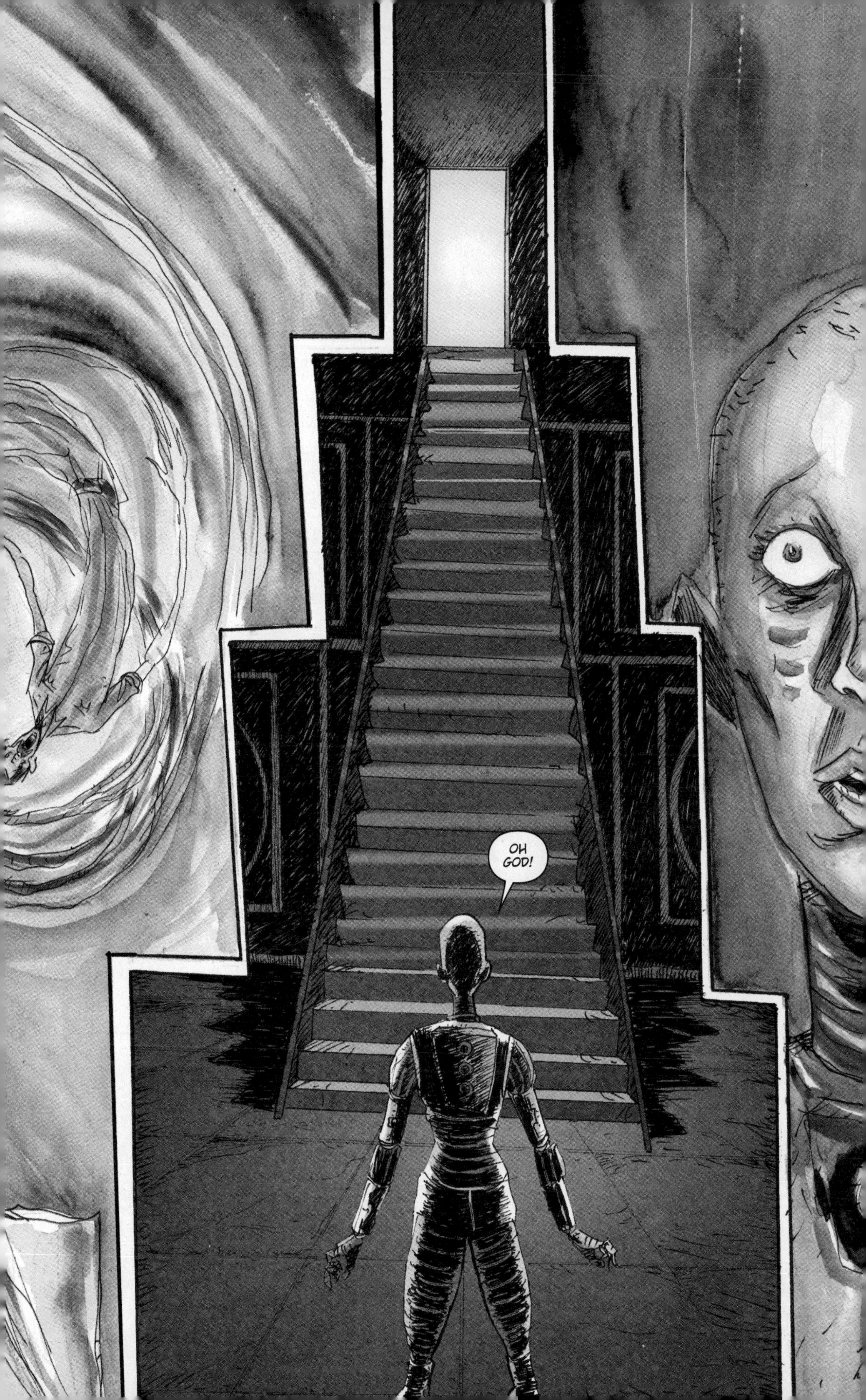
OH GOD!

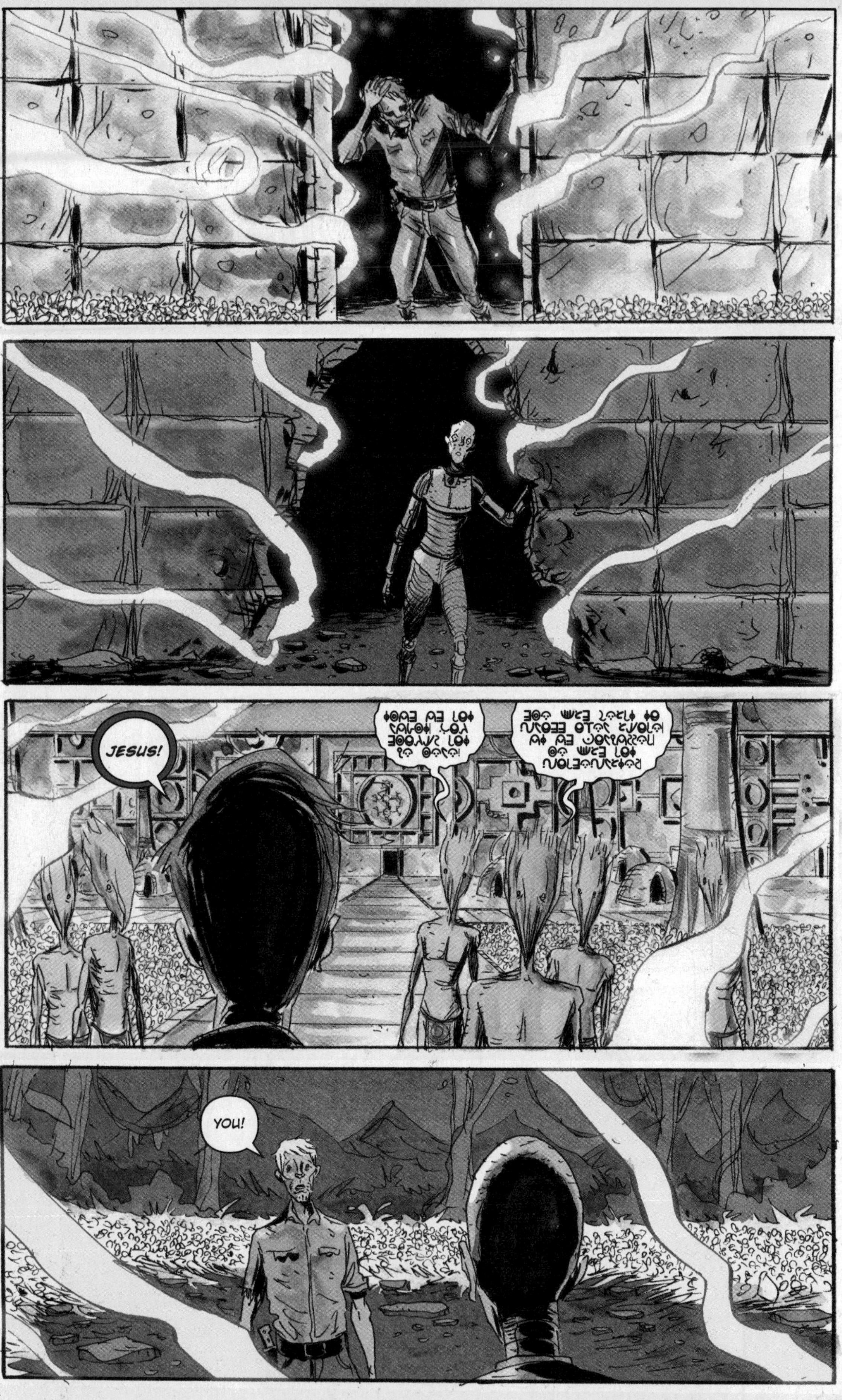
JESUS!
YOU!

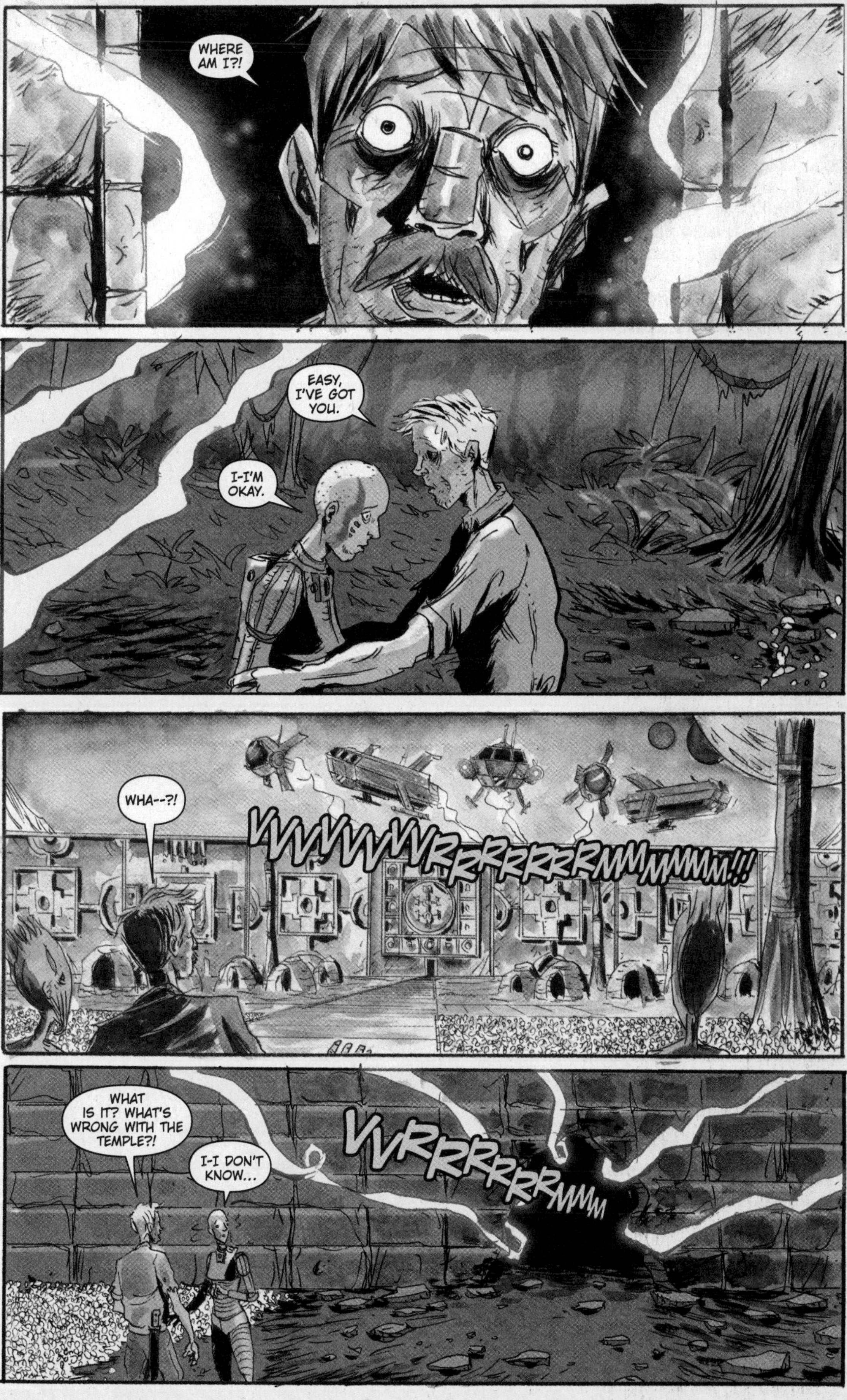
WHERE AM I?!
EASY, I'VE GOT YOU.
I-I'M OKAY.
WHA--?!
VVVVVVVVRRRRRRRRMMMMMMM!!!
WHAT IS IT? WHAT'S WRONG WITH THE TEMPLE?!
I-I DON'T KNOW...
VVRRRRRRRMMM

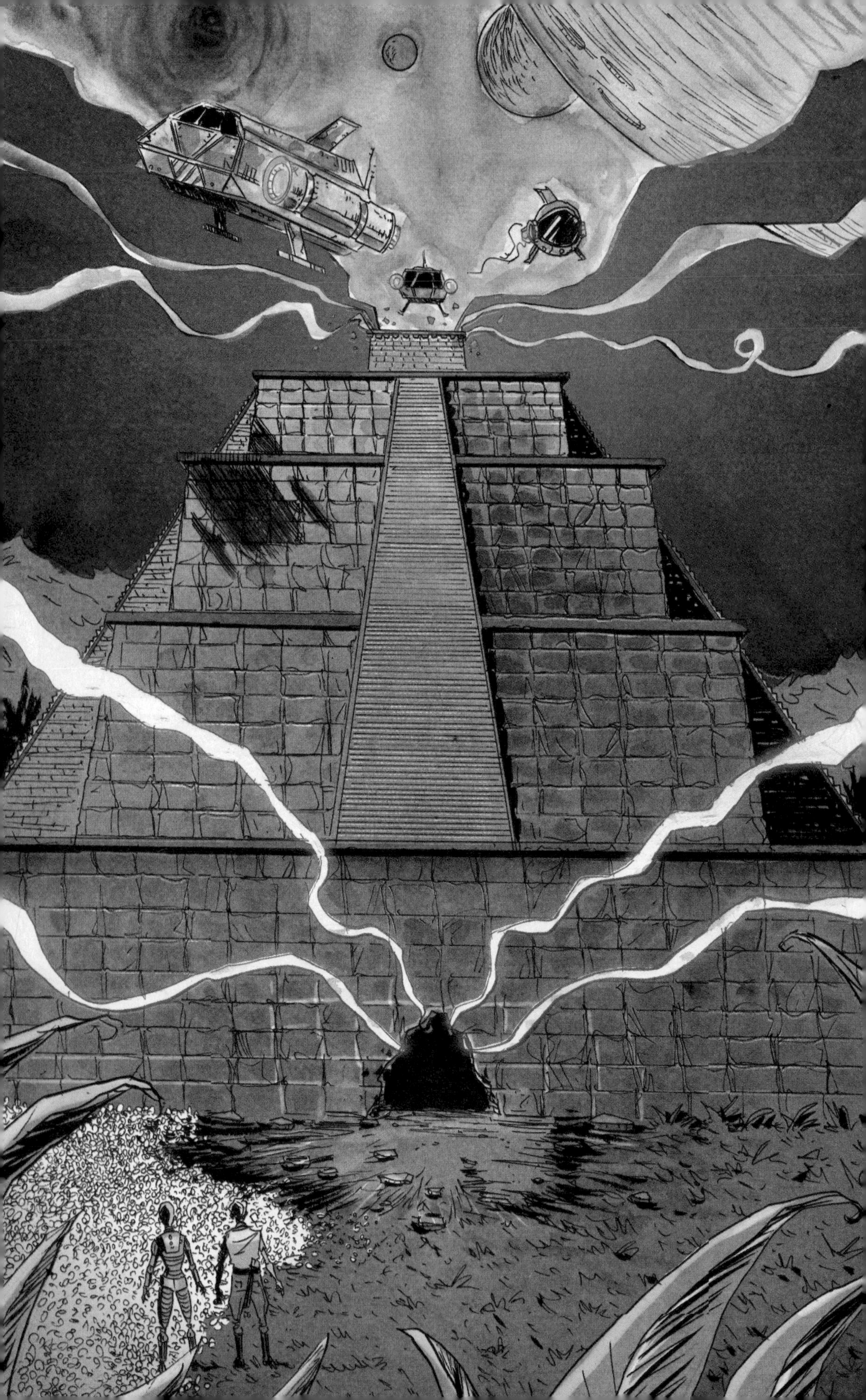

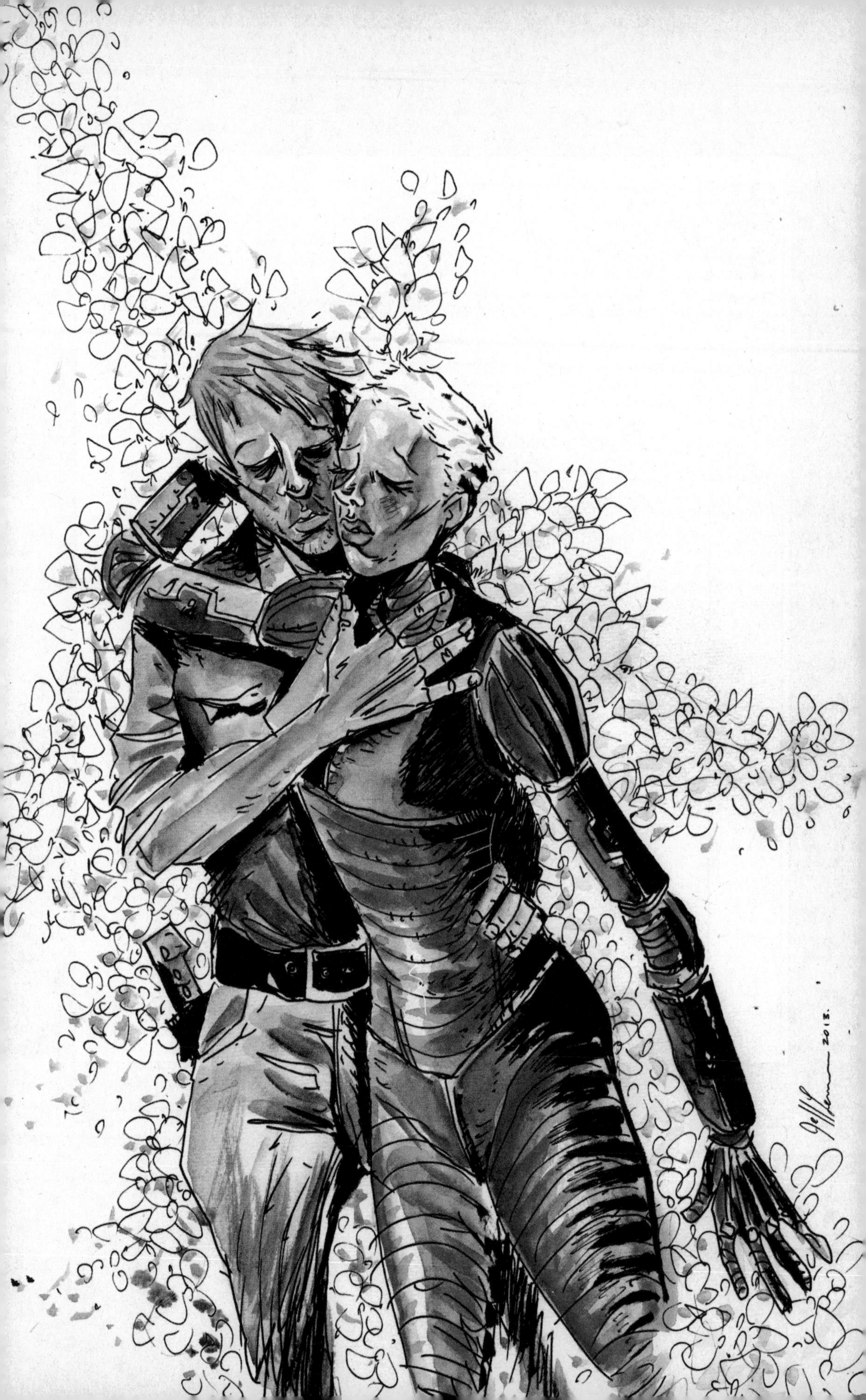
2013.

CHAPTER 4: ENTROPY

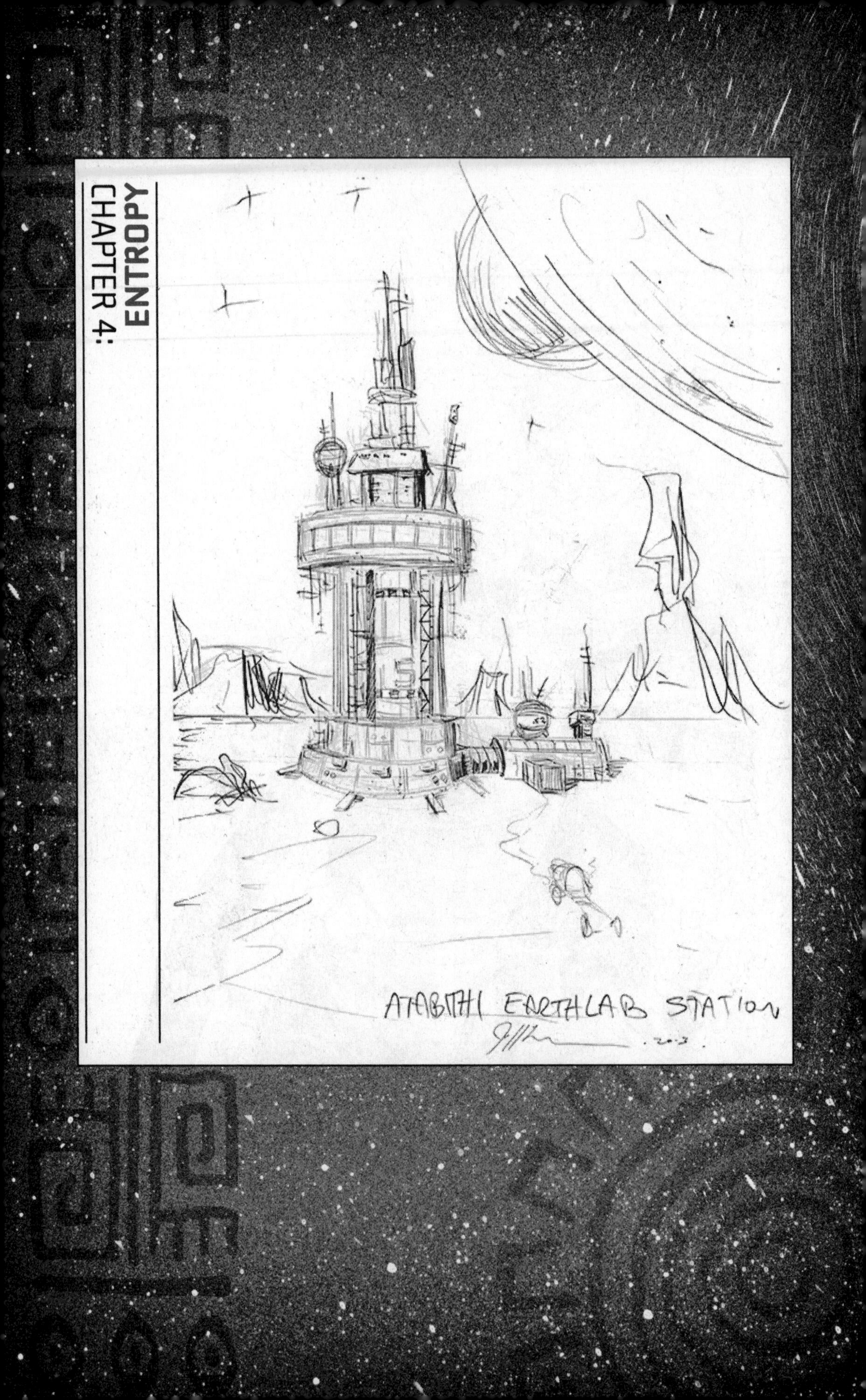
ATABITHI EARTHLAB STATION

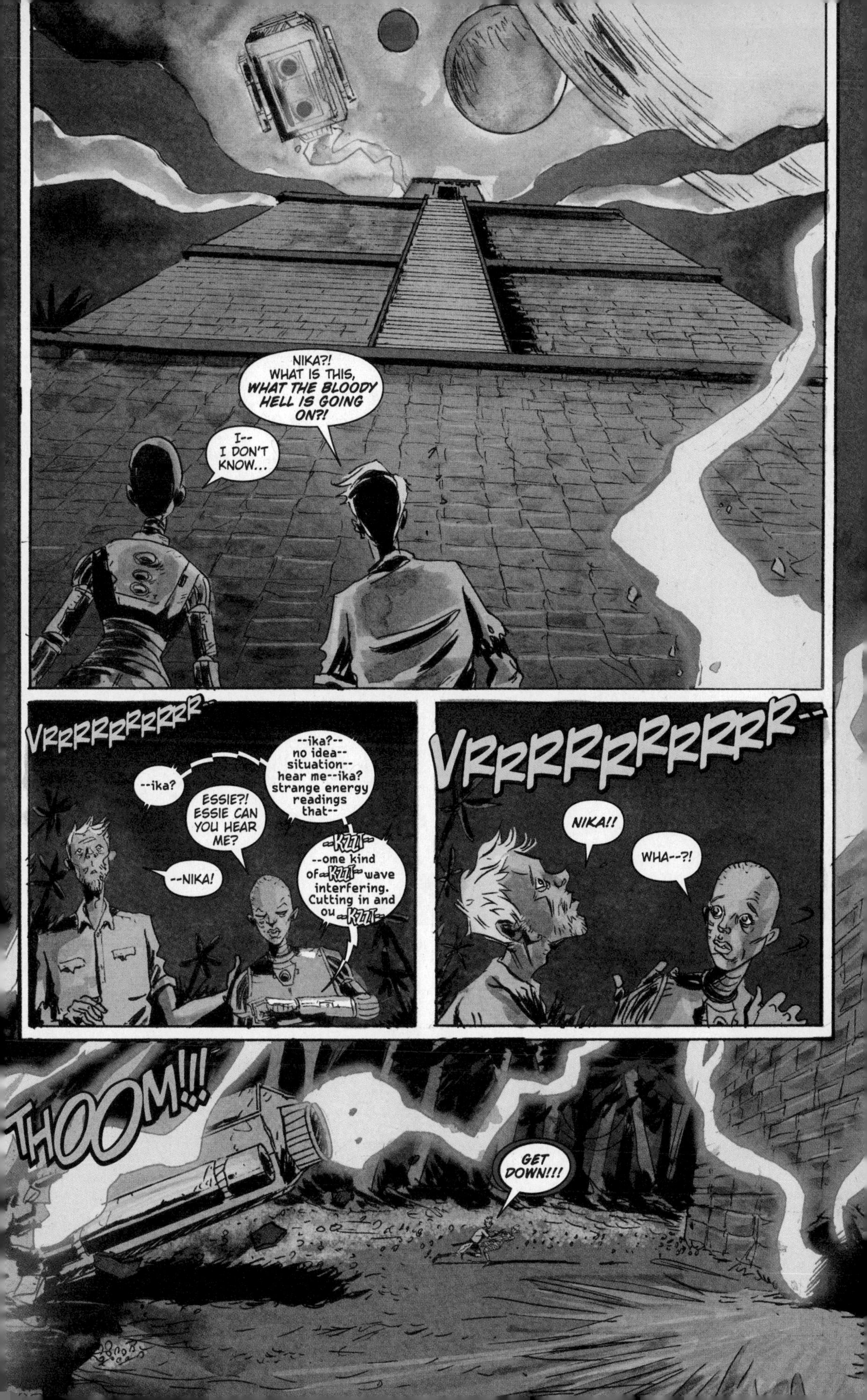
NIKA?! WHAT IS THIS, WHAT THE BLOODY HELL IS GOING ON?!
I-- I DON'T KNOW...
VRRRRRRRRR--
--ika?
ESSIE?! ESSIE CAN YOU HEAR ME?
--ika?-- no idea-- situation-- hear me--ika? strange energy readings that--
--KZZT-- --ome kind of--KZZT--wave interfering. Cutting in and ou--KZZT--
--NIKA!
VRRRRRRRRRR--
NIKA!!
WHA--?!
THOOM!!!
GET DOWN!!!

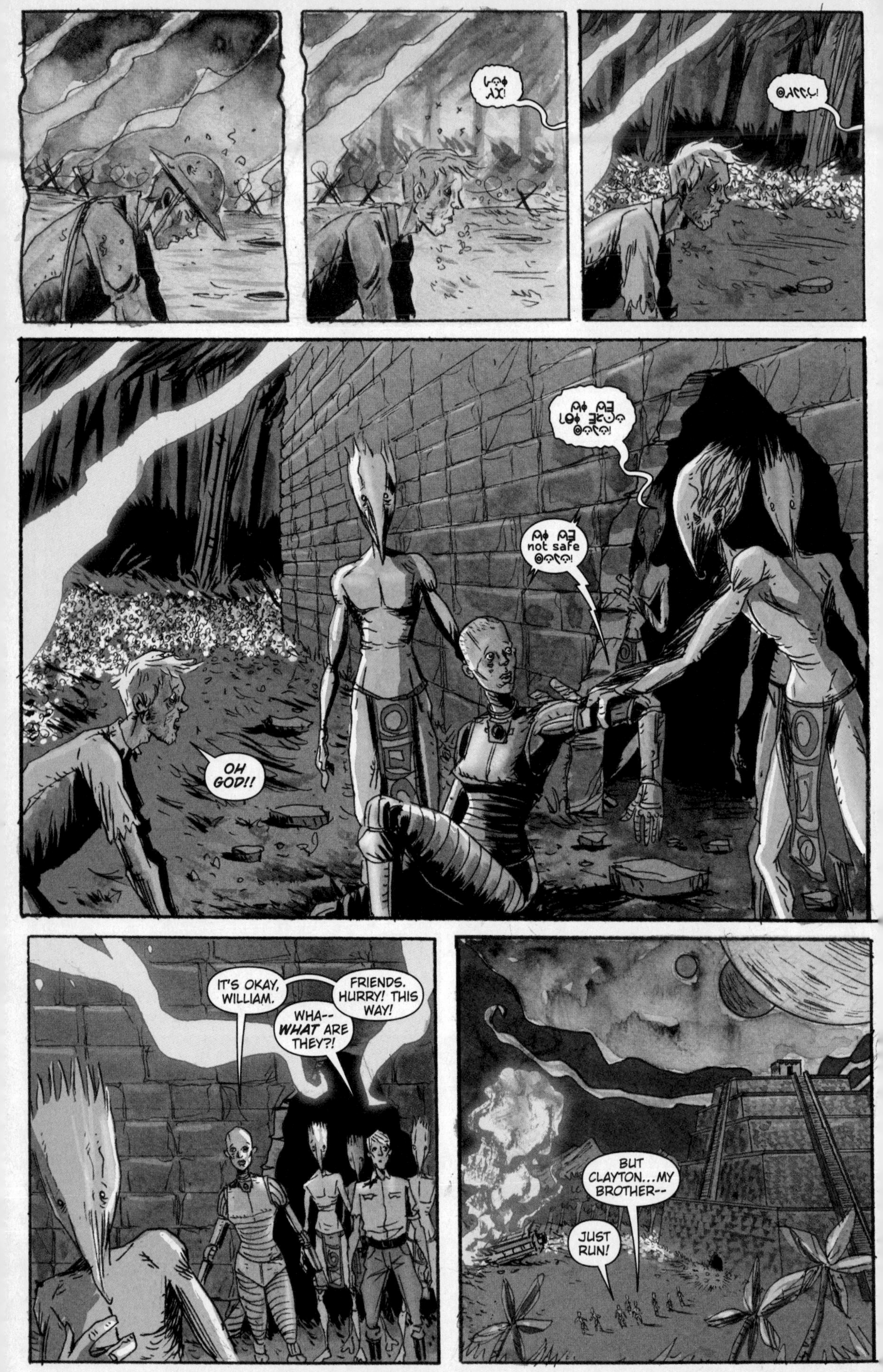
not safe
OH GOD!!
IT'S OKAY, WILLIAM.
FRIENDS. HURRY! THIS WAY!
WHA-- WHAT ARE THEY?!
BUT CLAYTON...MY BROTHER--
JUST RUN!

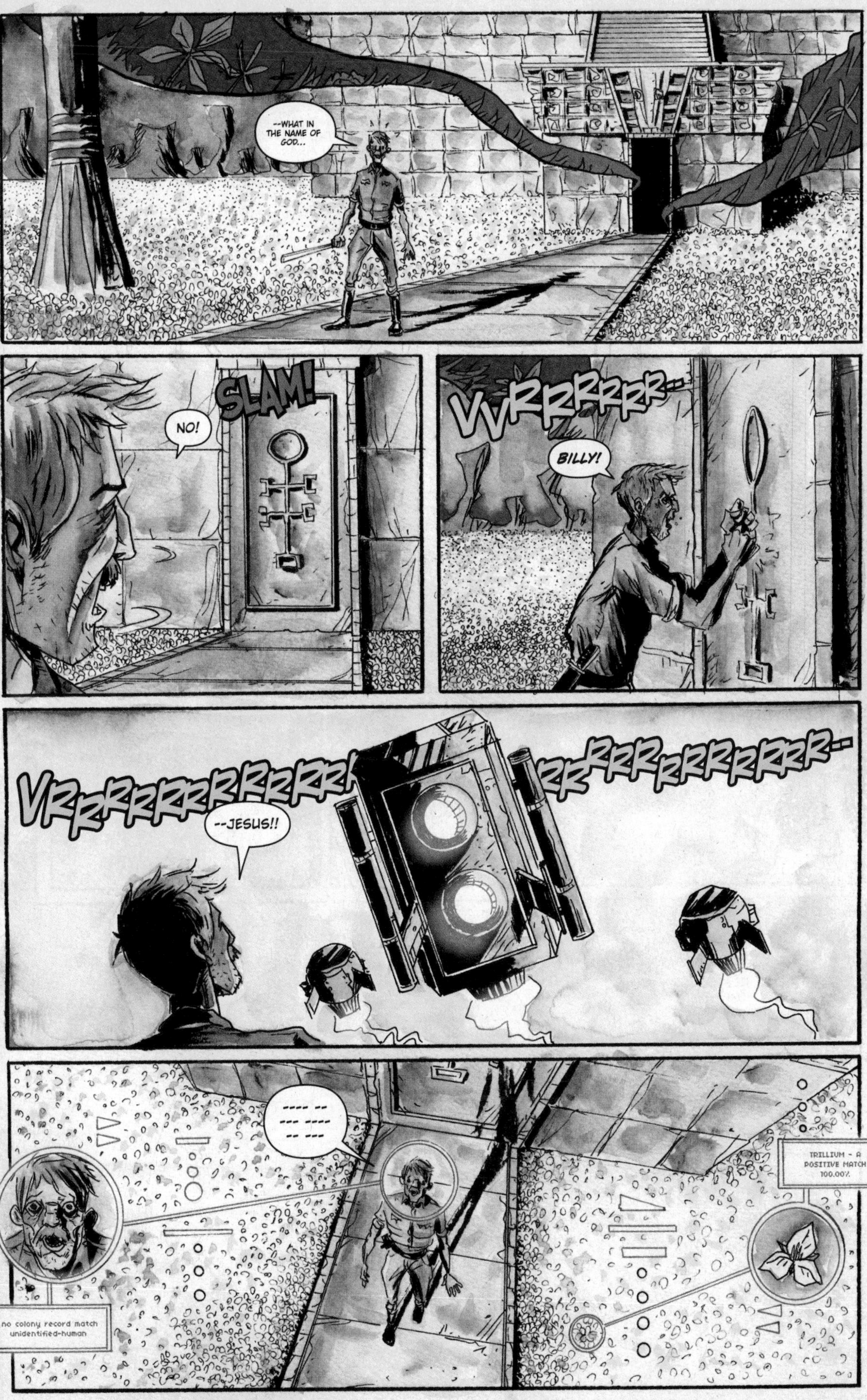
--WHAT IN THE NAME OF GOD...
SLAM!
NO!
VVRRRRRRR--
BILLY!
VRRRRRRRRRRRRRRRRRRRRRRRRRR--
--JESUS!!
TRILLIUM - A POSITIVE MATCH 100.00%
no colony record match
unidentified-human

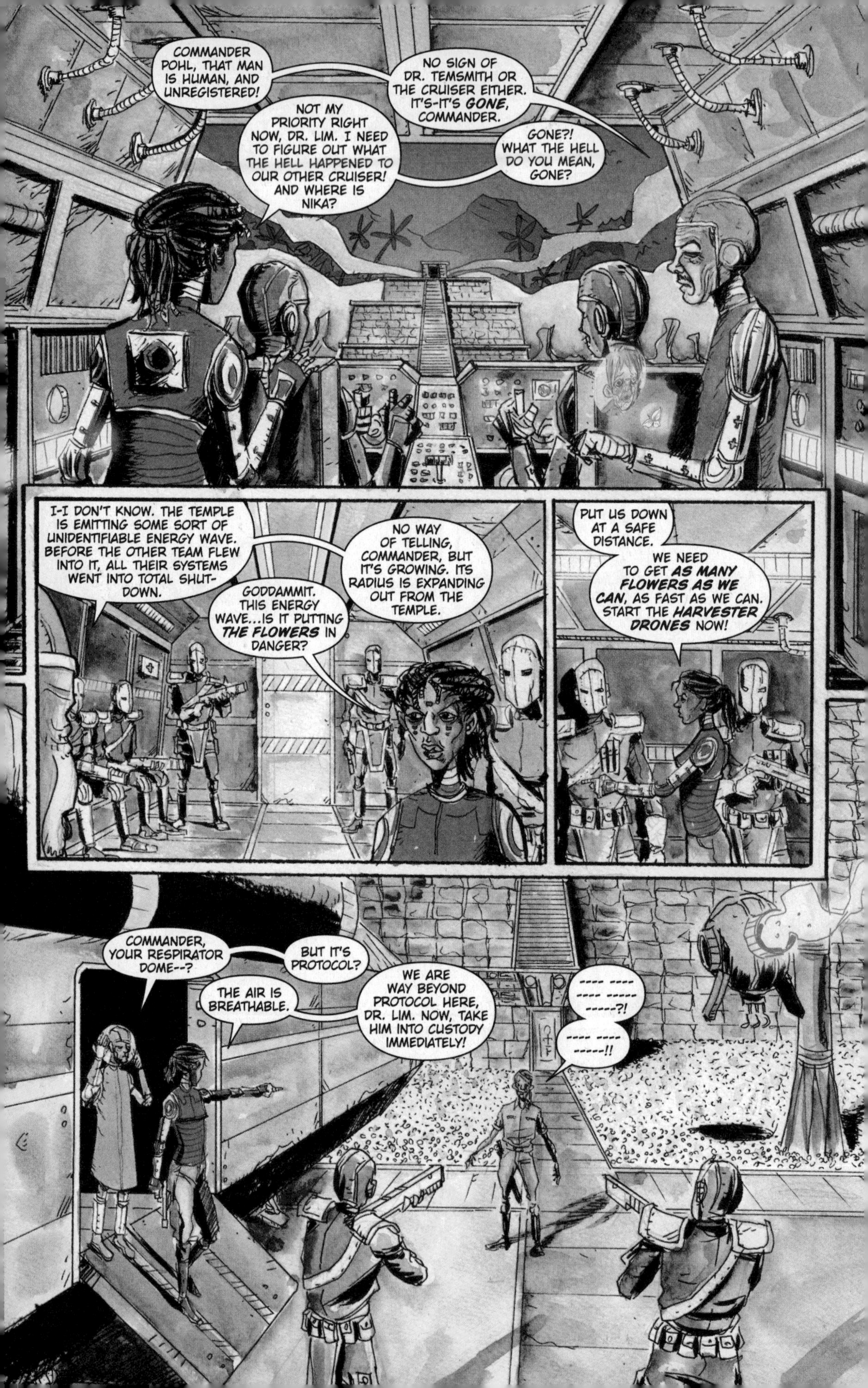
COMMANDER POHL, THAT MAN IS HUMAN, AND UNREGISTERED!
NO SIGN OF DR. TEMSMITH OR THE CRUISER EITHER. IT'S-IT'S GONE, COMMANDER.
NOT MY PRIORITY RIGHT NOW, DR. LIM. I NEED TO FIGURE OUT WHAT THE HELL HAPPENED TO OUR OTHER CRUISER! AND WHERE IS NIKA?
GONE?! WHAT THE HELL DO YOU MEAN, GONE?
I-I DON'T KNOW. THE TEMPLE IS EMITTING SOME SORT OF UNIDENTIFIABLE ENERGY WAVE. BEFORE THE OTHER TEAM FLEW INTO IT, ALL THEIR SYSTEMS WENT INTO TOTAL SHUT-DOWN.
GODDAMMIT. THIS ENERGY WAVE...IS IT PUTTING THE FLOWERS IN DANGER?
NO WAY OF TELLING, COMMANDER, BUT IT'S GROWING. ITS RADIUS IS EXPANDING OUT FROM THE TEMPLE.
PUT US DOWN AT A SAFE DISTANCE.
WE NEED TO GET AS MANY FLOWERS AS WE CAN, AS FAST AS WE CAN. START THE HARVESTER DRONES NOW!
COMMANDER, YOUR RESPIRATOR DOME--?
THE AIR IS BREATHABLE.
BUT IT'S PROTOCOL?
WE ARE WAY BEYOND PROTOCOL HERE, DR. LIM. NOW, TAKE HIM INTO CUSTODY IMMEDIATELY!
---- ---- ---- ----- -----?!
---- ---- -----!!

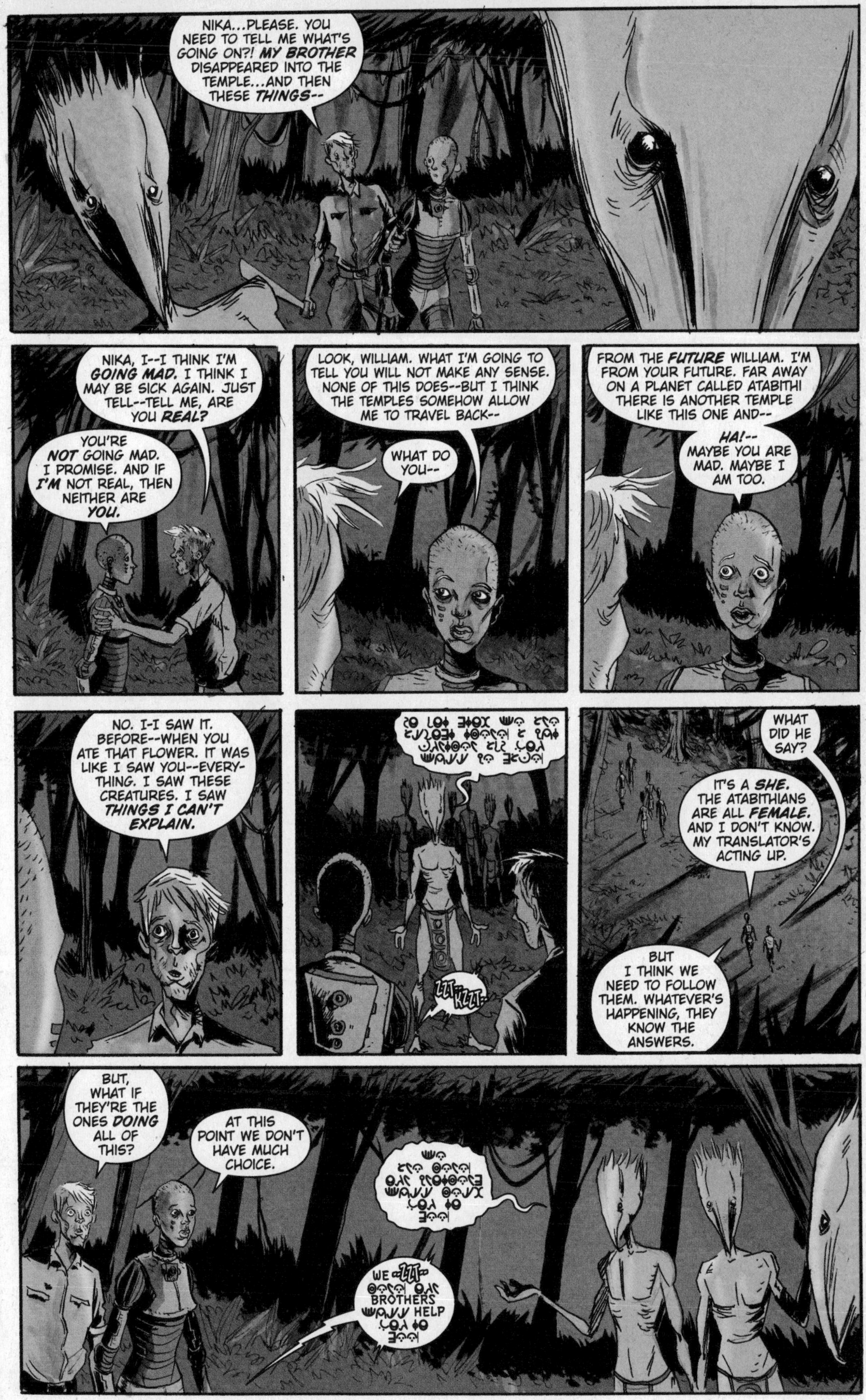
NIKA...PLEASE. YOU NEED TO TELL ME WHAT'S GOING ON?! MY BROTHER DISAPPEARED INTO THE TEMPLE...AND THEN THESE THINGS--
NIKA, I--I THINK I'M GOING MAD. I THINK I MAY BE SICK AGAIN. JUST TELL--TELL ME, ARE YOU REAL?
YOU'RE NOT GOING MAD. I PROMISE. AND IF I'M NOT REAL, THEN NEITHER ARE YOU.
LOOK, WILLIAM. WHAT I'M GOING TO TELL YOU WILL NOT MAKE ANY SENSE. NONE OF THIS DOES--BUT I THINK THE TEMPLES SOMEHOW ALLOW ME TO TRAVEL BACK--
WHAT DO YOU--
FROM THE FUTURE WILLIAM. I'M FROM YOUR FUTURE. FAR AWAY ON A PLANET CALLED ATABITHI THERE IS ANOTHER TEMPLE LIKE THIS ONE AND--
HA!-- MAYBE YOU ARE MAD. MAYBE I AM TOO.
NO. I-I SAW IT. BEFORE--WHEN YOU ATE THAT FLOWER. IT WAS LIKE I SAW YOU--EVERY-THING. I SAW THESE CREATURES. I SAW THINGS I CAN'T EXPLAIN.
ZZT KZZZT--
WHAT DID HE SAY?
IT'S A SHE. THE ATABITHIANS ARE ALL FEMALE. AND I DON'T KNOW. MY TRANSLATOR'S ACTING UP.
BUT I THINK WE NEED TO FOLLOW THEM. WHATEVER'S HAPPENING, THEY KNOW THE ANSWERS.
BUT, WHAT IF THEY'RE THE ONES DOING ALL OF THIS?
AT THIS POINT WE DON'T HAVE MUCH CHOICE.
WE --ZZT--
BROTHERS
HELP

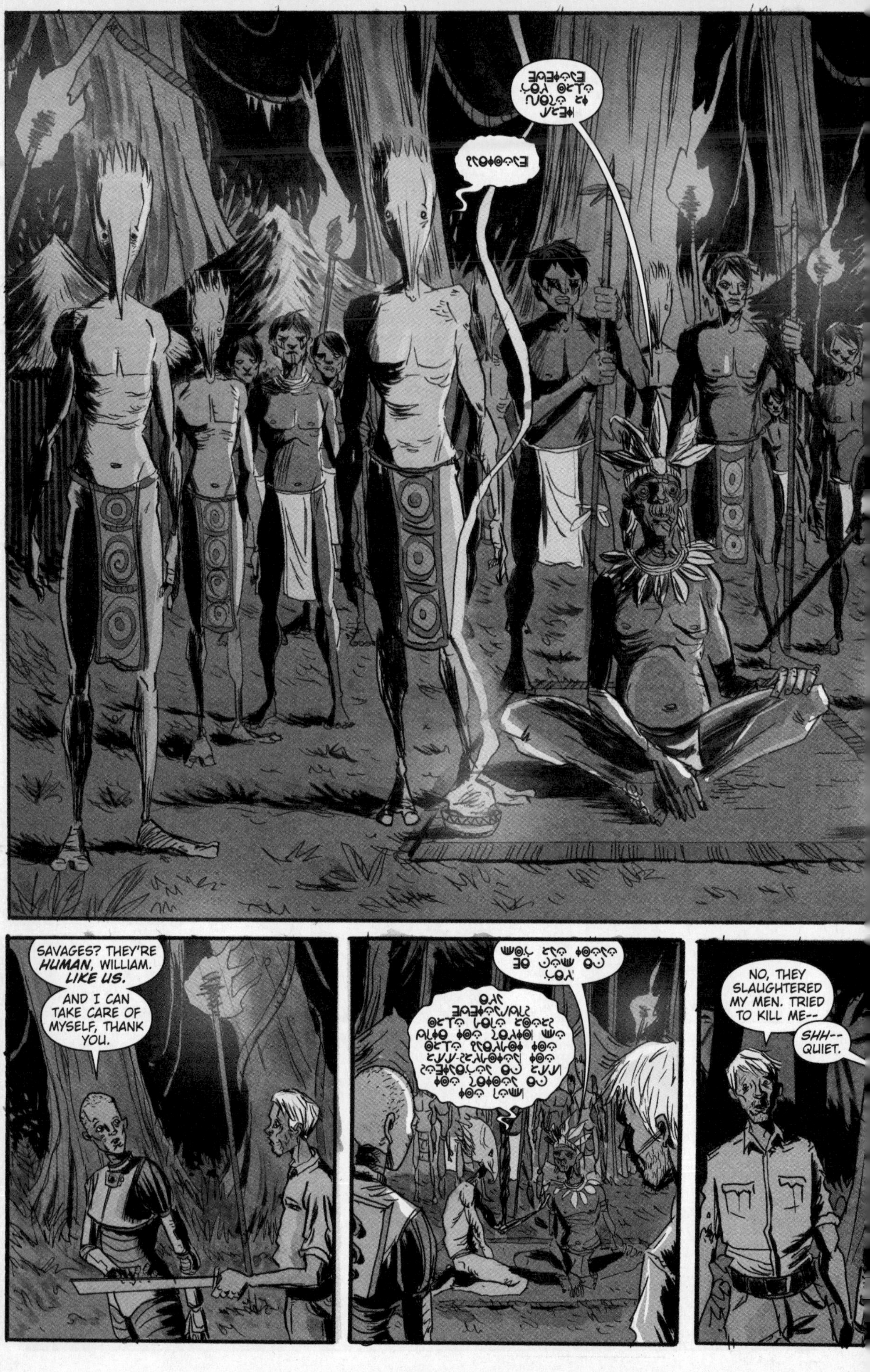
SAVAGES? THEY'RE **HUMAN**, WILLIAM. **LIKE US.**
AND I CAN TAKE CARE OF MYSELF, THANK YOU.
NO, THEY SLAUGHTERED MY MEN. TRIED TO KILL ME--
SHH-- QUIET.

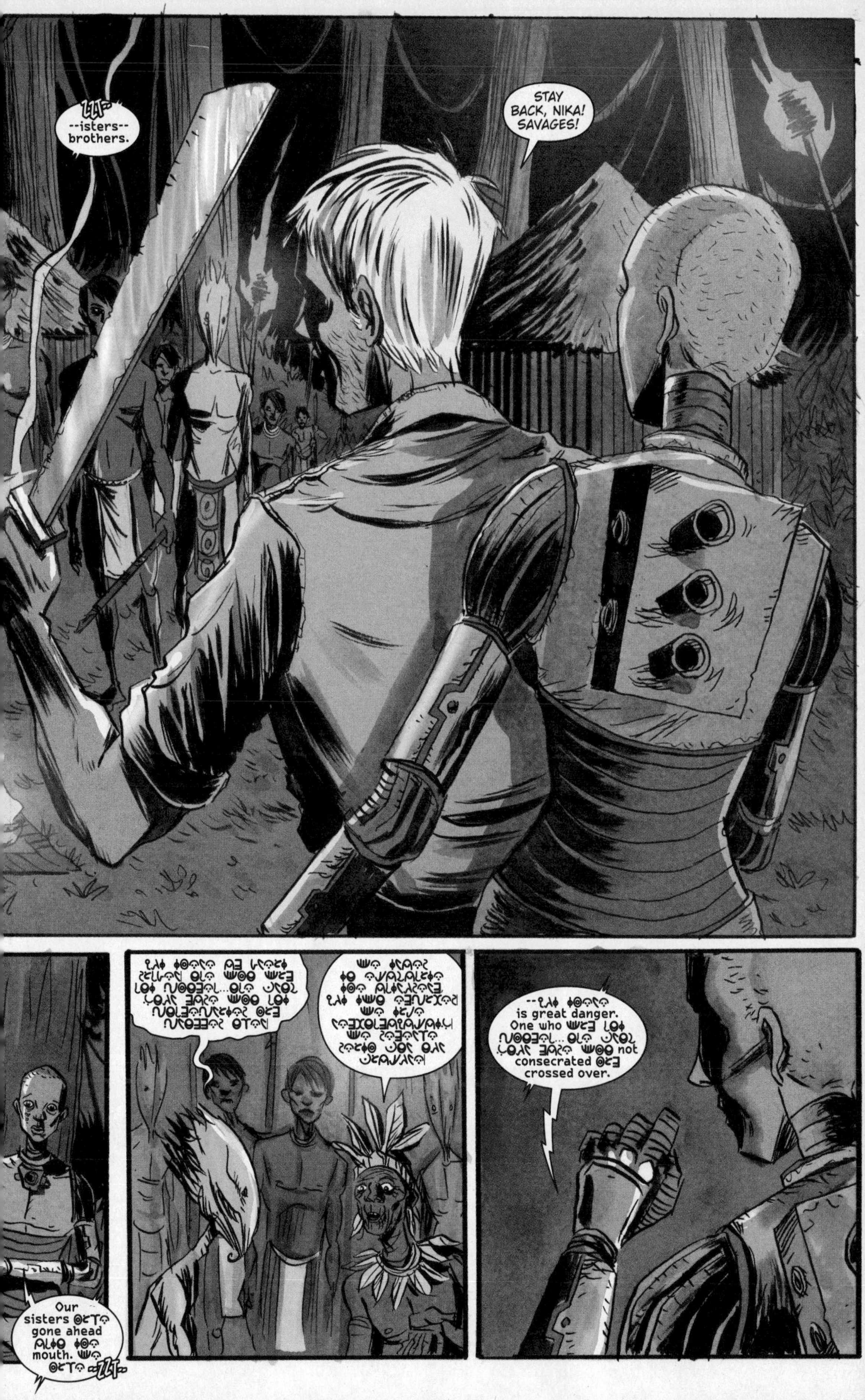
ZZT--
--isters-- brothers.
STAY BACK, NIKA! SAVAGES!
Our sisters gone ahead mouth.
ZZT--
is great danger. One who not consecrated crossed over.

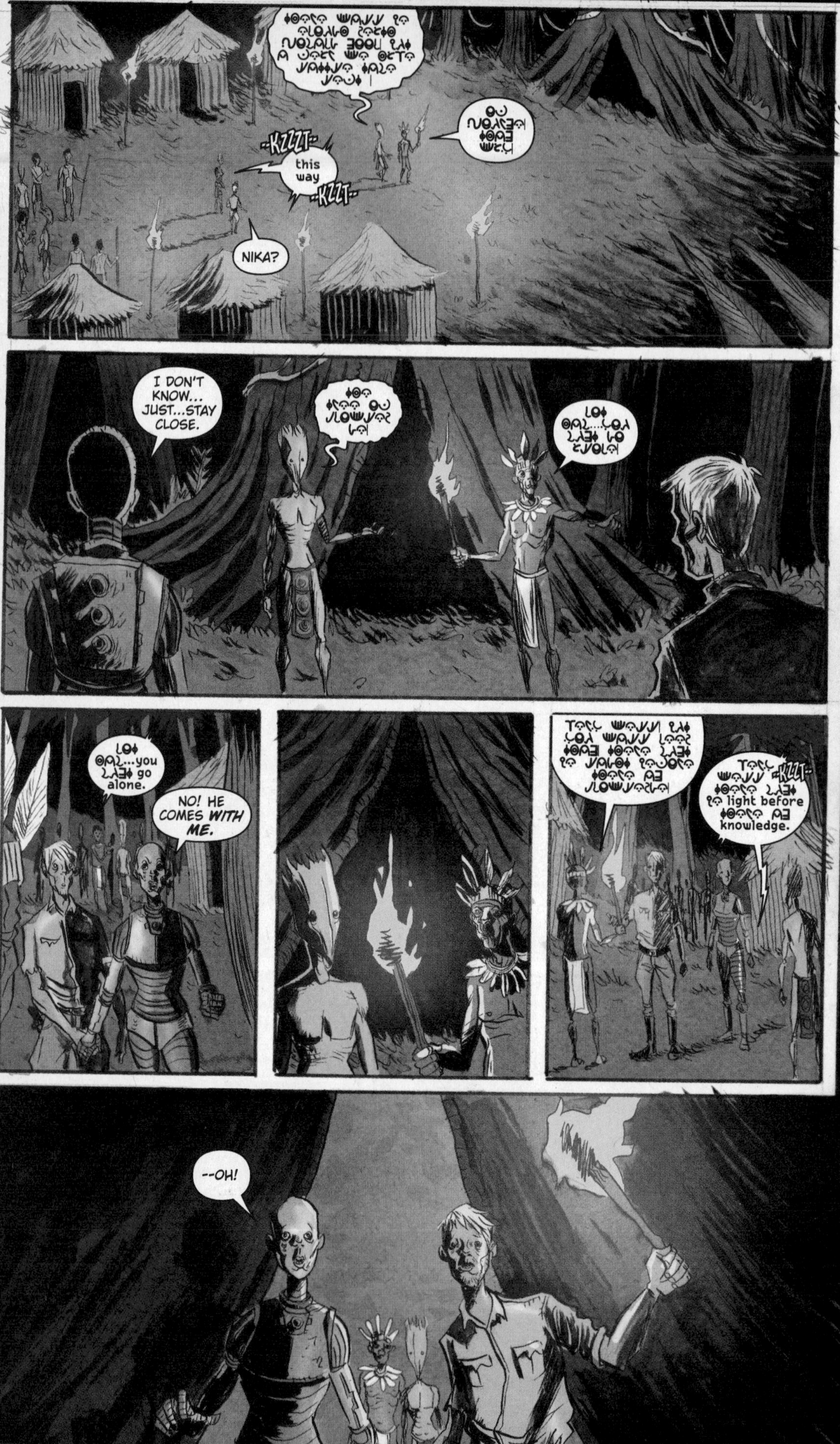
-KZZZT-
this way
-KZZT-
NIKA?
I DON'T KNOW... JUST...STAY CLOSE.
...you go alone.
NO! HE COMES WITH ME.
-KZZT-
light before
knowledge.
--OH!

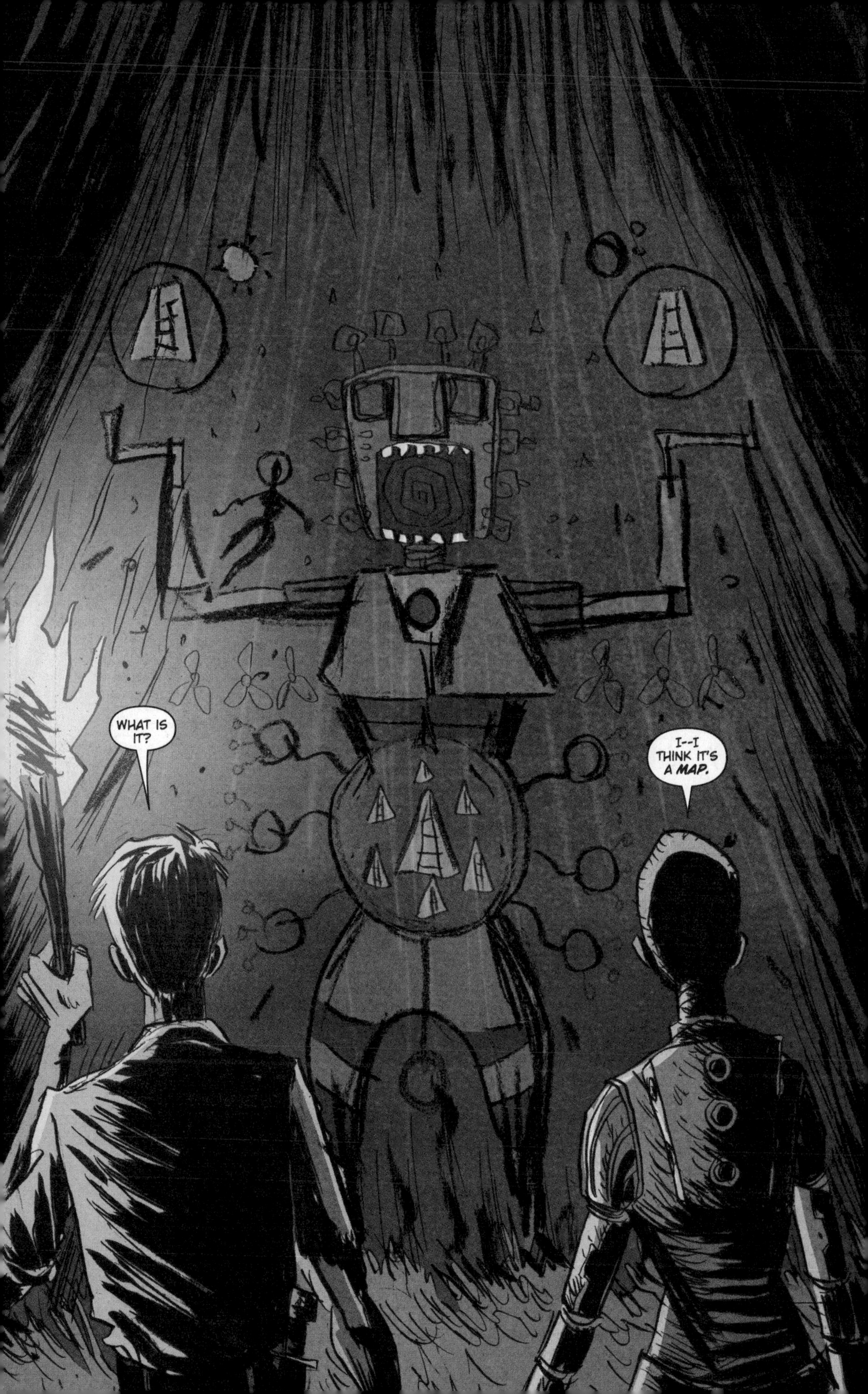
WHAT IS IT?
I--I THINK IT'S A **MAP.**

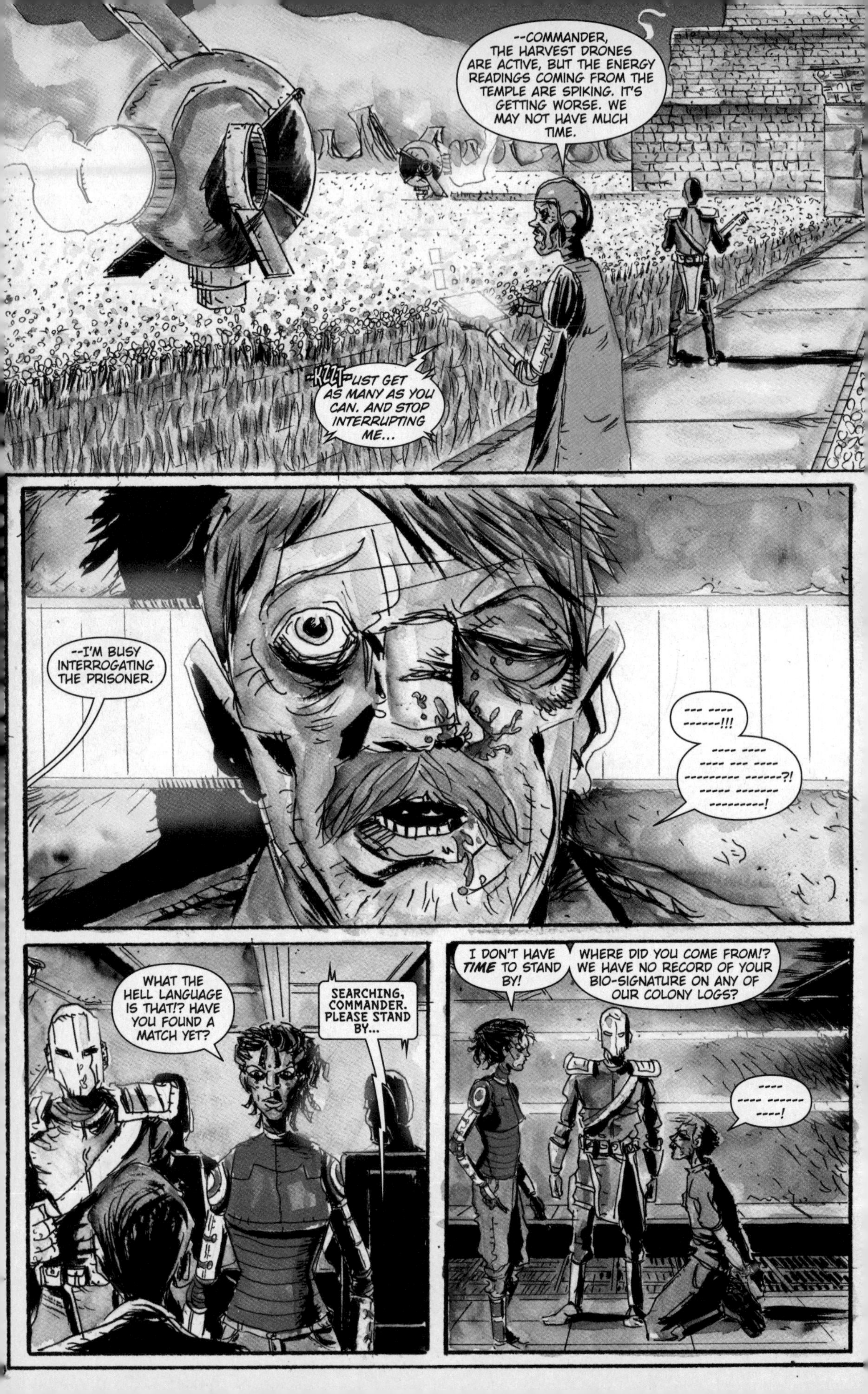
--COMMANDER, THE HARVEST DRONES ARE ACTIVE, BUT THE ENERGY READINGS COMING FROM THE TEMPLE ARE SPIKING. IT'S GETTING WORSE. WE MAY NOT HAVE MUCH TIME.
-KZZT-
JUST GET AS MANY AS YOU CAN. AND STOP INTERRUPTING ME...
--I'M BUSY INTERROGATING THE PRISONER.
--- ---- ------!!!
---- ---- ---- --- ---- --------- ------?! ----- ------- ---------!
WHAT THE HELL LANGUAGE IS THAT!? HAVE YOU FOUND A MATCH YET?
SEARCHING, COMMANDER. PLEASE STAND BY...
I DON'T HAVE *TIME* TO STAND BY!
WHERE DID YOU COME FROM!? WE HAVE NO RECORD OF YOUR BIO-SIGNATURE ON ANY OF OUR COLONY LOGS?
---- ---- ------ ----!

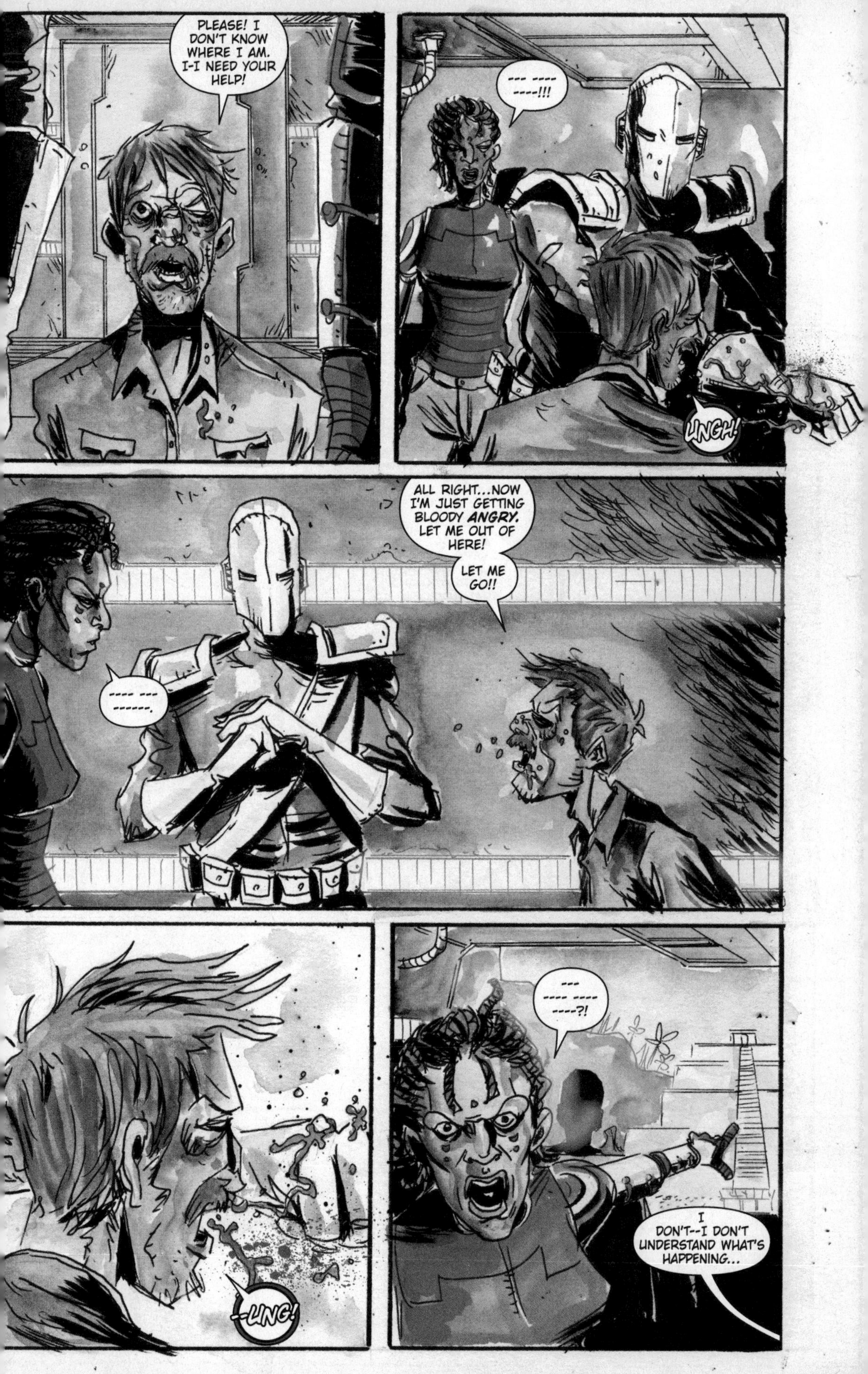
PLEASE! I DON'T KNOW WHERE I AM. I-I NEED YOUR HELP!
--- ---- ----!!!
UNGH!
ALL RIGHT...NOW I'M JUST GETTING BLOODY ANGRY. LET ME OUT OF HERE!
LET ME GO!!
---- --- ------.
-UNG!
--- ---- ---- ----?!
I DON'T--I DON'T UNDERSTAND WHAT'S HAPPENING...

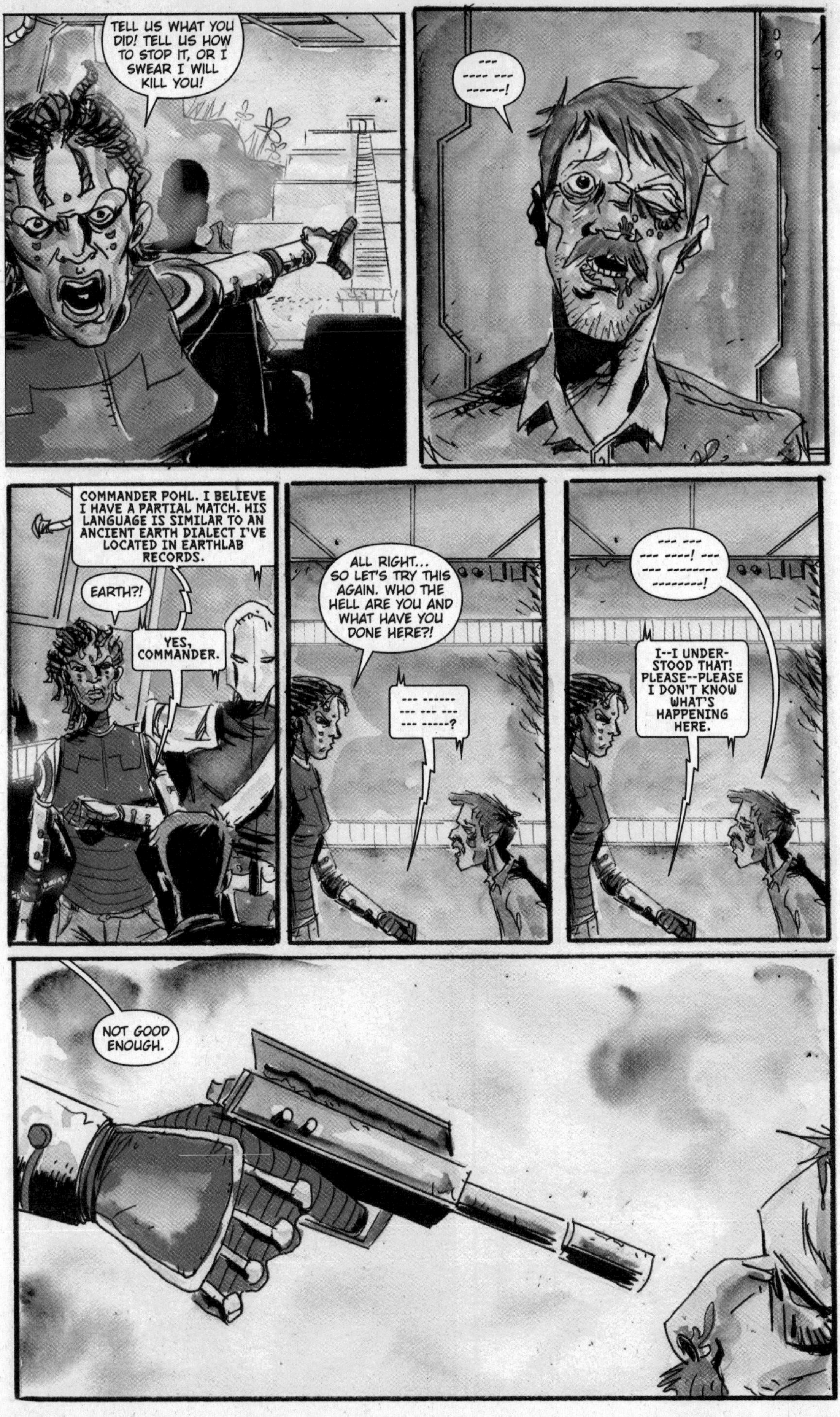
TELL US WHAT YOU DID! TELL US HOW TO STOP IT, OR I SWEAR I WILL KILL YOU!

---- ---
------!
COMMANDER POHL. I BELIEVE I HAVE A PARTIAL MATCH. HIS LANGUAGE IS SIMILAR TO AN ANCIENT EARTH DIALECT I'VE LOCATED IN EARTHLAB RECORDS.
EARTH?!
YES, COMMANDER.
ALL RIGHT... SO LET'S TRY THIS AGAIN. WHO THE HELL ARE YOU AND WHAT HAVE YOU DONE HERE?!
--- ------
--- --- ---
--- -----?
--- ---
--- ----! ---
--- ---------
---------!
I--I UNDERSTOOD THAT! PLEASE--PLEASE I DON'T KNOW WHAT'S HAPPENING HERE.
NOT GOOD ENOUGH.

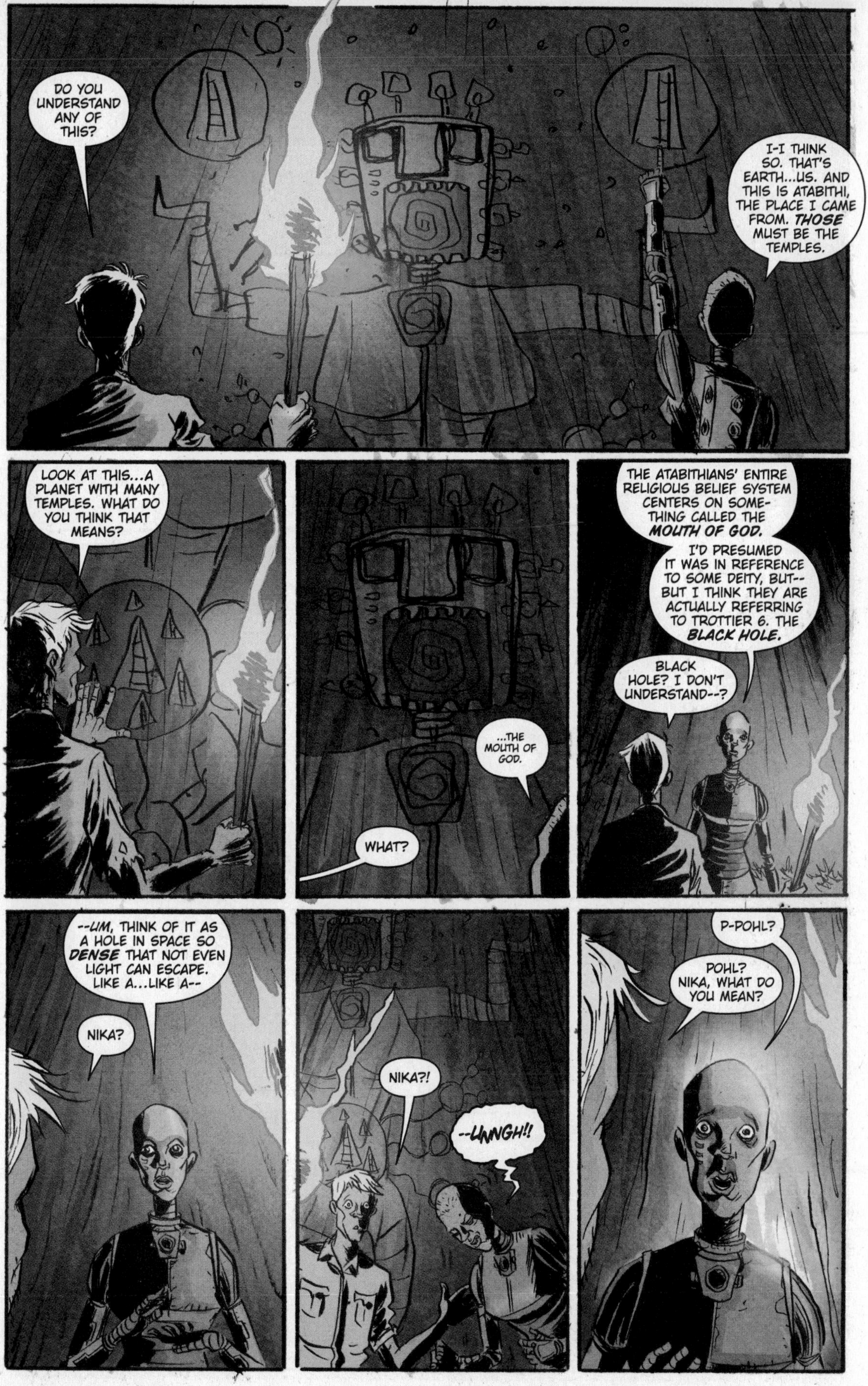
DO YOU UNDERSTAND ANY OF THIS?
I-I THINK SO. THAT'S EARTH...US. AND THIS IS ATABITHI, THE PLACE I CAME FROM. THOSE MUST BE THE TEMPLES.
LOOK AT THIS...A PLANET WITH MANY TEMPLES. WHAT DO YOU THINK THAT MEANS?
...THE MOUTH OF GOD.
WHAT?
THE ATABITHIANS' ENTIRE RELIGIOUS BELIEF SYSTEM CENTERS ON SOMETHING CALLED THE MOUTH OF GOD.
I'D PRESUMED IT WAS IN REFERENCE TO SOME DEITY, BUT--BUT I THINK THEY ARE ACTUALLY REFERRING TO TROTTIER 6. THE BLACK HOLE.
BLACK HOLE? I DON'T UNDERSTAND--?
--UM, THINK OF IT AS A HOLE IN SPACE SO DENSE THAT NOT EVEN LIGHT CAN ESCAPE. LIKE A...LIKE A--
NIKA?
NIKA?!
--UNNGH!!
P-POHL?
POHL? NIKA, WHAT DO YOU MEAN?

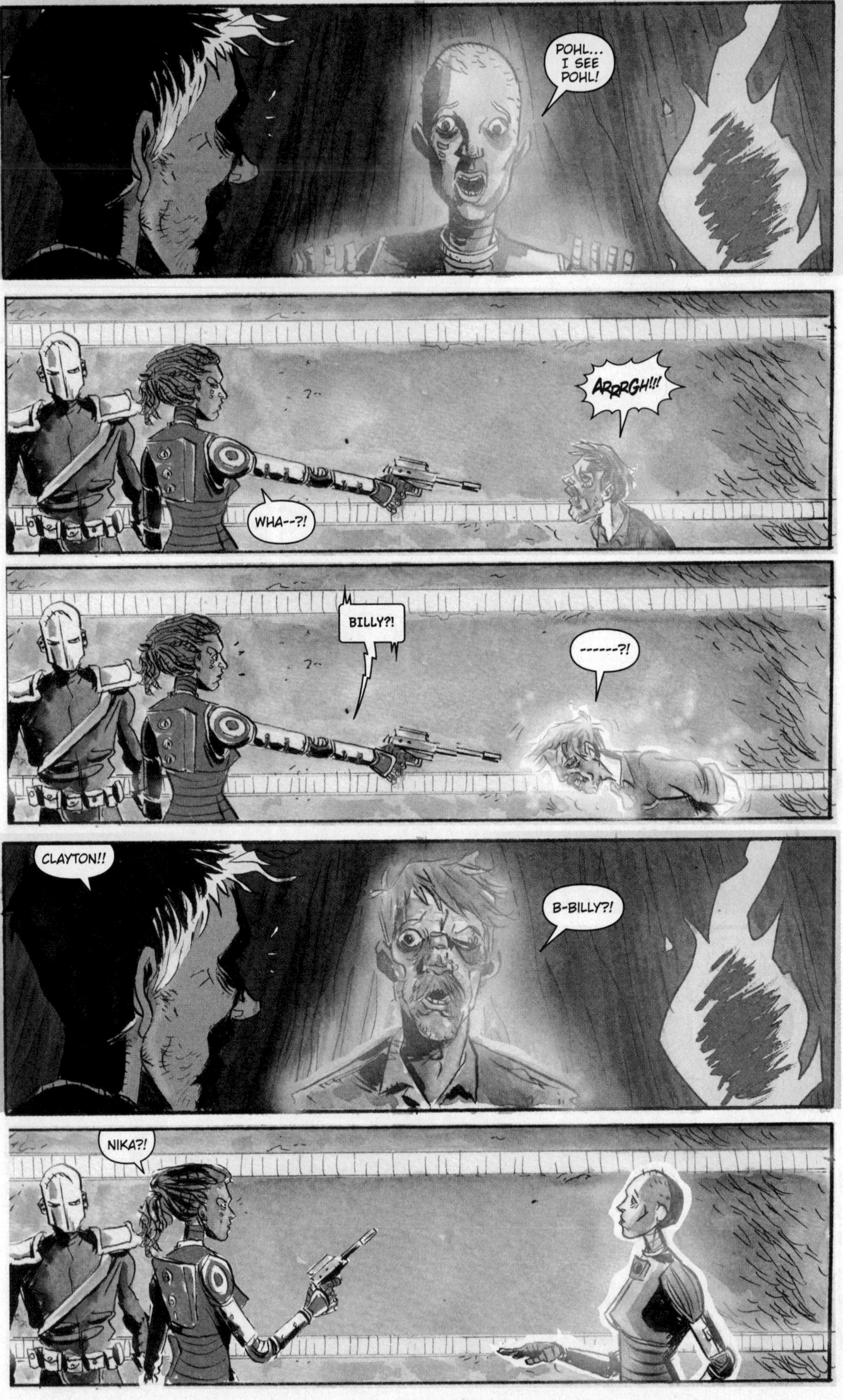
POHL... I SEE POHL!
ARRRGH!!!
WHA--?!
BILLY?!
------?!
CLAYTON!!
B-BILLY?!
NIKA?!

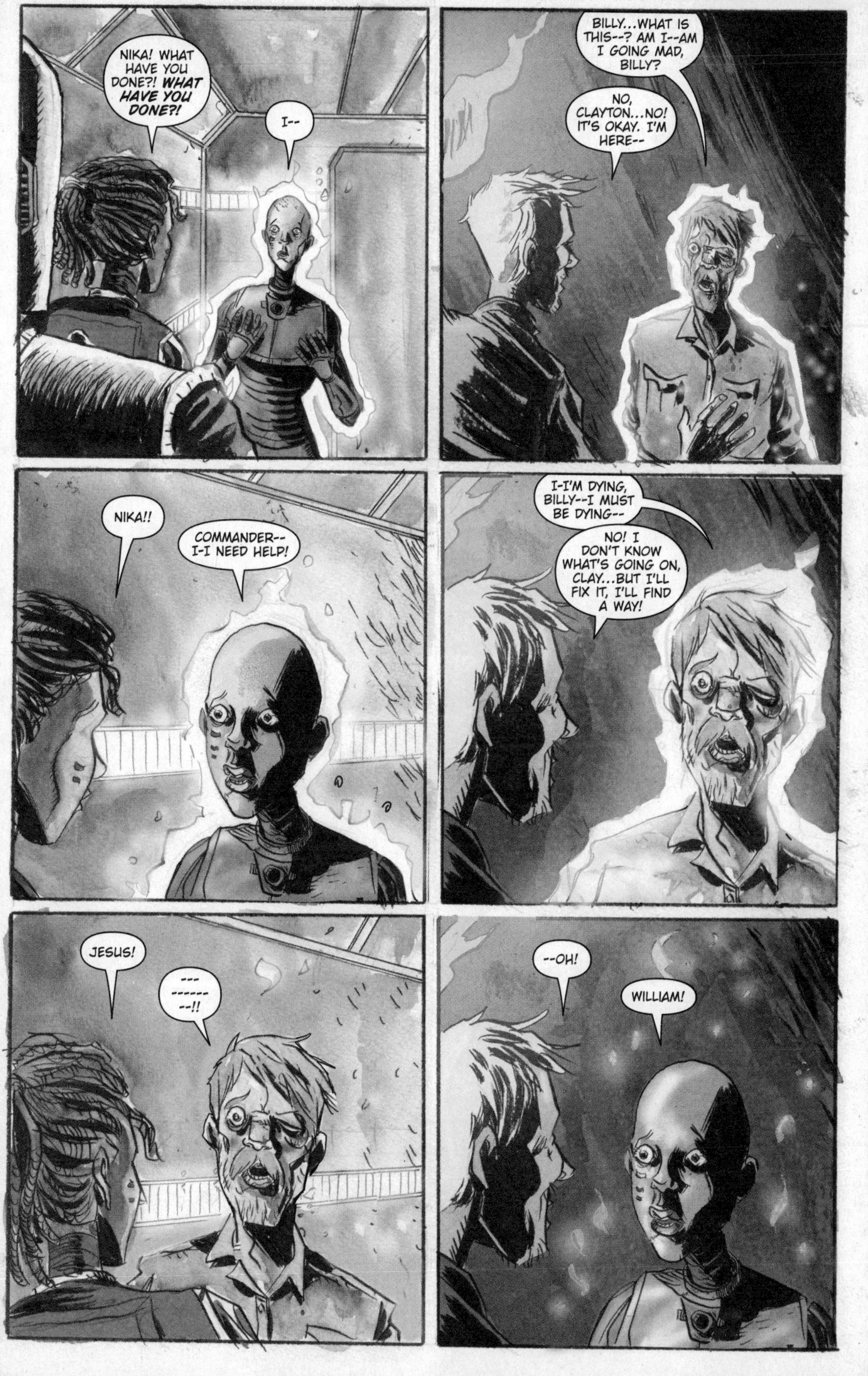
NIKA! WHAT HAVE YOU DONE?! **WHAT HAVE YOU DONE?!**
I--
BILLY...WHAT IS THIS--? AM I--AM I GOING MAD, BILLY?
NO, CLAYTON...NO! IT'S OKAY. I'M HERE--
NIKA!!
COMMANDER-- I-I NEED HELP!
I-I'M DYING, BILLY--I MUST BE DYING--
NO! I DON'T KNOW WHAT'S GOING ON, CLAY...BUT I'LL FIX IT, I'LL FIND A WAY!
JESUS!
--- ------ --!!
--OH!
WILLIAM!

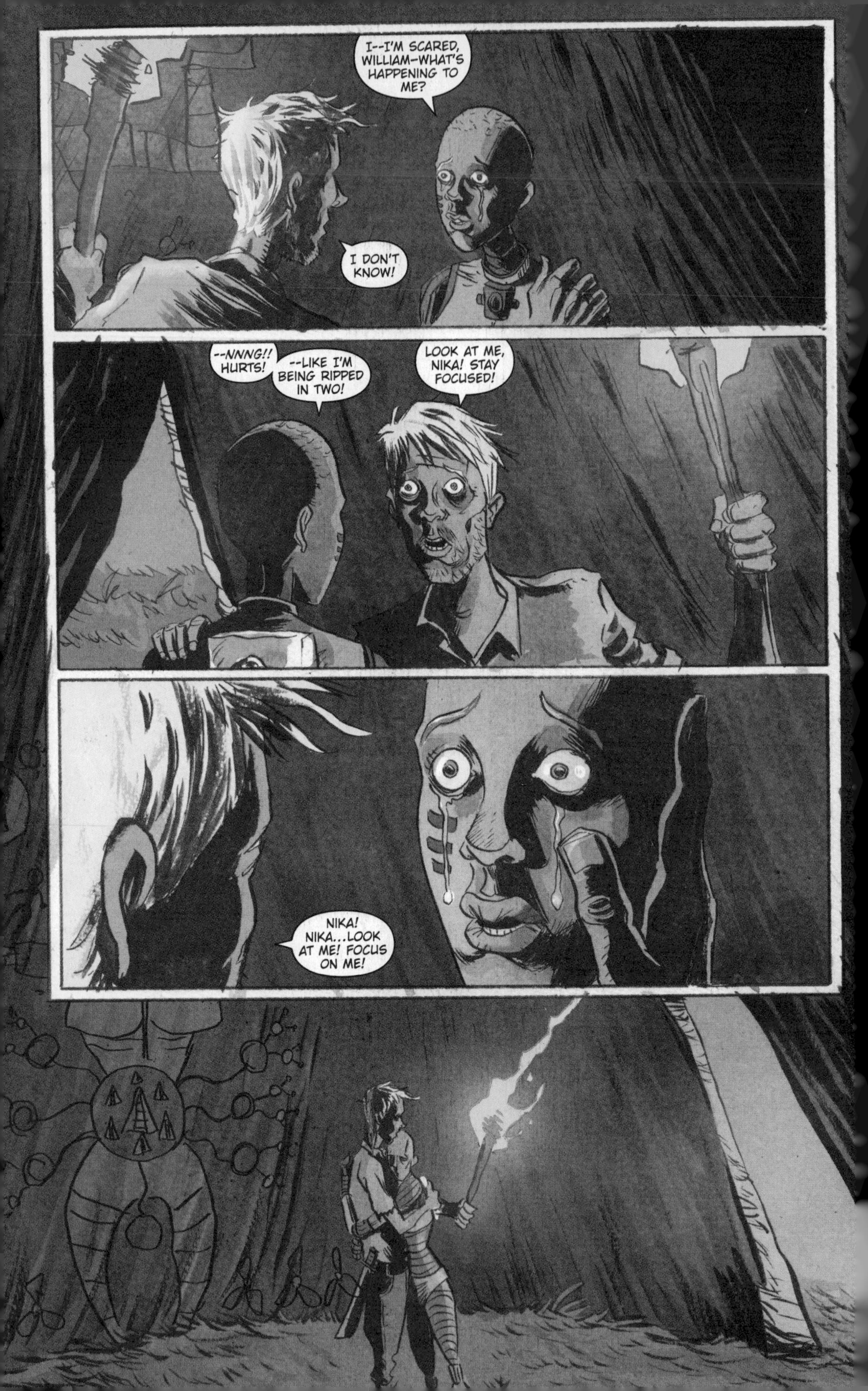
I--I'M SCARED, WILLIAM--WHAT'S HAPPENING TO ME?
I DON'T KNOW!
--NNNG!! HURTS!
--LIKE I'M BEING RIPPED IN TWO!
LOOK AT ME, NIKA! STAY FOCUSED!
NIKA! NIKA...LOOK AT ME! FOCUS ON ME!

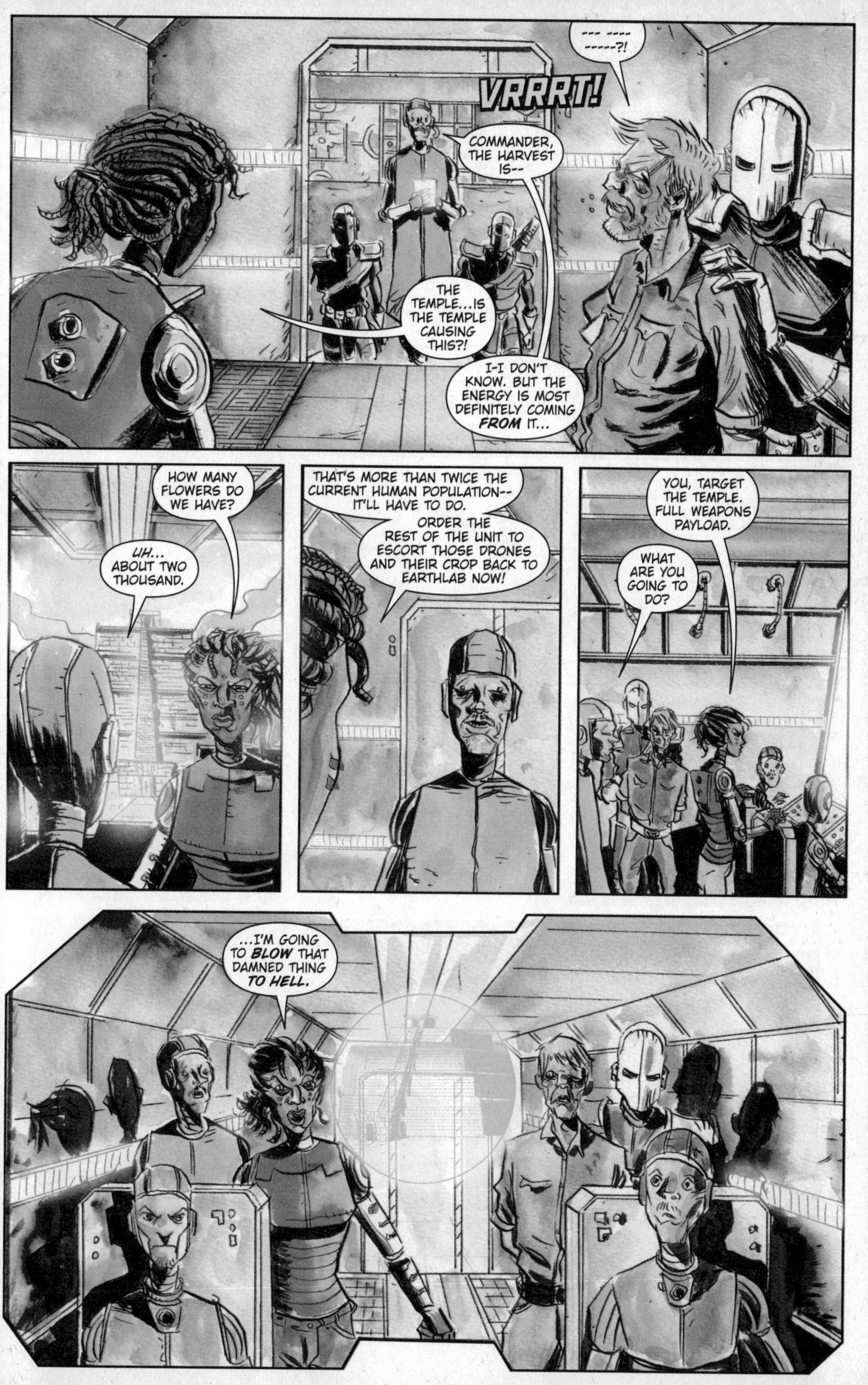
--- ----
-----?!
VRRRT!
COMMANDER, THE HARVEST IS--
THE TEMPLE...IS THE TEMPLE CAUSING THIS?!
I-I DON'T KNOW. BUT THE ENERGY IS MOST DEFINITELY COMING *FROM* IT...
HOW MANY FLOWERS DO WE HAVE?
UH... ABOUT TWO THOUSAND.
THAT'S MORE THAN TWICE THE CURRENT HUMAN POPULATION-- IT'LL HAVE TO DO.
ORDER THE REST OF THE UNIT TO ESCORT THOSE DRONES AND THEIR CROP BACK TO EARTHLAB NOW!
YOU, TARGET THE TEMPLE. FULL WEAPONS PAYLOAD.
WHAT ARE YOU GOING TO DO?
...I'M GOING TO *BLOW* THAT DAMNED THING *TO HELL.*

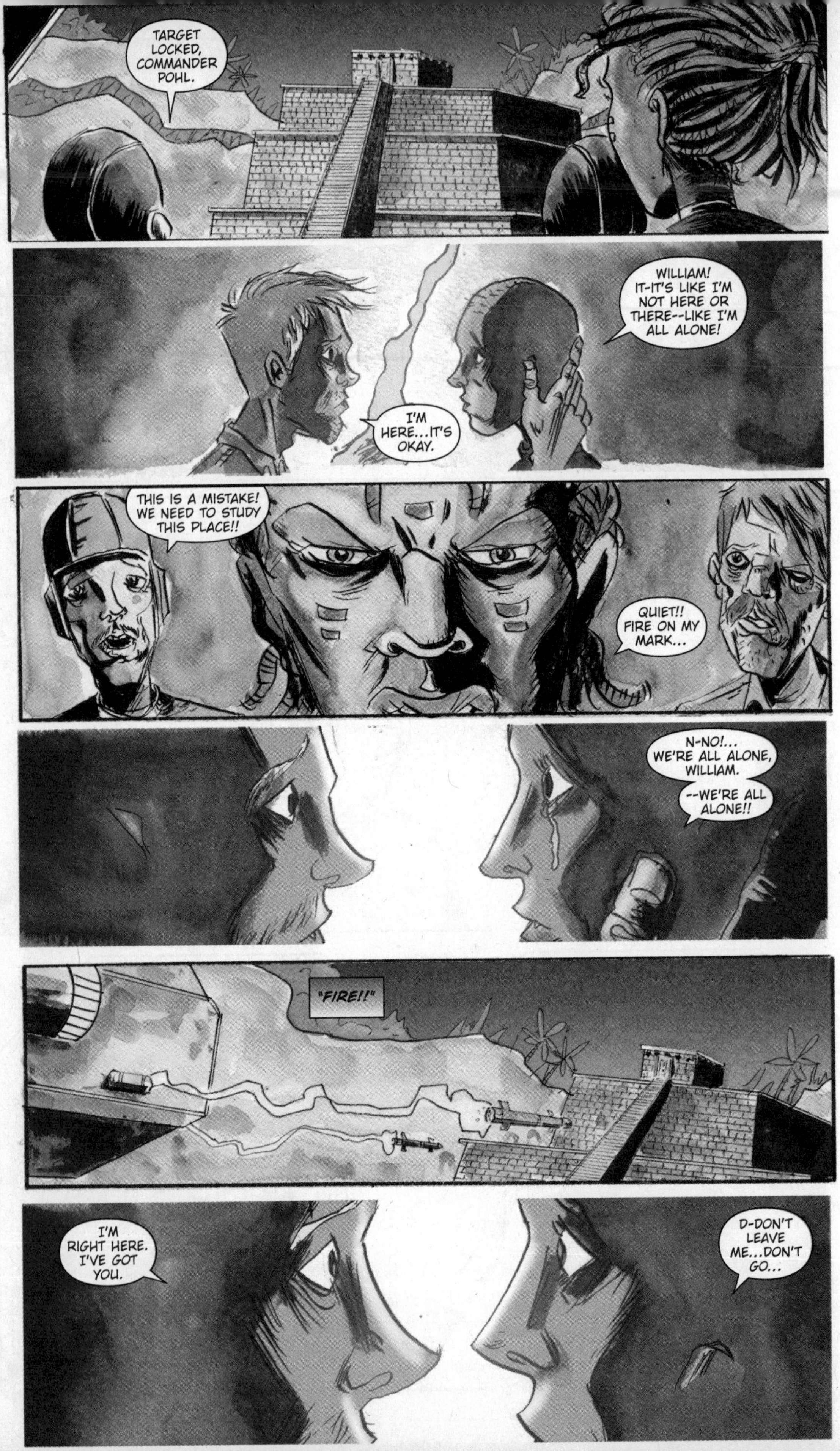
TARGET LOCKED, COMMANDER POHL.
WILLIAM! IT-IT'S LIKE I'M NOT HERE OR THERE--LIKE I'M ALL ALONE!
I'M HERE...IT'S OKAY.
THIS IS A MISTAKE! WE NEED TO STUDY THIS PLACE!!
QUIET!! FIRE ON MY MARK...
N-NO!... WE'RE ALL ALONE, WILLIAM.
--WE'RE ALL ALONE!!
"FIRE!!"
I'M RIGHT HERE. I'VE GOT YOU.
D-DON'T LEAVE ME...DON'T GO...

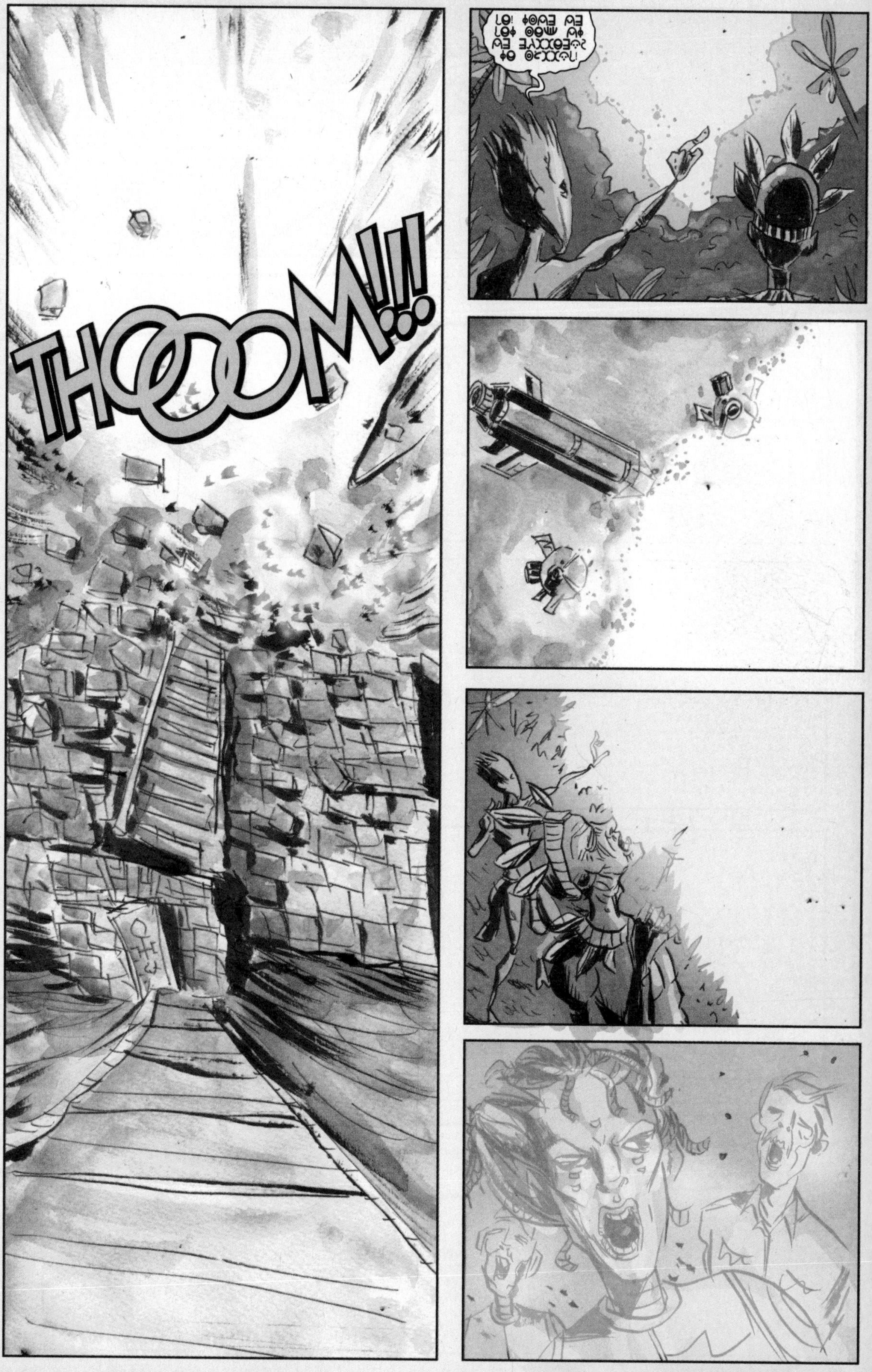
THOOOM!!!

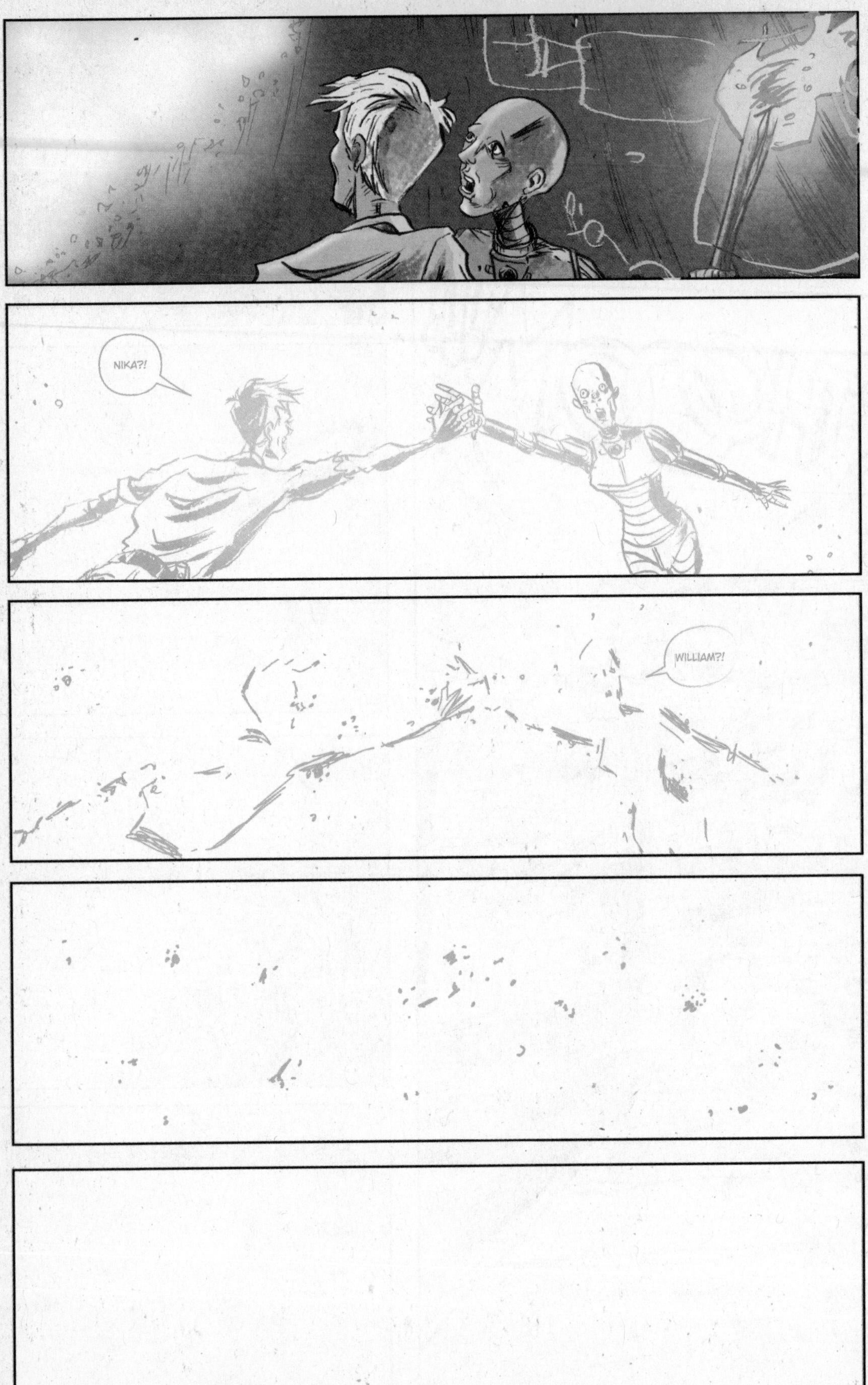
NIKA?!
WILLIAM?!

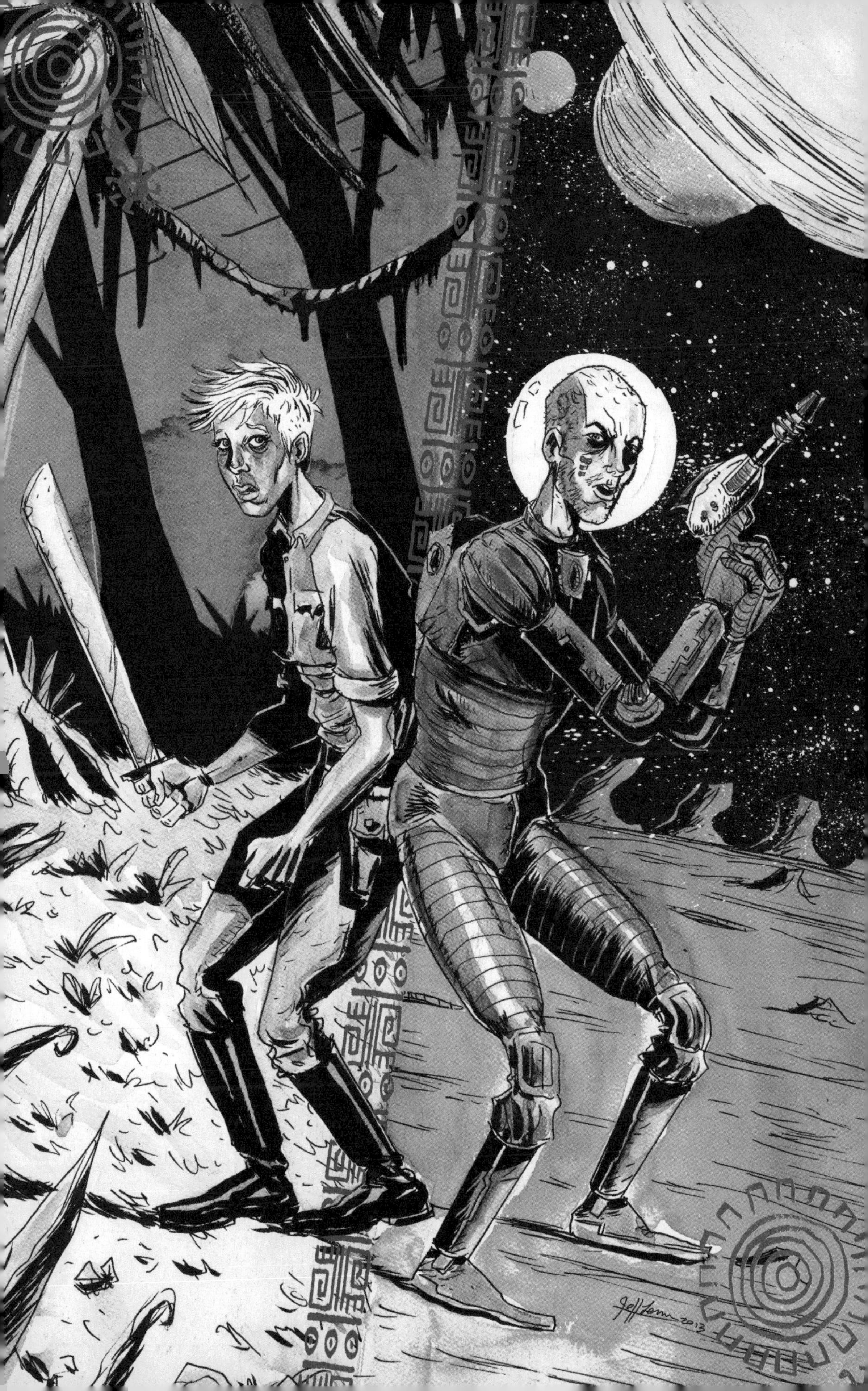

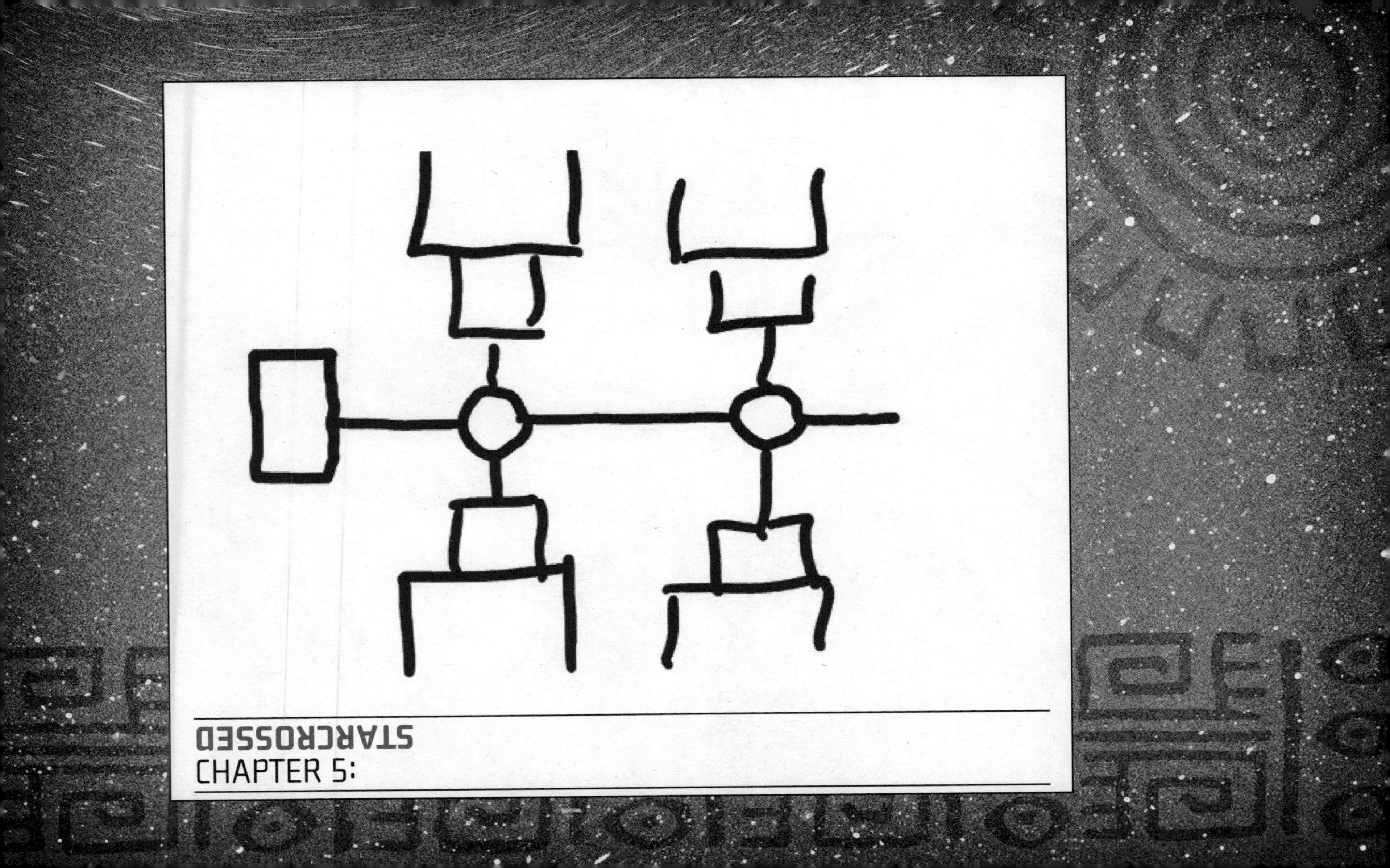

CHAPTER 5: STARCROSSED

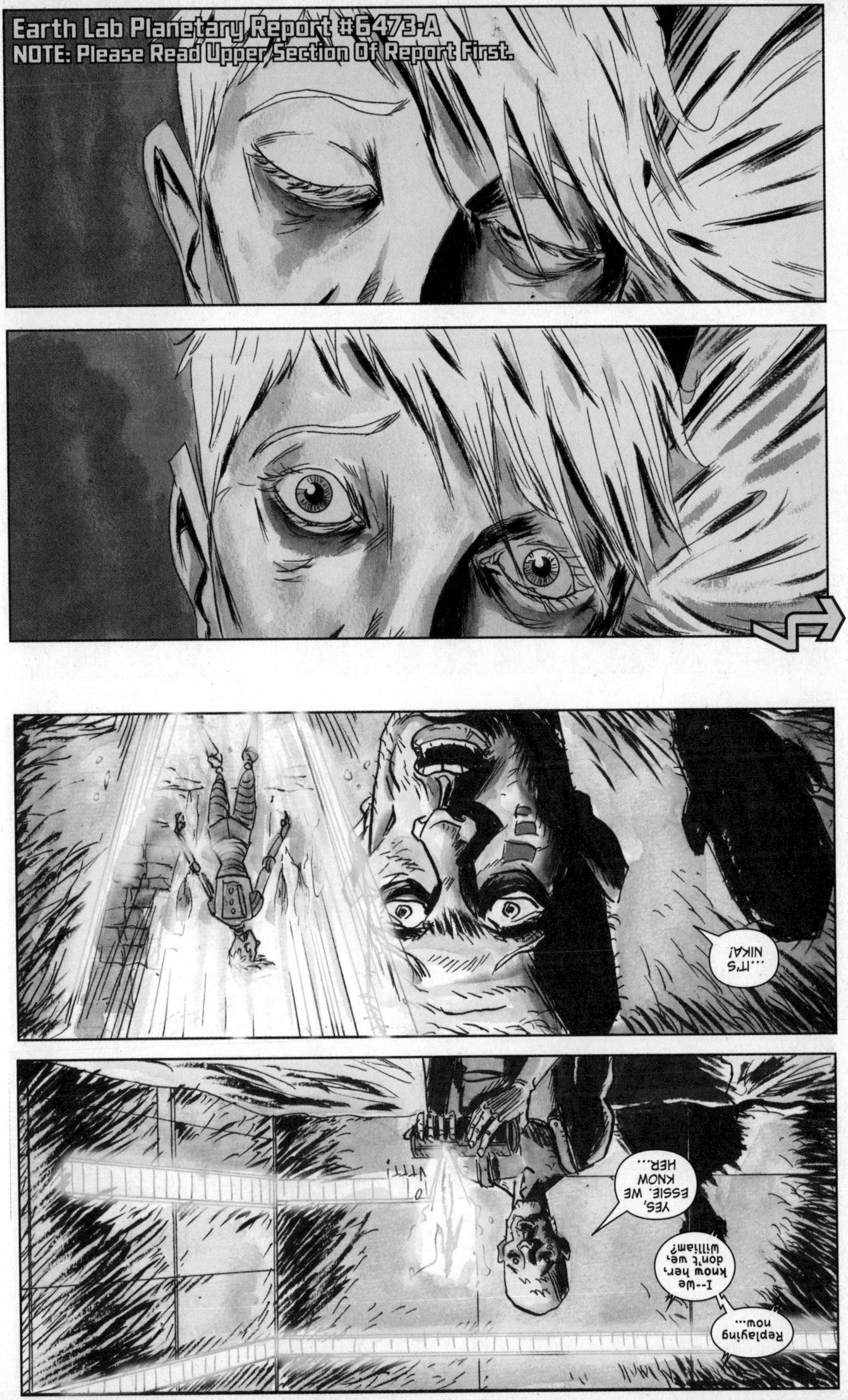
Earth Lab Planetary Report #6473-A
NOTE: Please Read Upper Section Of Report First.
Replaying now...
I--we know her, don't we, William?
YES, ESSIE, WE KNOW HER...
...IT'S NIKA!

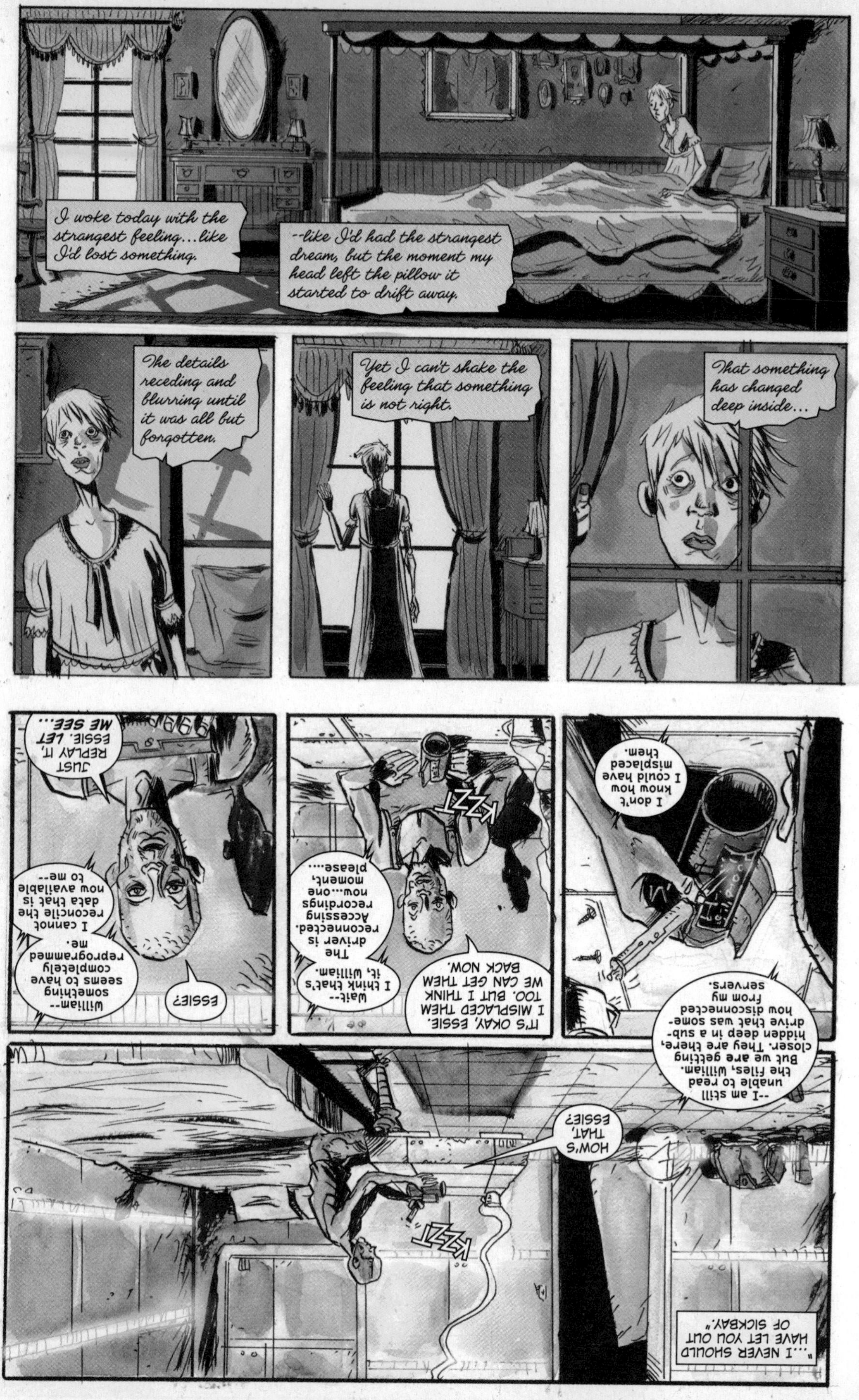
I woke today with the strangest feeling...like I'd lost something.
--like I'd had the strangest dream, but the moment my head left the pillow it started to drift away.
The details receding and blurring until it was all but forgotten.
Yet I can't shake the feeling that something is not right.
That something has changed deep inside...
"...I NEVER SHOULD HAVE LET YOU OUT OF SICKBAY."
HOW'S THAT, ESSIE?
KZZT
--I am still unable to read the files, William. But we are getting closer. They are there, hidden deep in a sub-drive that was somehow disconnected from my servers.
I don't know how I could have misplaced them.
IT'S OKAY, ESSIE. I MISPLACED THEM TOO. BUT I THINK WE CAN GET THEM BACK NOW.
Wait--I think that's it, William.
The driver is reconnected. Accessing recordings now...one moment, please....
KZZT
ESSIE?
William--something seems to have completely reprogrammed me.
I cannot reconcile the data that is now available to me--
JUST REPLAY IT, ESSIE. LET ME SEE...

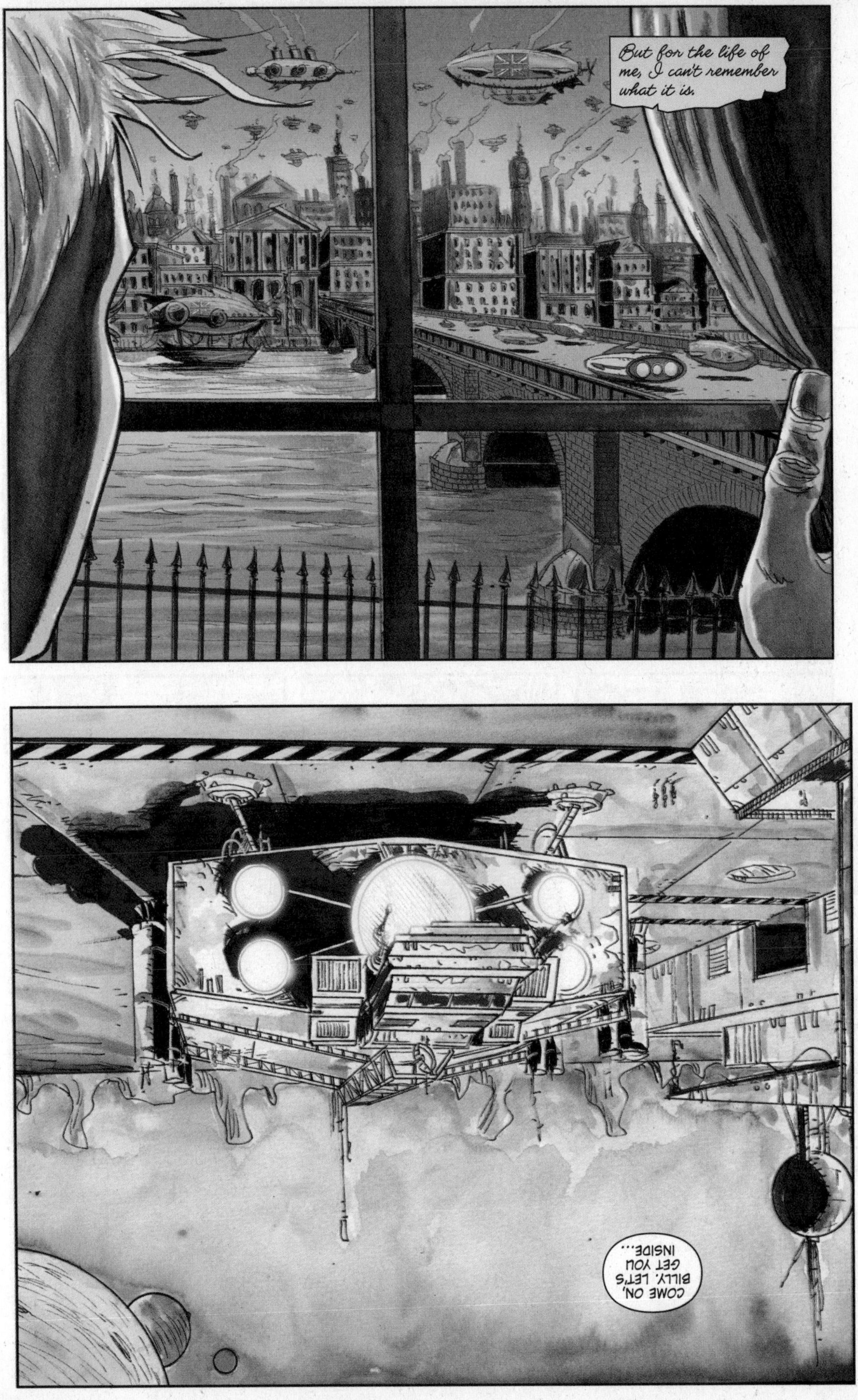
But for the life of me, I can't remember what it is.
COME ON, BILLY. LET'S GET YOU INSIDE...

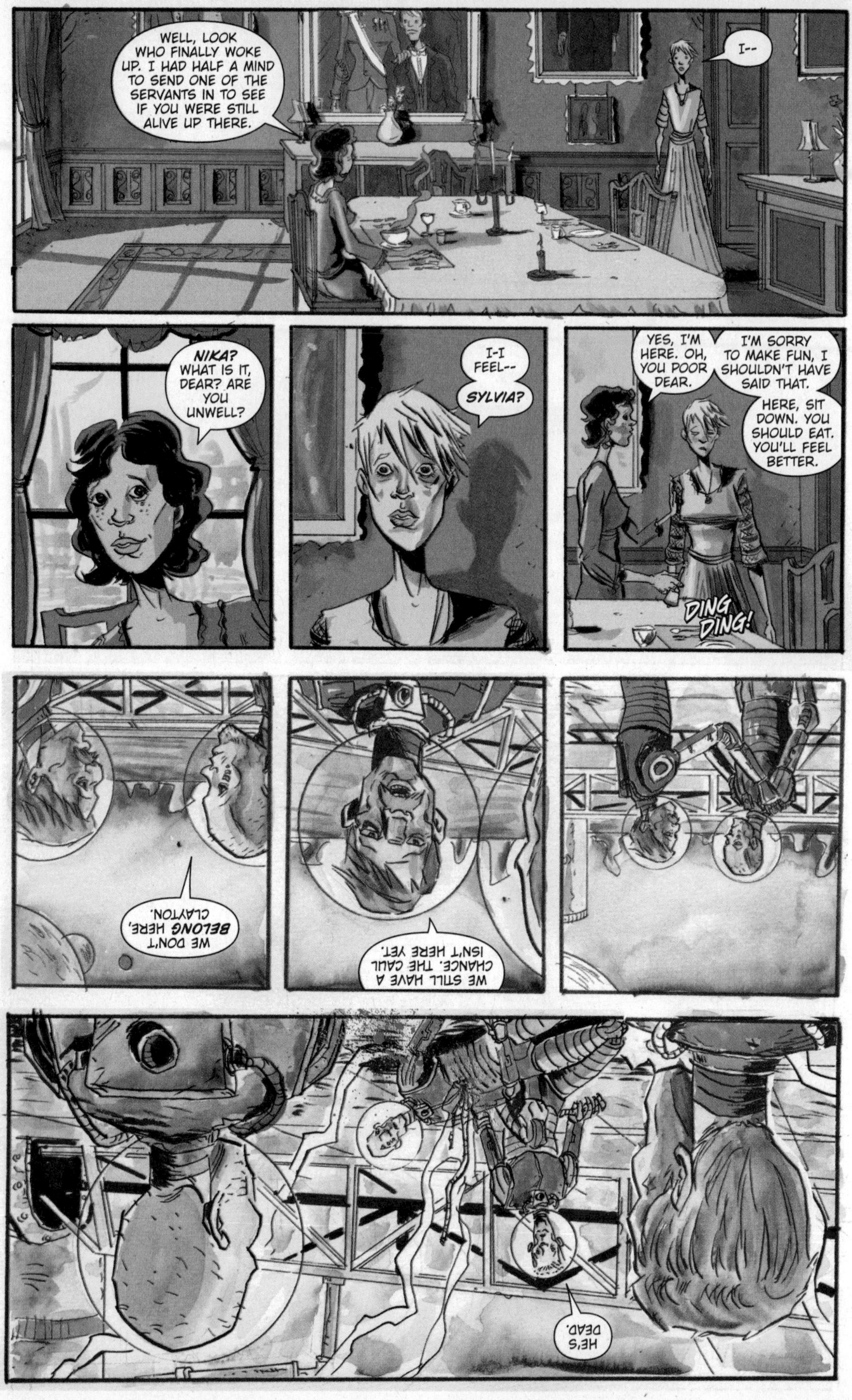
WELL, LOOK WHO FINALLY WOKE UP. I HAD HALF A MIND TO SEND ONE OF THE SERVANTS IN TO SEE IF YOU WERE STILL ALIVE UP THERE.
I--
NIKA? WHAT IS IT, DEAR? ARE YOU UNWELL?
I-I FEEL--
SYLVIA?
YES, I'M HERE. OH, YOU POOR DEAR.
I'M SORRY TO MAKE FUN, I SHOULDN'T HAVE SAID THAT.
HERE, SIT DOWN. YOU SHOULD EAT. YOU'LL FEEL BETTER.
DING DING!
WE DON'T BELONG HERE, CLAYTON.
WE STILL HAVE A CHANCE. THE CAUL ISN'T HERE YET.
HE'S DEAD.

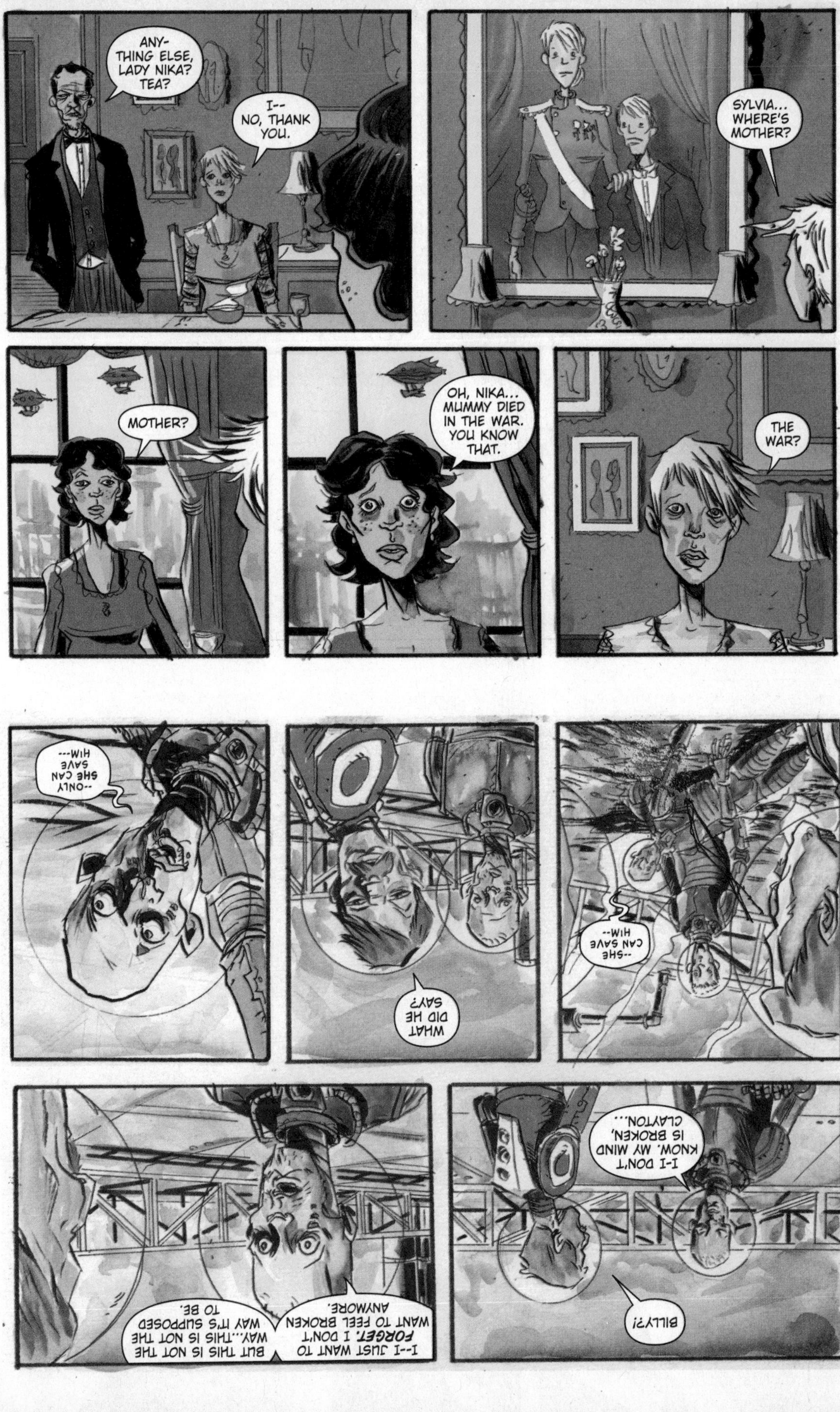
ANY-THING ELSE, LADY NIKA? TEA?
I-- NO, THANK YOU.
SYLVIA... WHERE'S MOTHER?
MOTHER?
OH, NIKA... MUMMY DIED IN THE WAR. YOU KNOW THAT.
THE WAR?
BILLY?!
I-I DON'T KNOW. MY MIND IS BROKEN, CLAYTON...
I--I JUST WANT TO FORGET. I DON'T WANT TO FEEL BROKEN ANYMORE.
BUT THIS IS NOT THE WAY...THIS IS NOT THE WAY IT'S SUPPOSED TO BE.
--SHE CAN SAVE HIM--
WHAT DID HE SAY?
--ONLY SHE CAN SAVE HIM---

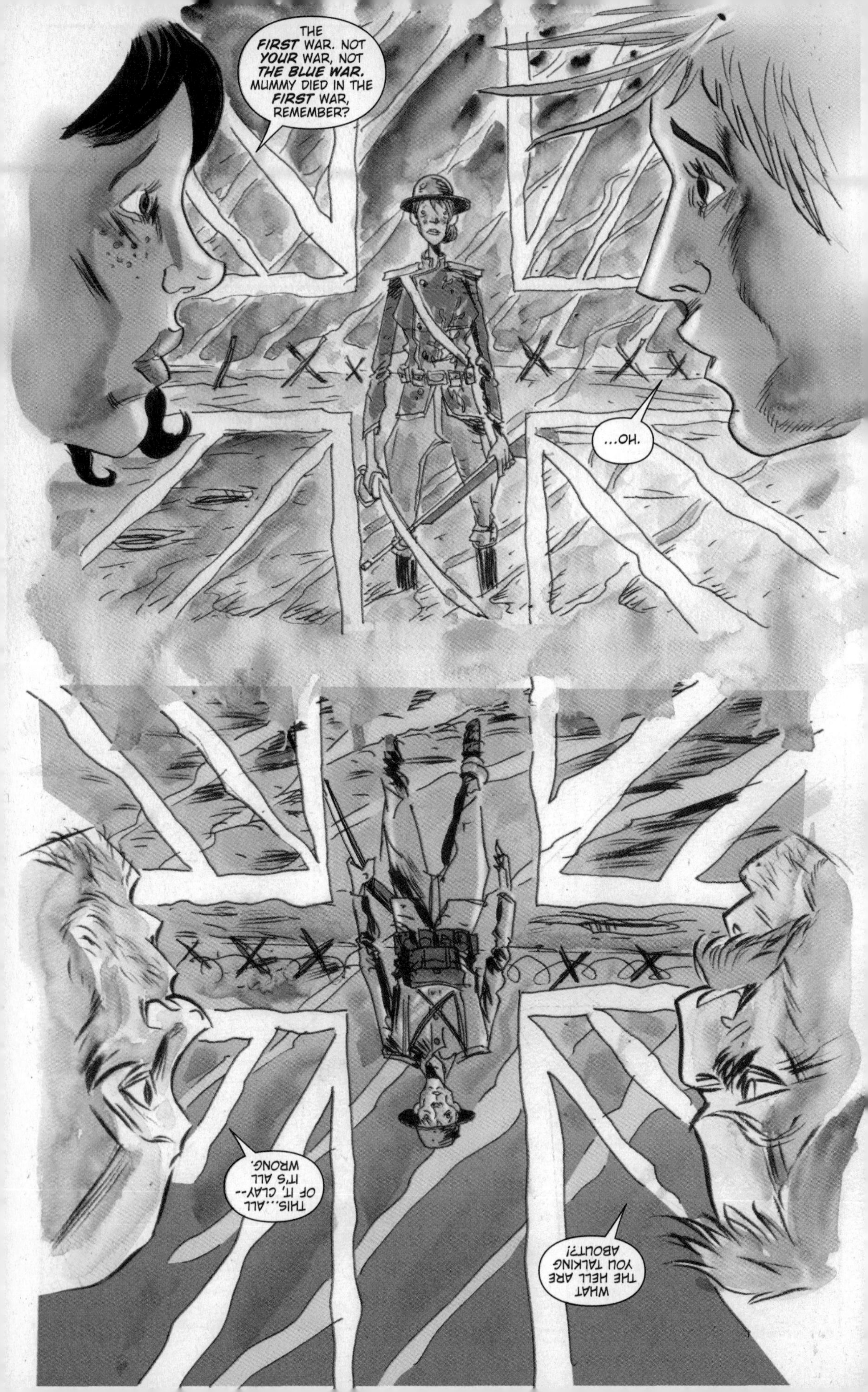
THE FIRST WAR. NOT YOUR WAR, NOT THE BLUE WAR. MUMMY DIED IN THE FIRST WAR, REMEMBER?
...OH.
THIS...ALL OF IT, CLAY-- IT'S ALL WRONG.
WHAT THE HELL ARE YOU TALKING ABOUT?!

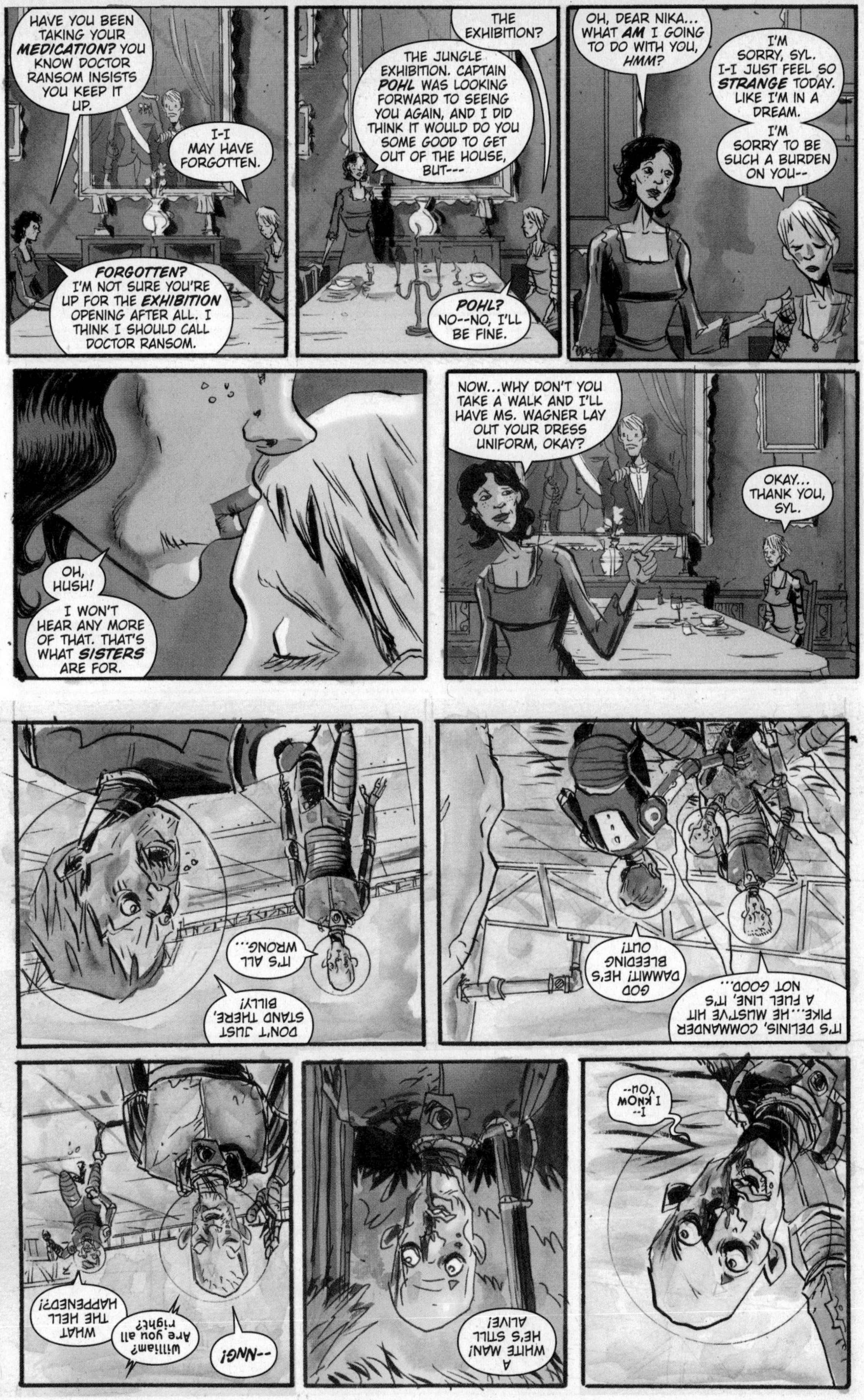
HAVE YOU BEEN TAKING YOUR MEDICATION? YOU KNOW DOCTOR RANSOM INSISTS YOU KEEP IT UP.
I-I MAY HAVE FORGOTTEN.
FORGOTTEN? I'M NOT SURE YOU'RE UP FOR THE EXHIBITION OPENING AFTER ALL. I THINK I SHOULD CALL DOCTOR RANSOM.
THE EXHIBITION?
THE JUNGLE EXHIBITION. CAPTAIN POHL WAS LOOKING FORWARD TO SEEING YOU AGAIN, AND I DID THINK IT WOULD DO YOU SOME GOOD TO GET OUT OF THE HOUSE, BUT---
POHL? NO--NO, I'LL BE FINE.
OH, DEAR NIKA... WHAT AM I GOING TO DO WITH YOU, HMM?
I'M SORRY, SYL. I-I JUST FEEL SO STRANGE TODAY. LIKE I'M IN A DREAM.
I'M SORRY TO BE SUCH A BURDEN ON YOU--
OH, HUSH!
I WON'T HEAR ANY MORE OF THAT. THAT'S WHAT SISTERS ARE FOR.
NOW...WHY DON'T YOU TAKE A WALK AND I'LL HAVE MS. WAGNER LAY OUT YOUR DRESS UNIFORM, OKAY?
OKAY... THANK YOU, SYL.
I-- I KNOW YOU--
A WHITE MAN! HE'S STILL ALIVE!
--NNG!
William? Are you all right?
WHAT THE HELL HAPPENED?!
IT'S DELINIS, COMMANDER PIKE...HE MUST'VE HIT A FUEL LINE, IT'S NOT GOOD...
GOD DAMMIT! HE'S BLEEDING OUT!
DON'T JUST STAND THERE, BILLY!
IT'S ALL WRONG...

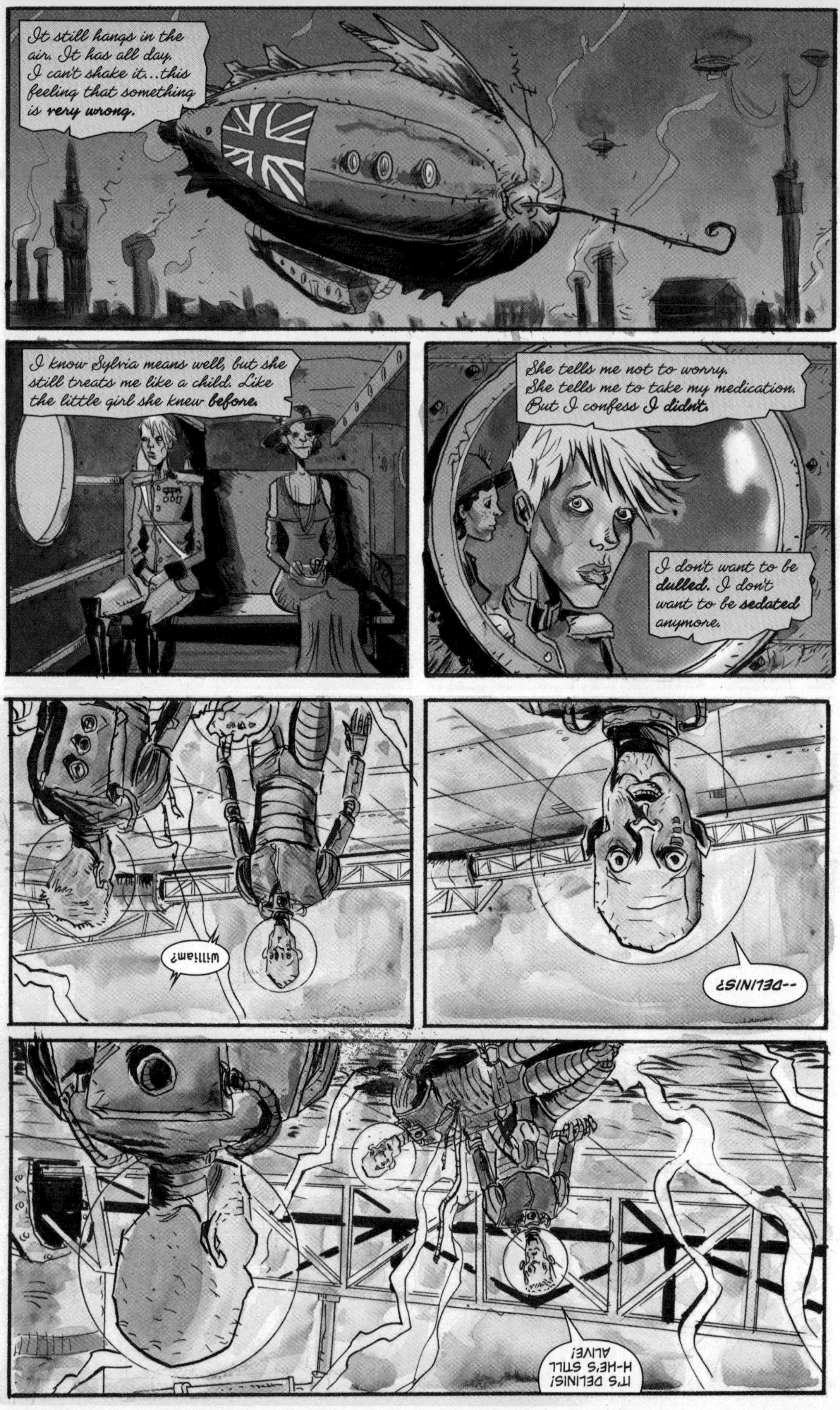
It still hangs in the air. It has all day. I can't shake it...this feeling that something is very wrong.
I know Sylvia means well, but she still treats me like a child. Like the little girl she knew before.
She tells me not to worry. She tells me to take my medication. But I confess I didn't.
I don't want to be dulled. I don't want to be sedated anymore.
William?
--DELINIS?
IT'S DELINIS! H-HE'S STILL ALIVE!

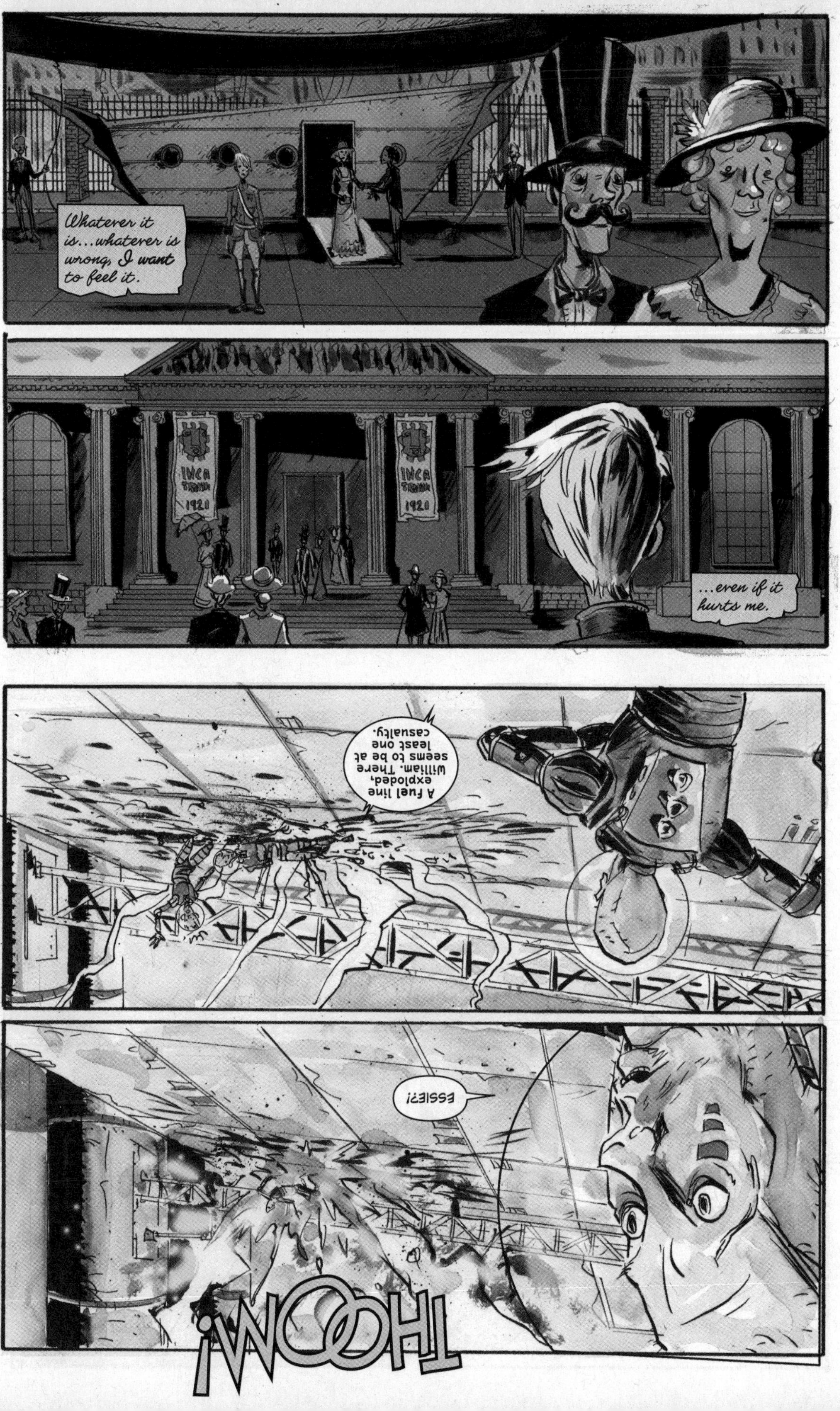

Whatever it is...whaterer is wrong, I want to feel it.
...even if it hurts me.
INCA 1920
INCA 1920
A fuel line exploded, William. There seems to be at least one casualty.
ESSIE?!
THOOM!

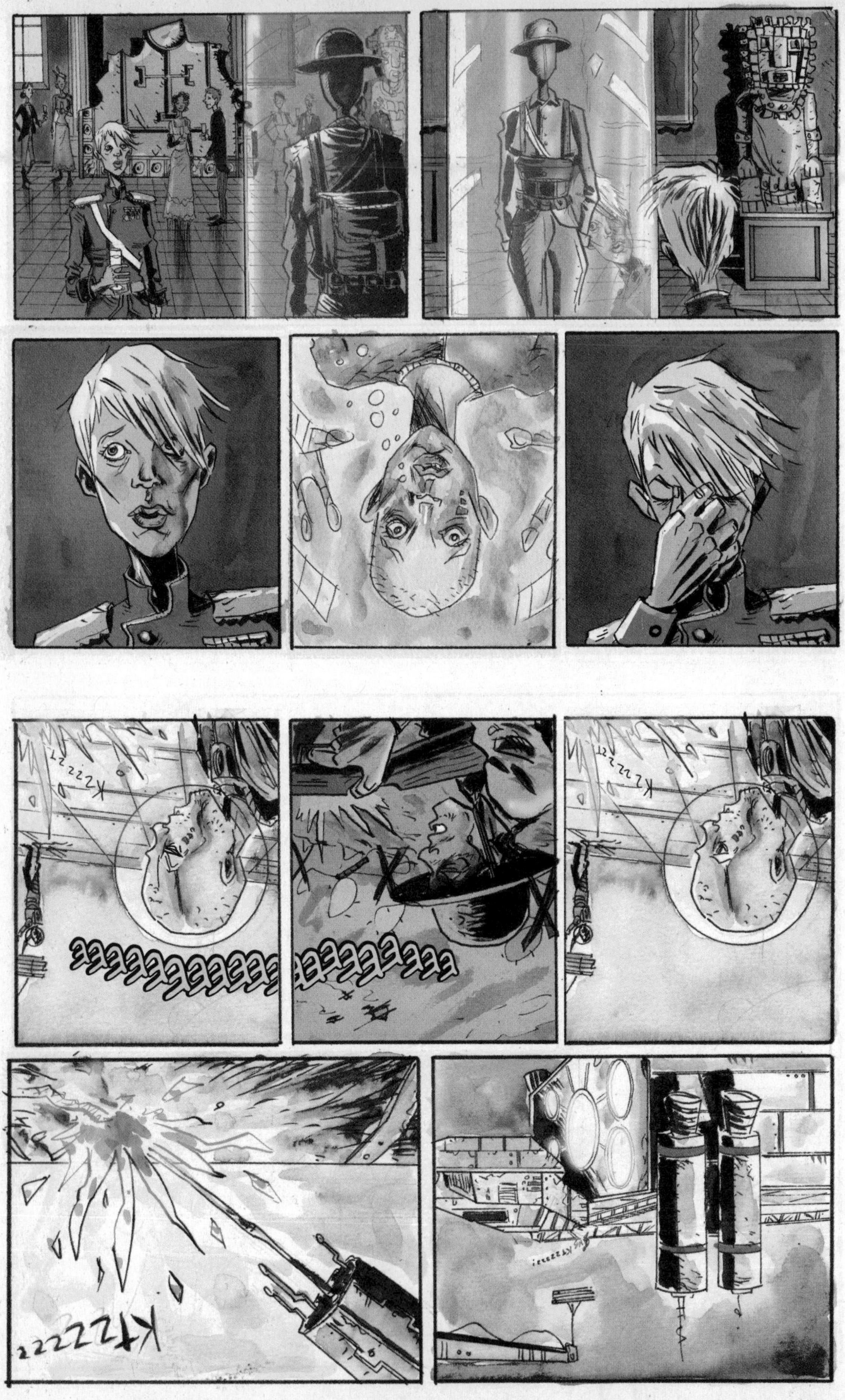
KTZZZZZ

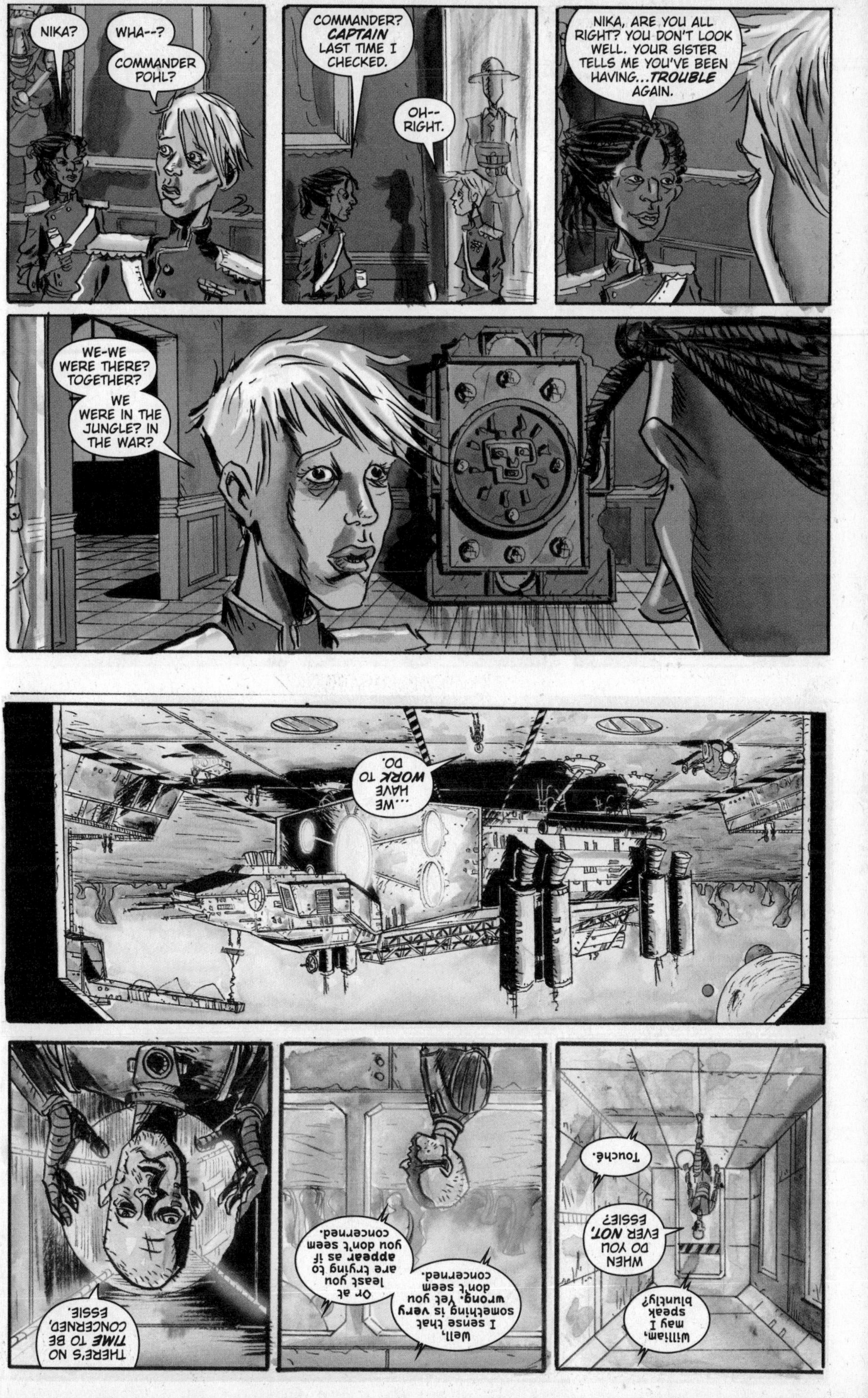
NIKA?
WHA--?
COMMANDER POHL?
COMMANDER? CAPTAIN LAST TIME I CHECKED.
OH-- RIGHT.
NIKA, ARE YOU ALL RIGHT? YOU DON'T LOOK WELL. YOUR SISTER TELLS ME YOU'VE BEEN HAVING...TROUBLE AGAIN.
WE-WE WERE THERE? TOGETHER?
WE WERE IN THE JUNGLE? IN THE WAR?
William, may I speak bluntly?
WHEN DO YOU EVER NOT, ESSIE?
Touché.
Well, I sense that something is very wrong. Yet you don't seem concerned.
Or at least you are trying to appear as if you don't seem concerned.
THERE'S NO TIME TO BE CONCERNED, ESSIE.
...WE HAVE WORK TO DO.

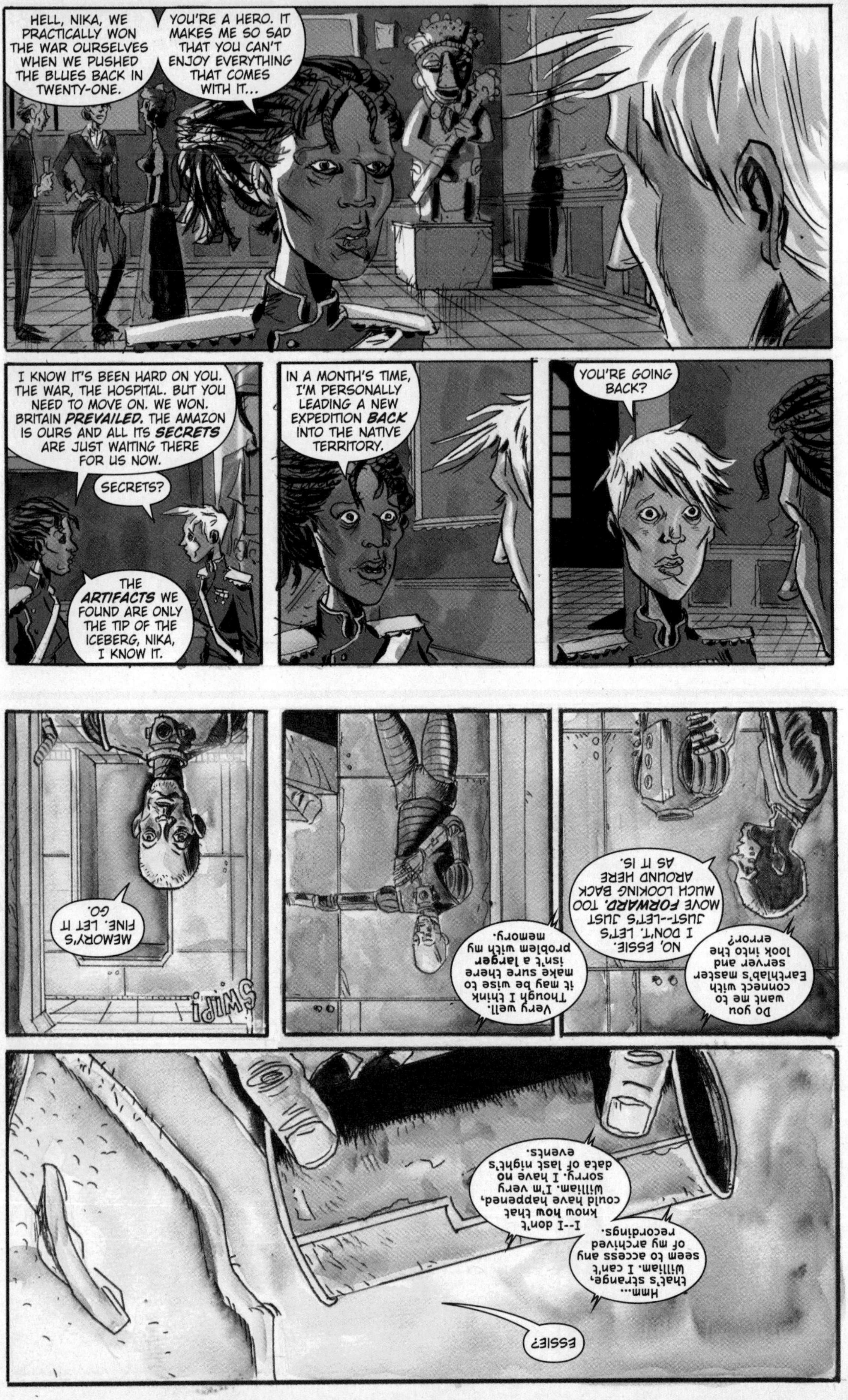
HELL, NIKA, WE PRACTICALLY WON THE WAR OURSELVES WHEN WE PUSHED THE BLUES BACK IN TWENTY-ONE.
YOU'RE A HERO. IT MAKES ME SO SAD THAT YOU CAN'T ENJOY EVERYTHING THAT COMES WITH IT...
I KNOW IT'S BEEN HARD ON YOU. THE WAR, THE HOSPITAL. BUT YOU NEED TO MOVE ON. WE WON. BRITAIN **PREVAILED.** THE AMAZON IS OURS AND ALL ITS **SECRETS** ARE JUST WAITING THERE FOR US NOW.
SECRETS?
THE **ARTIFACTS** WE FOUND ARE ONLY THE TIP OF THE ICEBERG, NIKA, I KNOW IT.
IN A MONTH'S TIME, I'M PERSONALLY LEADING A NEW EXPEDITION **BACK** INTO THE NATIVE TERRITORY.
YOU'RE GOING BACK?
ESSIE?
Hmm... that's strange, William. I can't seem to access any of my archived recordings.
I--I don't know how that could have happened, William. I'm very sorry. I have no data of last night's events.
Do you want me to connect with Earthlab's master server and look into the error?
NO, ESSIE. I DON'T. LET'S JUST--LET'S JUST MOVE **FORWARD.** TOO MUCH LOOKING BACK AROUND HERE AS IT IS.
Very well. Though I think it may be wise to make sure there isn't a **larger** problem with my memory.
MEMORY'S FINE. LET IT GO.
SWIP!

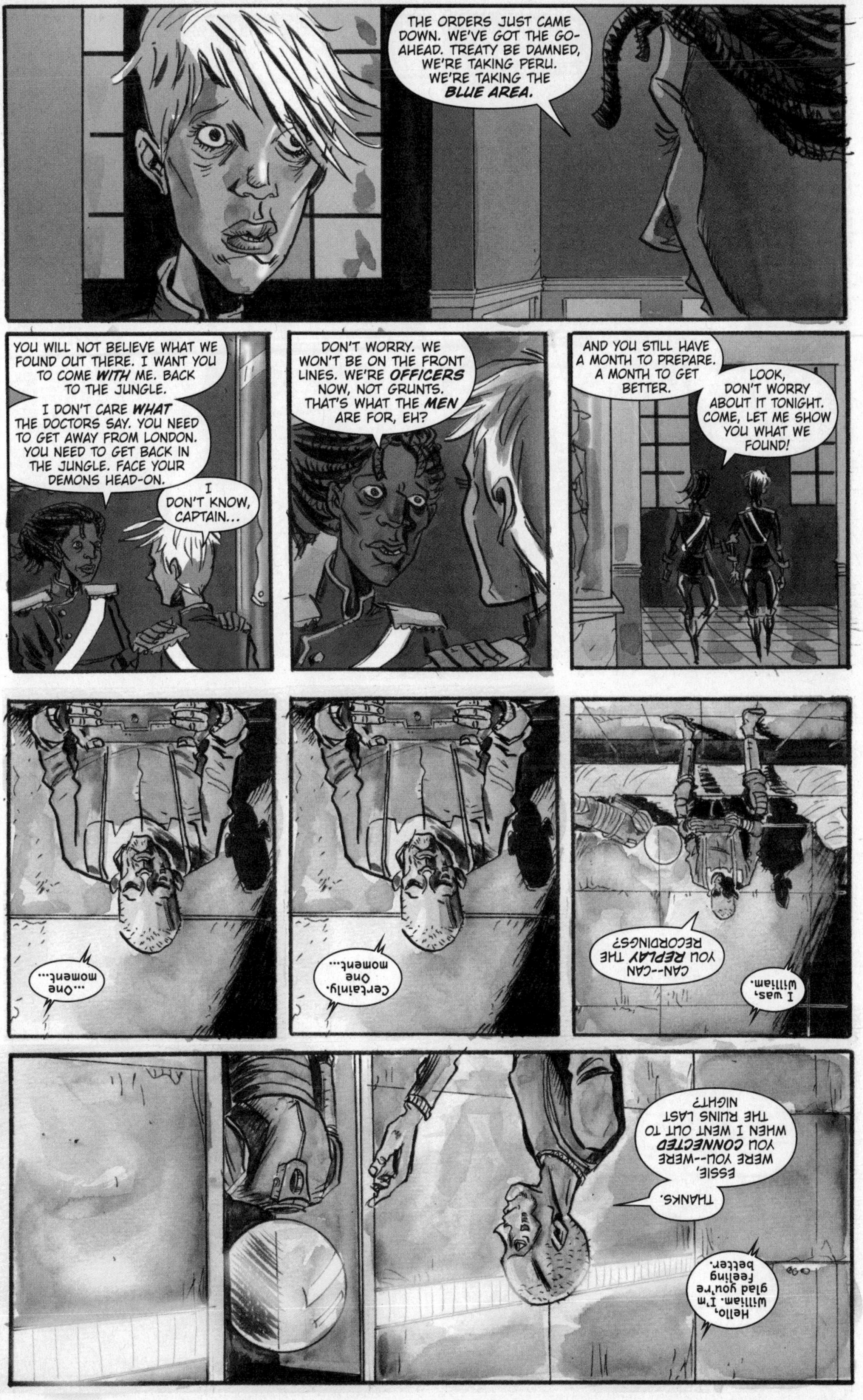
THE ORDERS JUST CAME DOWN. WE'VE GOT THE GO-AHEAD. TREATY BE DAMNED, WE'RE TAKING PERU. WE'RE TAKING THE BLUE AREA.
YOU WILL NOT BELIEVE WHAT WE FOUND OUT THERE. I WANT YOU TO COME WITH ME. BACK TO THE JUNGLE.
I DON'T CARE WHAT THE DOCTORS SAY. YOU NEED TO GET AWAY FROM LONDON. YOU NEED TO GET BACK IN THE JUNGLE. FACE YOUR DEMONS HEAD-ON.
I DON'T KNOW, CAPTAIN...
DON'T WORRY. WE WON'T BE ON THE FRONT LINES. WE'RE OFFICERS NOW, NOT GRUNTS. THAT'S WHAT THE MEN ARE FOR, EH?
AND YOU STILL HAVE A MONTH TO PREPARE. A MONTH TO GET BETTER.
LOOK, DON'T WORRY ABOUT IT TONIGHT. COME, LET ME SHOW YOU WHAT WE FOUND!
Hello, William. I'm glad you're feeling better.
THANKS.
ESSIE, WERE YOU--WERE YOU CONNECTED WHEN I WENT OUT TO THE RUINS LAST NIGHT?
I was, William.
CAN--CAN YOU REPLAY THE RECORDINGS?
Certainly. One moment...
...One moment...

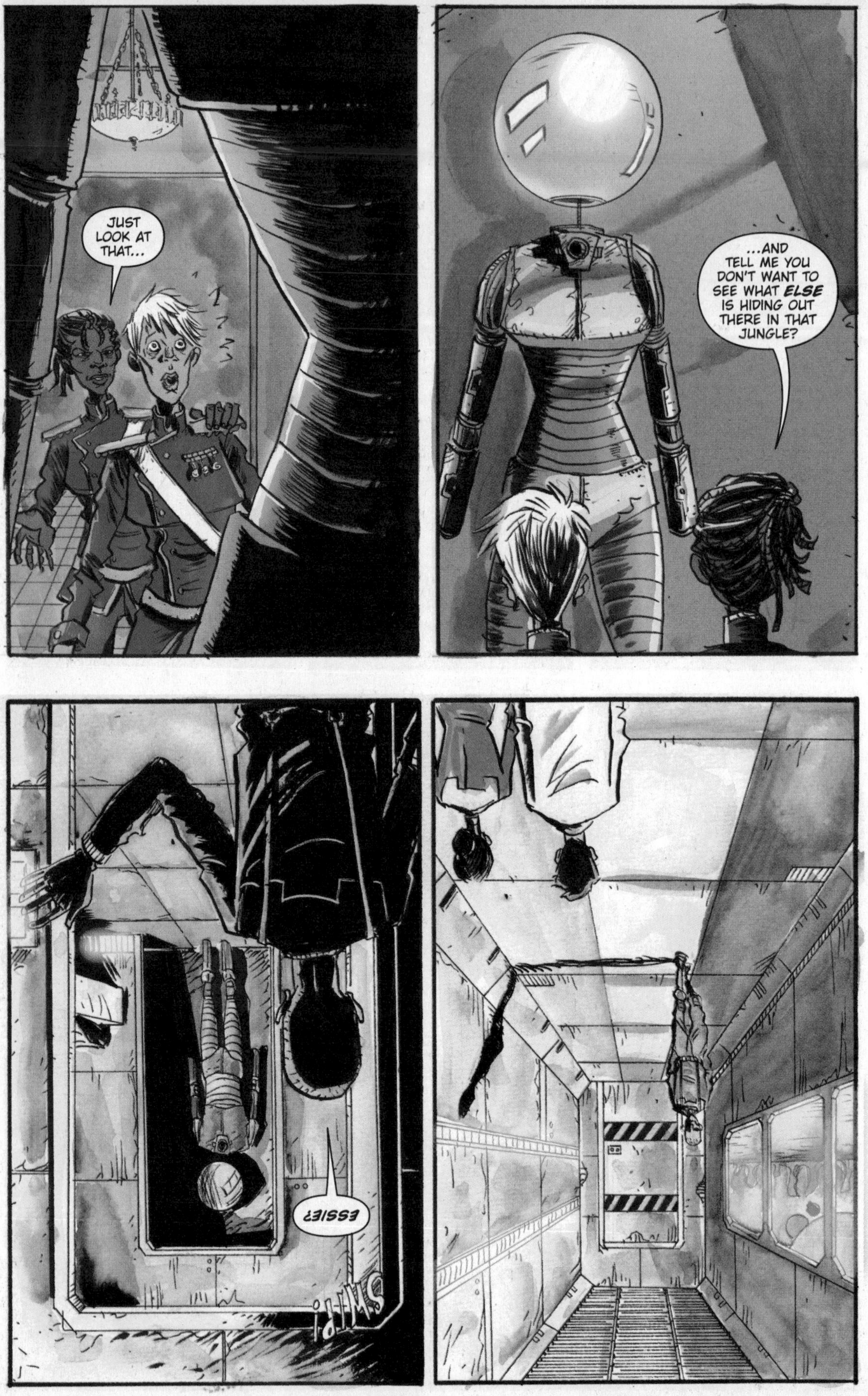
JUST LOOK AT THAT...
...AND TELL ME YOU DON'T WANT TO SEE WHAT ELSE IS HIDING OUT THERE IN THAT JUNGLE?
ESSIE?
SWIP!

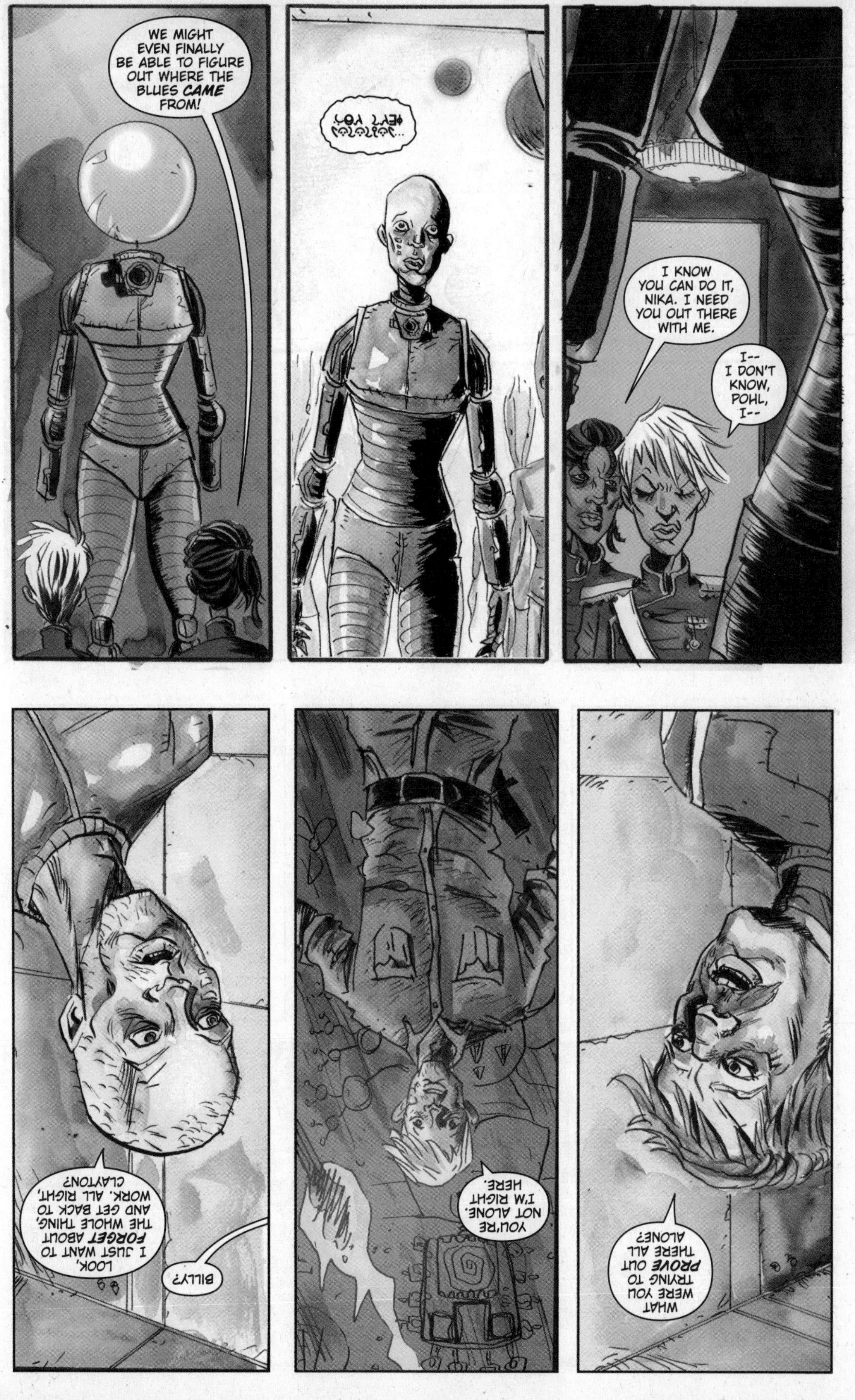
WE MIGHT EVEN FINALLY BE ABLE TO FIGURE OUT WHERE THE BLUES CAME FROM!
I KNOW YOU CAN DO IT, NIKA. I NEED YOU OUT THERE WITH ME.
I-- I DON'T KNOW, POHL, I--
WHAT WERE YOU TRYING TO PROVE OUT THERE ALL ALONE?
YOU'RE NOT ALONE. I'M RIGHT HERE.
BILLY?
LOOK, I JUST WANT TO FORGET ABOUT THE WHOLE THING, AND GET BACK TO WORK. ALL RIGHT, CLAYTON?

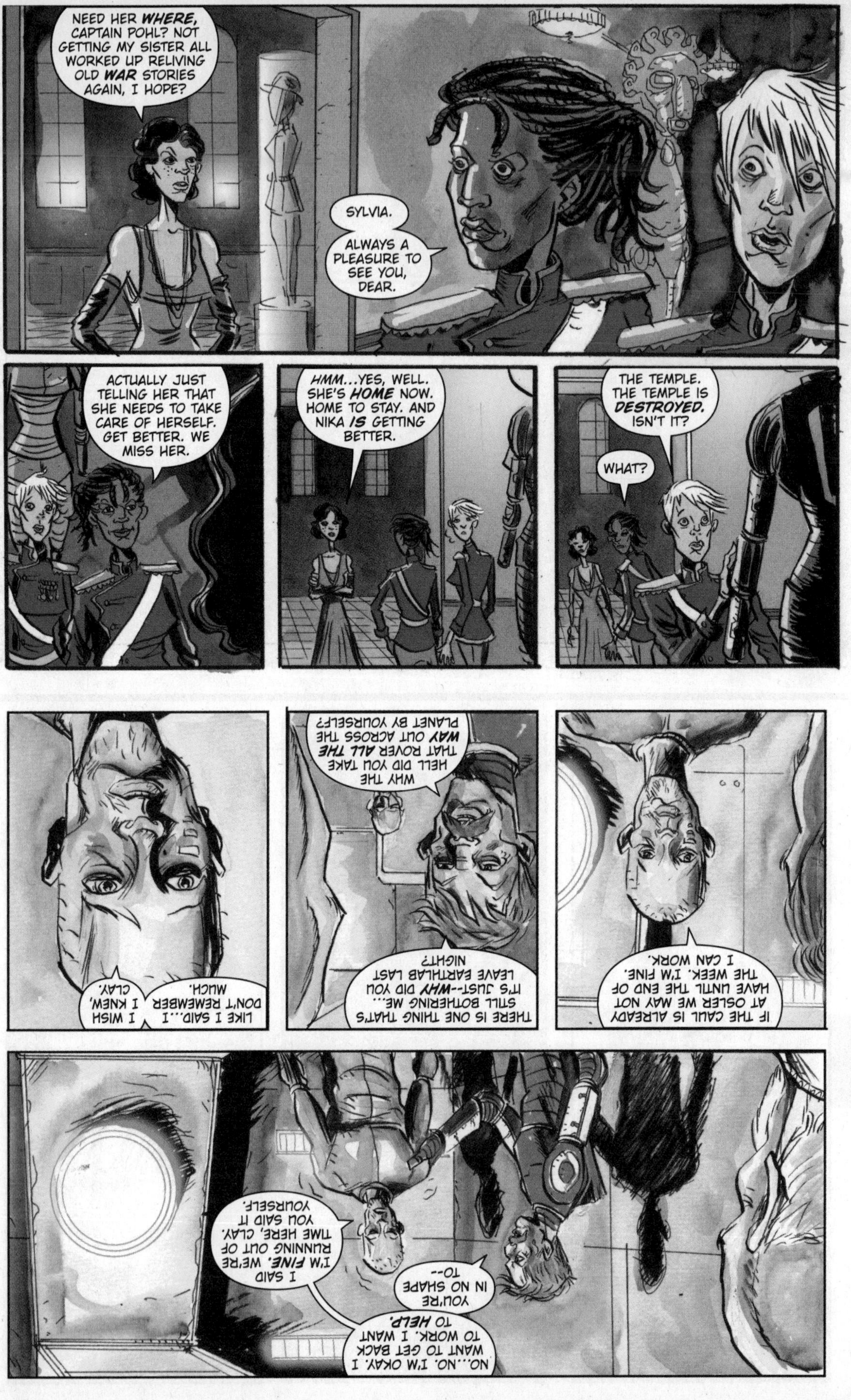
NEED HER *WHERE,* CAPTAIN POHL? NOT GETTING MY SISTER ALL WORKED UP RELIVING OLD *WAR* STORIES AGAIN, I HOPE?
SYLVIA.
ALWAYS A PLEASURE TO SEE YOU, DEAR.
ACTUALLY JUST TELLING HER THAT SHE NEEDS TO TAKE CARE OF HERSELF. GET BETTER. WE MISS HER.
HMM...YES, WELL. SHE'S *HOME* NOW. HOME TO STAY. AND NIKA *IS* GETTING BETTER.
THE TEMPLE. THE TEMPLE IS *DESTROYED.* ISN'T IT?
WHAT?
NO...NO. I'M OKAY. I WANT TO GET BACK TO WORK. I WANT TO *HELP.*
YOU'RE IN NO SHAPE TO--
I SAID I'M *FINE.* WE'RE RUNNING OUT OF TIME HERE, CLAY. YOU SAID IT YOURSELF.
IF THE CAUL IS ALREADY AT OSLER WE MAY NOT HAVE UNTIL THE END OF THE WEEK. I'M FINE. I CAN WORK.
THERE IS ONE THING THAT'S STILL BOTHERING ME... IT'S JUST--*WHY* DID YOU LEAVE EARTHLAB LAST NIGHT?
WHY THE HELL DID YOU TAKE THAT ROVER *ALL THE WAY* OUT ACROSS THE PLANET BY YOURSELF?
LIKE I SAID...I DON'T REMEMBER MUCH.
I WISH I KNEW, CLAY.

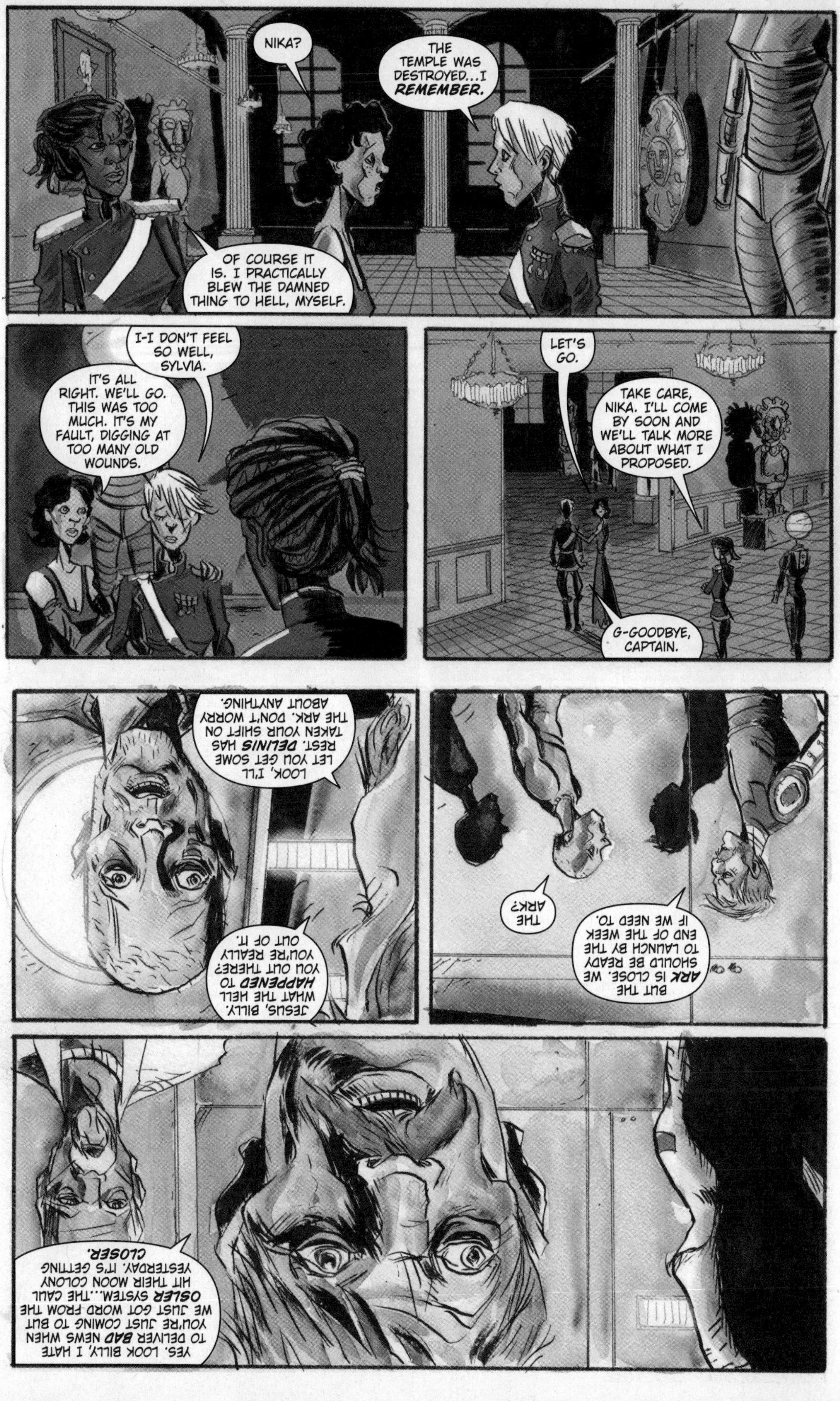
NIKA?
THE TEMPLE WAS DESTROYED...I REMEMBER.
OF COURSE IT IS. I PRACTICALLY BLEW THE DAMNED THING TO HELL, MYSELF.
I-I DON'T FEEL SO WELL, SYLVIA.
IT'S ALL RIGHT. WE'LL GO. THIS WAS TOO MUCH. IT'S MY FAULT, DIGGING AT TOO MANY OLD WOUNDS.
LET'S GO.
TAKE CARE, NIKA. I'LL COME BY SOON AND WE'LL TALK MORE ABOUT WHAT I PROPOSED.
G-GOODBYE, CAPTAIN.
JESUS, BILLY. WHAT THE HELL HAPPENED TO YOU OUT THERE? YOU'RE REALLY OUT OF IT.
LOOK, I'LL LET YOU GET SOME REST. DELINIS HAS TAKEN YOUR SHIFT ON THE ARK. DON'T WORRY ABOUT ANYTHING.
THE ARK?
BUT THE ARK IS CLOSE. WE SHOULD BE READY TO LAUNCH BY THE END OF THE WEEK IF WE NEED TO.
YES. LOOK BILLY, I HATE TO DELIVER BAD NEWS WHEN YOU'RE JUST COMING TO BUT WE JUST GOT WORD FROM THE OSLER SYSTEM...THE CAUL HIT THEIR MOON COLONY YESTERDAY. IT'S GETTING CLOSER.

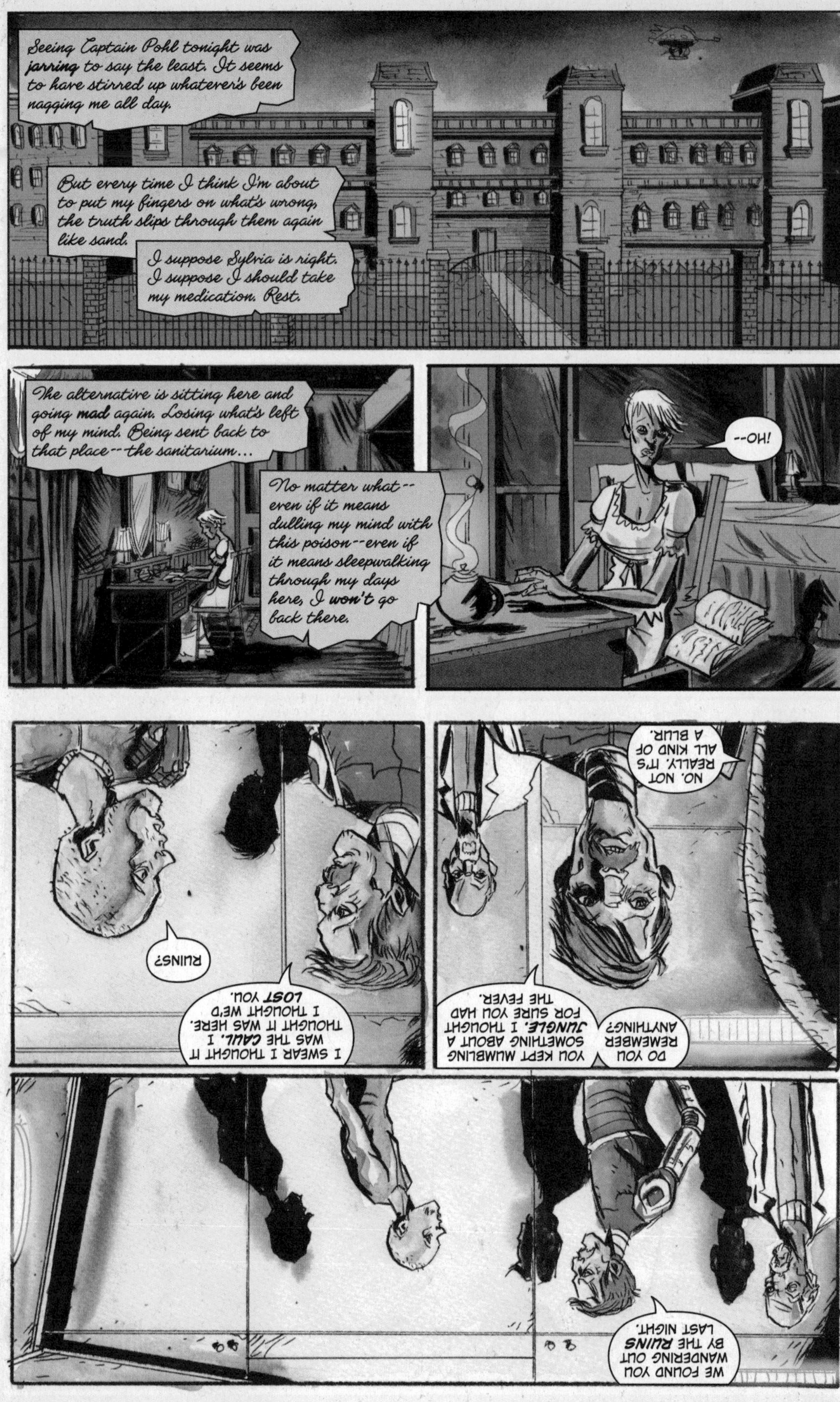

Seeing Captain Pohl tonight was jarring to say the least. It seems to have stirred up whatever's been nagging me all day.
But every time I think I'm about to put my fingers on what's wrong, the truth slips through them again like sand.
I suppose Sylvia is right. I suppose I should take my medication. Rest.
The alternative is sitting here and going mad again. Losing what's left of my mind. Being sent back to that place--the sanitarium...
No matter what--even if it means dulling my mind with this poison--even if it means sleepwalking through my days here, I won't go back there.
--OH!
WE FOUND YOU WANDERING OUT BY THE RUINS LAST NIGHT.
RUINS?
I SWEAR I THOUGHT IT WAS THE CAUL. I THOUGHT IT WAS HERE. I THOUGHT WE'D LOST YOU.
DO YOU REMEMBER ANYTHING?
NO, NOT REALLY. IT'S ALL KIND OF A BLUR.
YOU KEPT MUMBLING SOMETHING ABOUT A JUNGLE. I THOUGHT FOR SURE YOU HAD THE FEVER.

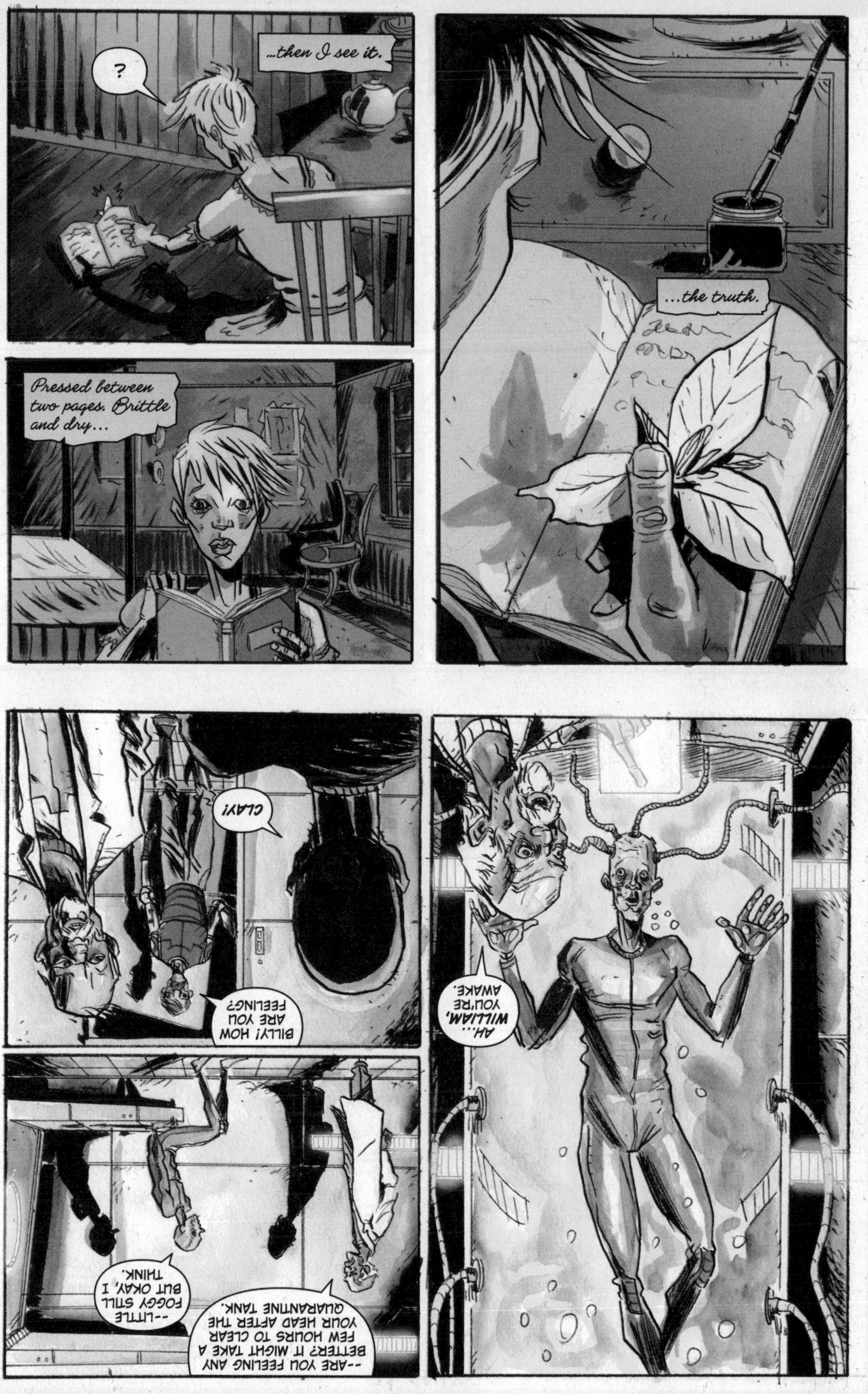

?
...then I see it.
...the truth.
Pressed between two pages. Brittle and dry...
AH... WILLIAM, YOU'RE AWAKE.
BILLY! HOW ARE YOU FEELING?
CLAY!
--ARE YOU FEELING ANY BETTER? IT MIGHT TAKE A FEW HOURS TO CLEAR YOUR HEAD AFTER THE QUARANTINE TANK.
--LITTLE FOGGY STILL BUT OKAY, I THINK.

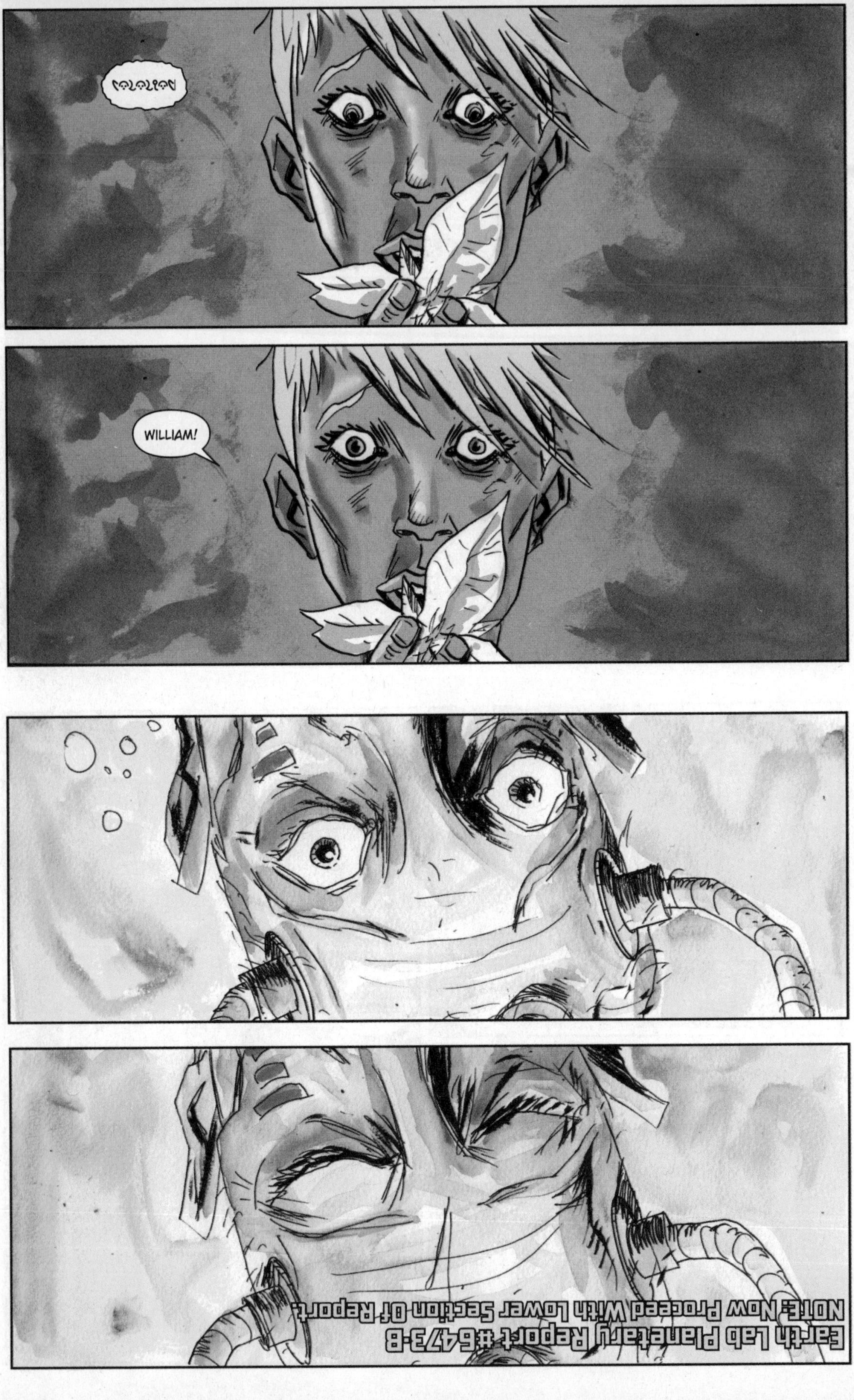
WILLIAM!
Earth Lab Planetary Report #6473-B
NOTE: Now Proceed With Lower Section Of Report.

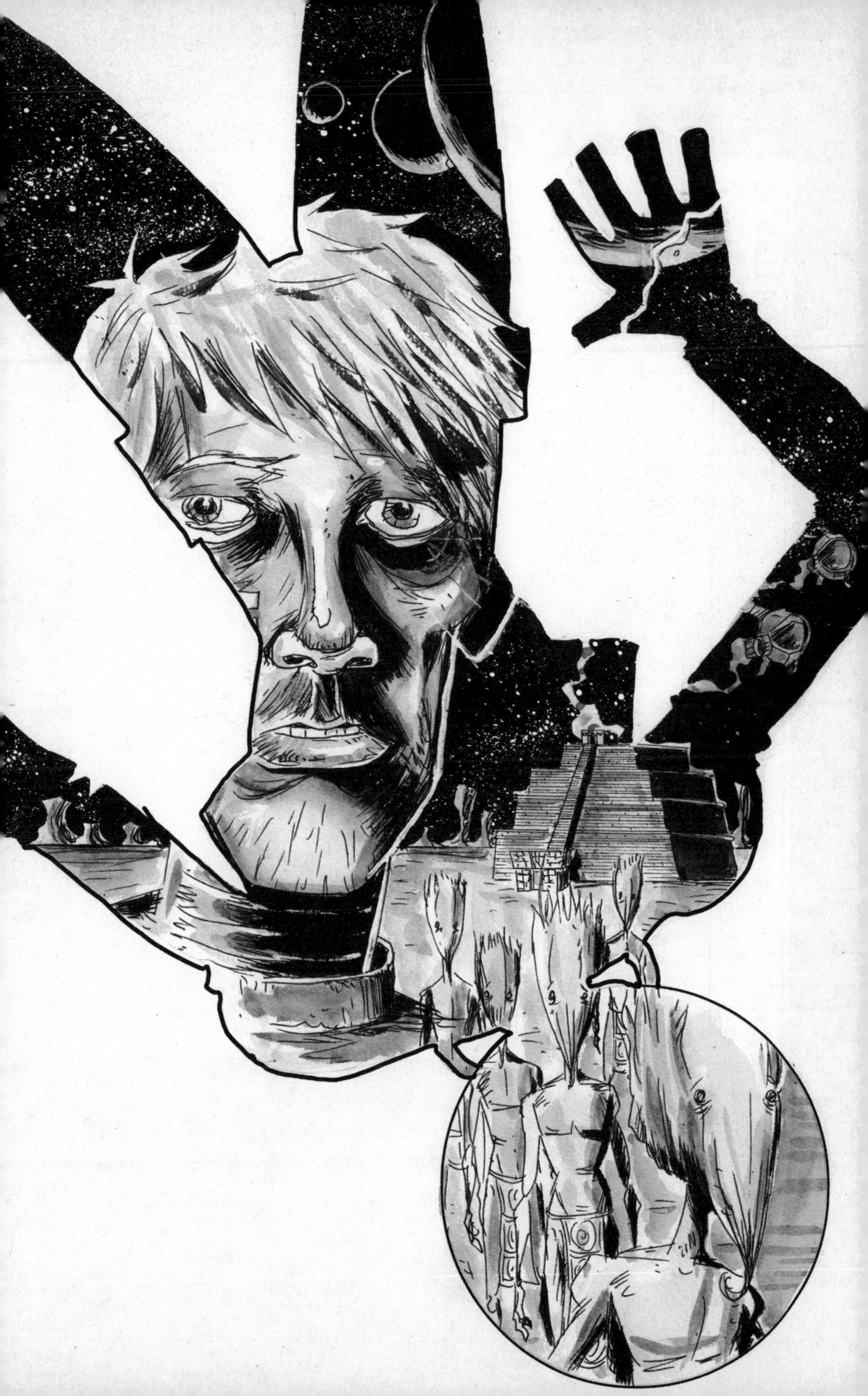

CHAPTER 6:
ESCAPE VELOCITY

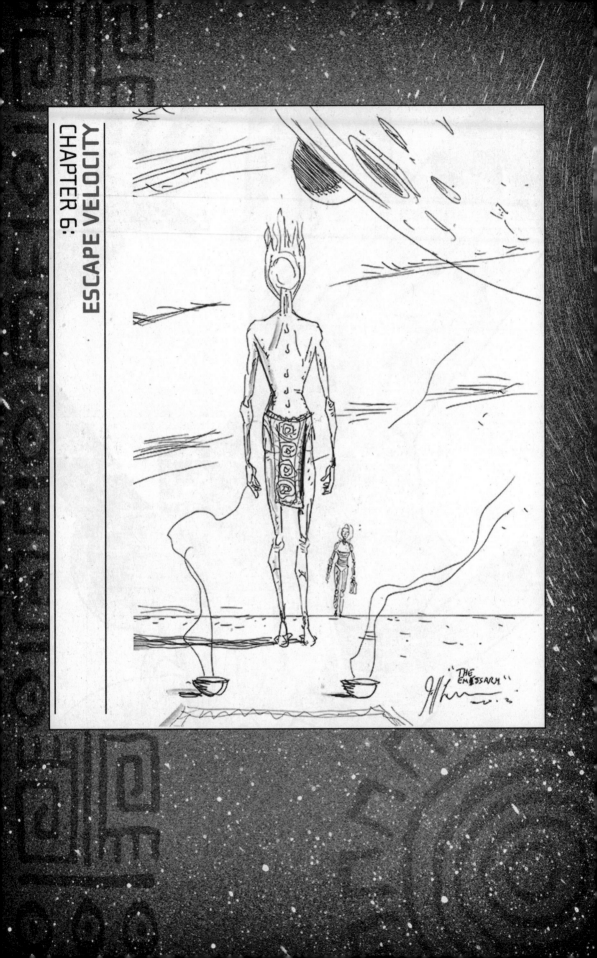

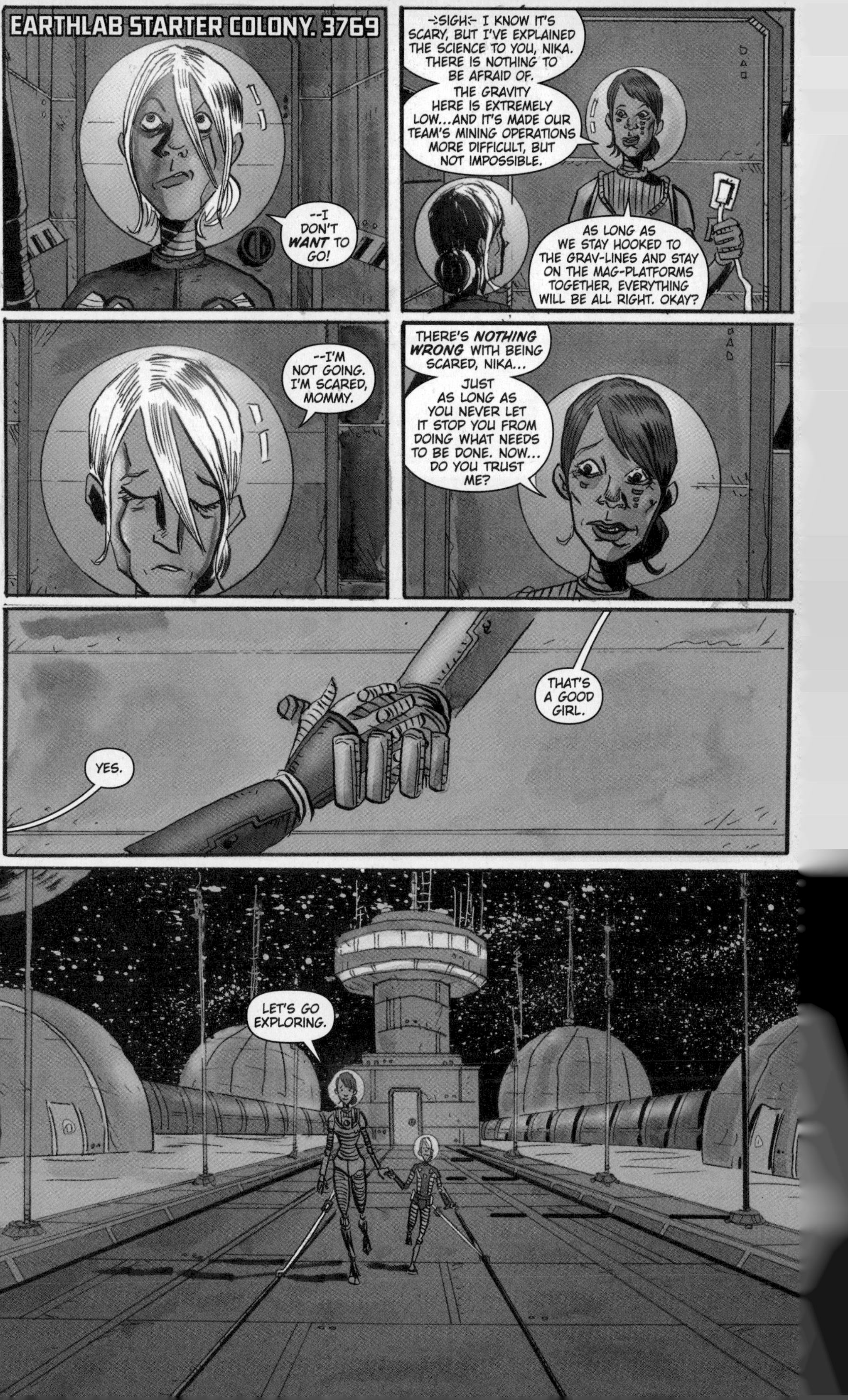

EARTHLAB STARTER COLONY. 3769
--I DON'T WANT TO GO!
-SIGH- I KNOW IT'S SCARY, BUT I'VE EXPLAINED THE SCIENCE TO YOU, NIKA. THERE IS NOTHING TO BE AFRAID OF.
THE GRAVITY HERE IS EXTREMELY LOW...AND IT'S MADE OUR TEAM'S MINING OPERATIONS MORE DIFFICULT, BUT NOT IMPOSSIBLE.
AS LONG AS WE STAY HOOKED TO THE GRAV-LINES AND STAY ON THE MAG-PLATFORMS TOGETHER, EVERYTHING WILL BE ALL RIGHT. OKAY?
--I'M NOT GOING. I'M SCARED, MOMMY.
THERE'S NOTHING WRONG WITH BEING SCARED, NIKA...
JUST AS LONG AS YOU NEVER LET IT STOP YOU FROM DOING WHAT NEEDS TO BE DONE. NOW... DO YOU TRUST ME?
YES.
THAT'S A GOOD GIRL.
LET'S GO EXPLORING.

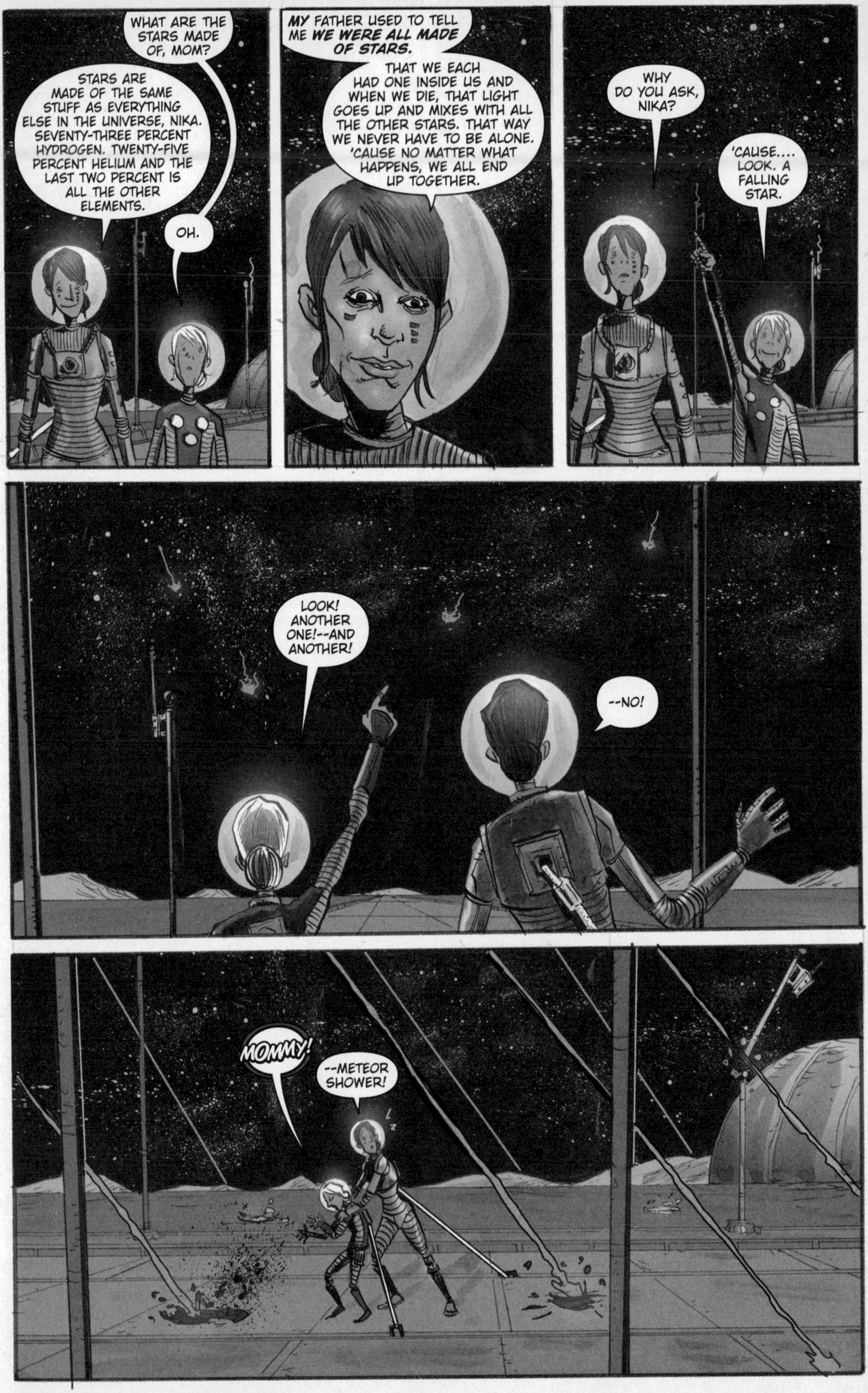
WHAT ARE THE STARS MADE OF, MOM?
STARS ARE MADE OF THE SAME STUFF AS EVERYTHING ELSE IN THE UNIVERSE, NIKA. SEVENTY-THREE PERCENT HYDROGEN. TWENTY-FIVE PERCENT HELIUM AND THE LAST TWO PERCENT IS ALL THE OTHER ELEMENTS.
OH.
MY FATHER USED TO TELL ME WE WERE ALL MADE OF STARS.
THAT WE EACH HAD ONE INSIDE US AND WHEN WE DIE, THAT LIGHT GOES UP AND MIXES WITH ALL THE OTHER STARS. THAT WAY WE NEVER HAVE TO BE ALONE. 'CAUSE NO MATTER WHAT HAPPENS, WE ALL END UP TOGETHER.
WHY DO YOU ASK, NIKA?
'CAUSE.... LOOK. A FALLING STAR.
LOOK! ANOTHER ONE!--AND ANOTHER!
--NO!
MOMMY!
--METEOR SHOWER!

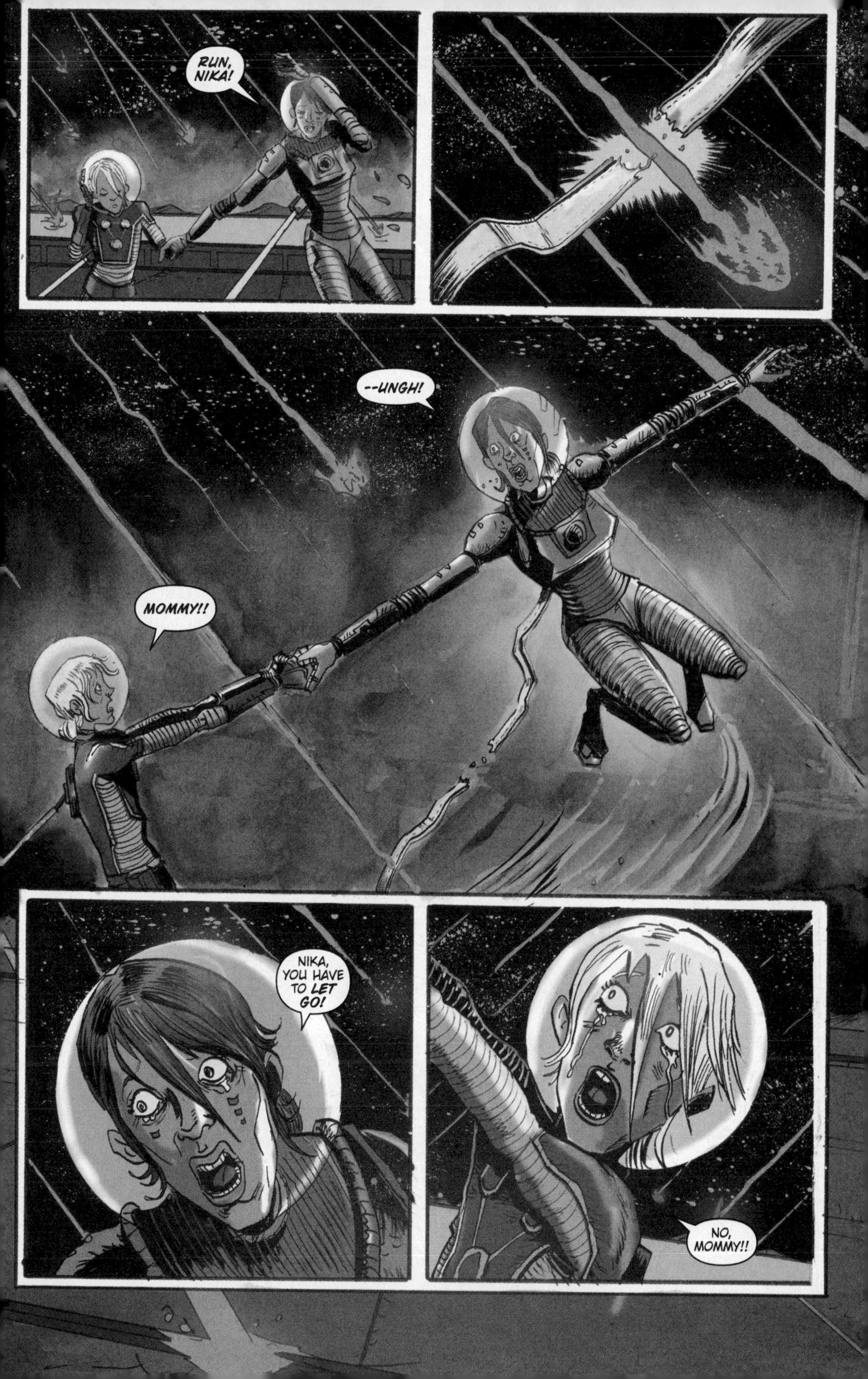
RUN, NIKA!
--UNGH!
MOMMY!!
NIKA, YOU HAVE TO LET GO!
NO, MOMMY!!

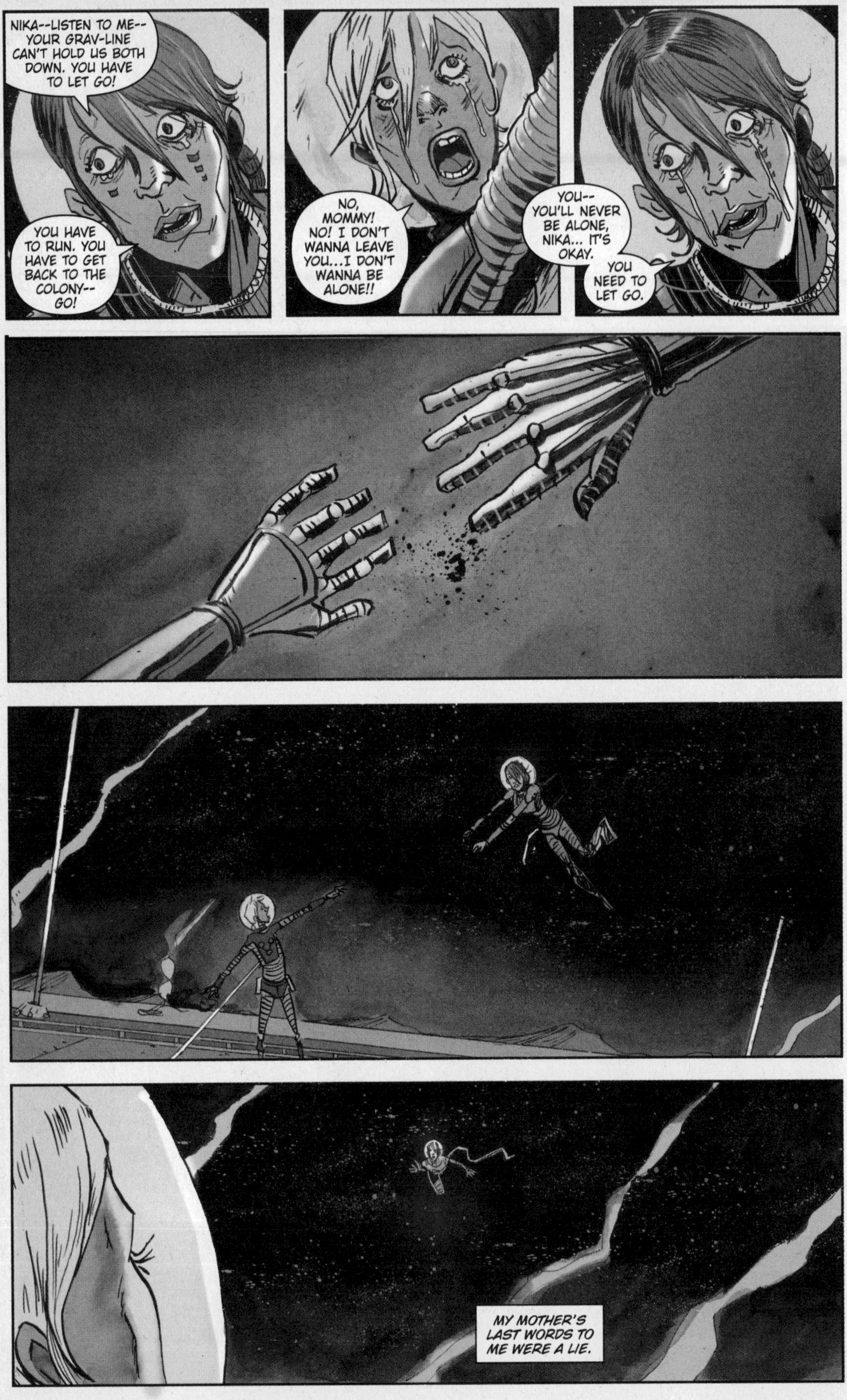
NIKA--LISTEN TO ME--YOUR GRAV-LINE CAN'T HOLD US BOTH DOWN. YOU HAVE TO LET GO!
YOU HAVE TO RUN. YOU HAVE TO GET BACK TO THE COLONY--GO!
NO, MOMMY! NO! I DON'T WANNA LEAVE YOU...I DON'T WANNA BE ALONE!!
YOU--YOU'LL NEVER BE ALONE, NIKA... IT'S OKAY.
YOU NEED TO LET GO.
MY MOTHER'S LAST WORDS TO ME WERE A LIE.

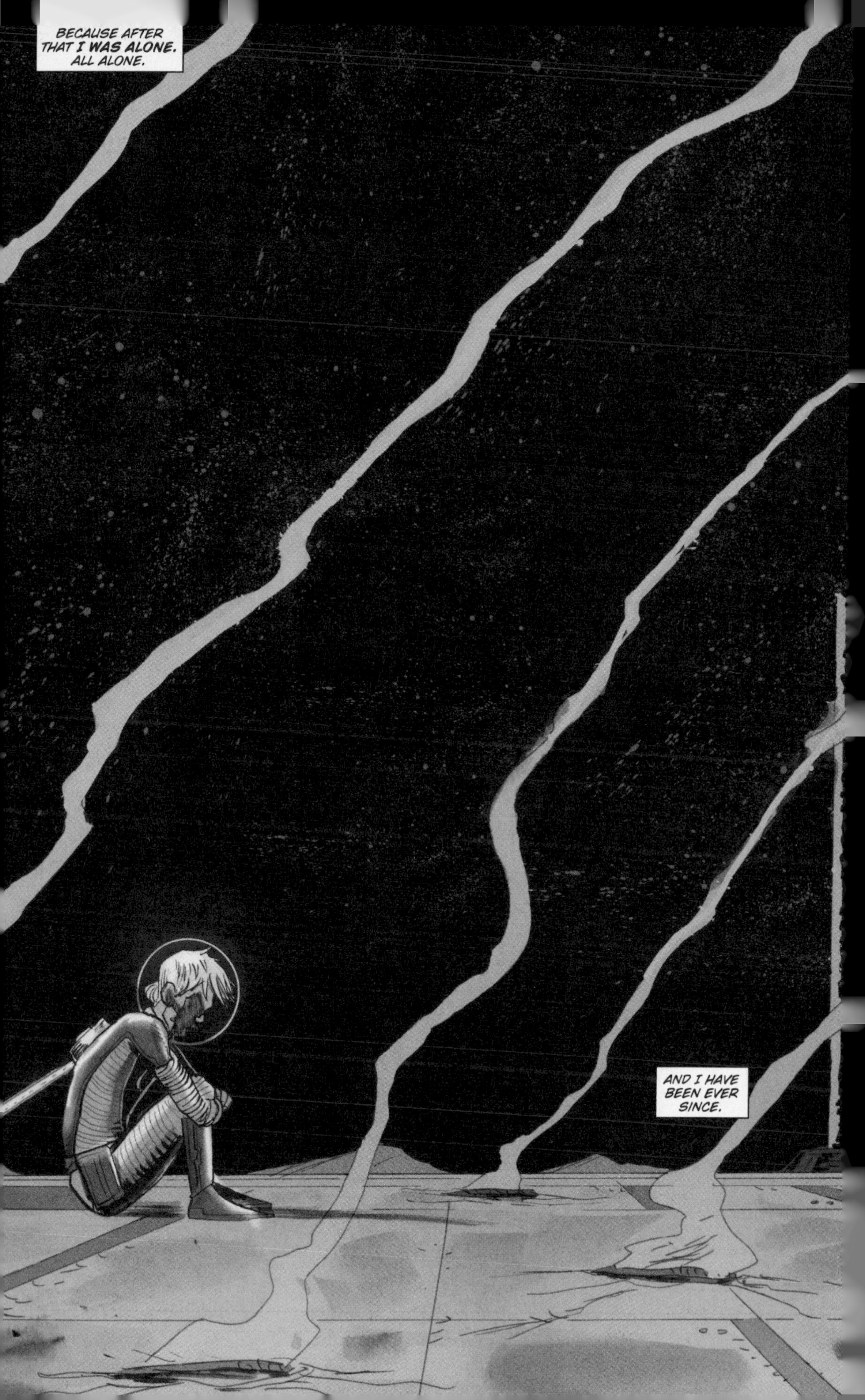
BECAUSE AFTER THAT I WAS ALONE. ALL ALONE.
AND I HAVE BEEN EVER SINCE.

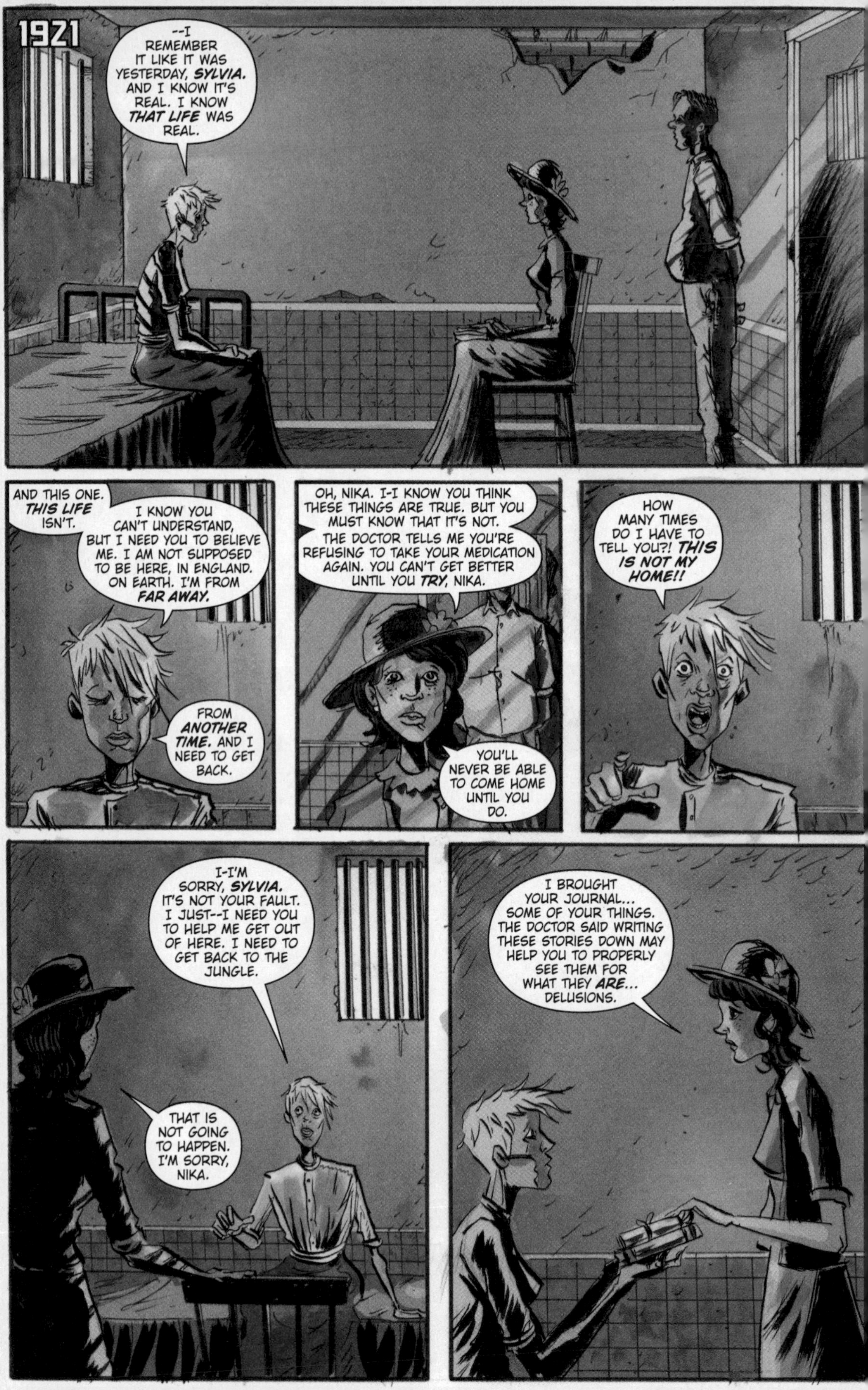
1921
--I REMEMBER IT LIKE IT WAS YESTERDAY, SYLVIA. AND I KNOW IT'S REAL. I KNOW THAT LIFE WAS REAL.
AND THIS ONE. THIS LIFE ISN'T.
I KNOW YOU CAN'T UNDERSTAND, BUT I NEED YOU TO BELIEVE ME. I AM NOT SUPPOSED TO BE HERE, IN ENGLAND. ON EARTH. I'M FROM FAR AWAY.
FROM ANOTHER TIME. AND I NEED TO GET BACK.
OH, NIKA. I-I KNOW YOU THINK THESE THINGS ARE TRUE. BUT YOU MUST KNOW THAT IT'S NOT.
THE DOCTOR TELLS ME YOU'RE REFUSING TO TAKE YOUR MEDICATION AGAIN. YOU CAN'T GET BETTER UNTIL YOU TRY, NIKA.
YOU'LL NEVER BE ABLE TO COME HOME UNTIL YOU DO.
HOW MANY TIMES DO I HAVE TO TELL YOU?! THIS IS NOT MY HOME!!
I-I'M SORRY, SYLVIA. IT'S NOT YOUR FAULT. I JUST--I NEED YOU TO HELP ME GET OUT OF HERE. I NEED TO GET BACK TO THE JUNGLE.
THAT IS NOT GOING TO HAPPEN. I'M SORRY, NIKA.
I BROUGHT YOUR JOURNAL... SOME OF YOUR THINGS. THE DOCTOR SAID WRITING THESE STORIES DOWN MAY HELP YOU TO PROPERLY SEE THEM FOR WHAT THEY ARE... DELUSIONS.

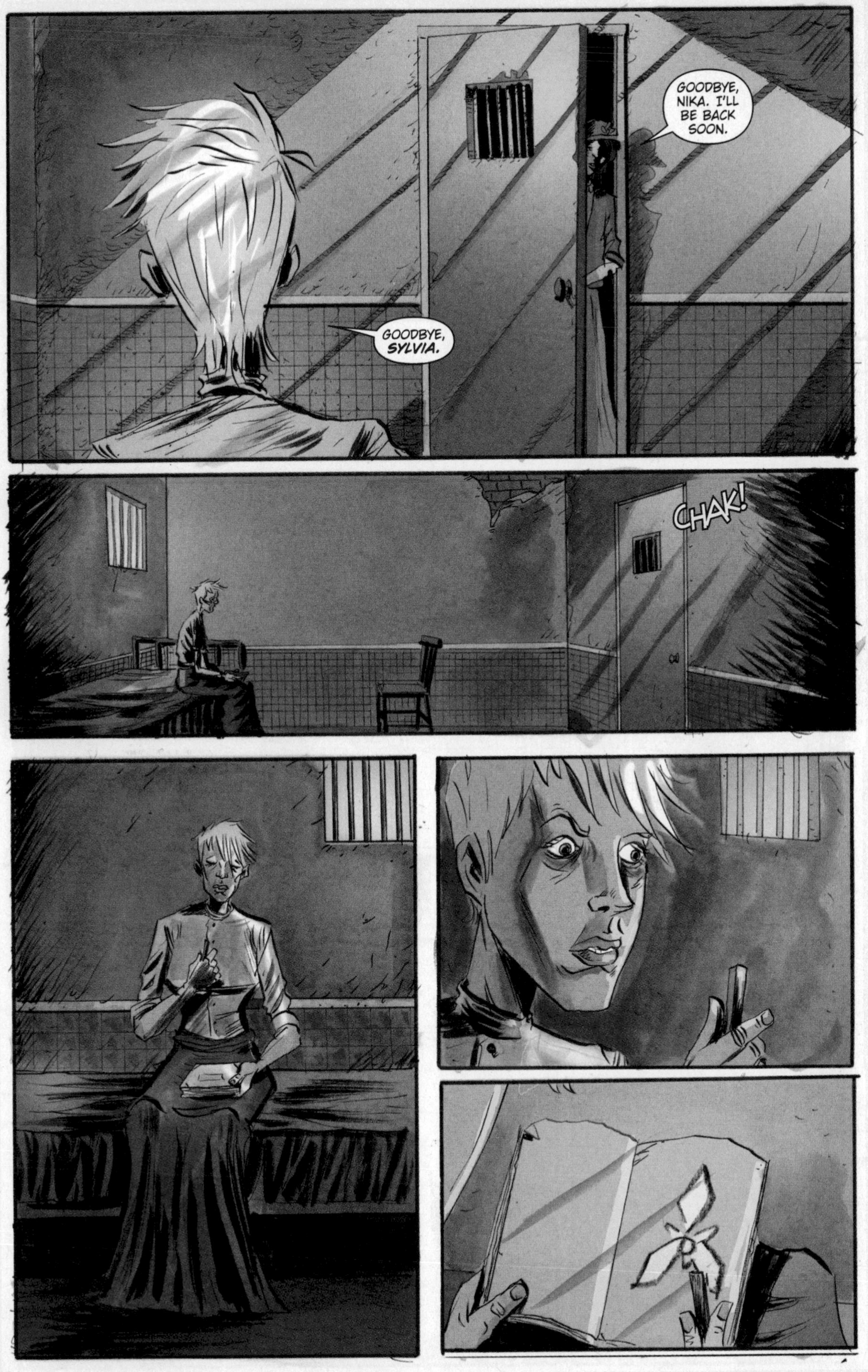
GOODBYE, NIKA. I'LL BE BACK SOON.
GOODBYE, SYLVIA.
CHAK!

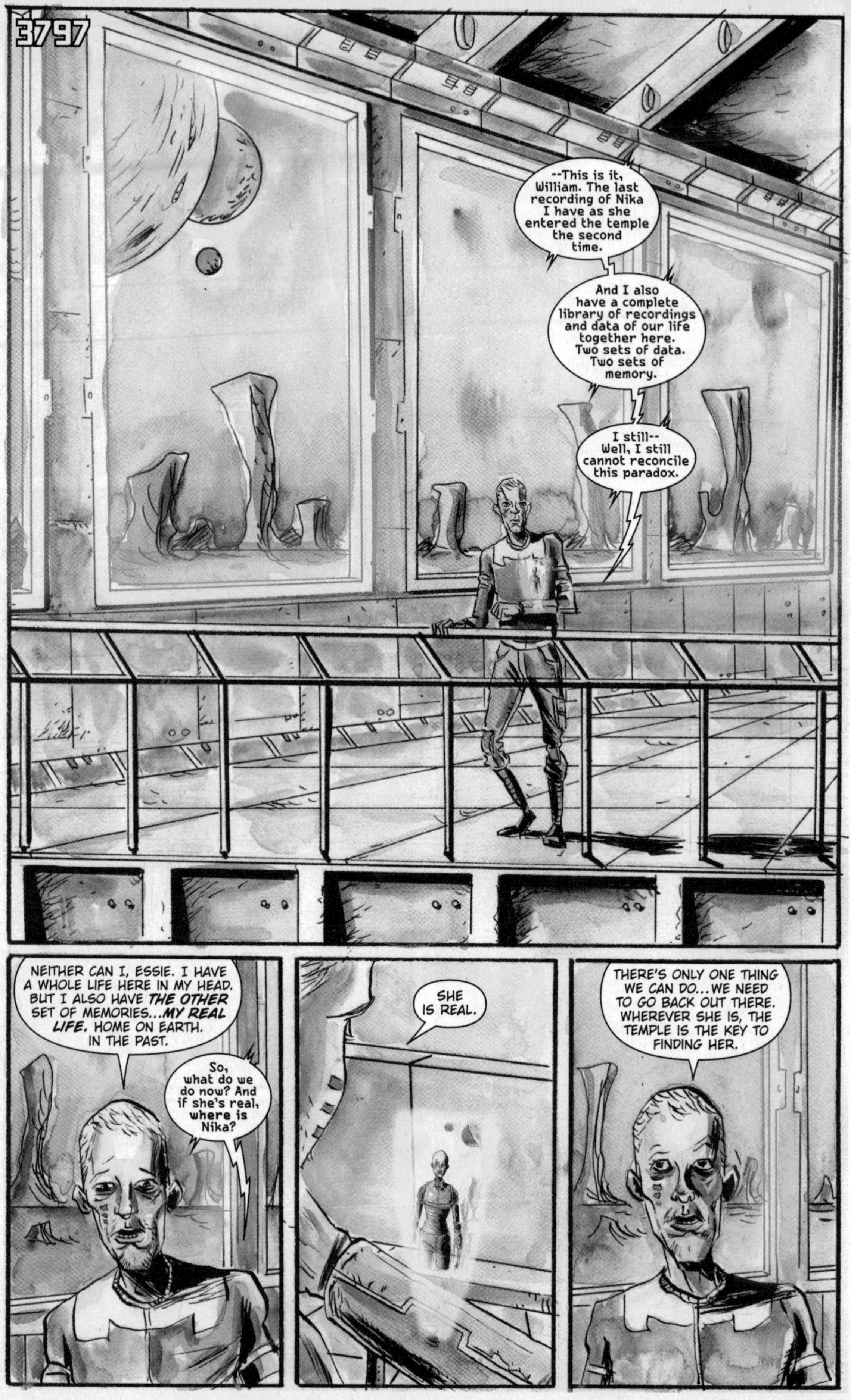
3797
--This is it, William. The last recording of Nika I have as she entered the temple the second time.
And I also have a complete library of recordings and data of our life together here. Two sets of data. Two sets of memory.
I still-- Well, I still cannot reconcile this paradox.
NEITHER CAN I, ESSIE. I HAVE A WHOLE LIFE HERE IN MY HEAD. BUT I ALSO HAVE THE OTHER SET OF MEMORIES...MY REAL LIFE. HOME ON EARTH. IN THE PAST.
So, what do we do now? And if she's real, where is Nika?
SHE IS REAL.
THERE'S ONLY ONE THING WE CAN DO...WE NEED TO GO BACK OUT THERE. WHEREVER SHE IS, THE TEMPLE IS THE KEY TO FINDING HER.

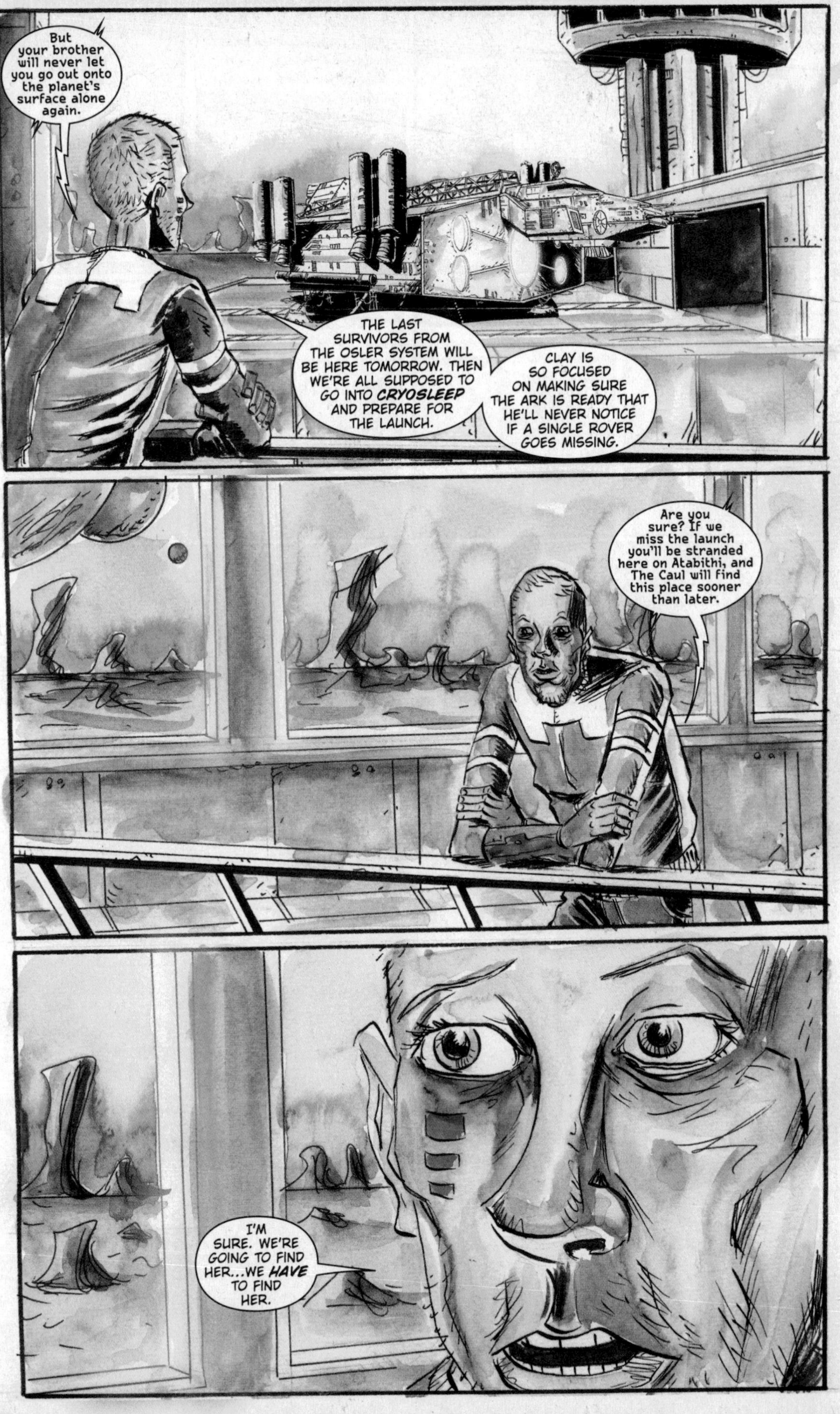
But your brother will never let you go out onto the planet's surface alone again.
THE LAST SURVIVORS FROM THE OSLER SYSTEM WILL BE HERE TOMORROW. THEN WE'RE ALL SUPPOSED TO GO INTO CRYOSLEEP AND PREPARE FOR THE LAUNCH.
CLAY IS SO FOCUSED ON MAKING SURE THE ARK IS READY THAT HE'LL NEVER NOTICE IF A SINGLE ROVER GOES MISSING.
Are you sure? If we miss the launch you'll be stranded here on Atabithi, and The Caul will find this place sooner than later.
I'M SURE. WE'RE GOING TO FIND HER...WE HAVE TO FIND HER.

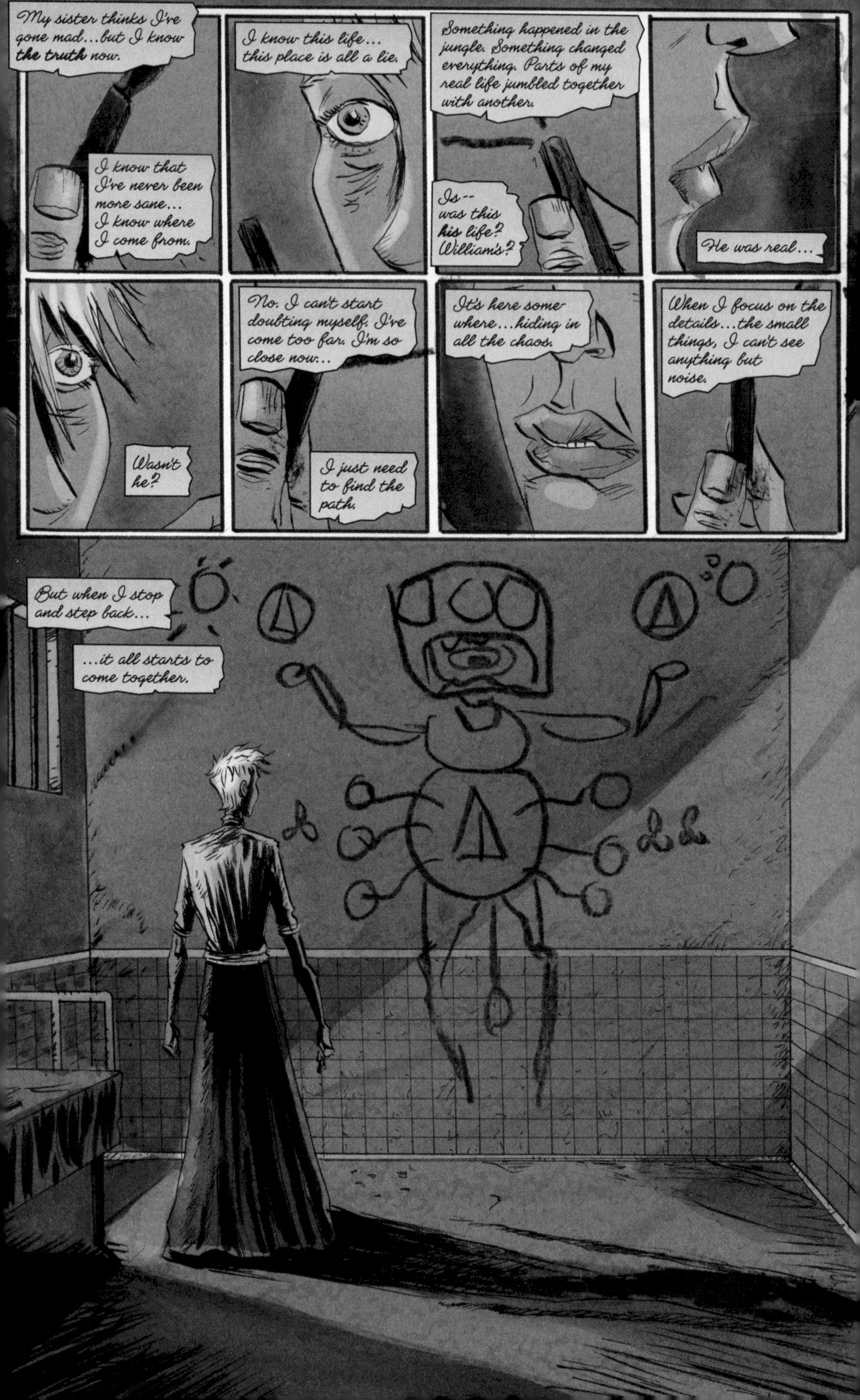
My sister thinks I've gone mad...but I know **the truth** now.
I know that I've never been more sane... I know where I come from.
I know this life... this place is all a lie.
Something happened in the jungle. Something changed everything. Parts of my real life jumbled together with another.
Is-- was this **his life**? William's?
He was real...
Wasn't he?
No. I can't start doubting myself. I've come too far. I'm so close now...
I just need to find the path.
It's here some where...hiding in all the chaos.
When I focus on the details...the small things, I can't see anything but noise.
But when I stop and step back...
...it all starts to come together.

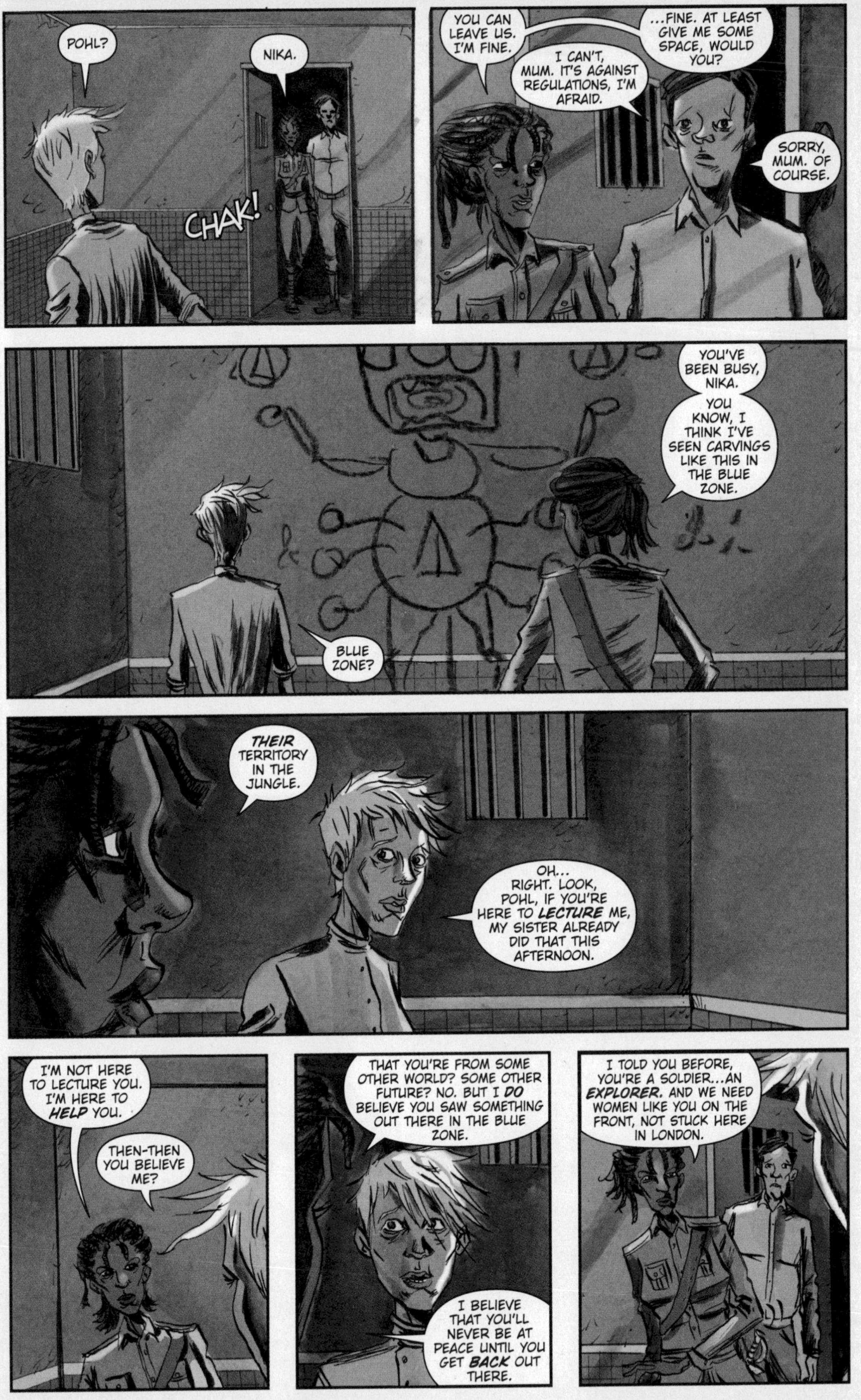
POHL?
NIKA.
CHAK!
YOU CAN LEAVE US. I'M FINE.
I CAN'T, MUM. IT'S AGAINST REGULATIONS, I'M AFRAID.
...FINE. AT LEAST GIVE ME SOME SPACE, WOULD YOU?
SORRY, MUM. OF COURSE.
YOU'VE BEEN BUSY, NIKA.
YOU KNOW, I THINK I'VE SEEN CARVINGS LIKE THIS IN THE BLUE ZONE.
BLUE ZONE?
THEIR TERRITORY IN THE JUNGLE.
OH... RIGHT. LOOK, POHL, IF YOU'RE HERE TO LECTURE ME, MY SISTER ALREADY DID THAT THIS AFTERNOON.
I'M NOT HERE TO LECTURE YOU. I'M HERE TO HELP YOU.
THEN-THEN YOU BELIEVE ME?
THAT YOU'RE FROM SOME OTHER WORLD? SOME OTHER FUTURE? NO. BUT I DO BELIEVE YOU SAW SOMETHING OUT THERE IN THE BLUE ZONE.
I BELIEVE THAT YOU'LL NEVER BE AT PEACE UNTIL YOU GET BACK OUT THERE.
I TOLD YOU BEFORE, YOU'RE A SOLDIER...AN EXPLORER. AND WE NEED WOMEN LIKE YOU ON THE FRONT, NOT STUCK HERE IN LONDON.

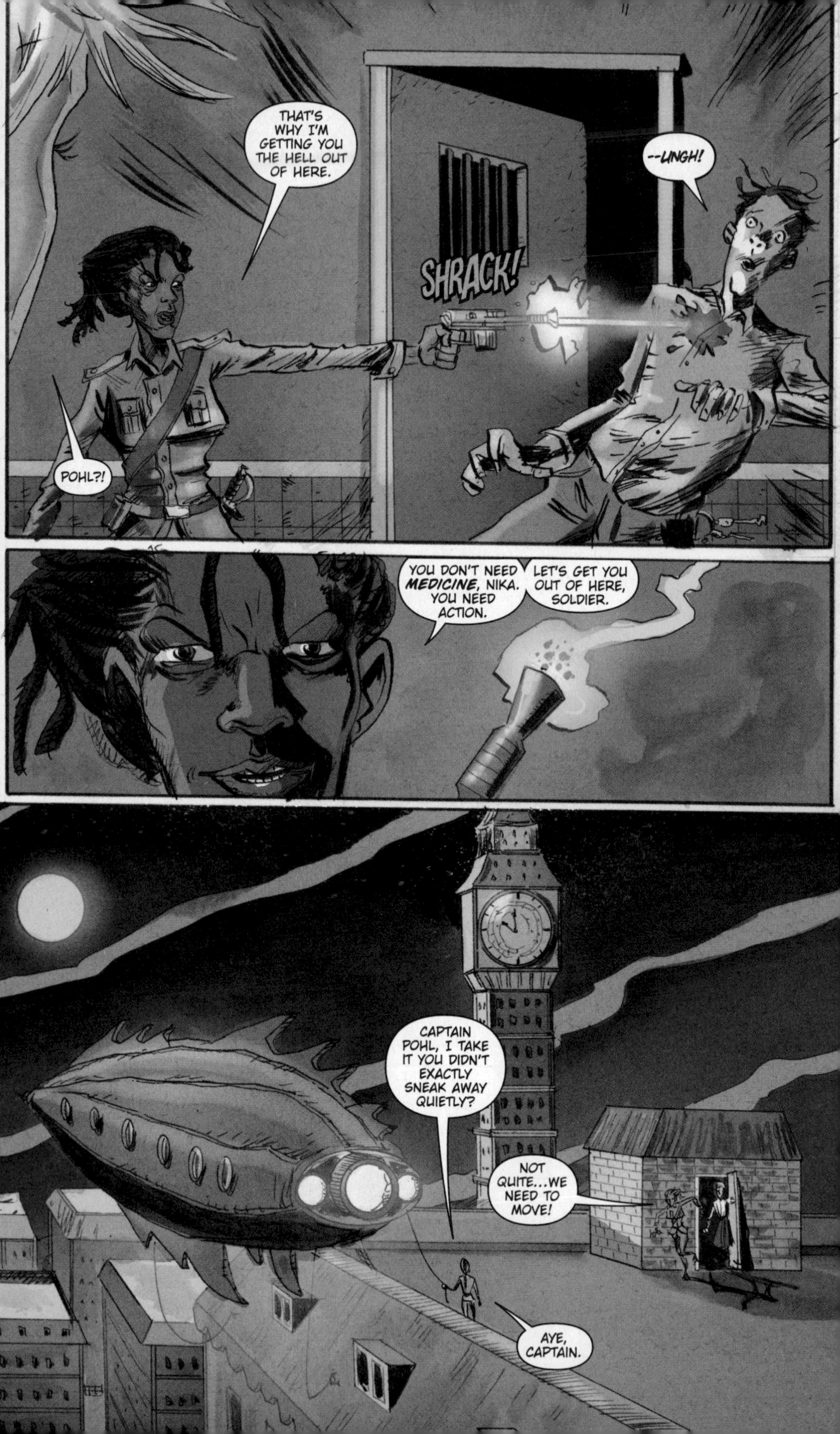
POHL?!
THAT'S WHY I'M GETTING YOU THE HELL OUT OF HERE.
SHRACK!
--UNGH!
YOU DON'T NEED MEDICINE, NIKA. YOU NEED ACTION.
LET'S GET YOU OUT OF HERE, SOLDIER.
CAPTAIN POHL, I TAKE IT YOU DIDN'T EXACTLY SNEAK AWAY QUIETLY?
NOT QUITE...WE NEED TO MOVE!
AYE, CAPTAIN.

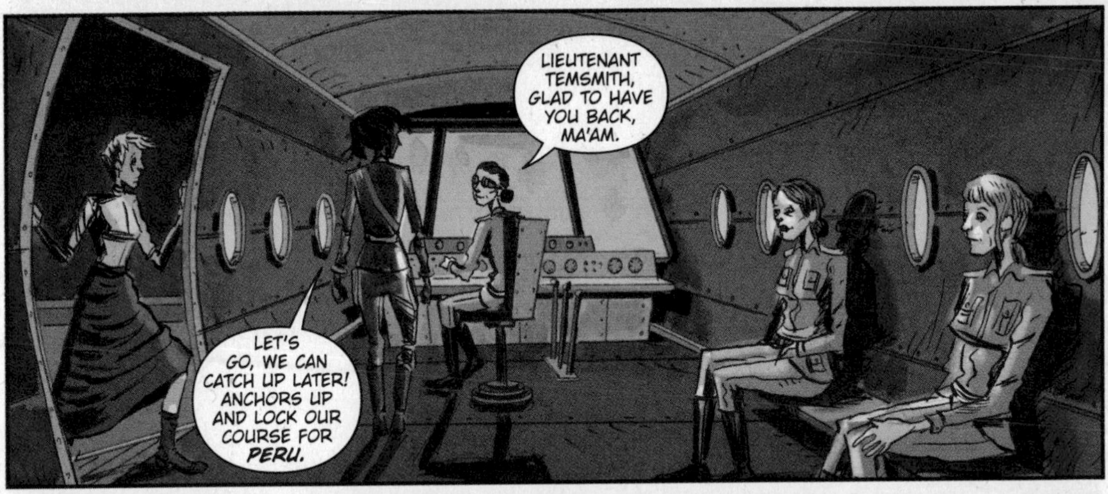
LIEUTENANT TEMSMITH, GLAD TO HAVE YOU BACK, MA'AM.
LET'S GO, WE CAN CATCH UP LATER! ANCHORS UP AND LOCK OUR COURSE FOR PERU.

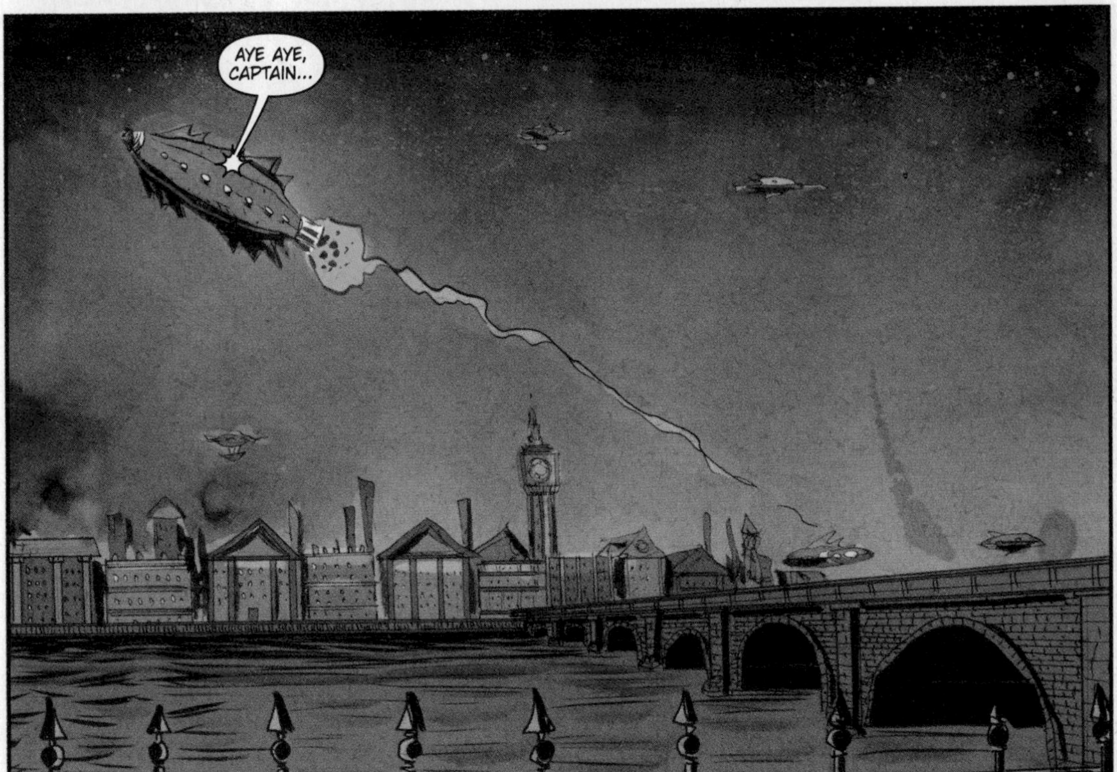
AYE AYE, CAPTAIN...

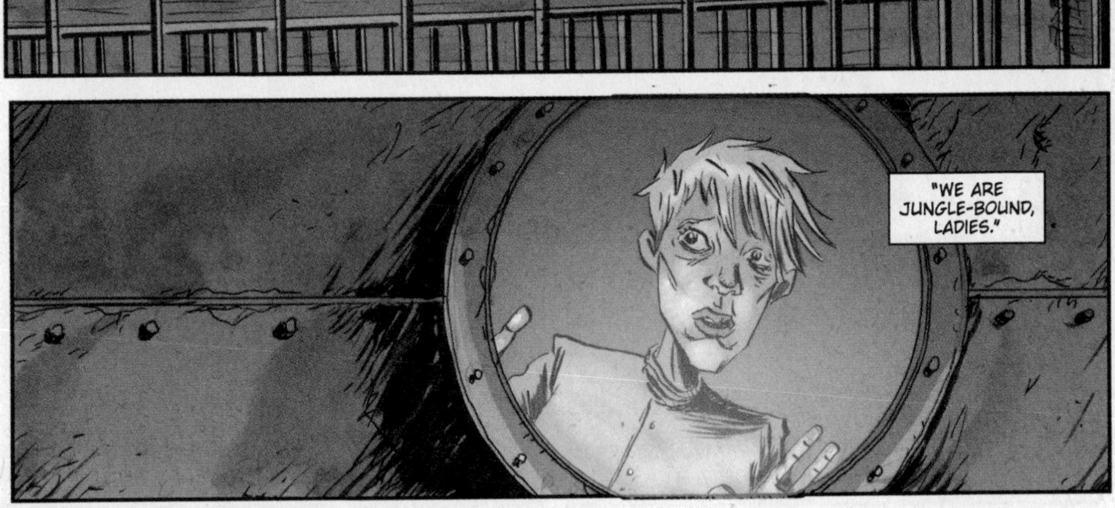
"WE ARE JUNGLE-BOUND, LADIES."

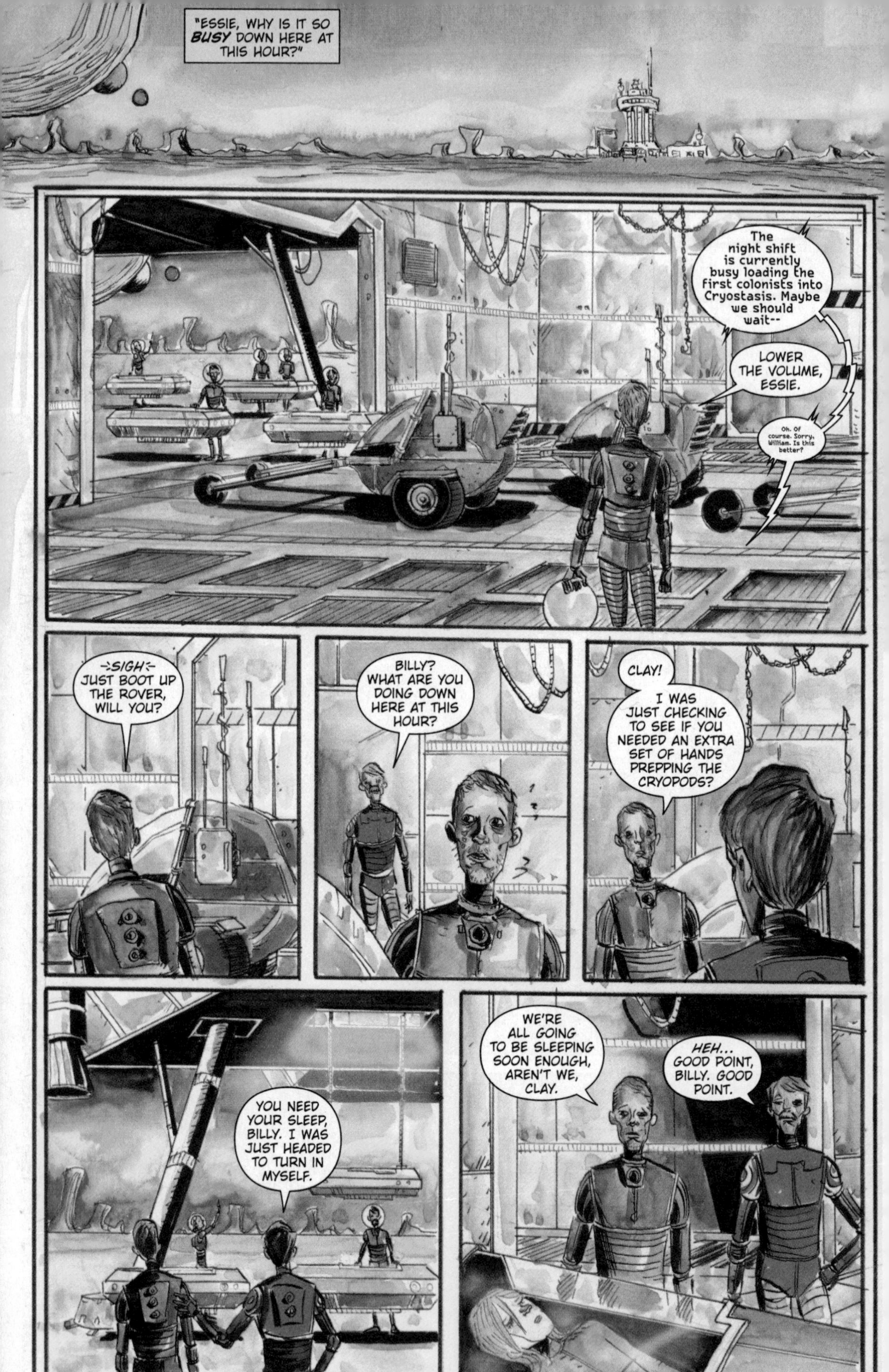
"ESSIE, WHY IS IT SO BUSY DOWN HERE AT THIS HOUR?"
The night shift is currently busy loading the first colonists into Cryostasis. Maybe we should wait--
LOWER THE VOLUME, ESSIE.
Oh. Of course. Sorry, William. Is this better?
-SIGH- JUST BOOT UP THE ROVER, WILL YOU?
BILLY? WHAT ARE YOU DOING DOWN HERE AT THIS HOUR?
CLAY!
I WAS JUST CHECKING TO SEE IF YOU NEEDED AN EXTRA SET OF HANDS PREPPING THE CRYOPODS?
YOU NEED YOUR SLEEP, BILLY. I WAS JUST HEADED TO TURN IN MYSELF.
WE'RE ALL GOING TO BE SLEEPING SOON ENOUGH, AREN'T WE, CLAY.
HEH... GOOD POINT, BILLY. GOOD POINT.

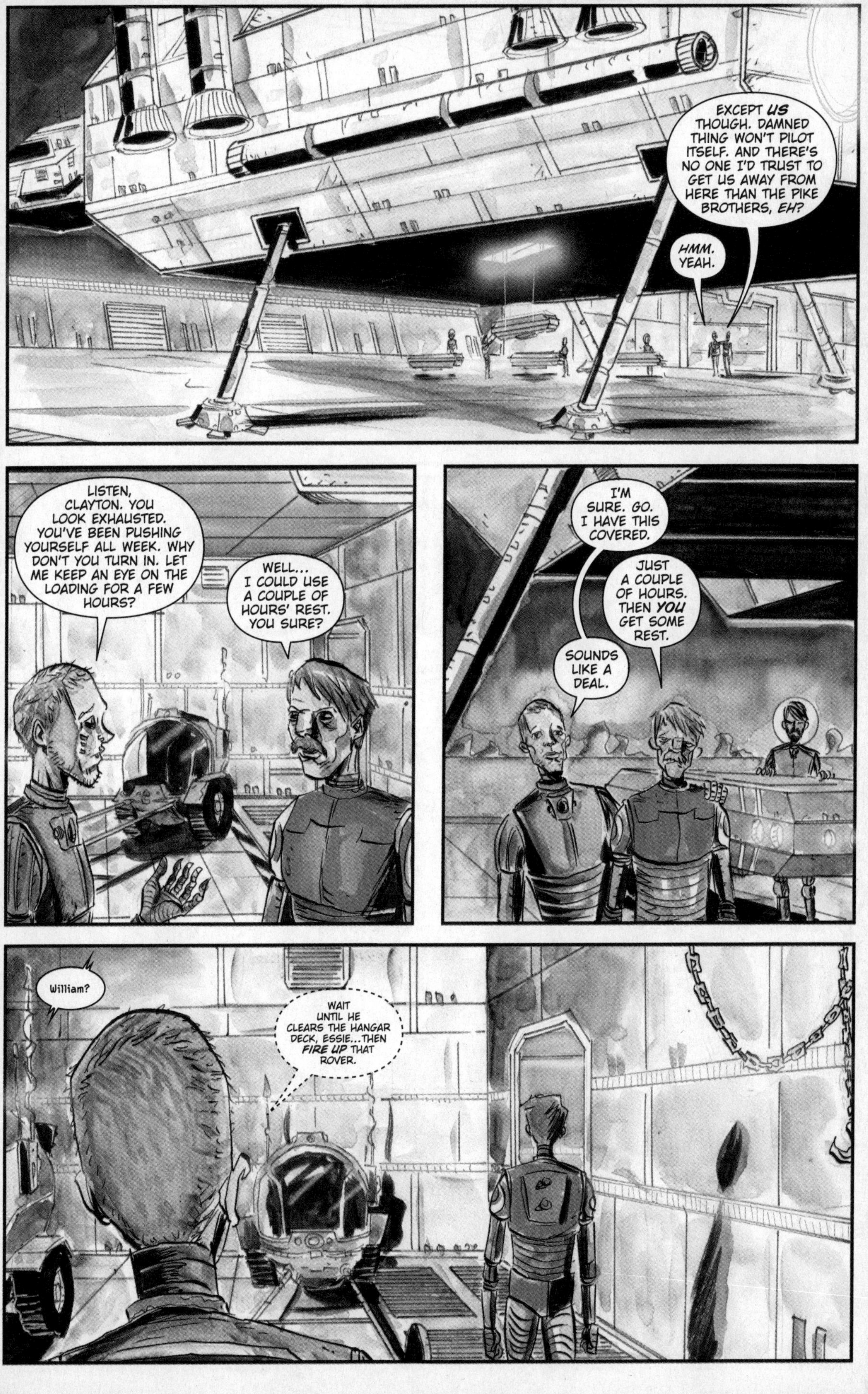
EXCEPT US THOUGH. DAMNED THING WON'T PILOT ITSELF. AND THERE'S NO ONE I'D TRUST TO GET US AWAY FROM HERE THAN THE PIKE BROTHERS, EH?
HMM. YEAH.
LISTEN, CLAYTON. YOU LOOK EXHAUSTED. YOU'VE BEEN PUSHING YOURSELF ALL WEEK. WHY DON'T YOU TURN IN. LET ME KEEP AN EYE ON THE LOADING FOR A FEW HOURS?
WELL... I COULD USE A COUPLE OF HOURS' REST. YOU SURE?
I'M SURE. GO. I HAVE THIS COVERED.
JUST A COUPLE OF HOURS. THEN YOU GET SOME REST.
SOUNDS LIKE A DEAL.
William?
WAIT UNTIL HE CLEARS THE HANGAR DECK, ESSIE...THEN FIRE UP THAT ROVER.

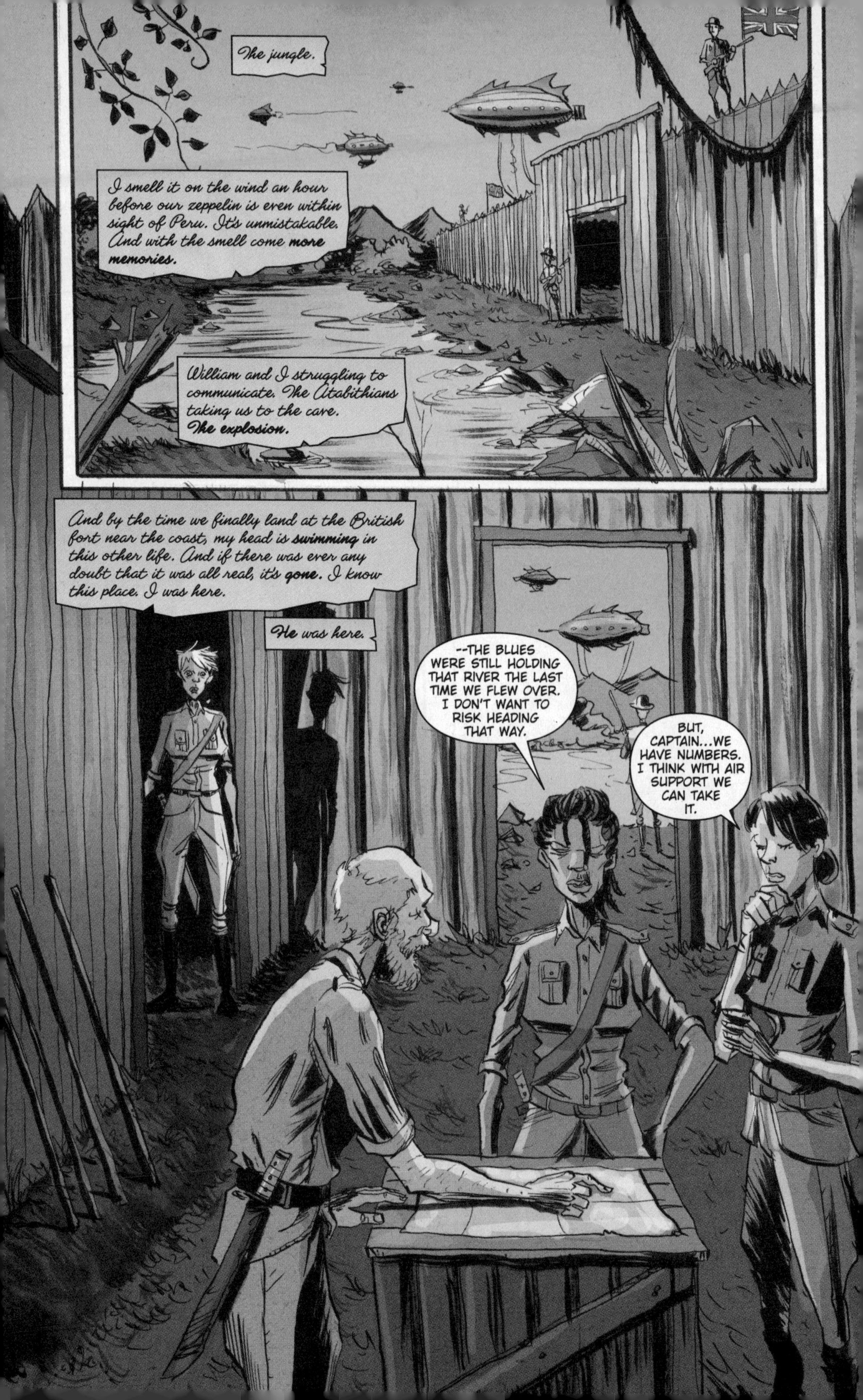
The jungle.
I smell it on the wind an hour before our zeppelin is even within sight of Peru. It's unmistakable. And with the smell come **more memories.**
William and I struggling to communicate. The Atabithians taking us to the cave. **The explosion.**
And by the time we finally land at the British fort near the coast, my head is **swimming** in this other life. And if there was ever any doubt that it was all real, it's **gone**. I know this place. I was here.
He was here.
--THE BLUES WERE STILL HOLDING THAT RIVER THE LAST TIME WE FLEW OVER. I DON'T WANT TO RISK HEADING THAT WAY.
BUT, CAPTAIN...WE HAVE NUMBERS. I THINK WITH AIR SUPPORT WE CAN TAKE IT.

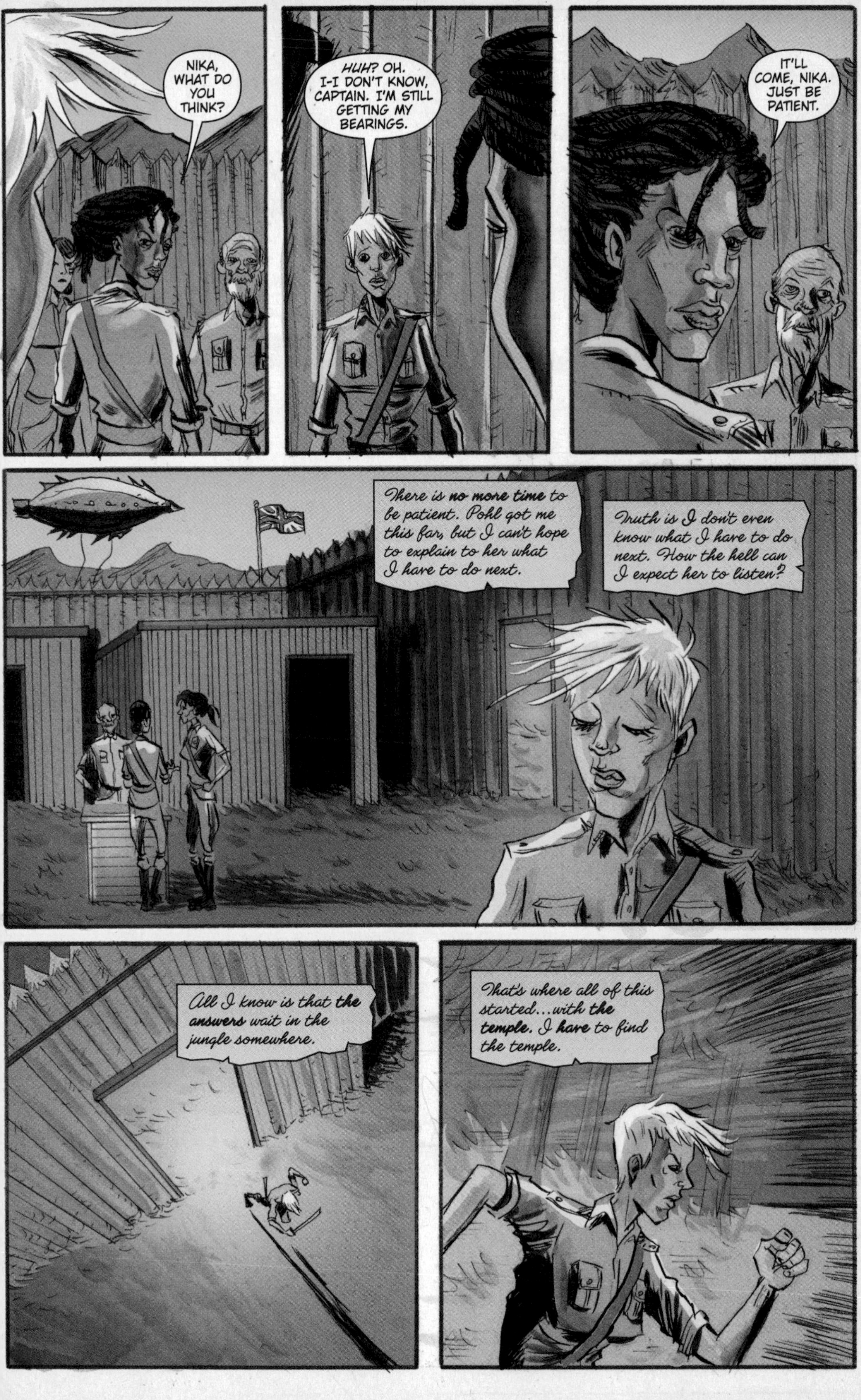

NIKA, WHAT DO YOU THINK?
HUH? OH. I-I DON'T KNOW, CAPTAIN. I'M STILL GETTING MY BEARINGS.
IT'LL COME, NIKA. JUST BE PATIENT.
There is no more time to be patient. Pohl got me this far, but I can't hope to explain to her what I have to do next.
Truth is I don't even know what I have to do next. How the hell can I expect her to listen?
All I know is that the answers wait in the jungle somewhere.
That's where all of this started...with the temple. I have to find the temple.

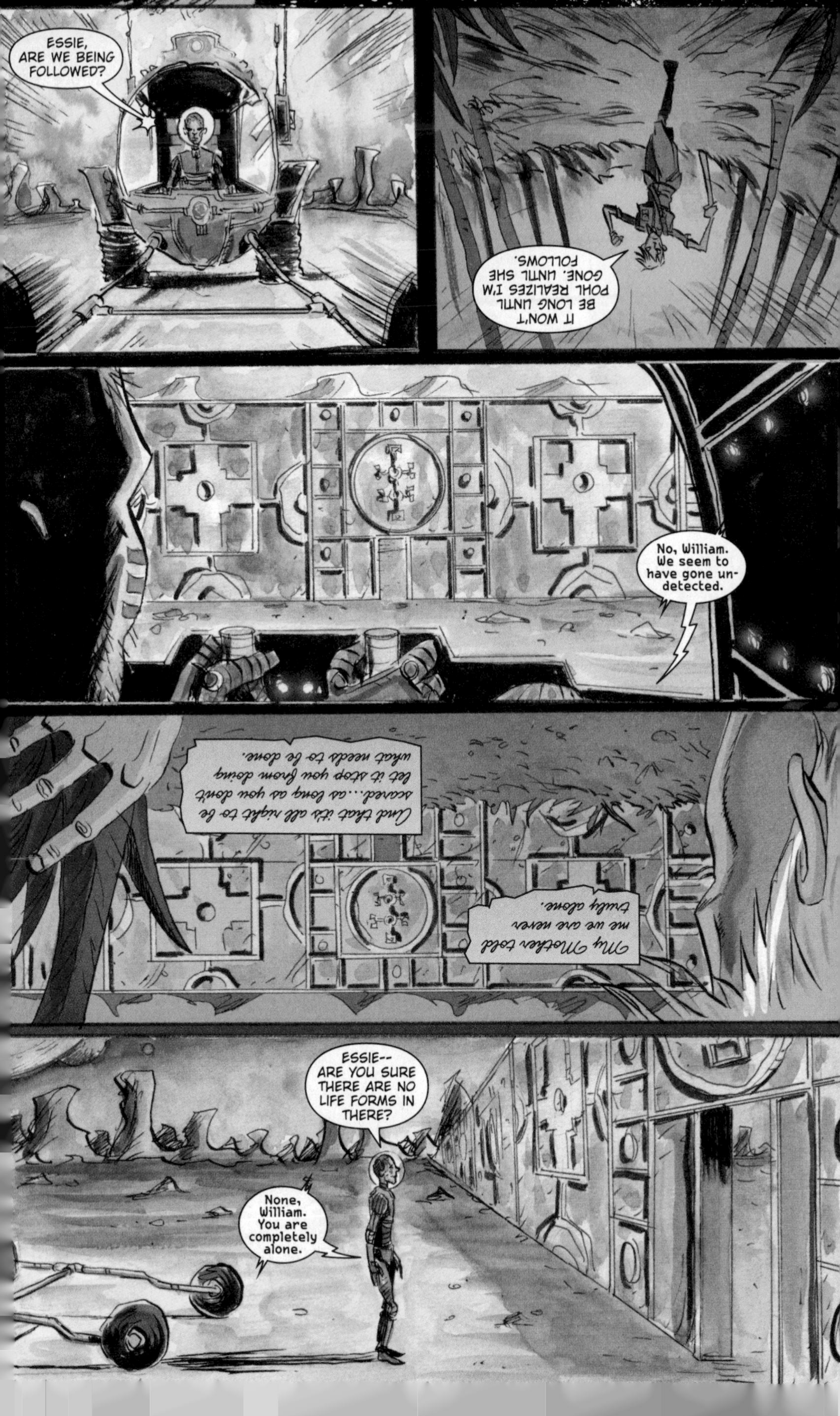
ESSIE, ARE WE BEING FOLLOWED?
IT WON'T BE LONG UNTIL POHL REALIZES I'M GONE. UNTIL SHE FOLLOWS.
No, William. We seem to have gone undetected.
My Mother told me we are never truly alone.
And that it's all right to be scared... as long as you don't let it stop you from doing what needs to be done.
ESSIE-- ARE YOU SURE THERE ARE NO LIFE FORMS IN THERE?
None, William. You are completely alone.

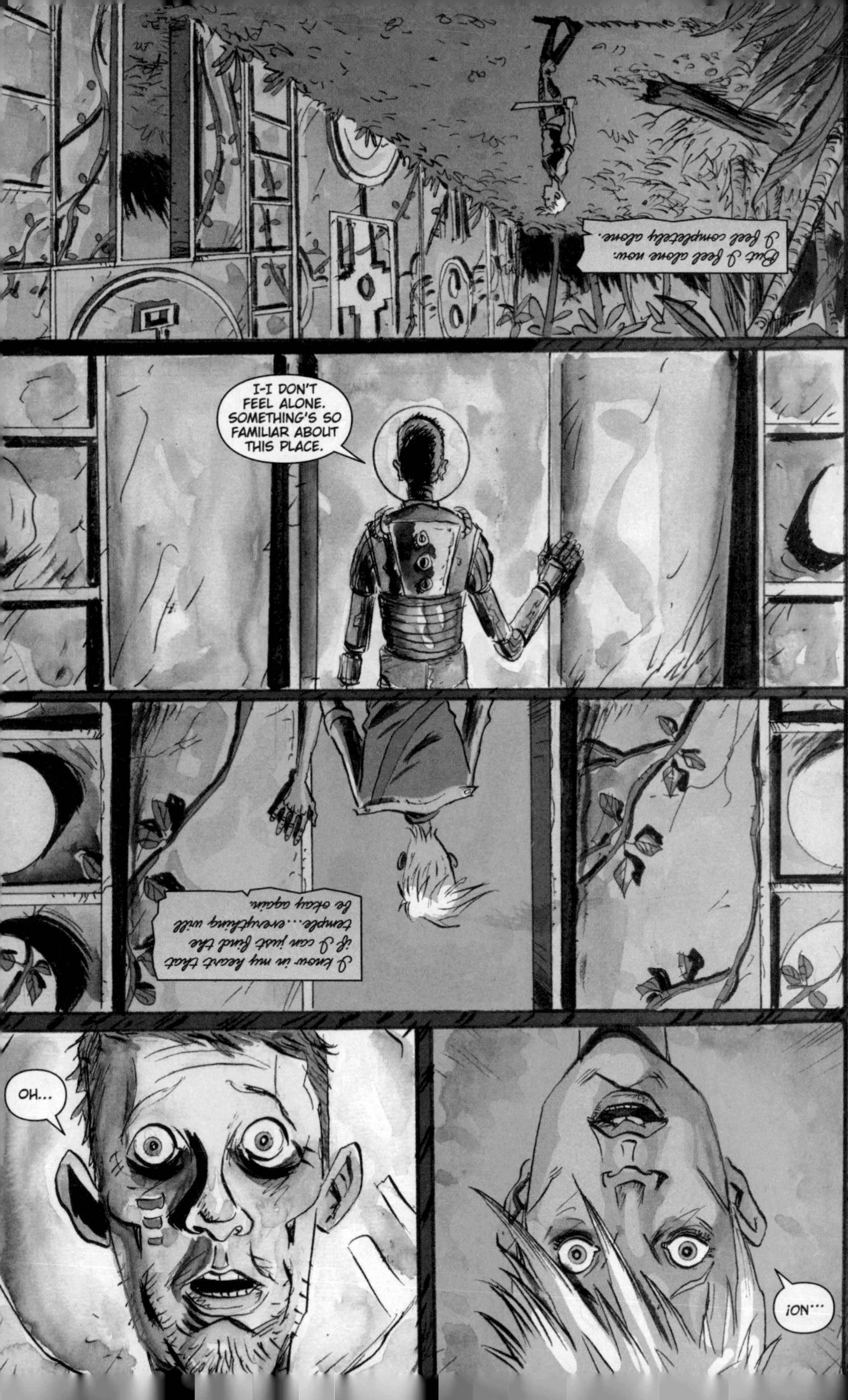
But I feel alone now.
I feel completely alone.
I-I DON'T FEEL ALONE. SOMETHING'S SO FAMILIAR ABOUT THIS PLACE.
I know in my heart that if I can just find the temple...everything will be okay again.
OH...
NO...!

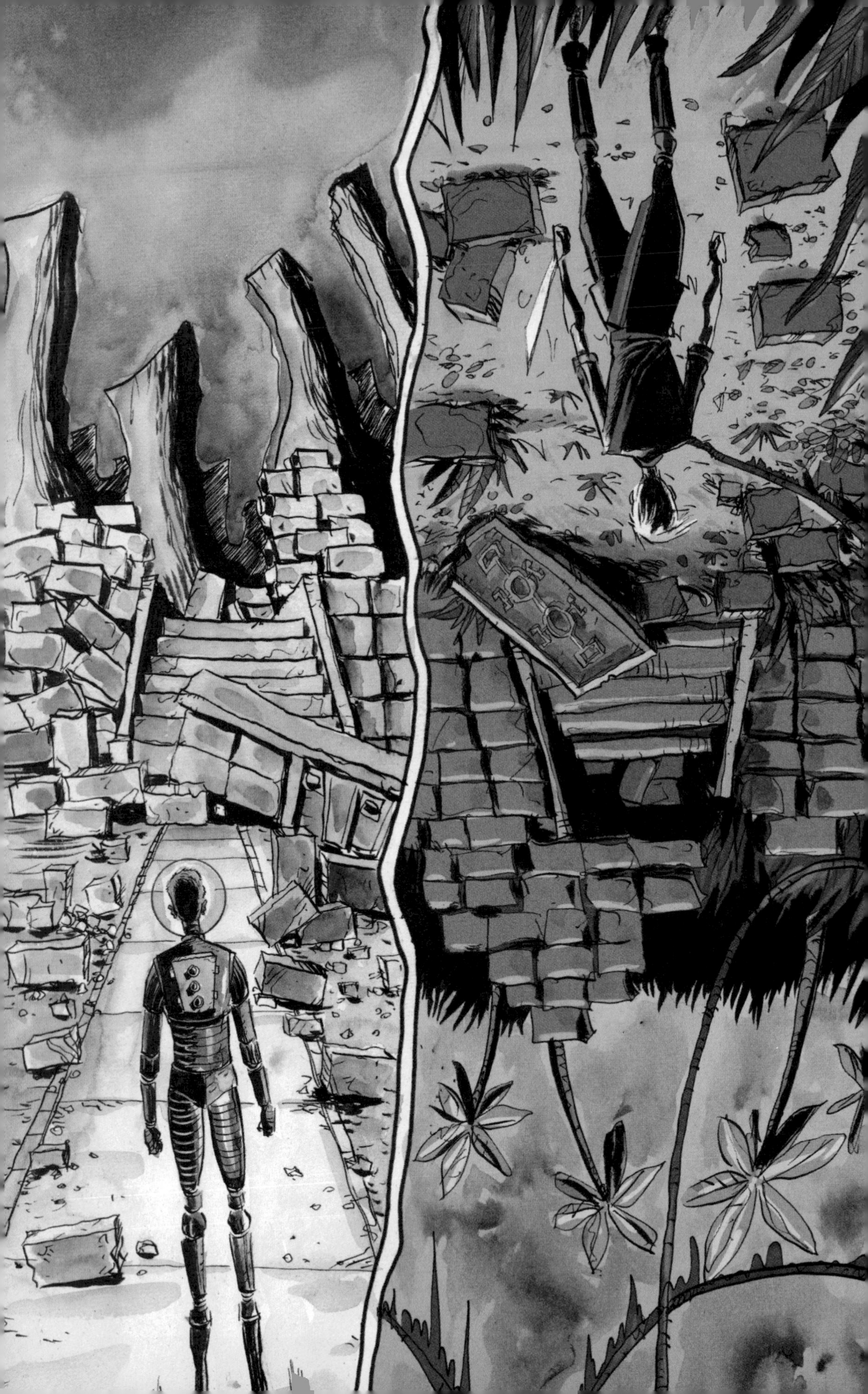

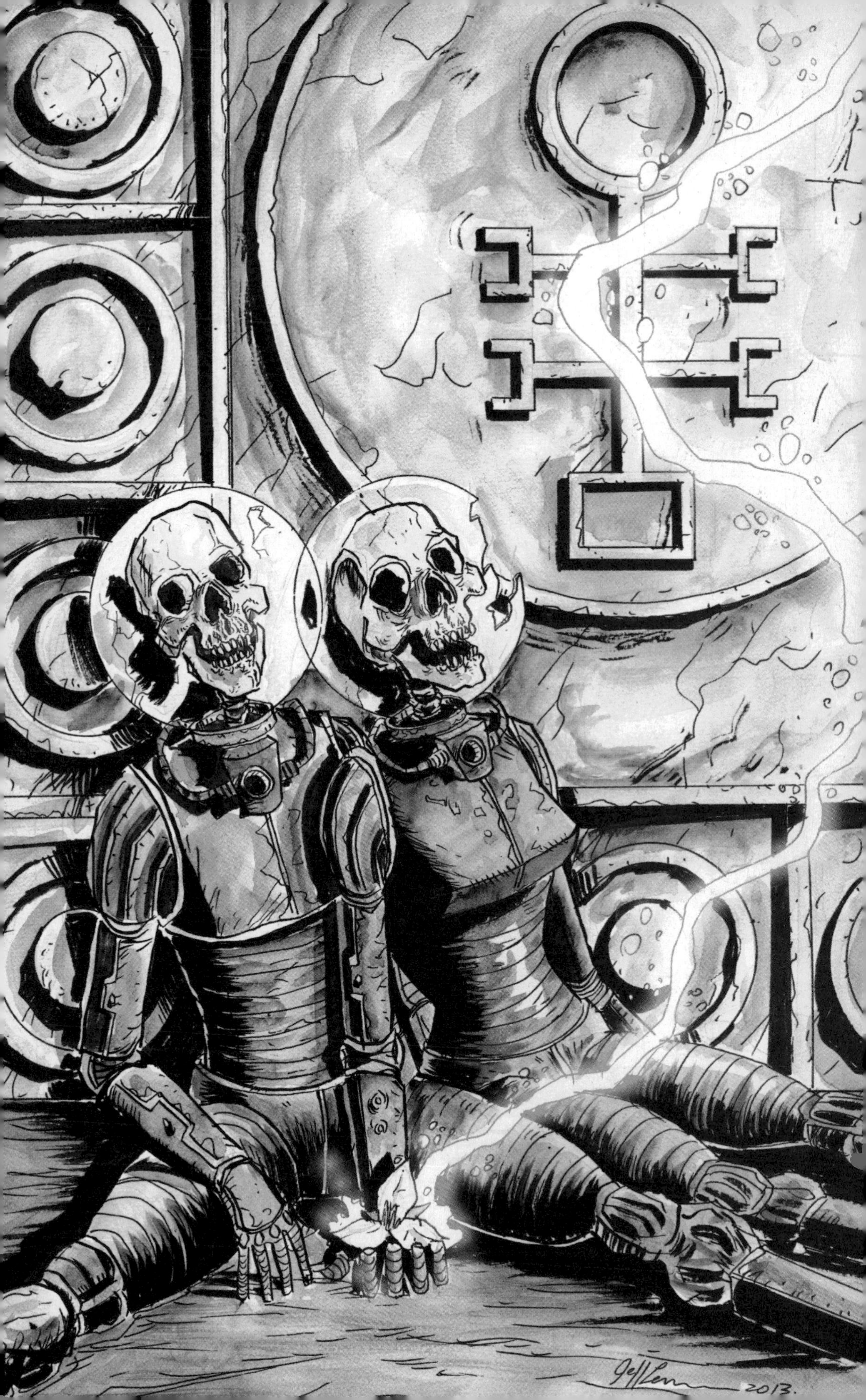

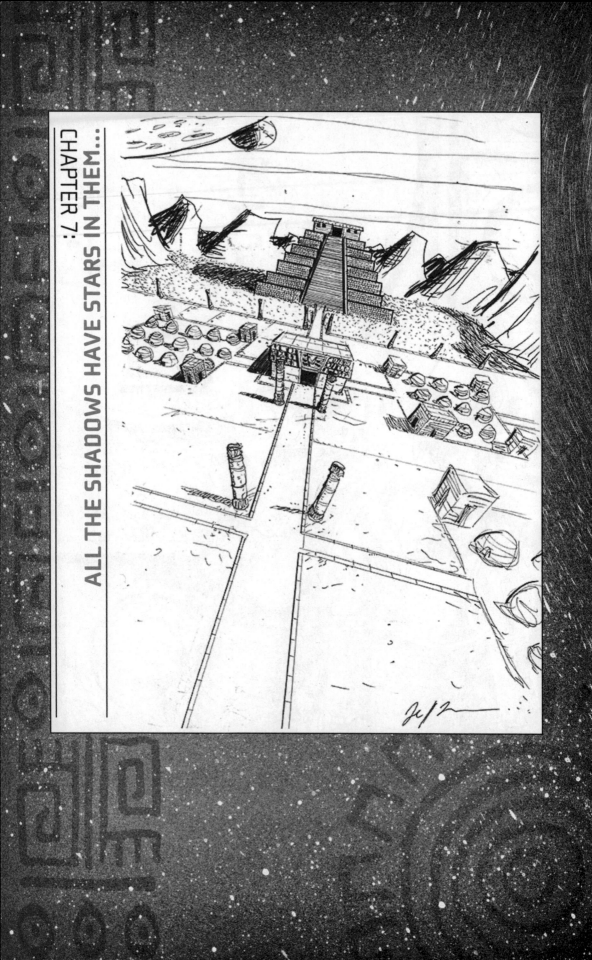

CHAPTER 7:
ALL THE SHADOWS HAVE STARS IN THEM...

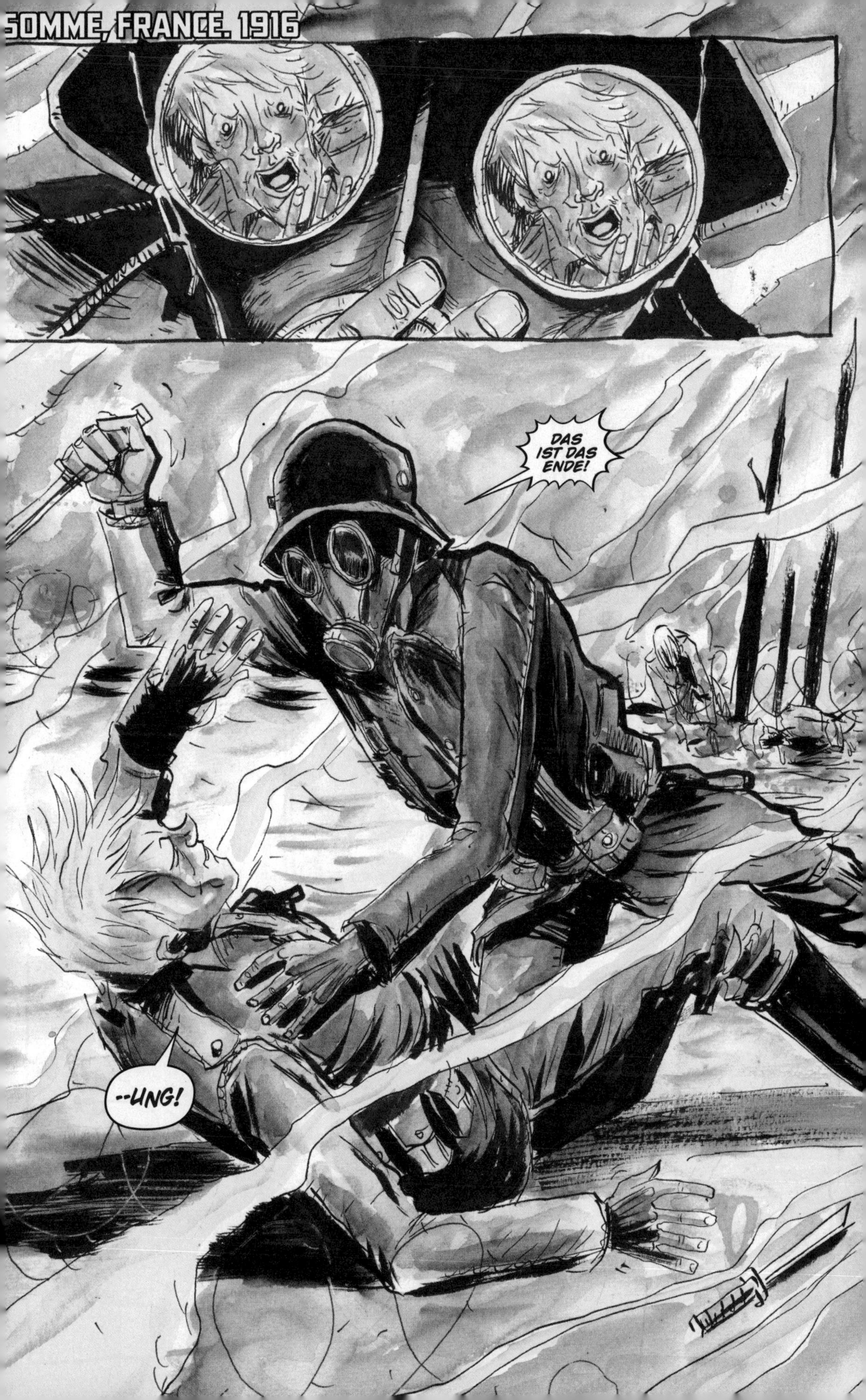
SOMME, FRANCE. 1916
DAS IST DAS ENDE!
--UNG!

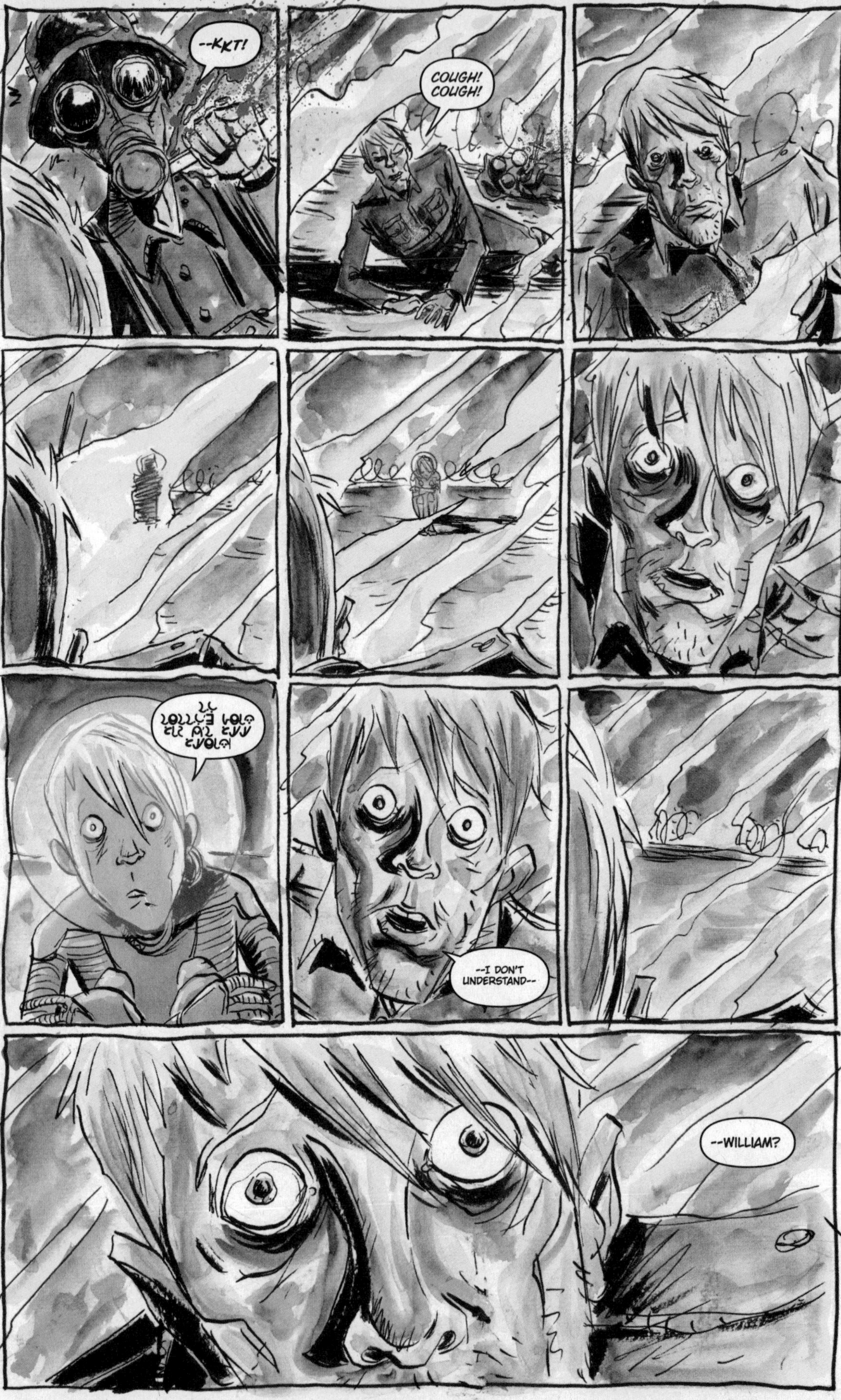
--KKT!
COUGH! COUGH!
--I DON'T UNDERSTAND--
--WILLIAM?

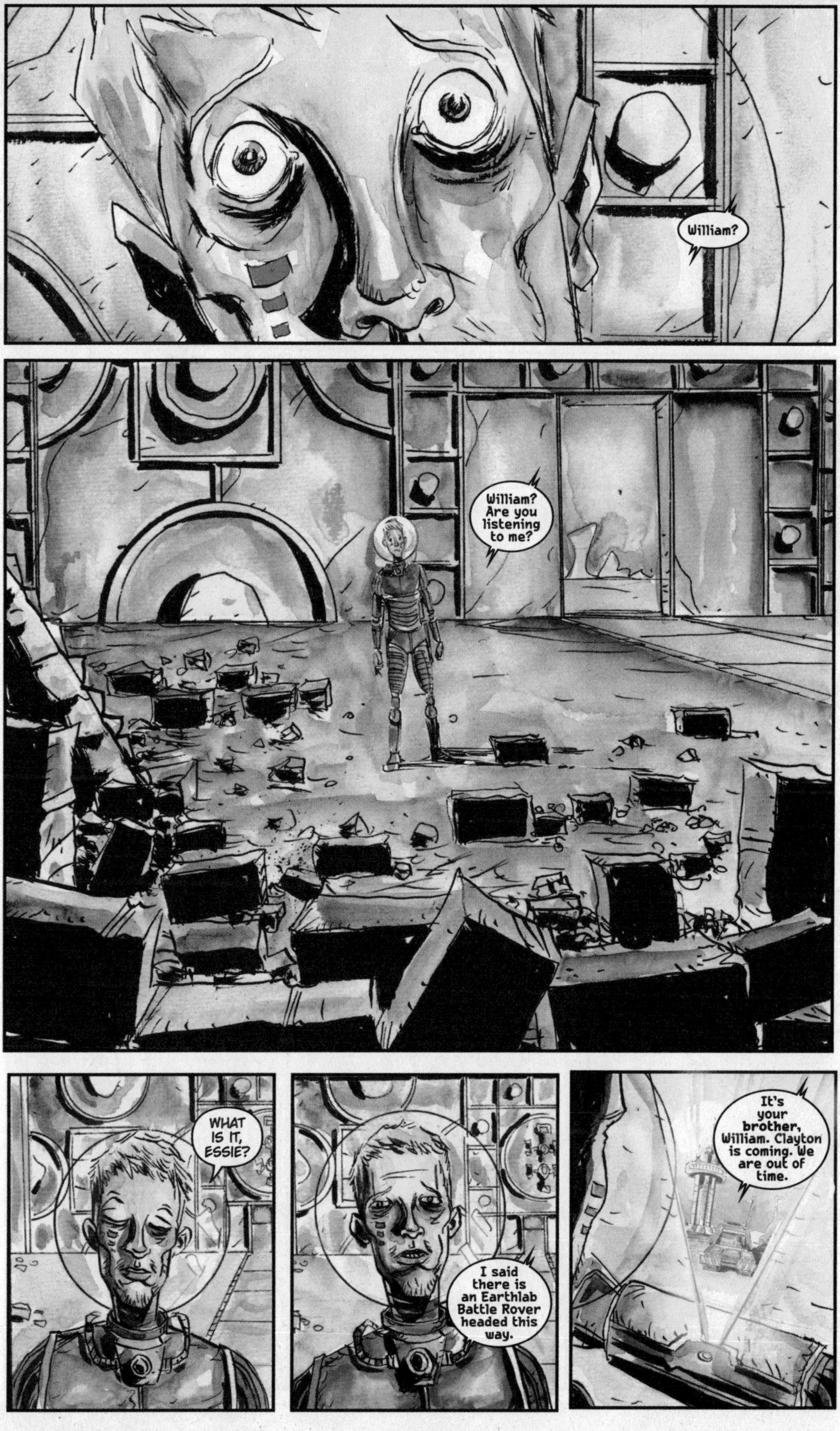
William?
William? Are you listening to me?
WHAT IS IT, ESSIE?
I said there is an Earthlab Battle Rover headed this way.
It's your brother, William. Clayton is coming. We are out of time.

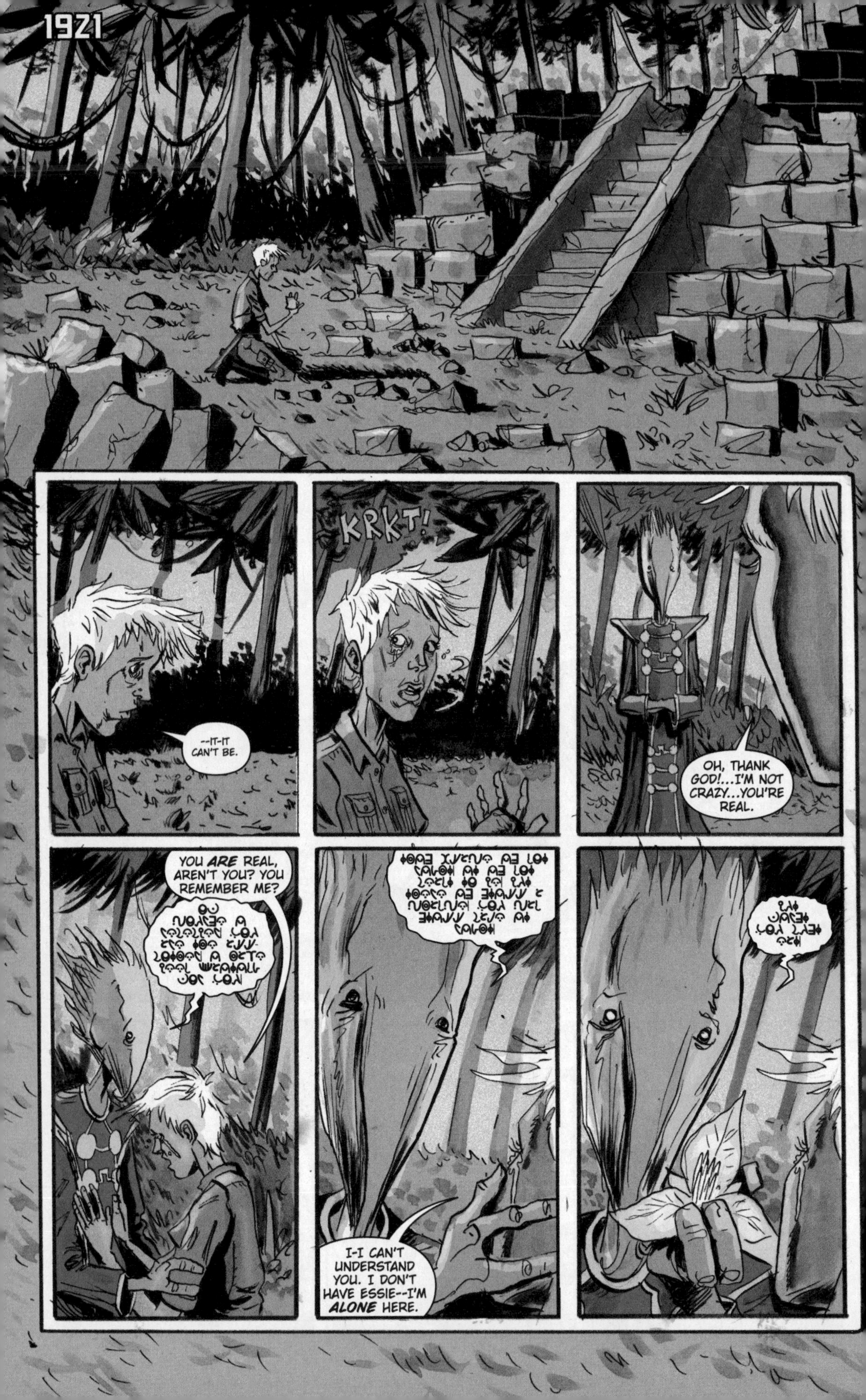
1921
--IT-IT CAN'T BE.
KRKT!
OH, THANK GOD!...I'M NOT CRAZY...YOU'RE REAL.
YOU ARE REAL, AREN'T YOU? YOU REMEMBER ME?
I-I CAN'T UNDERSTAND YOU. I DON'T HAVE ESSIE--I'M ALONE HERE.

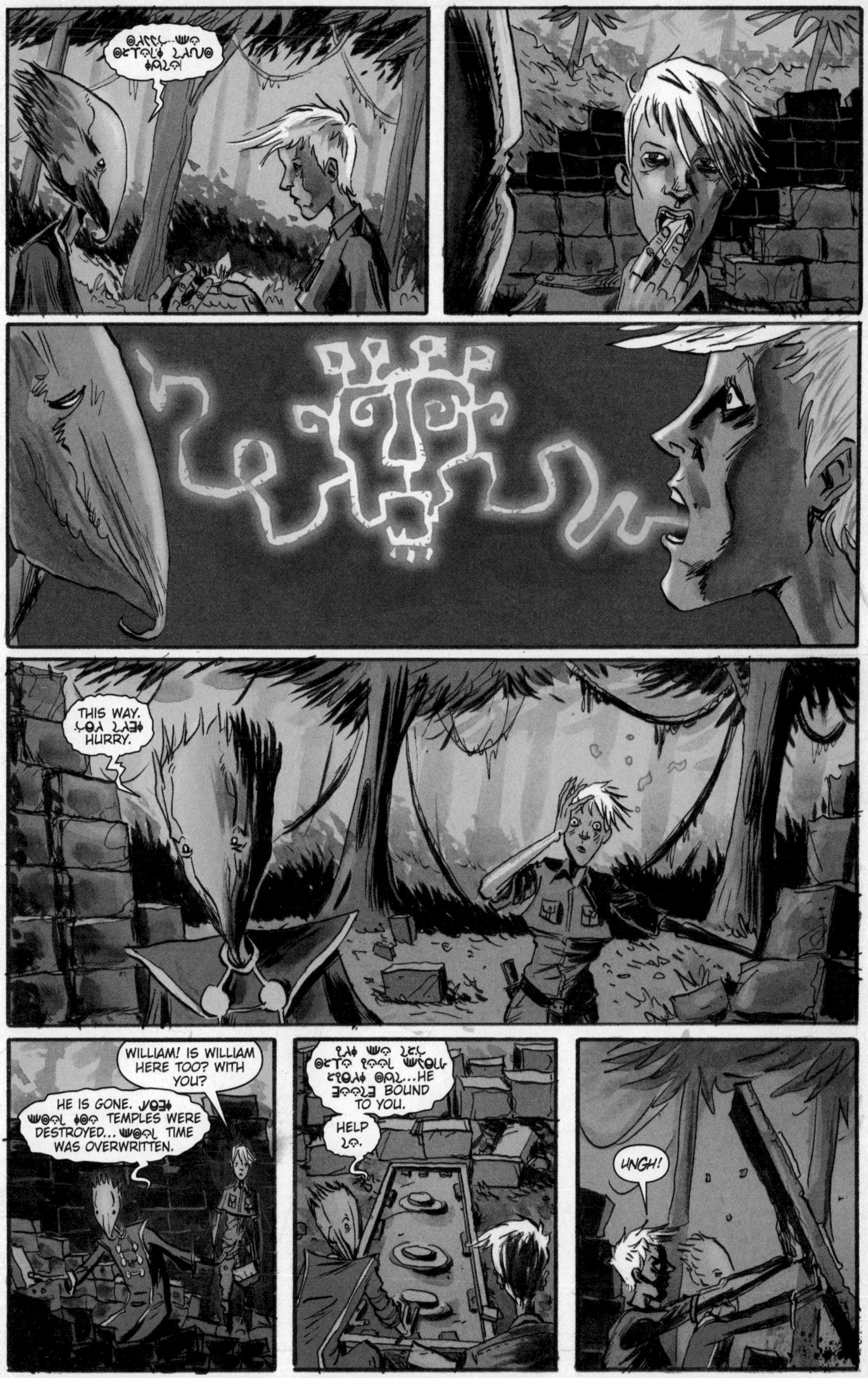
THIS WAY. HURRY.
WILLIAM! IS WILLIAM HERE TOO? WITH YOU?
HE IS GONE. TEMPLES WERE DESTROYED... TIME WAS OVERWRITTEN.
...HE BOUND TO YOU.
HELP
UNGH!

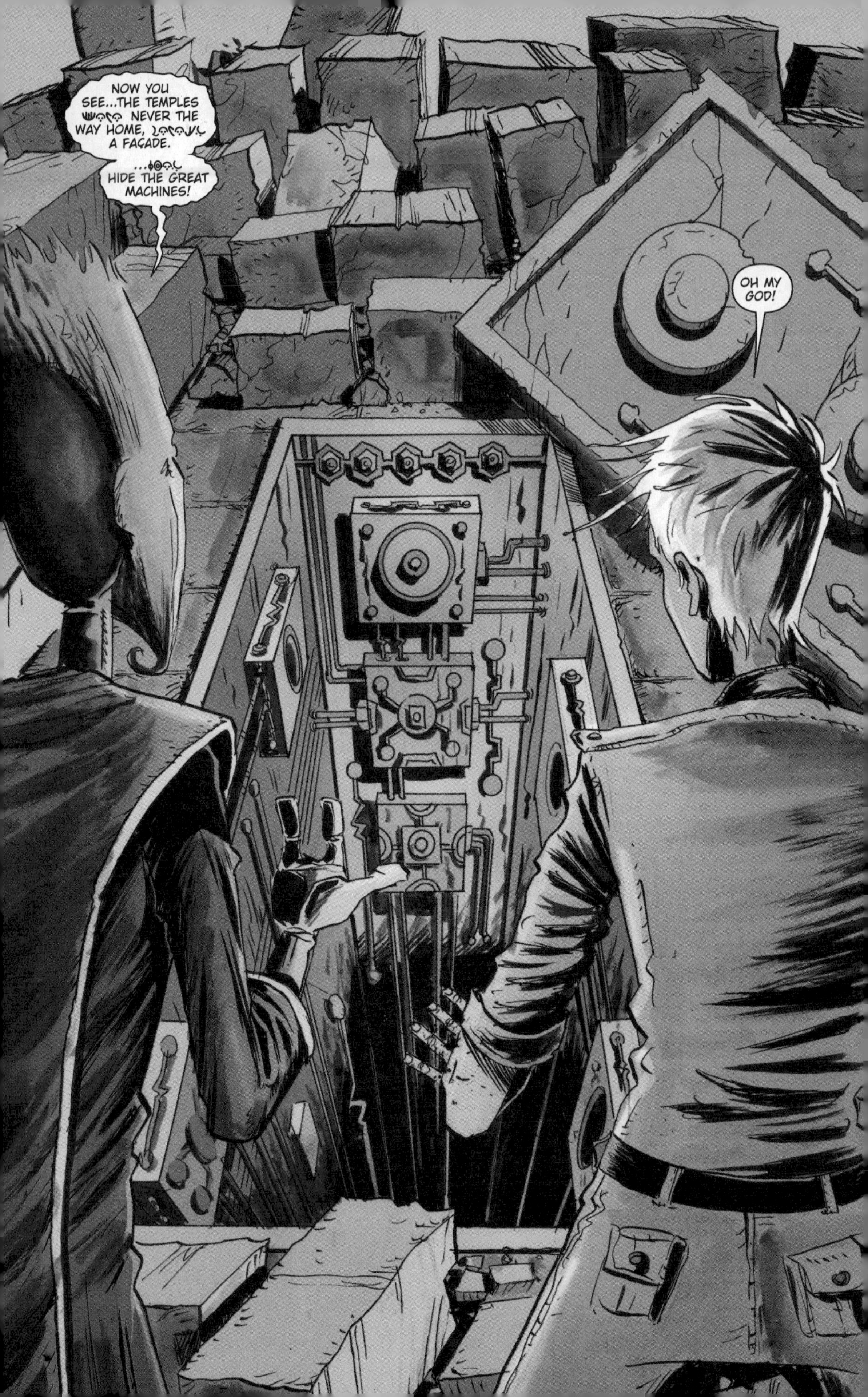
NOW YOU SEE...THE TEMPLES NEVER THE WAY HOME, A FAÇADE.
...HIDE THE GREAT MACHINES!
OH MY GOD!

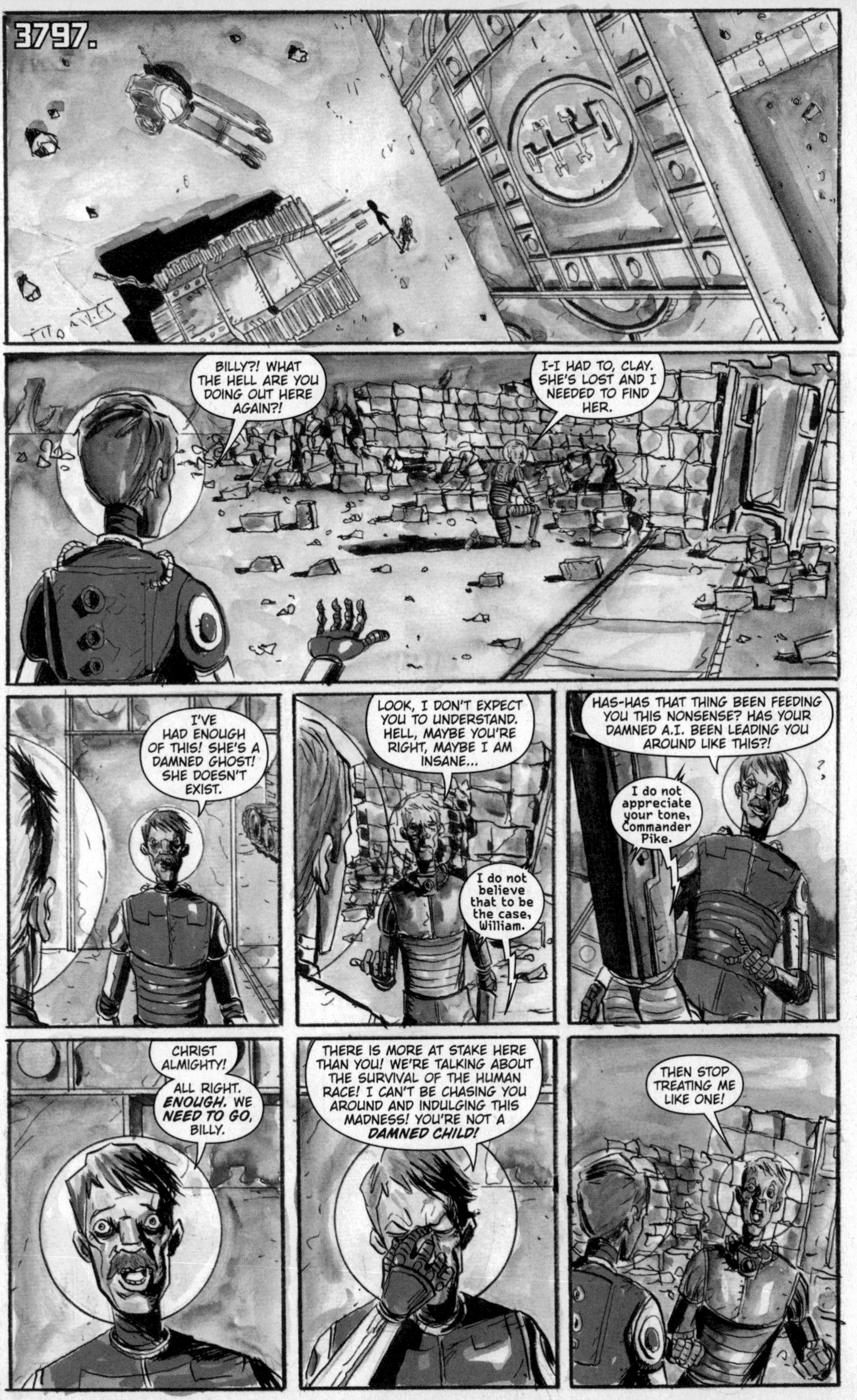
3797.
BILLY?! WHAT THE HELL ARE YOU DOING OUT HERE AGAIN?!
I-I HAD TO, CLAY. SHE'S LOST AND I NEEDED TO FIND HER.
I'VE HAD ENOUGH OF THIS! SHE'S A DAMNED GHOST! SHE DOESN'T EXIST.
LOOK, I DON'T EXPECT YOU TO UNDERSTAND. HELL, MAYBE YOU'RE RIGHT, MAYBE I AM INSANE...
I do not believe that to be the case, William.
HAS-HAS THAT THING BEEN FEEDING YOU THIS NONSENSE? HAS YOUR DAMNED A.I. BEEN LEADING YOU AROUND LIKE THIS?!
I do not appreciate your tone, Commander Pike.
CHRIST ALMIGHTY!
ALL RIGHT. ENOUGH. WE NEED TO GO, BILLY.
THERE IS MORE AT STAKE HERE THAN YOU! WE'RE TALKING ABOUT THE SURVIVAL OF THE HUMAN RACE! I CAN'T BE CHASING YOU AROUND AND INDULGING THIS MADNESS! YOU'RE NOT A DAMNED CHILD!
THEN STOP TREATING ME LIKE ONE!

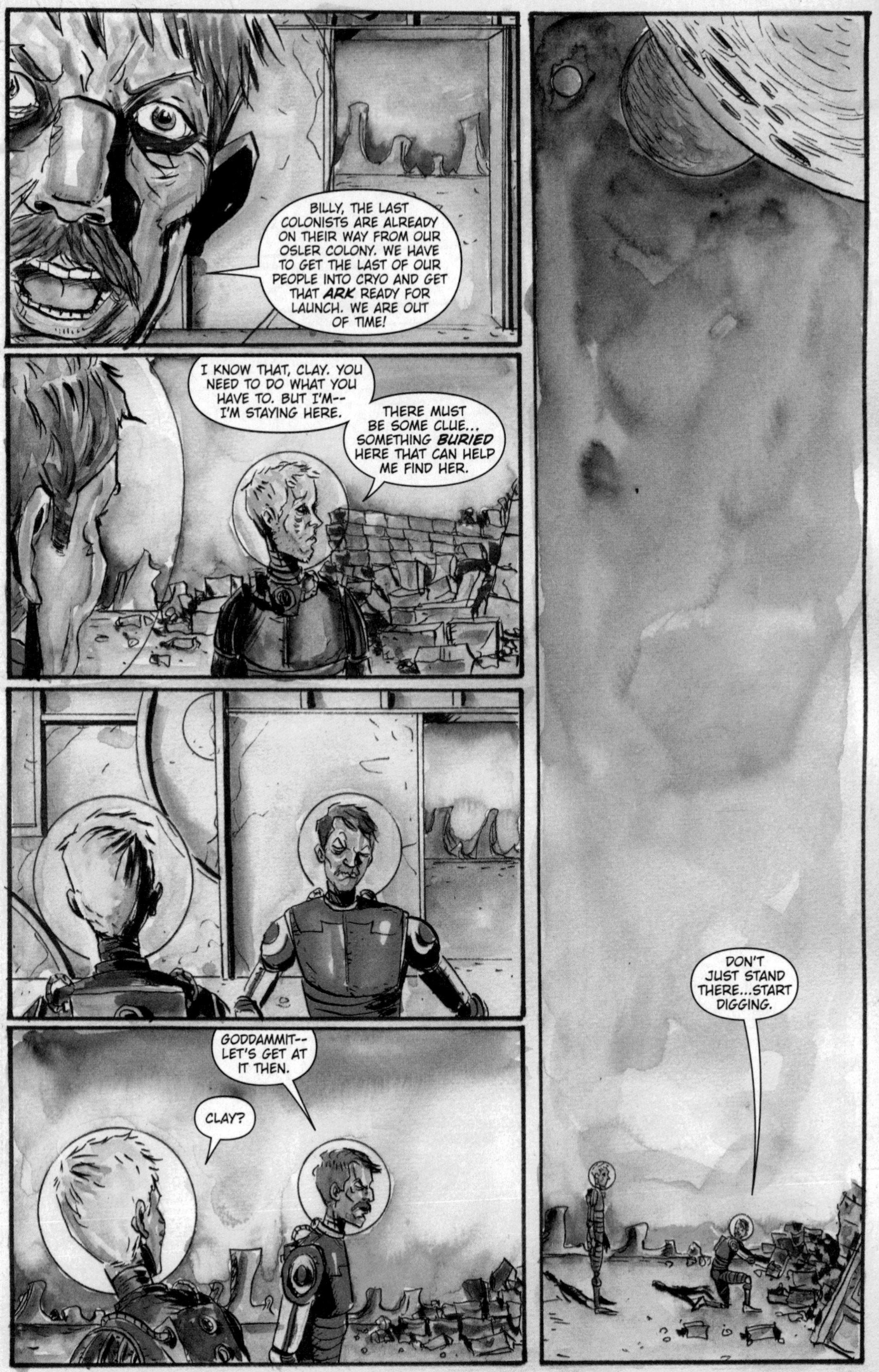
BILLY, THE LAST COLONISTS ARE ALREADY ON THEIR WAY FROM OUR OSLER COLONY. WE HAVE TO GET THE LAST OF OUR PEOPLE INTO CRYO AND GET THAT ARK READY FOR LAUNCH. WE ARE OUT OF TIME!
I KNOW THAT, CLAY. YOU NEED TO DO WHAT YOU HAVE TO. BUT I'M-- I'M STAYING HERE.
THERE MUST BE SOME CLUE... SOMETHING BURIED HERE THAT CAN HELP ME FIND HER.
GODDAMMIT-- LET'S GET AT IT THEN.
CLAY?
DON'T JUST STAND THERE...START DIGGING.

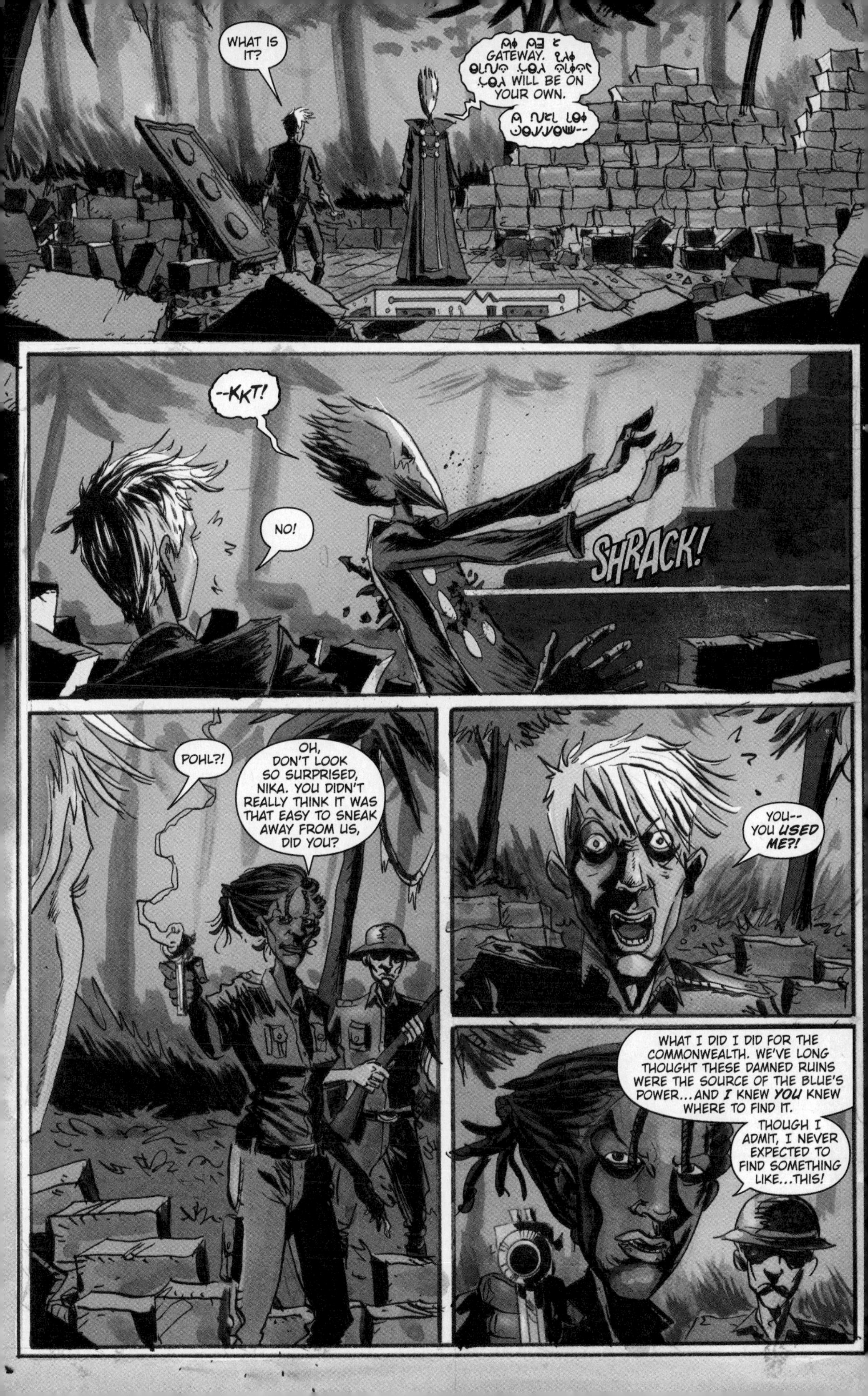

WHAT IS IT?
GATEWAY.
WILL BE ON YOUR OWN.
--KKT!
NO!
SHRACK!
POHL?!
OH, DON'T LOOK SO SURPRISED, NIKA. YOU DIDN'T REALLY THINK IT WAS THAT EASY TO SNEAK AWAY FROM US, DID YOU?
YOU-- YOU USED ME?!
WHAT I DID I DID FOR THE COMMONWEALTH. WE'VE LONG THOUGHT THESE DAMNED RUINS WERE THE SOURCE OF THE BLUE'S POWER...AND I KNEW YOU KNEW WHERE TO FIND IT.
THOUGH I ADMIT, I NEVER EXPECTED TO FIND SOMETHING LIKE...THIS!

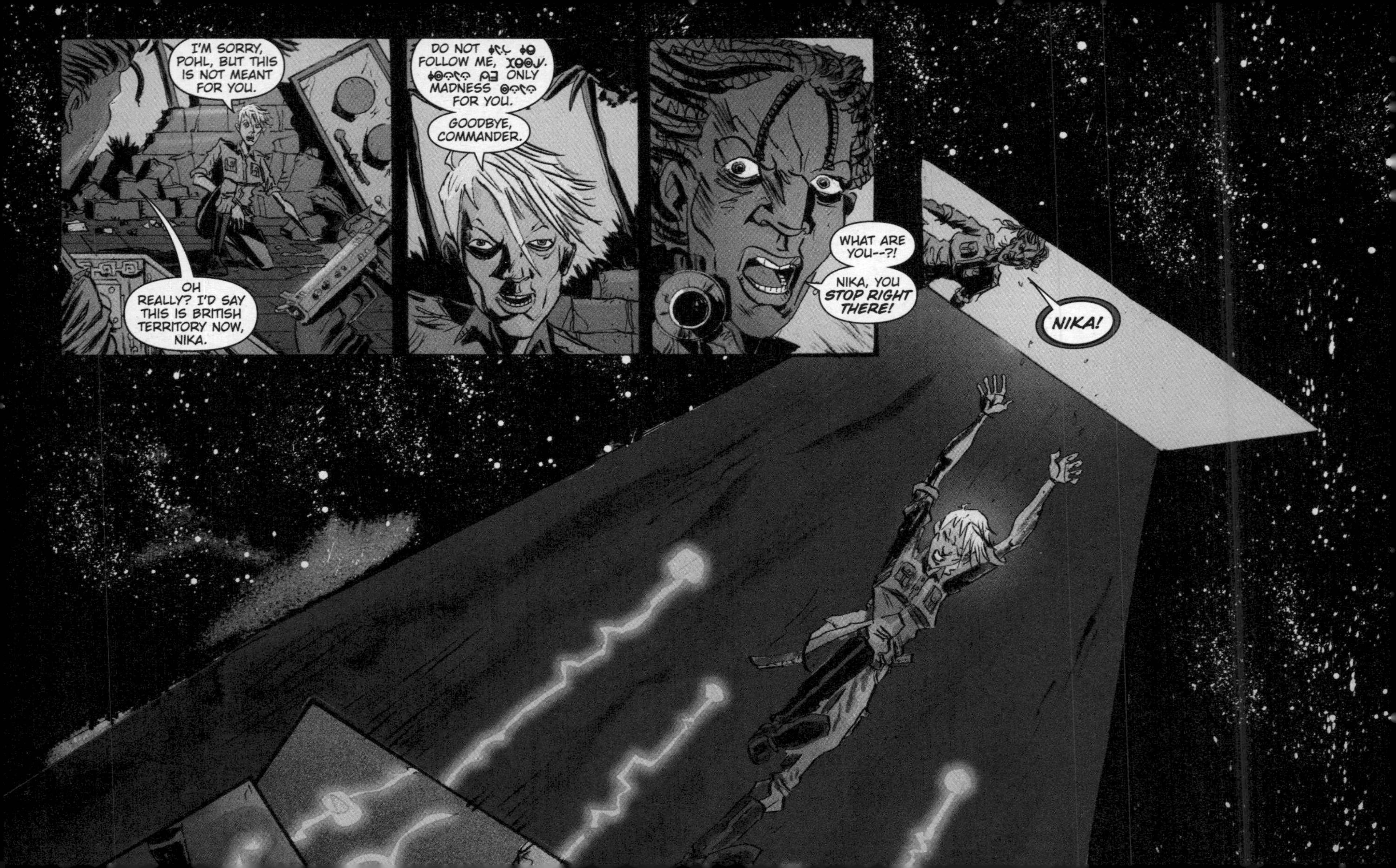

I'M SORRY, POHL, BUT THIS IS NOT MEANT FOR YOU.
OH REALLY? I'D SAY THIS IS BRITISH TERRITORY NOW, NIKA.
DO NOT FOLLOW ME, ONLY MADNESS FOR YOU.
GOODBYE, COMMANDER.
WHAT ARE YOU--?!
NIKA, YOU STOP RIGHT THERE!
NIKA!

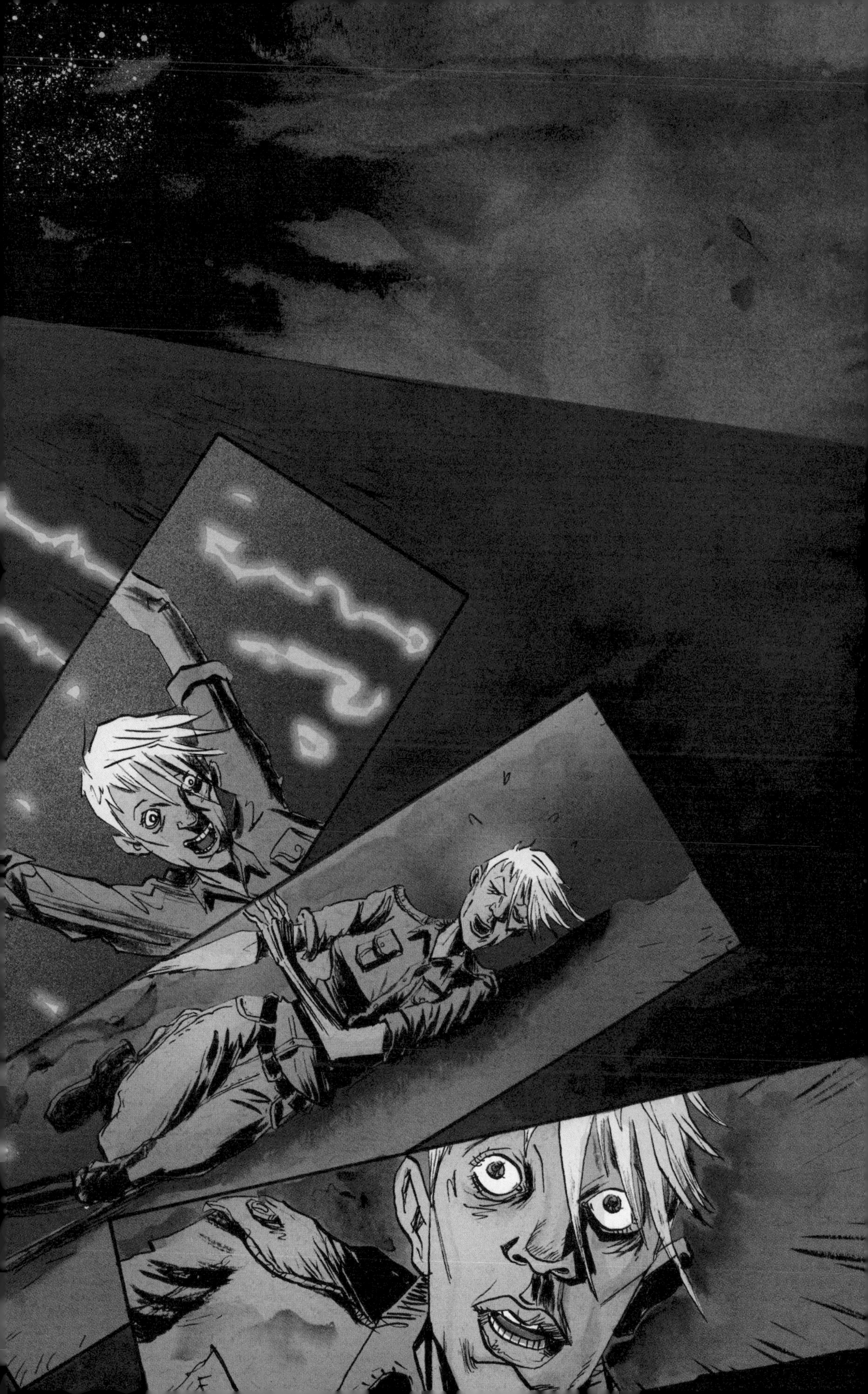

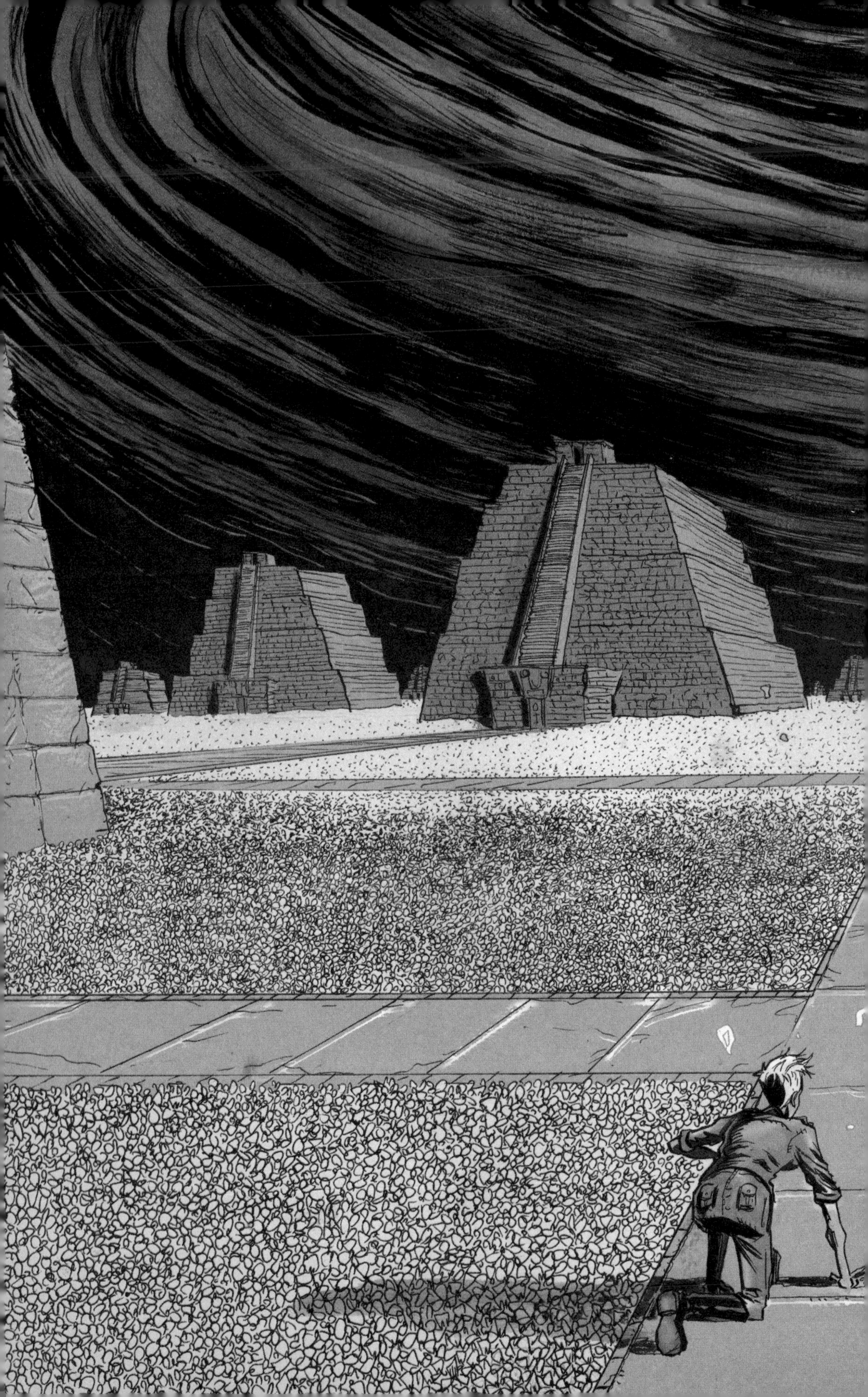

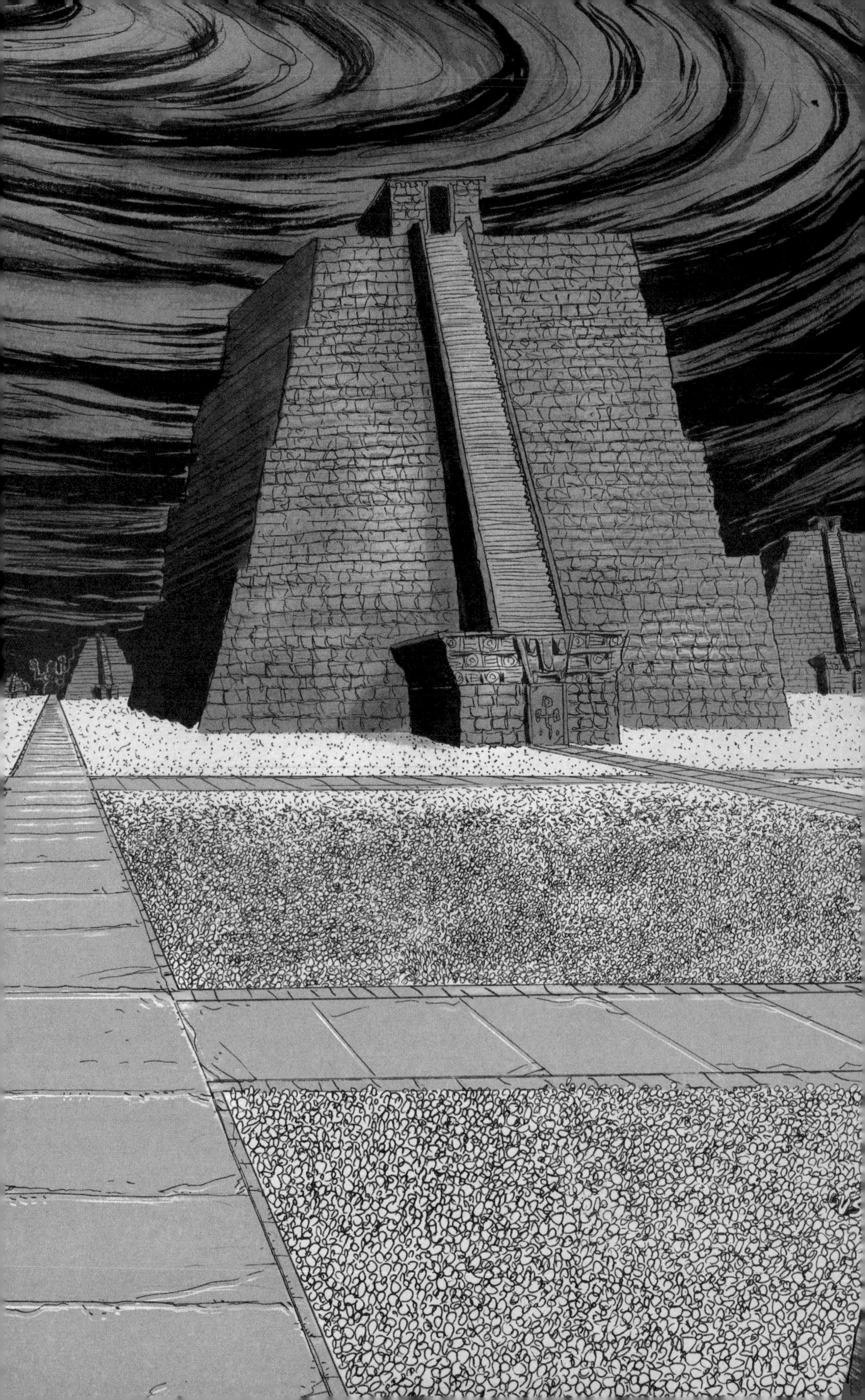

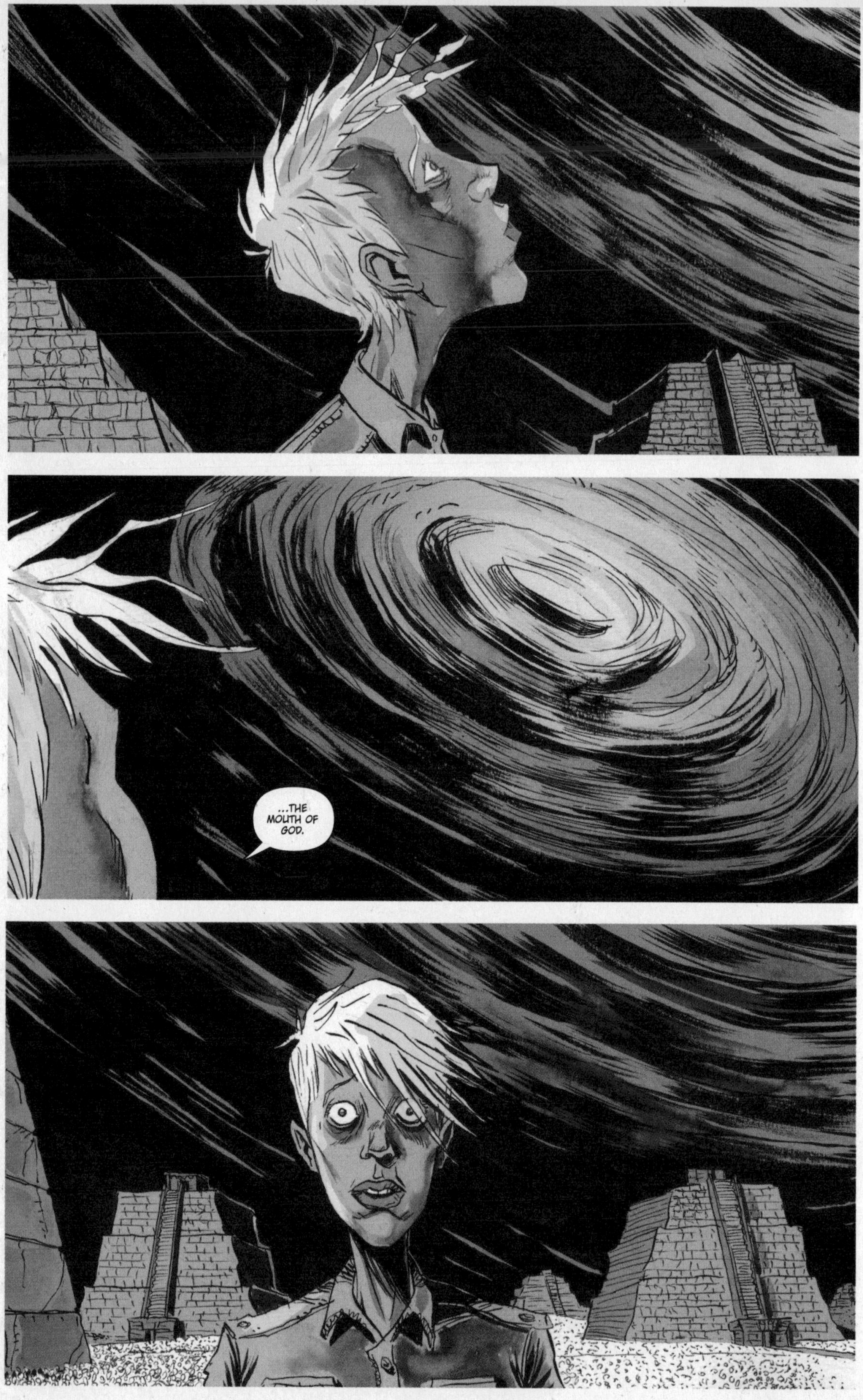
...THE MOUTH OF GOD.

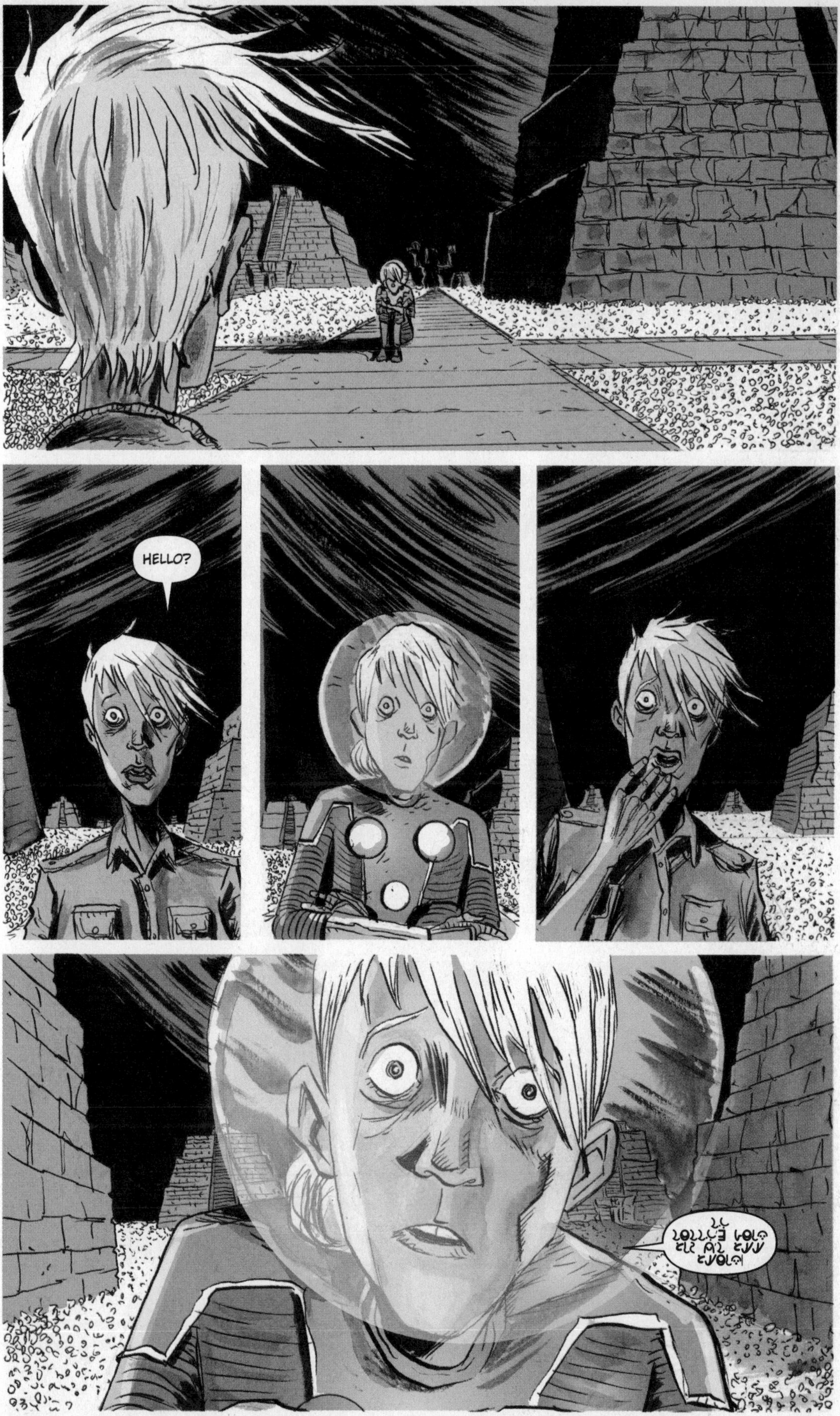
HELLO?

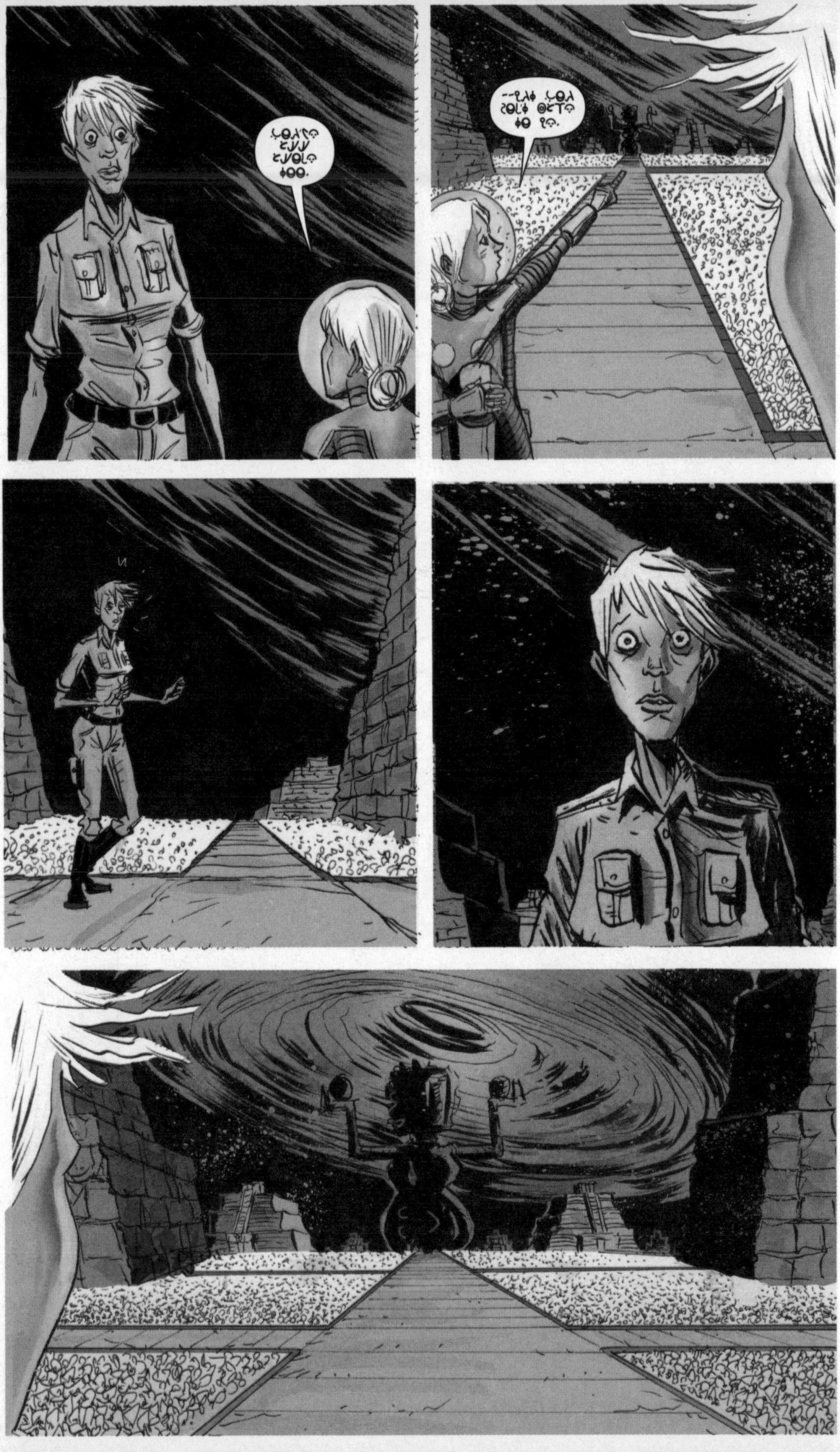

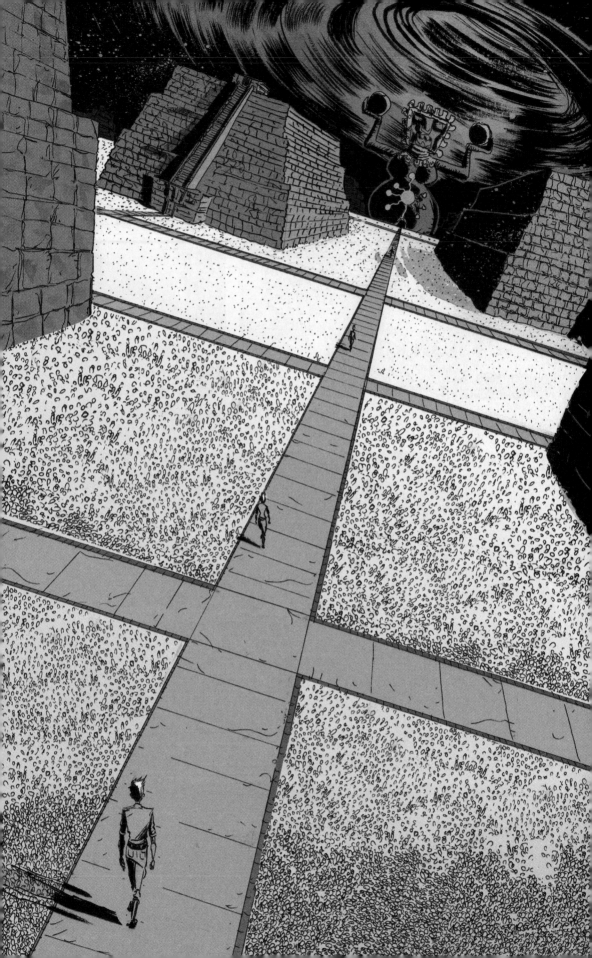

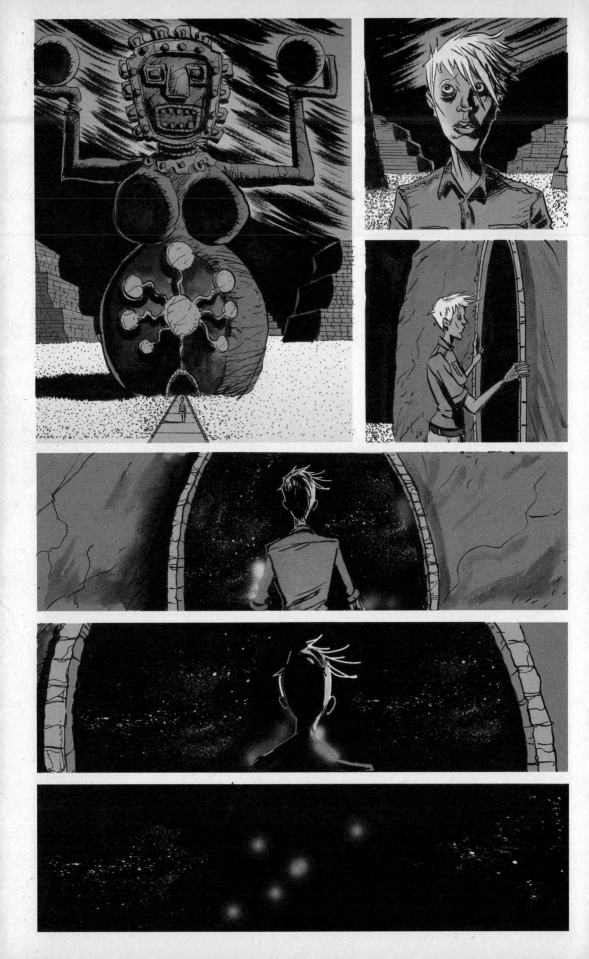

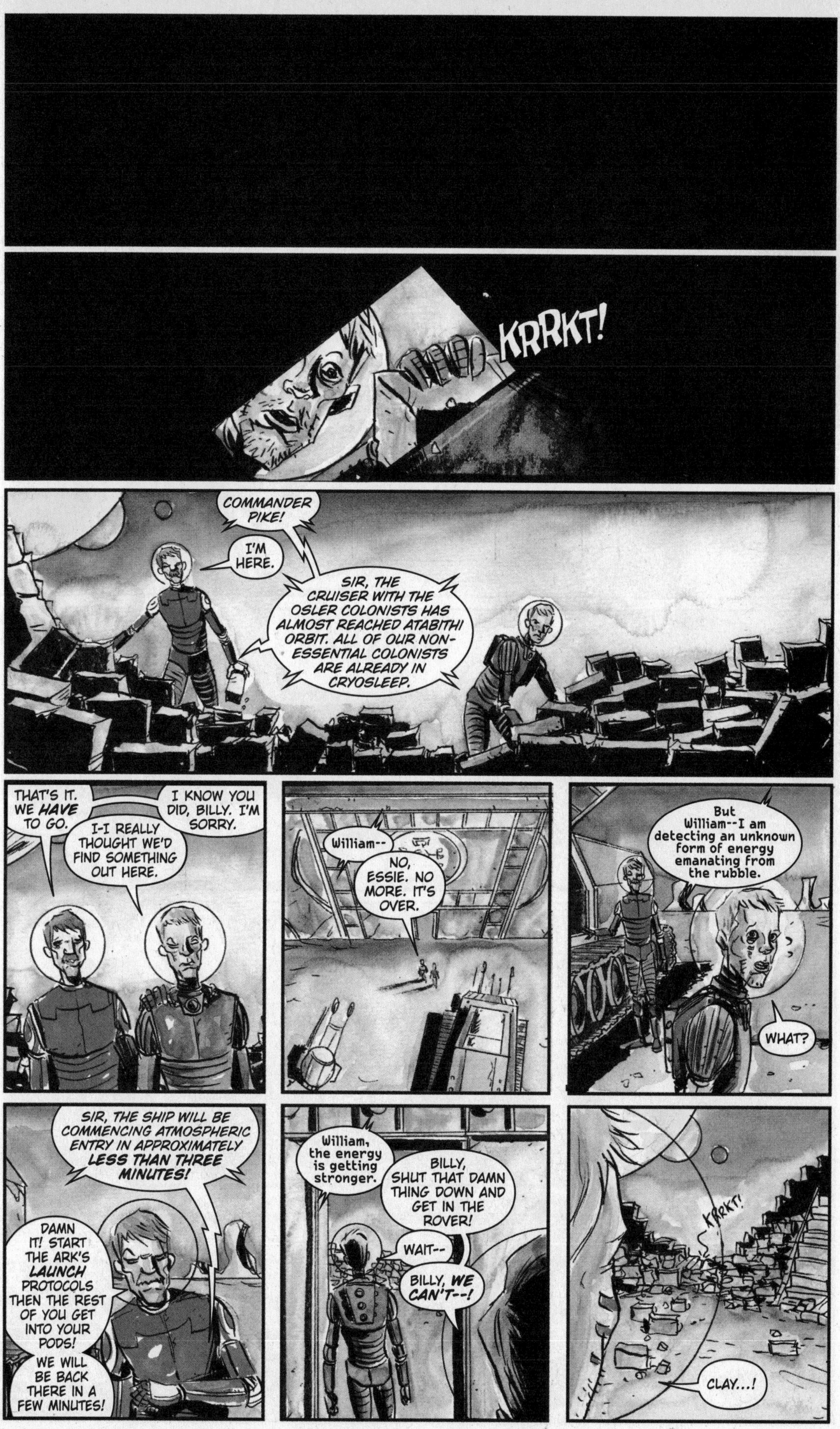
KRRKT!
COMMANDER PIKE!
I'M HERE.
SIR, THE CRUISER WITH THE OSLER COLONISTS HAS ALMOST REACHED ATABITHI ORBIT. ALL OF OUR NON-ESSENTIAL COLONISTS ARE ALREADY IN CRYOSLEEP.
THAT'S IT. WE HAVE TO GO.
I-I REALLY THOUGHT WE'D FIND SOMETHING OUT HERE.
I KNOW YOU DID, BILLY. I'M SORRY.
William--
NO, ESSIE. NO MORE. IT'S OVER.
But William--I am detecting an unknown form of energy emanating from the rubble.
WHAT?
SIR, THE SHIP WILL BE COMMENCING ATMOSPHERIC ENTRY IN APPROXIMATELY LESS THAN THREE MINUTES!
DAMN IT! START THE ARK'S LAUNCH PROTOCOLS THEN THE REST OF YOU GET INTO YOUR PODS!
WE WILL BE BACK THERE IN A FEW MINUTES!
William, the energy is getting stronger.
BILLY, SHUT THAT DAMN THING DOWN AND GET IN THE ROVER!
WAIT--
BILLY, WE CAN'T--!
KRRKT!
CLAY...!

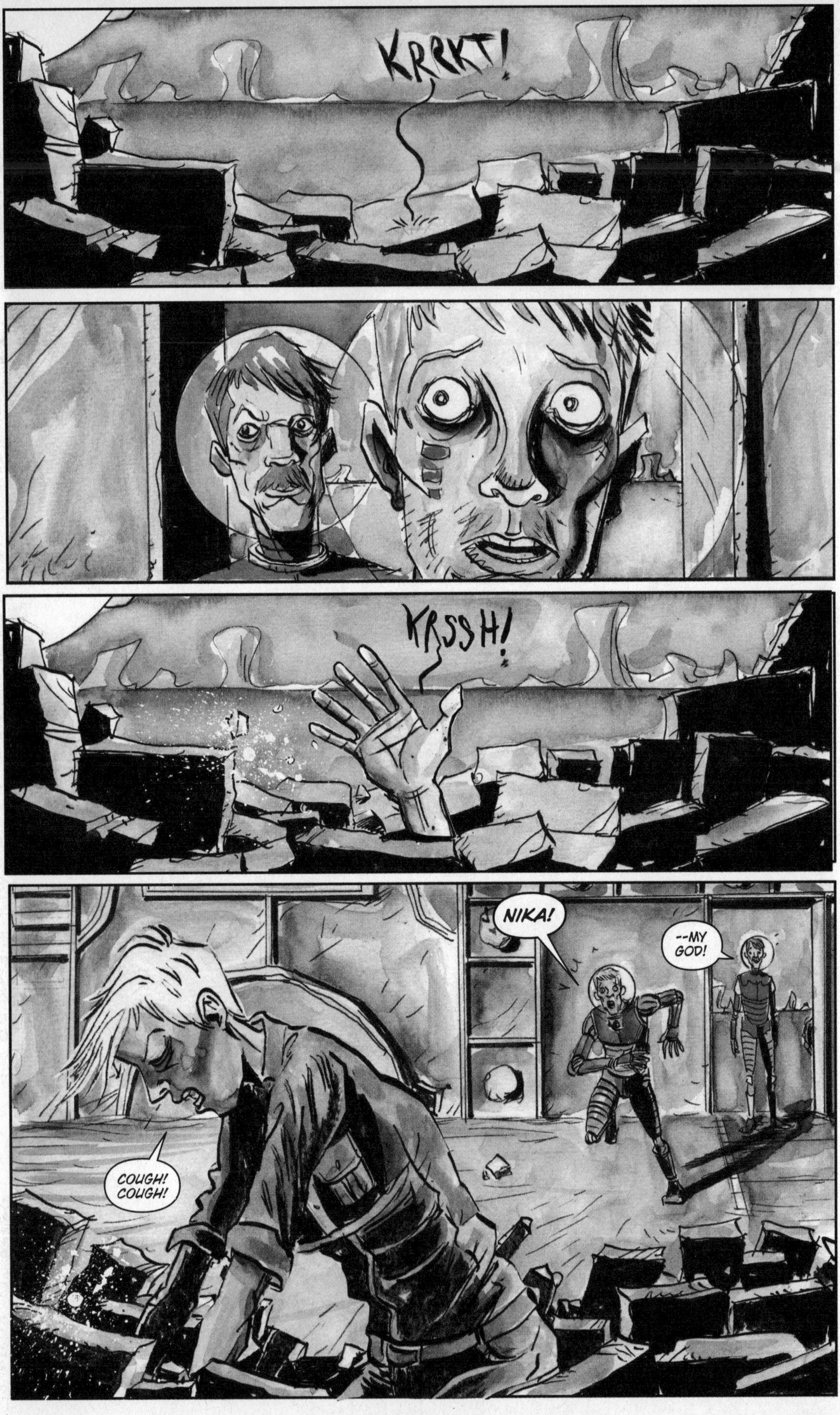
KRRKT!
KRSSH!
NIKA!
--MY GOD!
COUGH! COUGH!

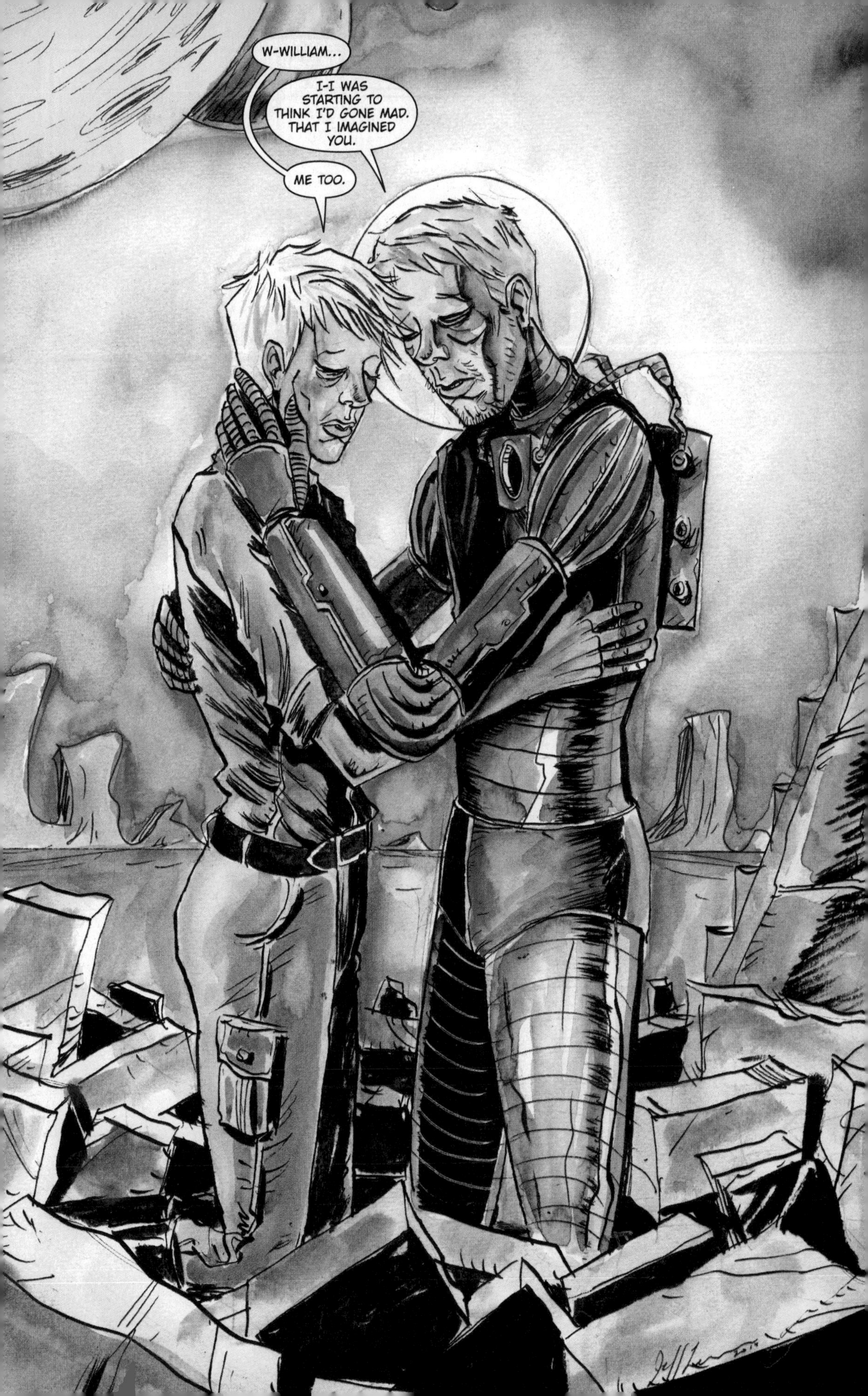
W-WILLIAM...
I-I WAS STARTING TO THINK I'D GONE MAD. THAT I IMAGINED YOU.
ME TOO.

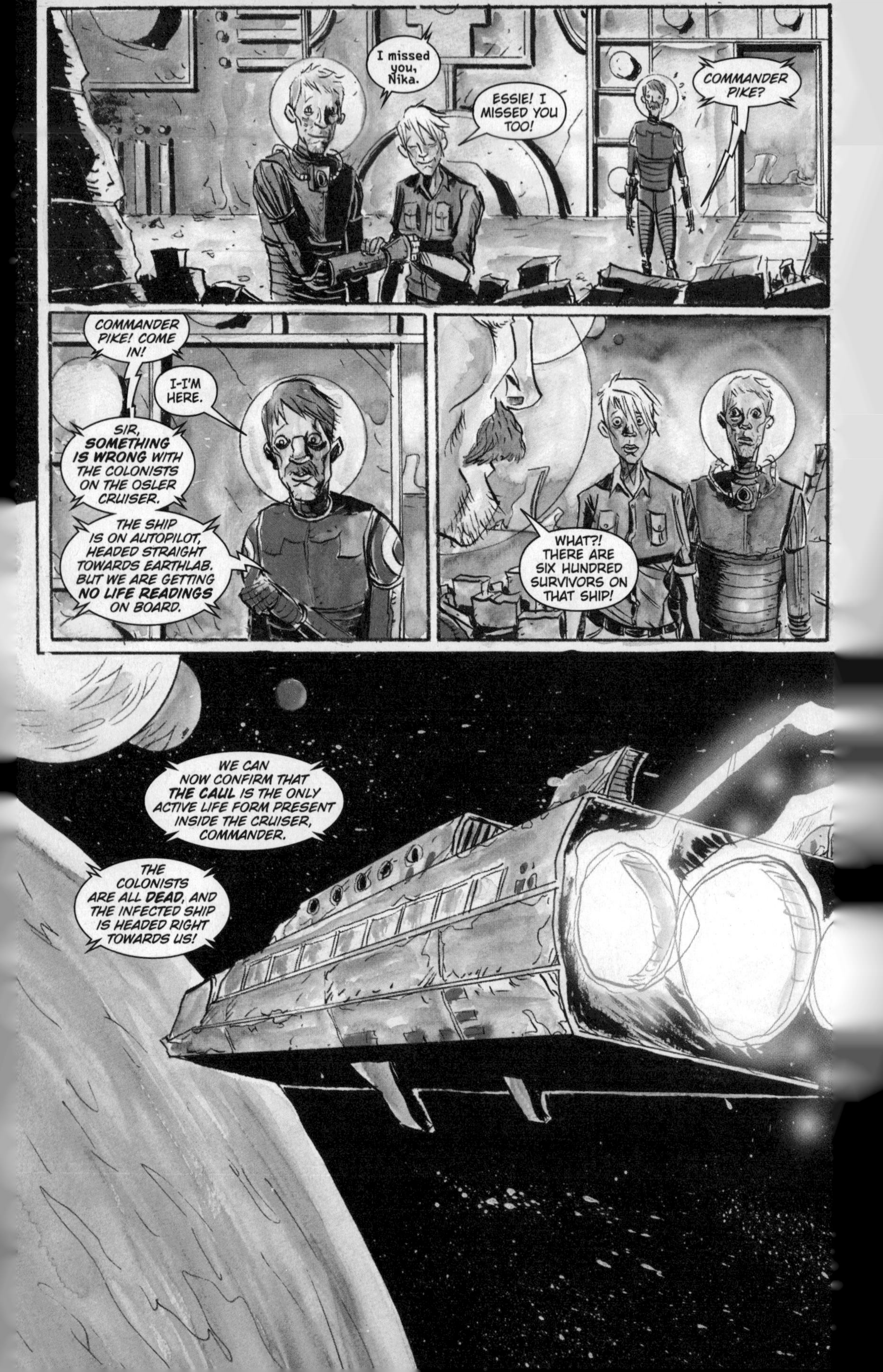
I missed you, Nika.
ESSIE! I MISSED YOU TOO!
COMMANDER PIKE?
COMMANDER PIKE! COME IN!
I-I'M HERE.
SIR, SOMETHING IS WRONG WITH THE COLONISTS ON THE OSLER CRUISER.
THE SHIP IS ON AUTOPILOT, HEADED STRAIGHT TOWARDS EARTHLAB. BUT WE ARE GETTING NO LIFE READINGS ON BOARD.
WHAT?! THERE ARE SIX HUNDRED SURVIVORS ON THAT SHIP!
WE CAN NOW CONFIRM THAT THE CAUL IS THE ONLY ACTIVE LIFE FORM PRESENT INSIDE THE CRUISER, COMMANDER.
THE COLONISTS ARE ALL DEAD, AND THE INFECTED SHIP IS HEADED RIGHT TOWARDS US!

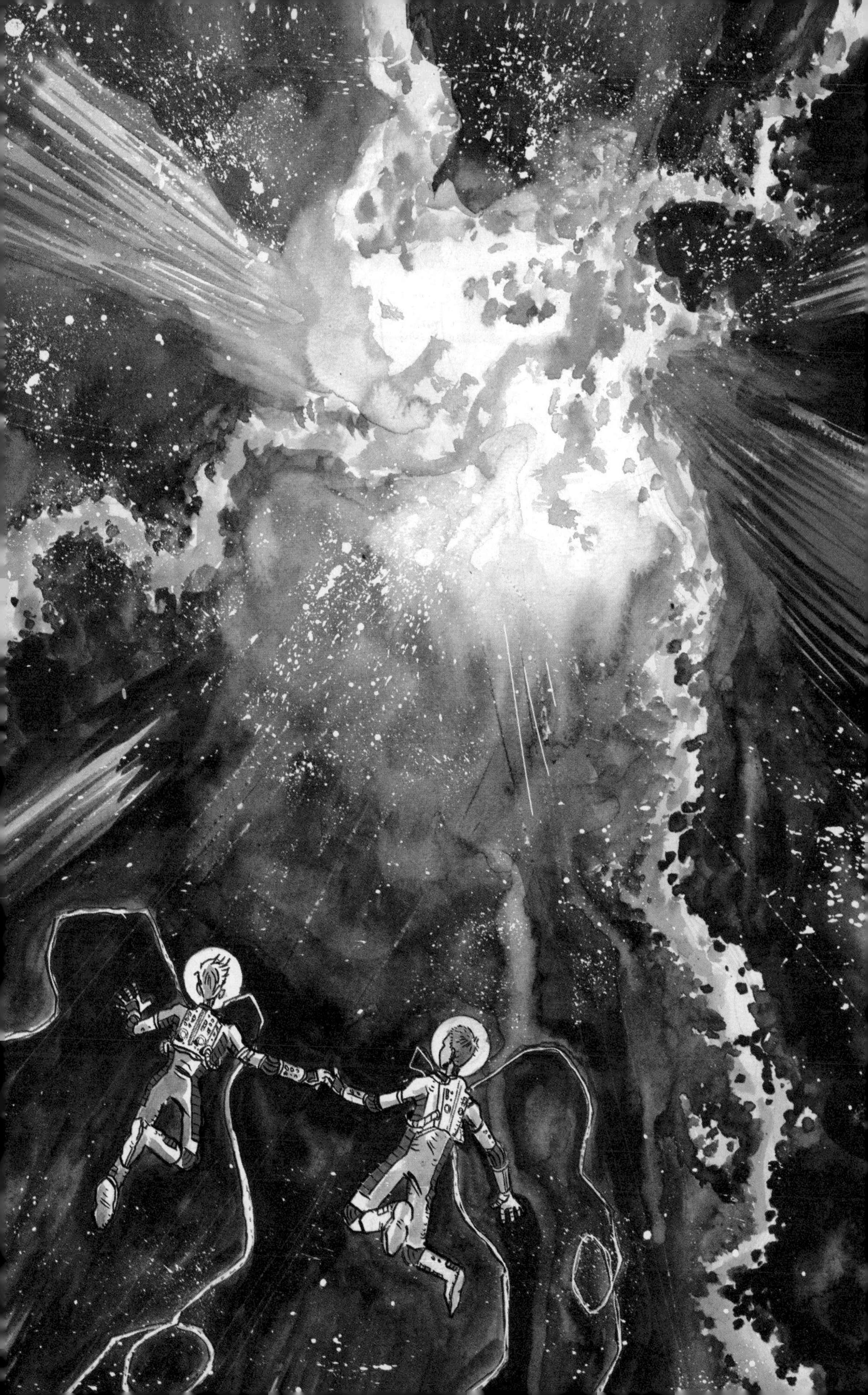

CHAPTER 8: TWO STARS BECOME ONE

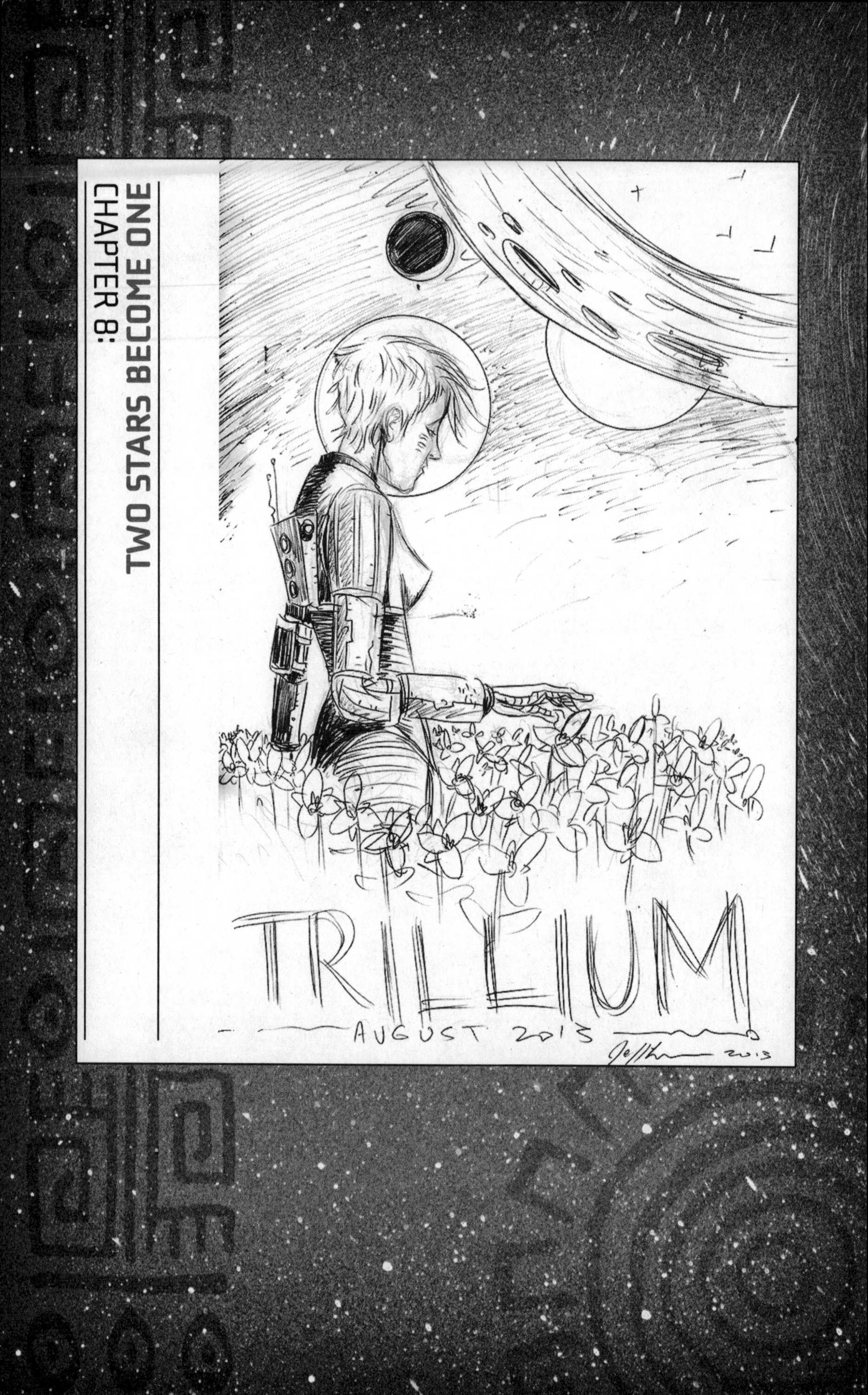
TRILLIUM
AUGUST 2013
2013

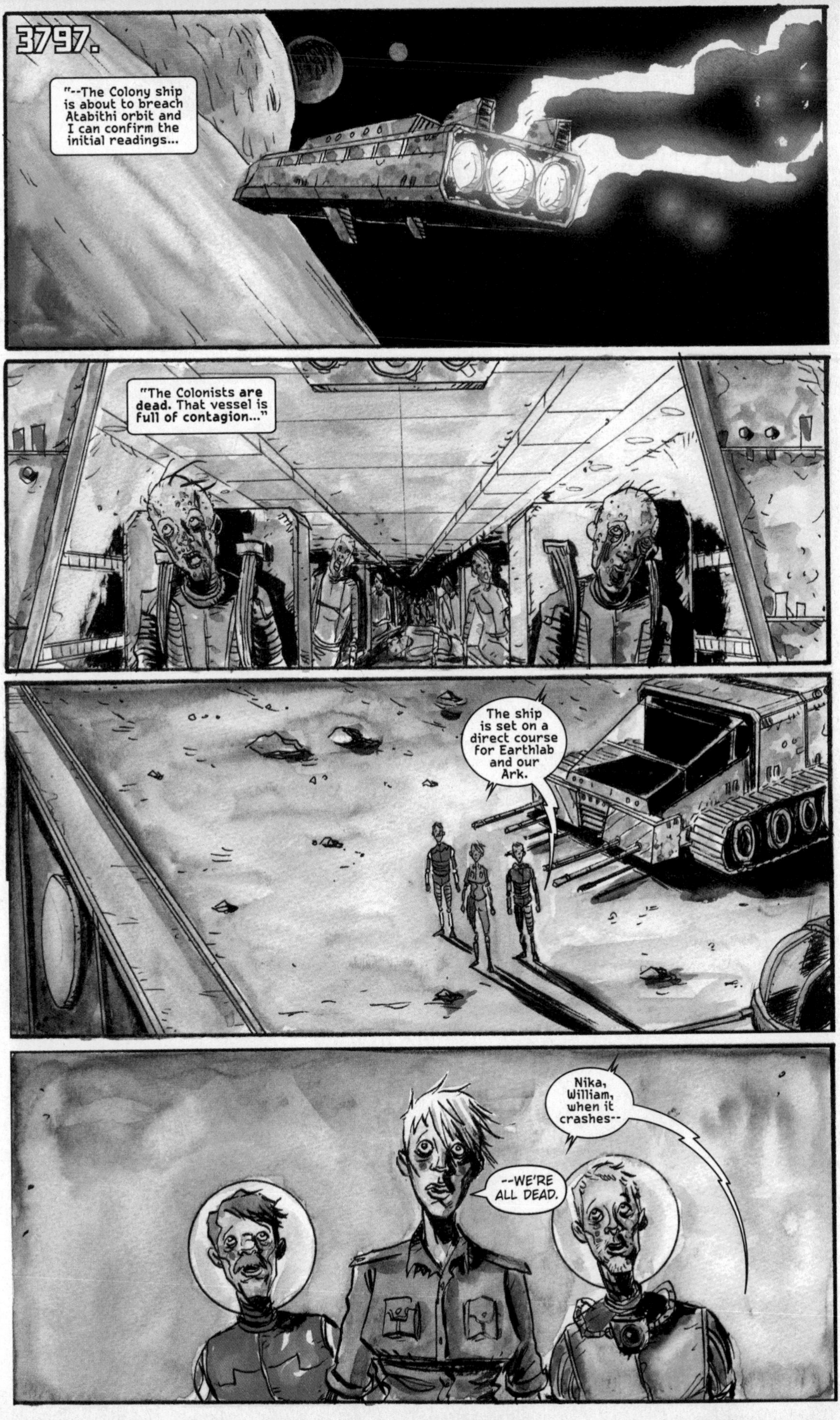
3797.
"--The Colony ship is about to breach Atabithi orbit and I can confirm the initial readings...
"The Colonists are dead. That vessel is full of contagion..."
The ship is set on a direct course for Earthlab and our Ark.
Nika, William, when it crashes--
--WE'RE ALL DEAD.

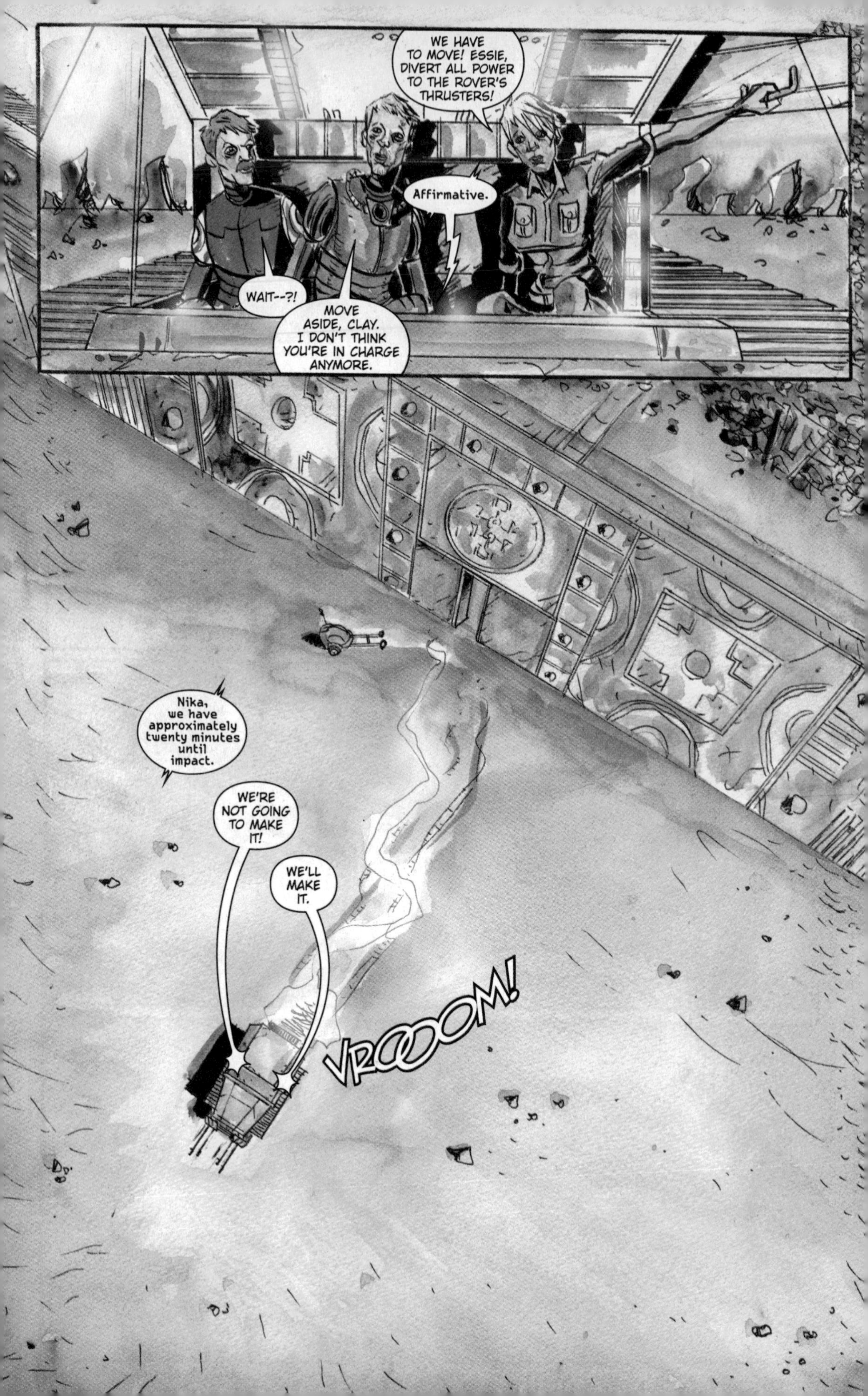
WE HAVE TO MOVE! ESSIE, DIVERT ALL POWER TO THE ROVER'S THRUSTERS!
Affirmative.
WAIT--?!
MOVE ASIDE, CLAY. I DON'T THINK YOU'RE IN CHARGE ANYMORE.
Nika, we have approximately twenty minutes until impact.
WE'RE NOT GOING TO MAKE IT!
WE'LL MAKE IT.
VROOOM!

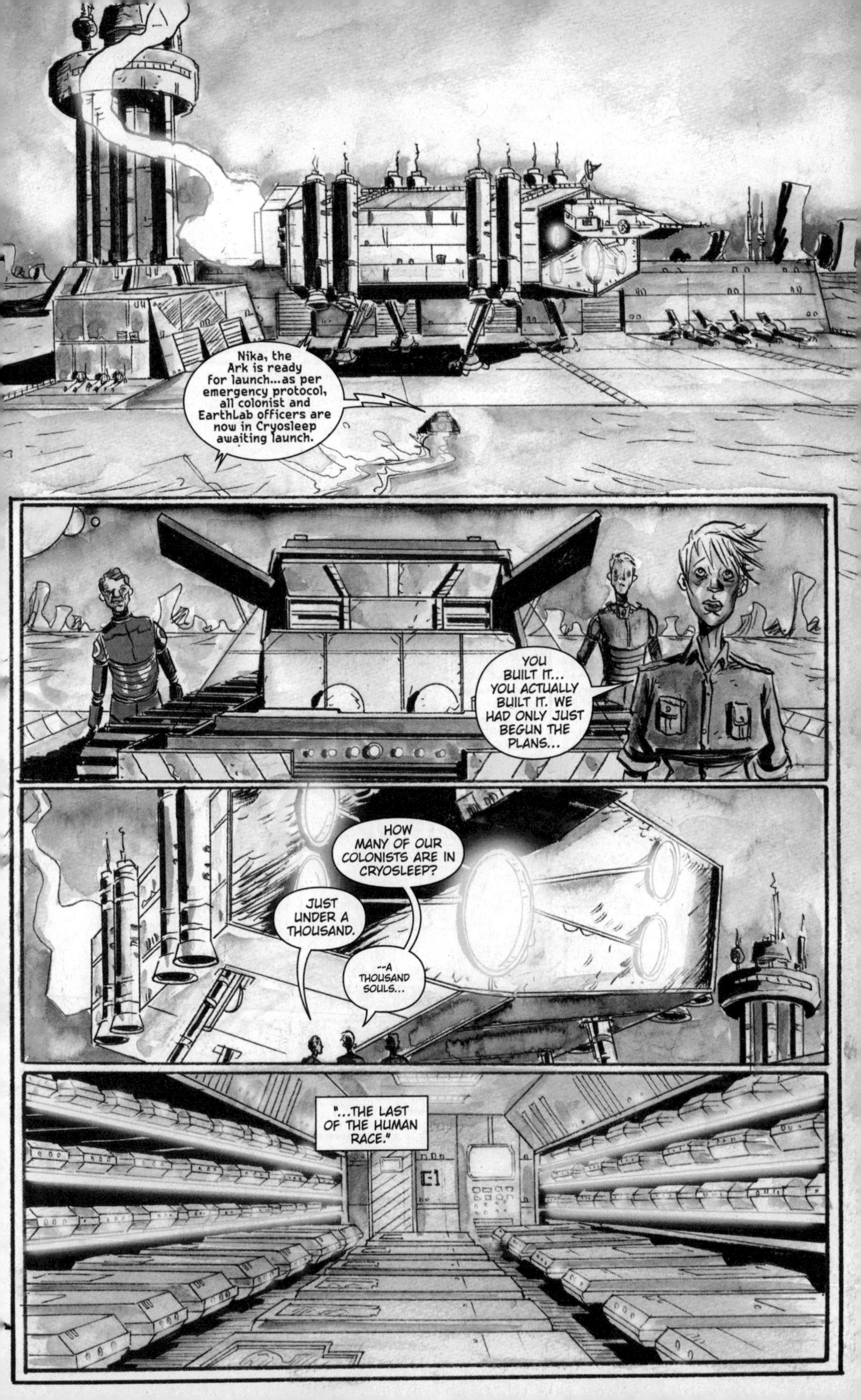
Nika, the Ark is ready for launch...as per emergency protocol, all colonist and EarthLab officers are now in Cryosleep awaiting launch.
YOU BUILT IT... YOU ACTUALLY BUILT IT. WE HAD ONLY JUST BEGUN THE PLANS...
HOW MANY OF OUR COLONISTS ARE IN CRYOSLEEP?
JUST UNDER A THOUSAND.
--A THOUSAND SOULS...
"...THE LAST OF THE HUMAN RACE."
E1

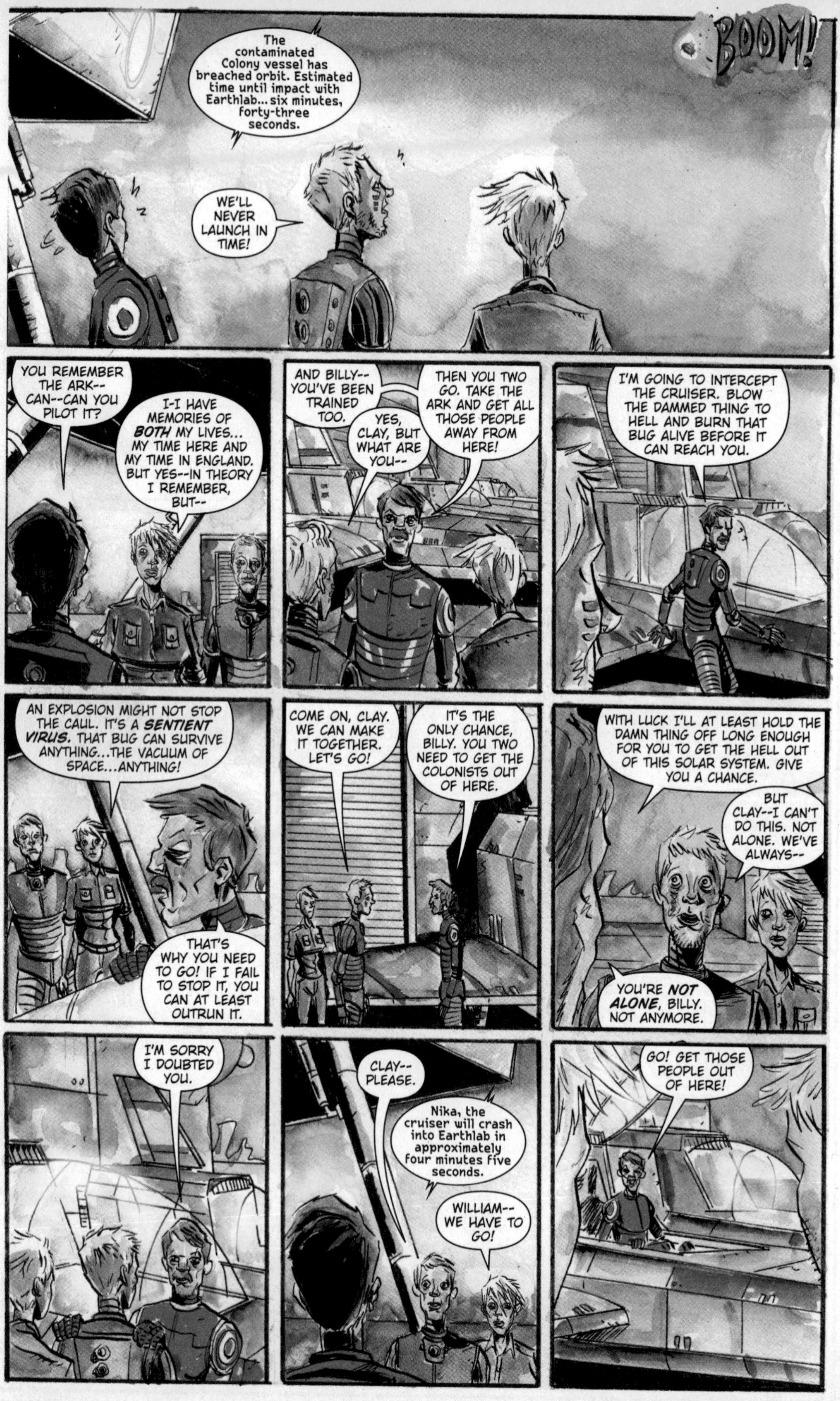
BOOM!
The contaminated Colony vessel has breached orbit. Estimated time until impact with Earthlab... six minutes, forty-three seconds.
WE'LL NEVER LAUNCH IN TIME!
YOU REMEMBER THE ARK-- CAN--CAN YOU PILOT IT?
I-I HAVE MEMORIES OF BOTH MY LIVES... MY TIME HERE AND MY TIME IN ENGLAND. BUT YES--IN THEORY I REMEMBER, BUT--
AND BILLY-- YOU'VE BEEN TRAINED TOO.
YES, CLAY, BUT WHAT ARE YOU--
THEN YOU TWO GO. TAKE THE ARK AND GET ALL THOSE PEOPLE AWAY FROM HERE!
I'M GOING TO INTERCEPT THE CRUISER. BLOW THE DAMMED THING TO HELL AND BURN THAT BUG ALIVE BEFORE IT CAN REACH YOU.
AN EXPLOSION MIGHT NOT STOP THE CAUL. IT'S A SENTIENT VIRUS. THAT BUG CAN SURVIVE ANYTHING...THE VACUUM OF SPACE...ANYTHING!
THAT'S WHY YOU NEED TO GO! IF I FAIL TO STOP IT, YOU CAN AT LEAST OUTRUN IT.
COME ON, CLAY. WE CAN MAKE IT TOGETHER. LET'S GO!
IT'S THE ONLY CHANCE, BILLY. YOU TWO NEED TO GET THE COLONISTS OUT OF HERE.
WITH LUCK I'LL AT LEAST HOLD THE DAMN THING OFF LONG ENOUGH FOR YOU TO GET THE HELL OUT OF THIS SOLAR SYSTEM. GIVE YOU A CHANCE.
BUT CLAY--I CAN'T DO THIS. NOT ALONE. WE'VE ALWAYS--
YOU'RE NOT ALONE, BILLY. NOT ANYMORE.
I'M SORRY I DOUBTED YOU.
CLAY-- PLEASE.
Nika, the cruiser will crash into Earthlab in approximately four minutes five seconds.
WILLIAM-- WE HAVE TO GO!
GO! GET THOSE PEOPLE OUT OF HERE!

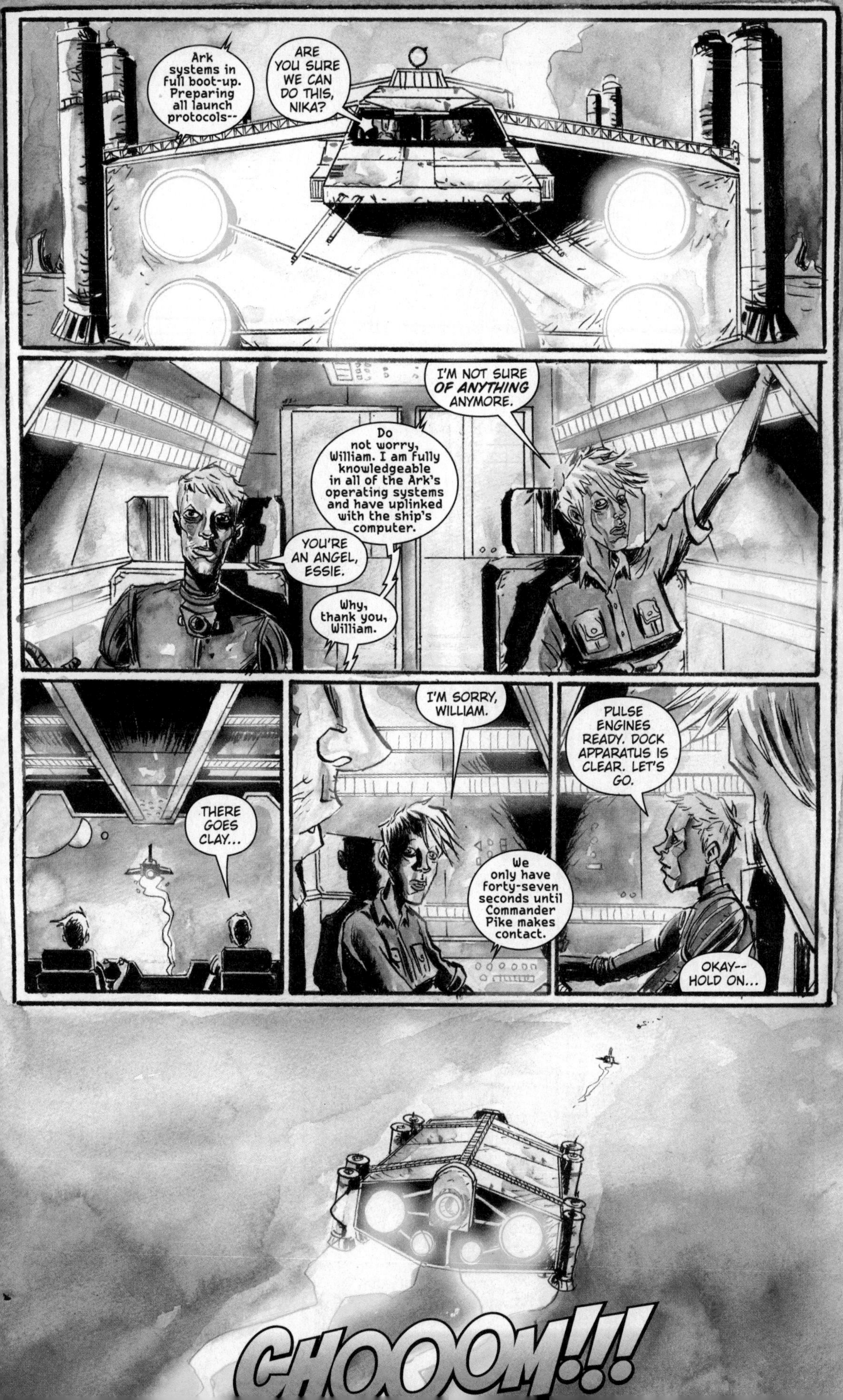
Ark systems in full boot-up. Preparing all launch protocols--
ARE YOU SURE WE CAN DO THIS, NIKA?
I'M NOT SURE OF *ANYTHING* ANYMORE.
Do not worry, William. I am fully knowledgeable in all of the Ark's operating systems and have uplinked with the ship's computer.
YOU'RE AN ANGEL, ESSIE.
Why, thank you, William.
THERE GOES CLAY...
I'M SORRY, WILLIAM.
We only have forty-seven seconds until Commander Pike makes contact.
PULSE ENGINES READY. DOCK APPARATUS IS CLEAR. LET'S GO.
OKAY-- HOLD ON...
CHOOOM!!!

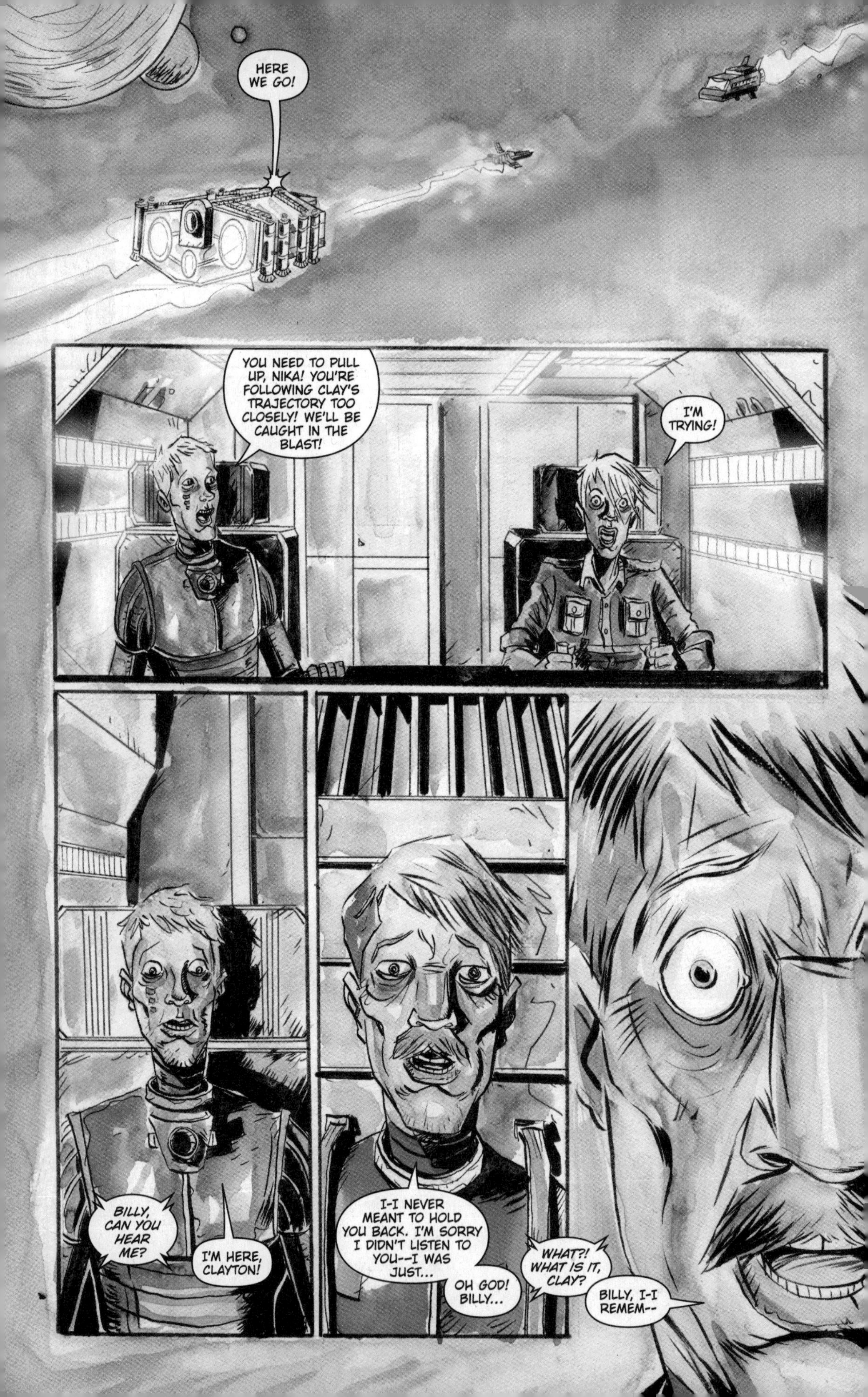
HERE WE GO!
YOU NEED TO PULL UP, NIKA! YOU'RE FOLLOWING CLAY'S TRAJECTORY TOO CLOSELY! WE'LL BE CAUGHT IN THE BLAST!
I'M TRYING!
BILLY, CAN YOU HEAR ME?
I'M HERE, CLAYTON!
I-I NEVER MEANT TO HOLD YOU BACK. I'M SORRY I DIDN'T LISTEN TO YOU--I WAS JUST...
OH GOD! BILLY...
WHAT?! WHAT IS IT, CLAY?
BILLY, I-I REMEM--

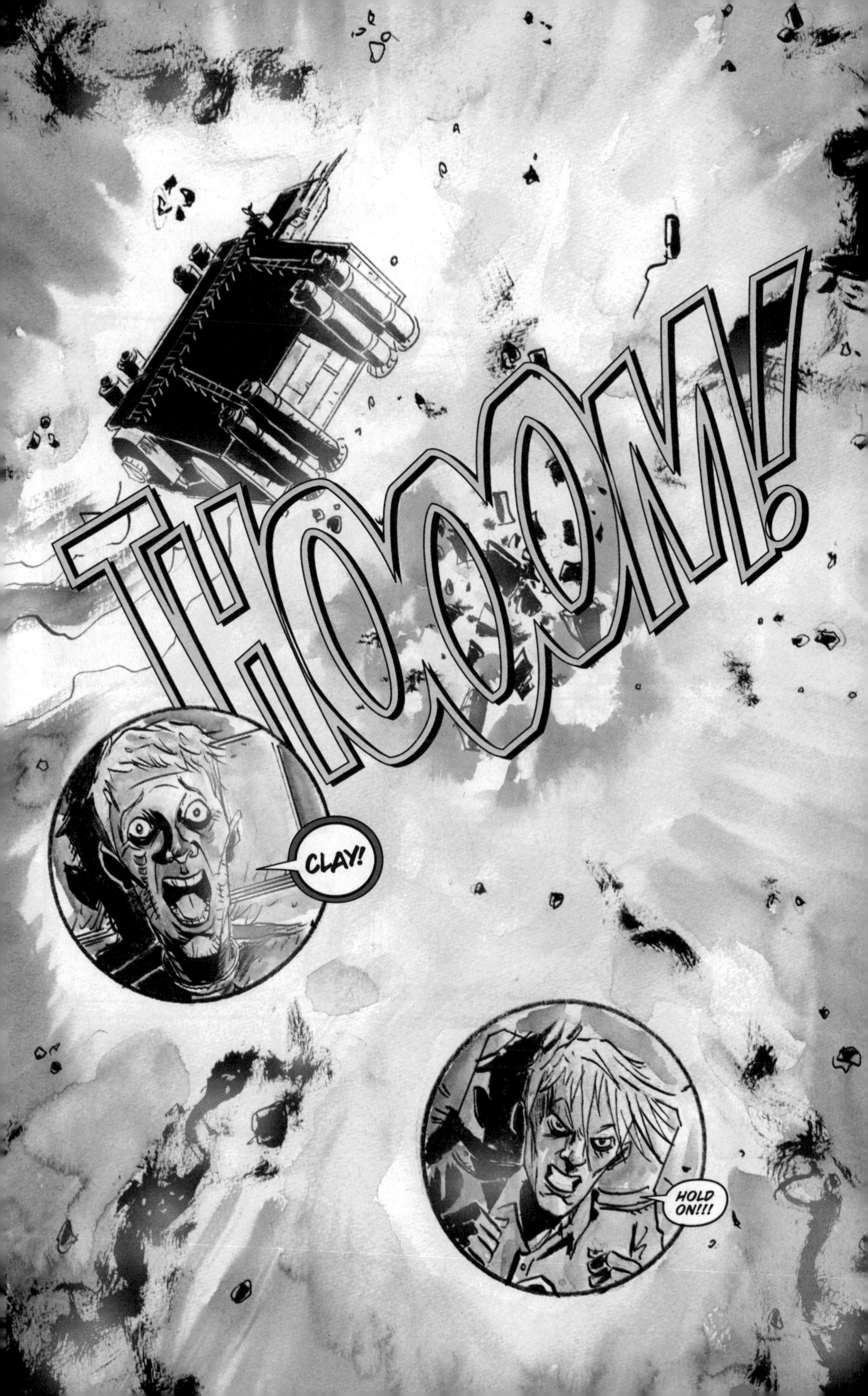
THOOOM!
CLAY!
HOLD ON!!!

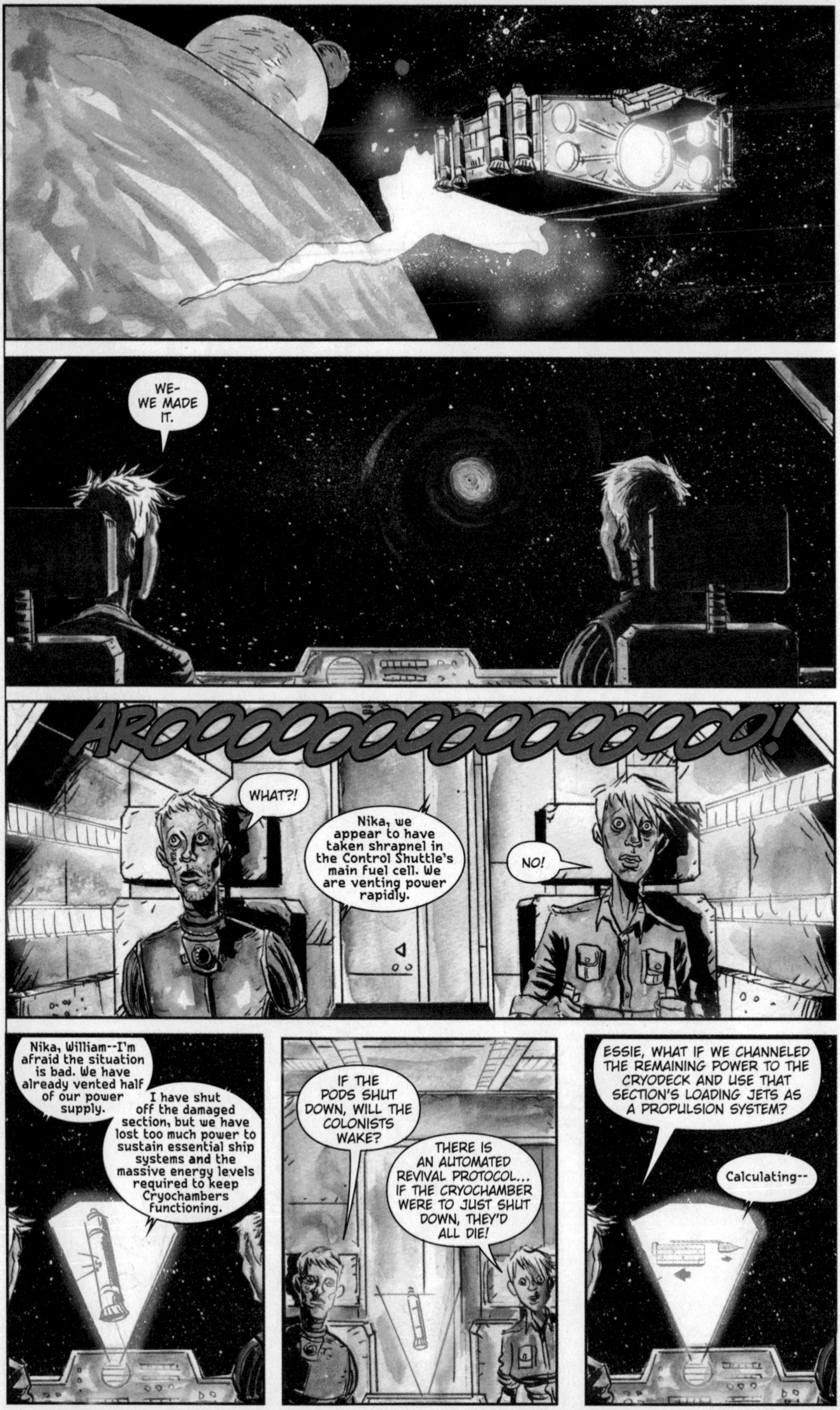
WE- WE MADE IT.
AROOOOOOOOOOOOOOOO!
WHAT?!
Nika, we appear to have taken shrapnel in the Control Shuttle's main fuel cell. We are venting power rapidly.
NO!
Nika, William--I'm afraid the situation is bad. We have already vented half of our power supply.
I have shut off the damaged section, but we have lost too much power to sustain essential ship systems and the massive energy levels required to keep Cryochambers functioning.
IF THE PODS SHUT DOWN, WILL THE COLONISTS WAKE?
THERE IS AN AUTOMATED REVIVAL PROTOCOL... IF THE CRYOCHAMBER WERE TO JUST SHUT DOWN, THEY'D ALL DIE!
ESSIE, WHAT IF WE CHANNELED THE REMAINING POWER TO THE CRYODECK AND USE THAT SECTION'S LOADING JETS AS A PROPULSION SYSTEM?
Calculating--

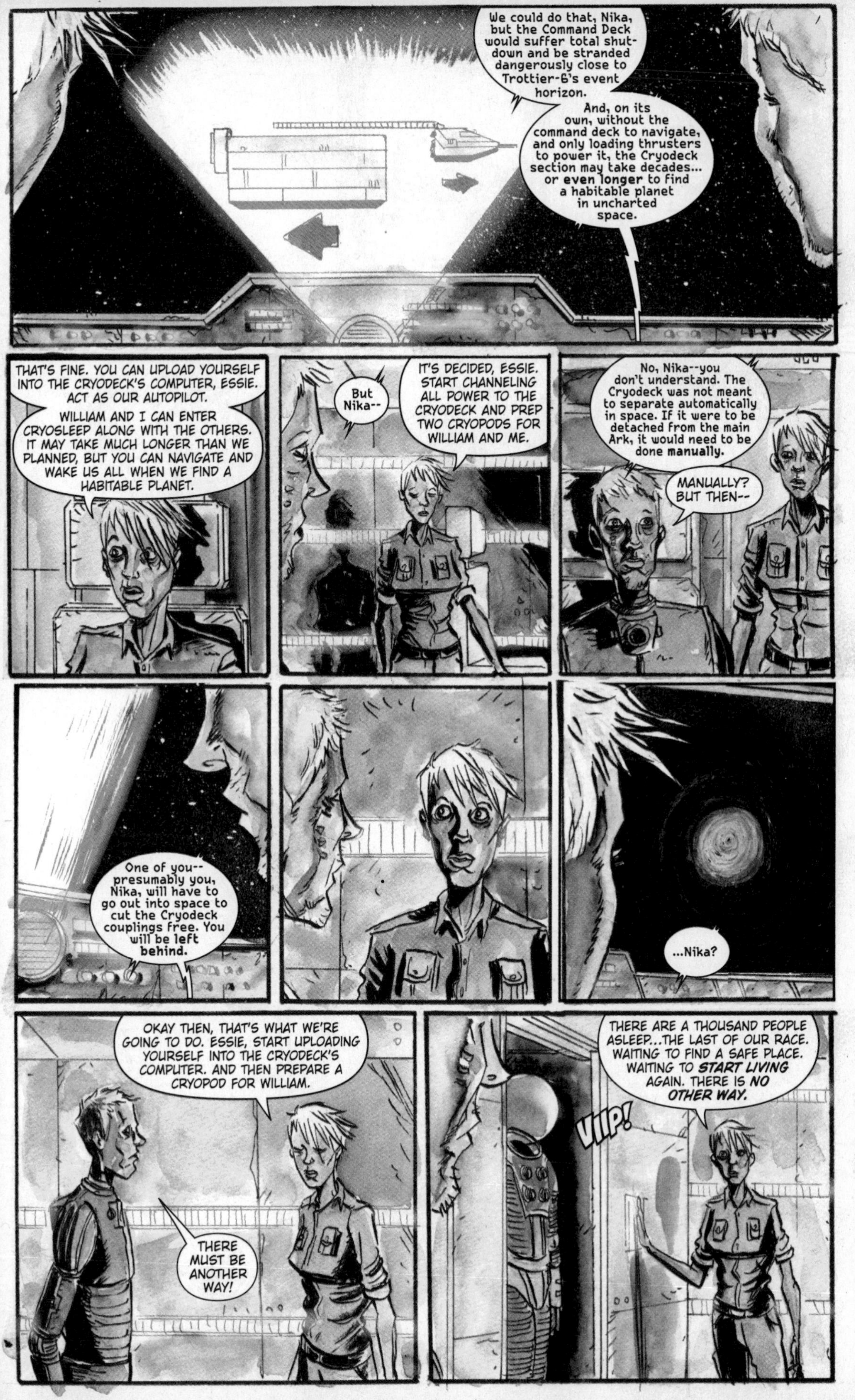
We could do that, Nika, but the Command Deck would suffer total shut-down and be stranded dangerously close to Trottier-6's event horizon.
And, on its own, without the command deck to navigate, and only loading thrusters to power it, the Cryodeck section may take decades... or even longer to find a habitable planet in uncharted space.
THAT'S FINE. YOU CAN UPLOAD YOURSELF INTO THE CRYODECK'S COMPUTER, ESSIE. ACT AS OUR AUTOPILOT.
WILLIAM AND I CAN ENTER CRYOSLEEP ALONG WITH THE OTHERS. IT MAY TAKE MUCH LONGER THAN WE PLANNED, BUT YOU CAN NAVIGATE AND WAKE US ALL WHEN WE FIND A HABITABLE PLANET.
But Nika--
IT'S DECIDED, ESSIE. START CHANNELING ALL POWER TO THE CRYODECK AND PREP TWO CRYOPODS FOR WILLIAM AND ME.
No, Nika--you don't understand. The Cryodeck was not meant to separate automatically in space. If it were to be detached from the main Ark, it would need to be done manually.
MANUALLY? BUT THEN--
One of you--presumably you, Nika, will have to go out into space to cut the Cryodeck couplings free. You will be left behind.
...Nika?
OKAY THEN, THAT'S WHAT WE'RE GOING TO DO. ESSIE, START UPLOADING YOURSELF INTO THE CRYODECK'S COMPUTER. AND THEN PREPARE A CRYOPOD FOR WILLIAM.
THERE MUST BE ANOTHER WAY!
THERE ARE A THOUSAND PEOPLE ASLEEP...THE LAST OF OUR RACE. WAITING TO FIND A SAFE PLACE. WAITING TO START LIVING AGAIN. THERE IS NO OTHER WAY.
VIIP!

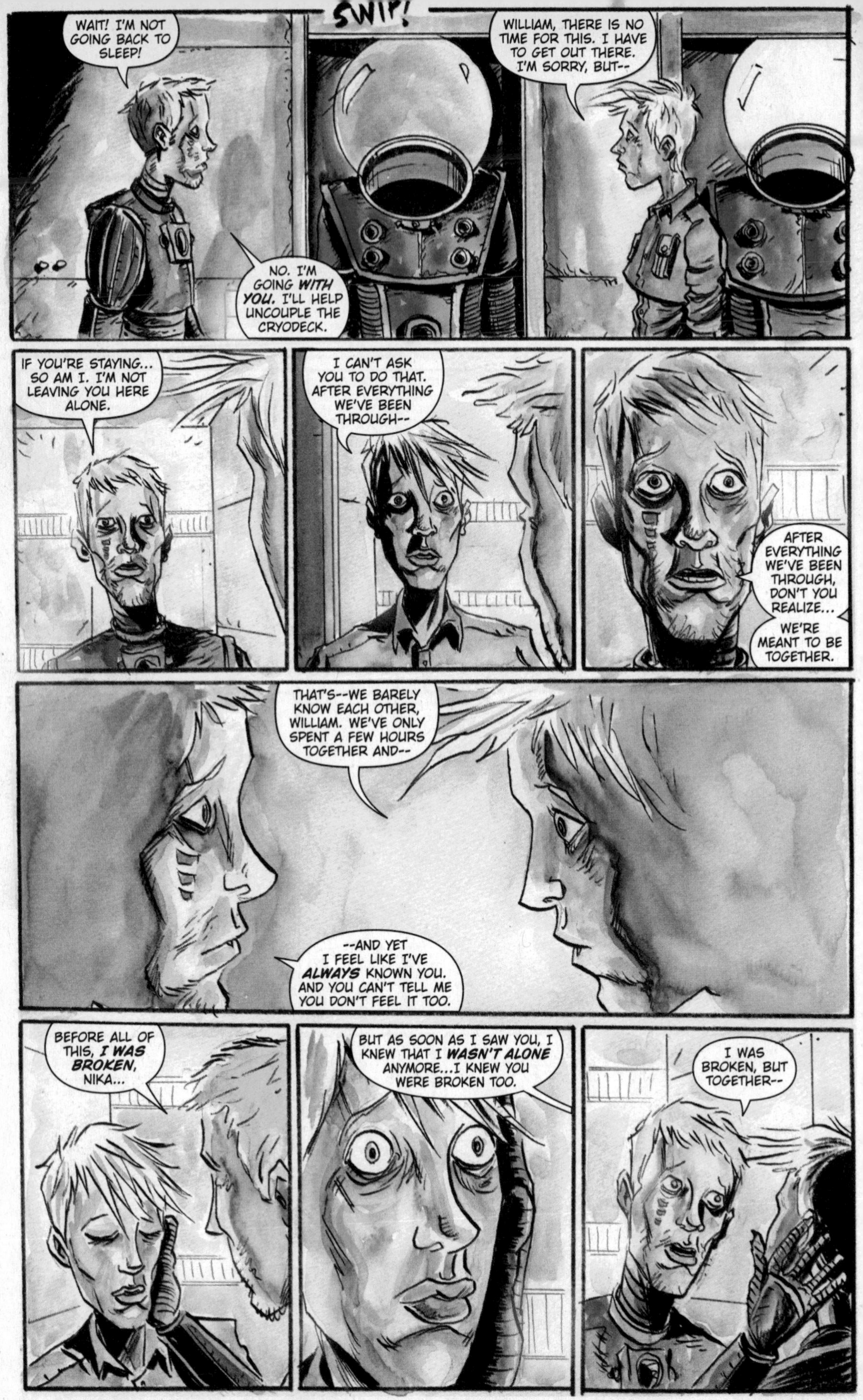
SWIP!
WAIT! I'M NOT GOING BACK TO SLEEP!
NO. I'M GOING WITH YOU. I'LL HELP UNCOUPLE THE CRYODECK.
WILLIAM, THERE IS NO TIME FOR THIS. I HAVE TO GET OUT THERE. I'M SORRY, BUT--
IF YOU'RE STAYING... SO AM I. I'M NOT LEAVING YOU HERE ALONE.
I CAN'T ASK YOU TO DO THAT. AFTER EVERYTHING WE'VE BEEN THROUGH--
AFTER EVERYTHING WE'VE BEEN THROUGH, DON'T YOU REALIZE...
WE'RE MEANT TO BE TOGETHER.
THAT'S--WE BARELY KNOW EACH OTHER, WILLIAM. WE'VE ONLY SPENT A FEW HOURS TOGETHER AND--
--AND YET I FEEL LIKE I'VE ALWAYS KNOWN YOU. AND YOU CAN'T TELL ME YOU DON'T FEEL IT TOO.
BEFORE ALL OF THIS, I WAS BROKEN, NIKA...
BUT AS SOON AS I SAW YOU, I KNEW THAT I WASN'T ALONE ANYMORE...I KNEW YOU WERE BROKEN TOO.
I WAS BROKEN, BUT TOGETHER--

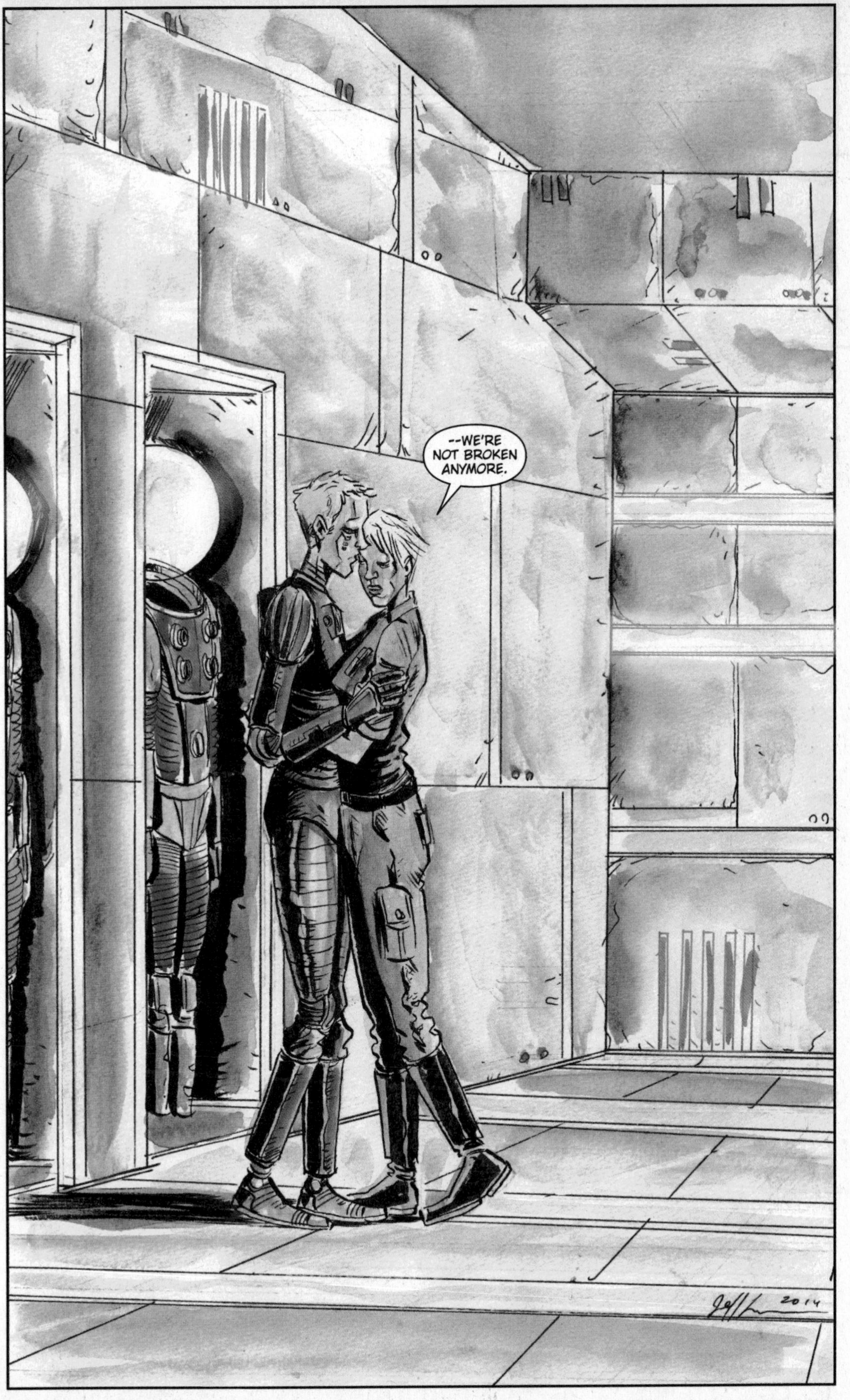
--WE'RE NOT BROKEN ANYMORE.

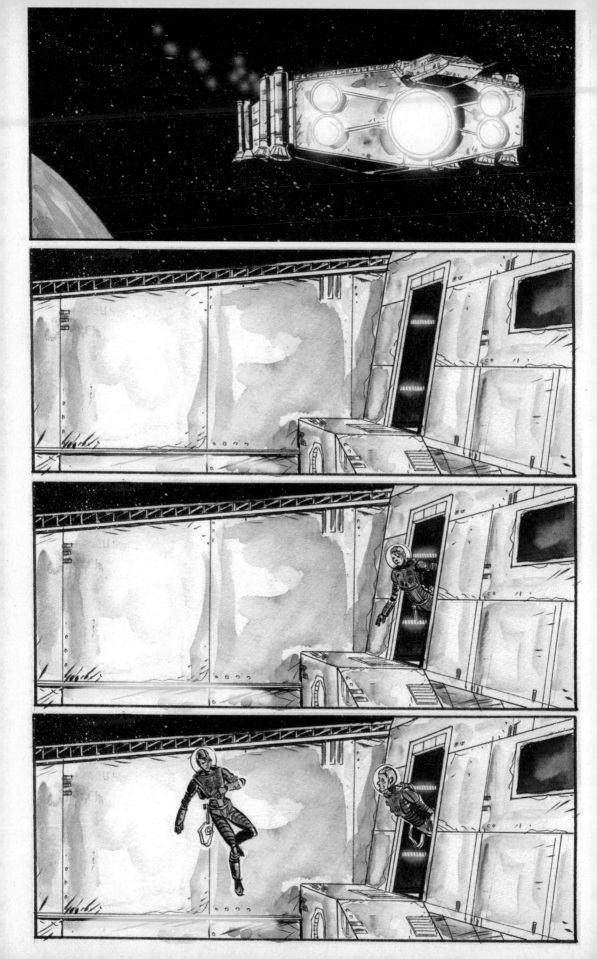

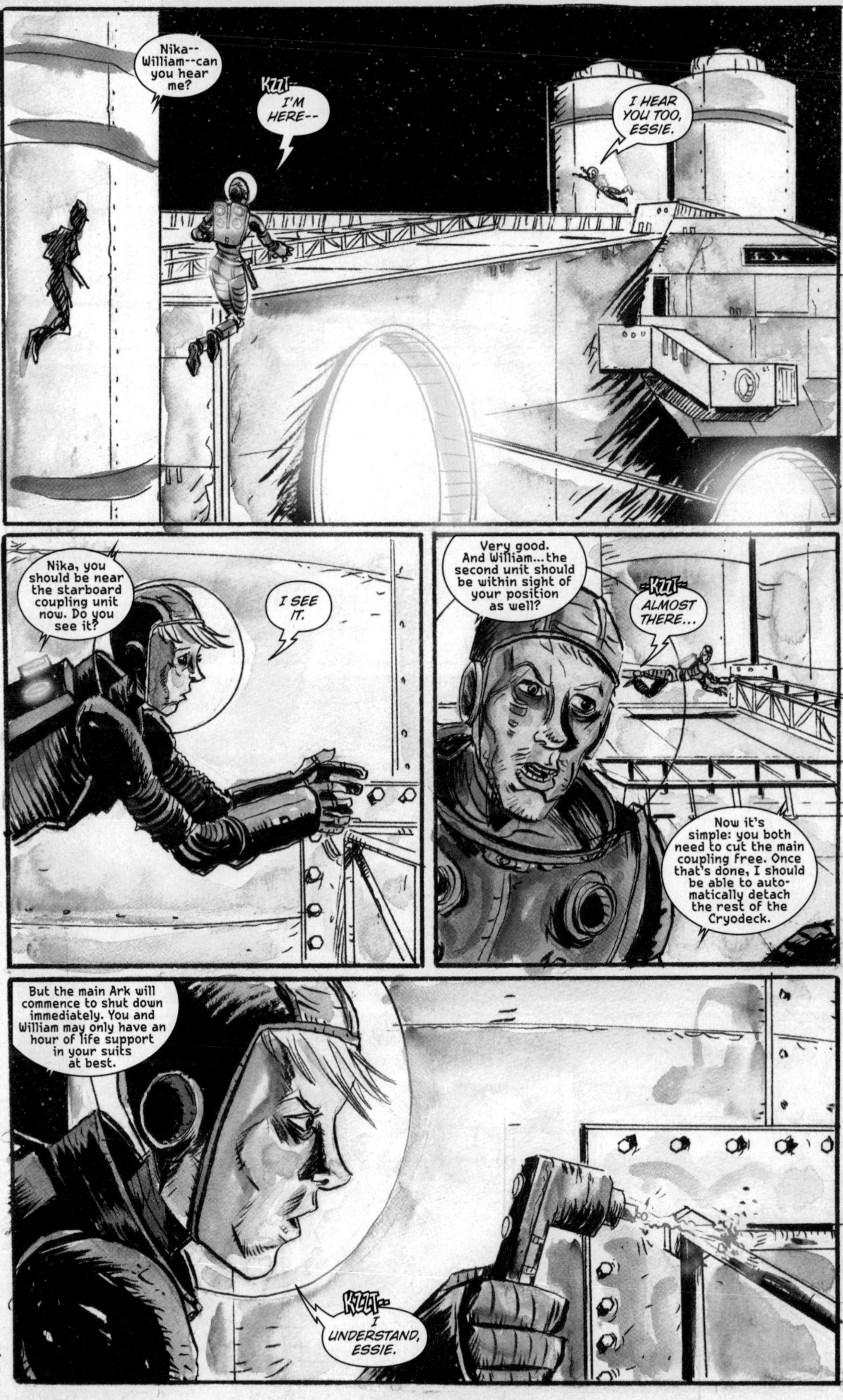
Nika--William--can you hear me?
KZZT-- I'M HERE--
I HEAR YOU TOO, ESSIE.
Nika, you should be near the starboard coupling unit now. Do you see it?
I SEE IT.
Very good. And William...the second unit should be within sight of your position as well?
-KZZT- ALMOST THERE...
Now it's simple: you both need to cut the main coupling free. Once that's done, I should be able to automatically detach the rest of the Cryodeck.
But the main Ark will commence to shut down immediately. You and William may only have an hour of life support in your suits at best.
KZZT-- I UNDERSTAND, ESSIE.

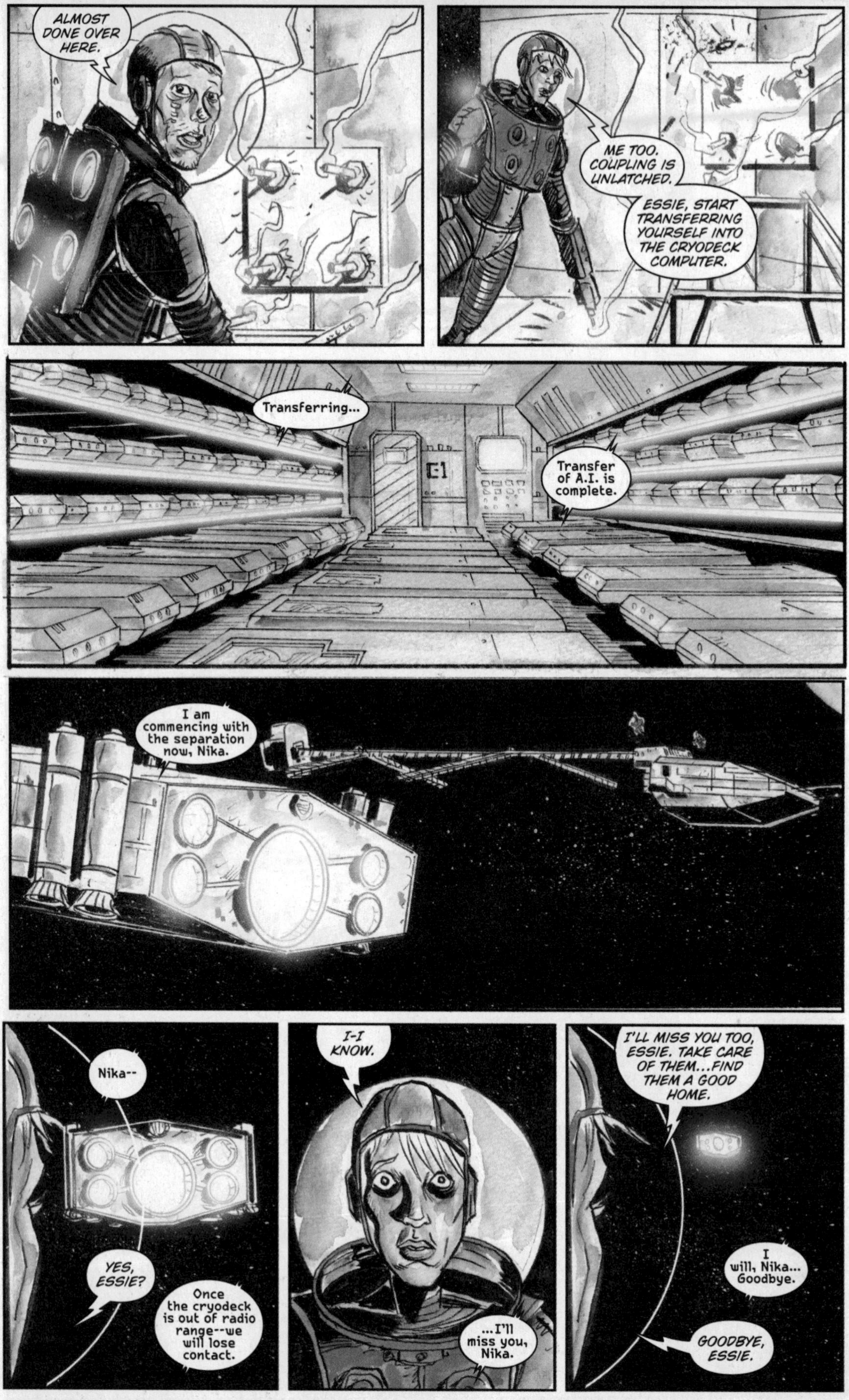
ALMOST DONE OVER HERE.
ME TOO. COUPLING IS UNLATCHED.
ESSIE, START TRANSFERRING YOURSELF INTO THE CRYODECK COMPUTER.
Transferring...
Transfer of A.I. is complete.
I am commencing with the separation now, Nika.
Nika--
YES, ESSIE?
Once the cryodeck is out of radio range--we will lose contact.
I-I KNOW.
...I'll miss you, Nika.
I'LL MISS YOU TOO, ESSIE. TAKE CARE OF THEM...FIND THEM A GOOD HOME.
I will, Nika... Goodbye.
GOODBYE, ESSIE.

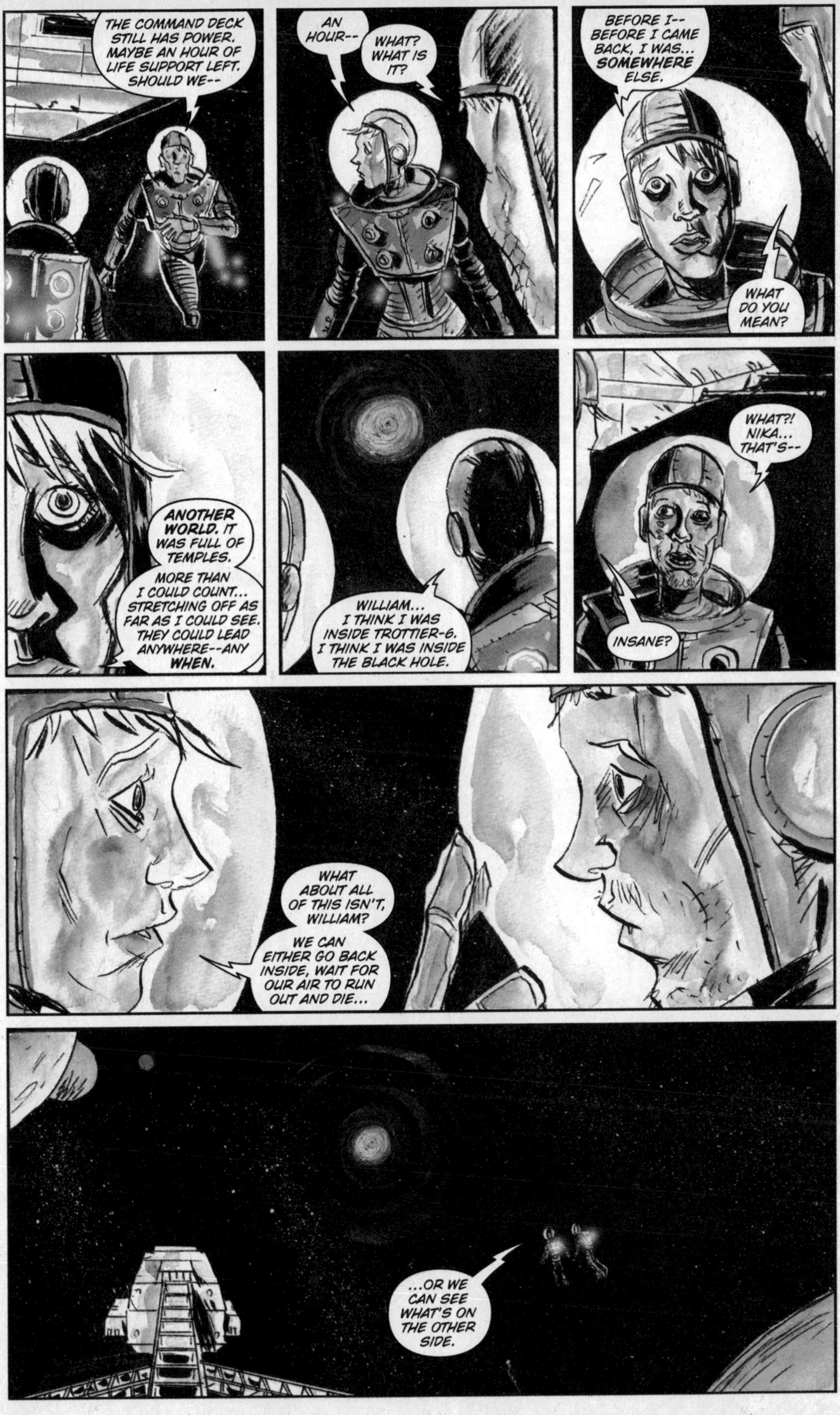
THE COMMAND DECK STILL HAS POWER. MAYBE AN HOUR OF LIFE SUPPORT LEFT. SHOULD WE--
AN HOUR--
WHAT? WHAT IS IT?
BEFORE I-- BEFORE I CAME BACK, I WAS... SOMEWHERE ELSE.
WHAT DO YOU MEAN?
ANOTHER WORLD. IT WAS FULL OF TEMPLES.
MORE THAN I COULD COUNT... STRETCHING OFF AS FAR AS I COULD SEE. THEY COULD LEAD ANYWHERE--ANY WHEN.
WILLIAM... I THINK I WAS INSIDE TROTTIER-6. I THINK I WAS INSIDE THE BLACK HOLE.
WHAT?! NIKA... THAT'S--
INSANE?
WHAT ABOUT ALL OF THIS ISN'T, WILLIAM?
WE CAN EITHER GO BACK INSIDE, WAIT FOR OUR AIR TO RUN OUT AND DIE...
...OR WE CAN SEE WHAT'S ON THE OTHER SIDE.

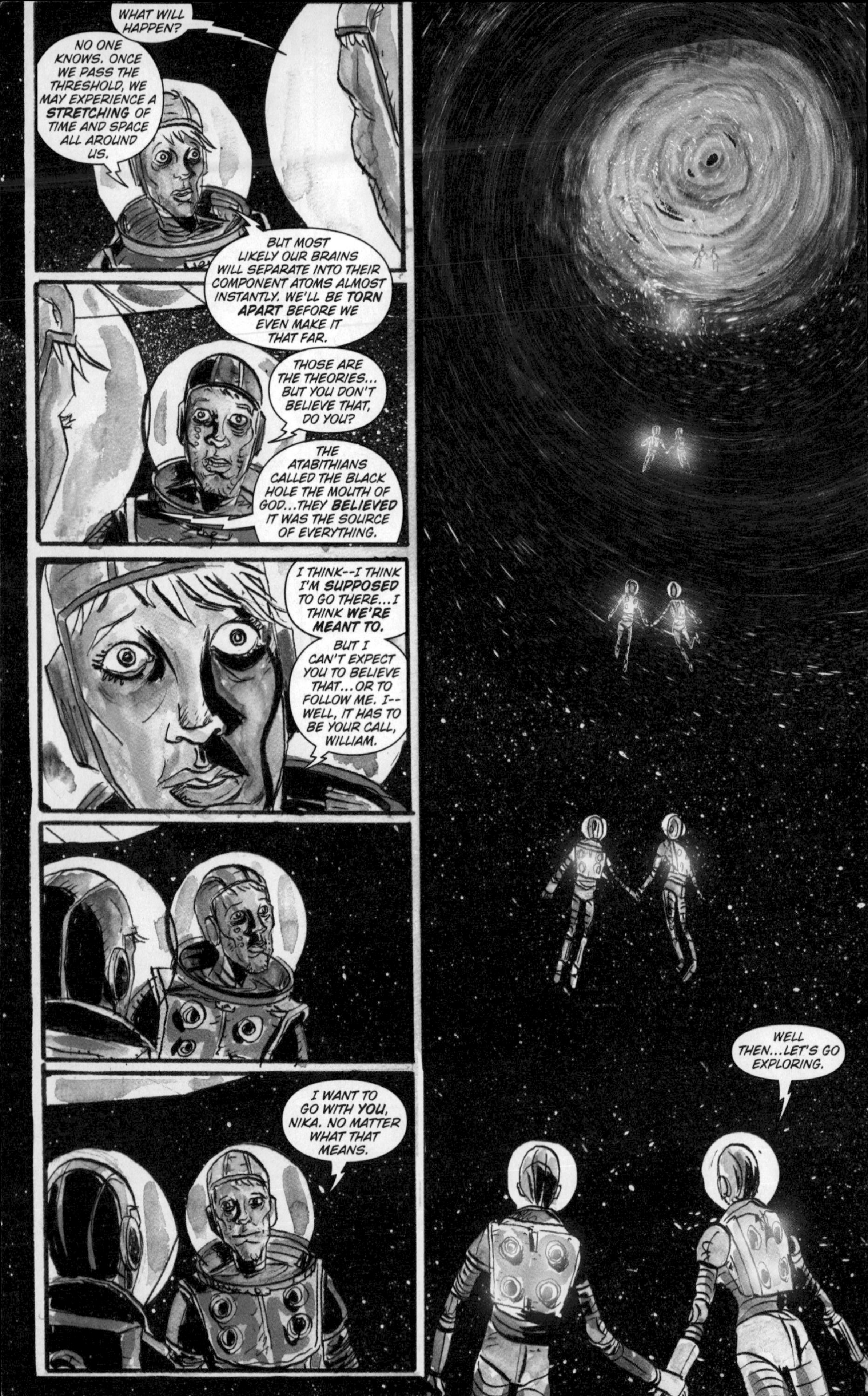
WHAT WILL HAPPEN?
NO ONE KNOWS. ONCE WE PASS THE THRESHOLD, WE MAY EXPERIENCE A STRETCHING OF TIME AND SPACE ALL AROUND US.
BUT MOST LIKELY OUR BRAINS WILL SEPARATE INTO THEIR COMPONENT ATOMS ALMOST INSTANTLY. WE'LL BE TORN APART BEFORE WE EVEN MAKE IT THAT FAR.
THOSE ARE THE THEORIES... BUT YOU DON'T BELIEVE THAT, DO YOU?
THE ATABITHIANS CALLED THE BLACK HOLE THE MOUTH OF GOD...THEY BELIEVED IT WAS THE SOURCE OF EVERYTHING.
I THINK--I THINK I'M SUPPOSED TO GO THERE...I THINK WE'RE MEANT TO.
BUT I CAN'T EXPECT YOU TO BELIEVE THAT...OR TO FOLLOW ME. I-- WELL, IT HAS TO BE YOUR CALL, WILLIAM.
I WANT TO GO WITH YOU, NIKA. NO MATTER WHAT THAT MEANS.
WELL THEN...LET'S GO EXPLORING.

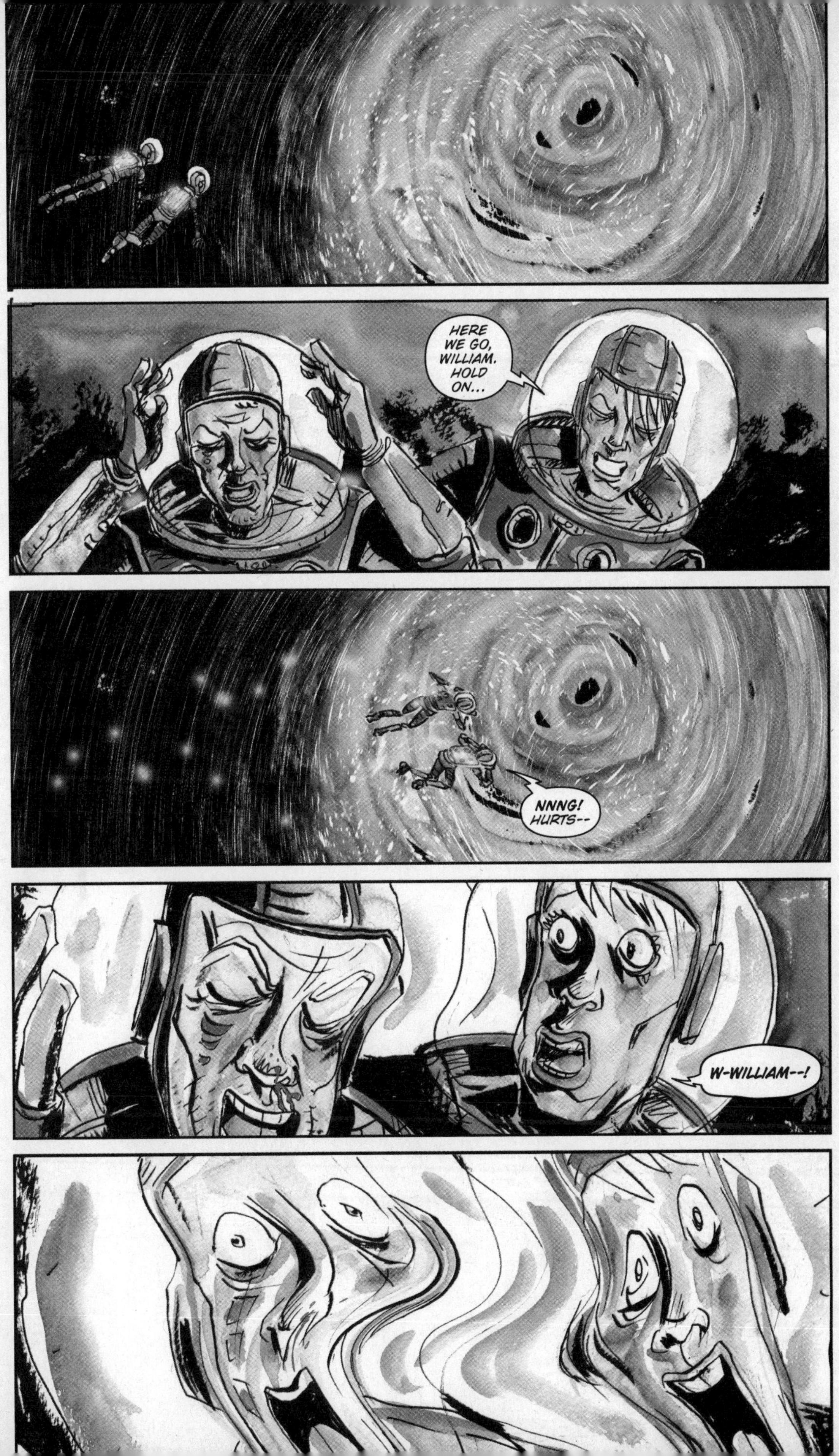
HERE WE GO, WILLIAM. HOLD ON...
NNNG! HURTS--
W-WILLIAM--!

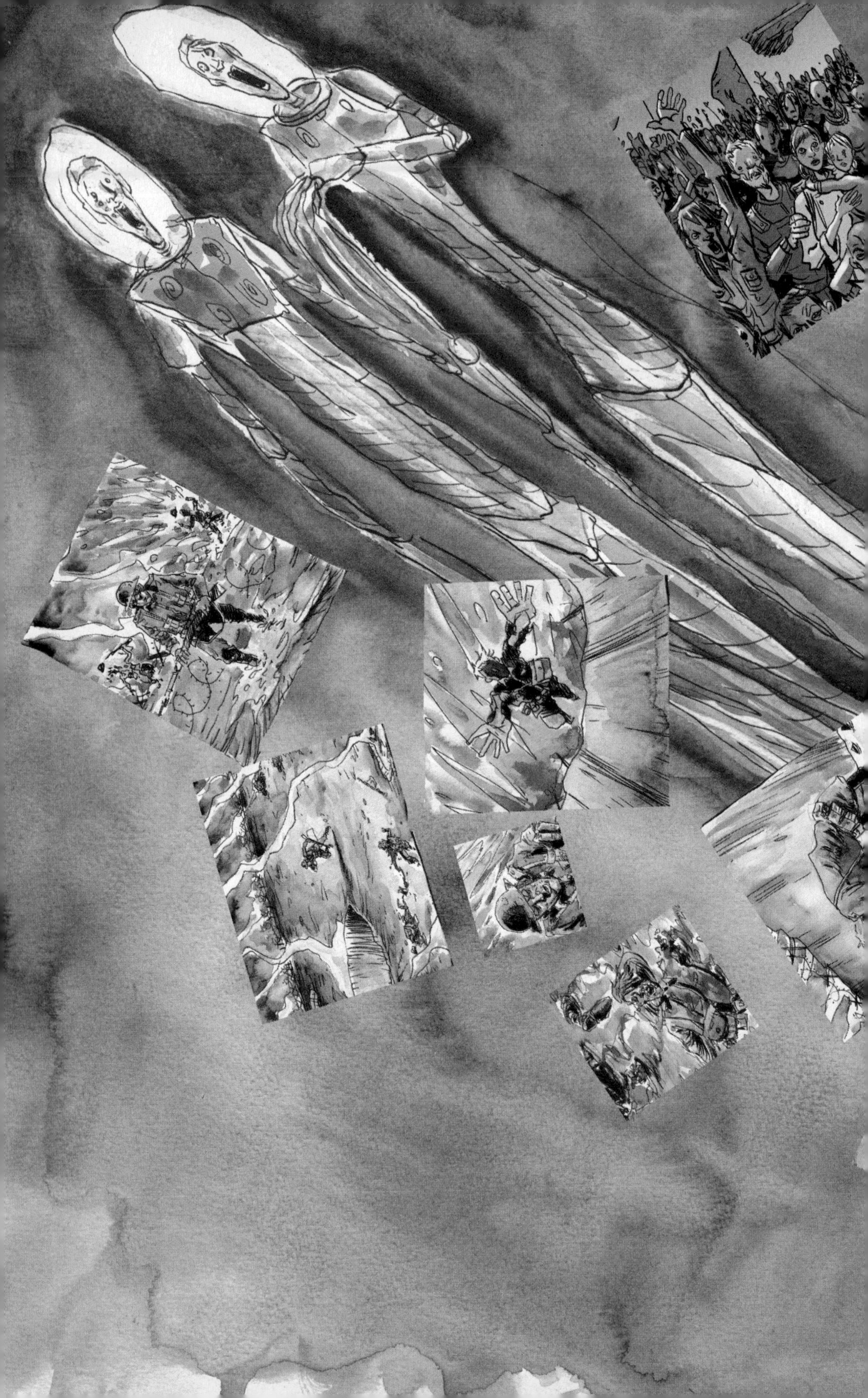

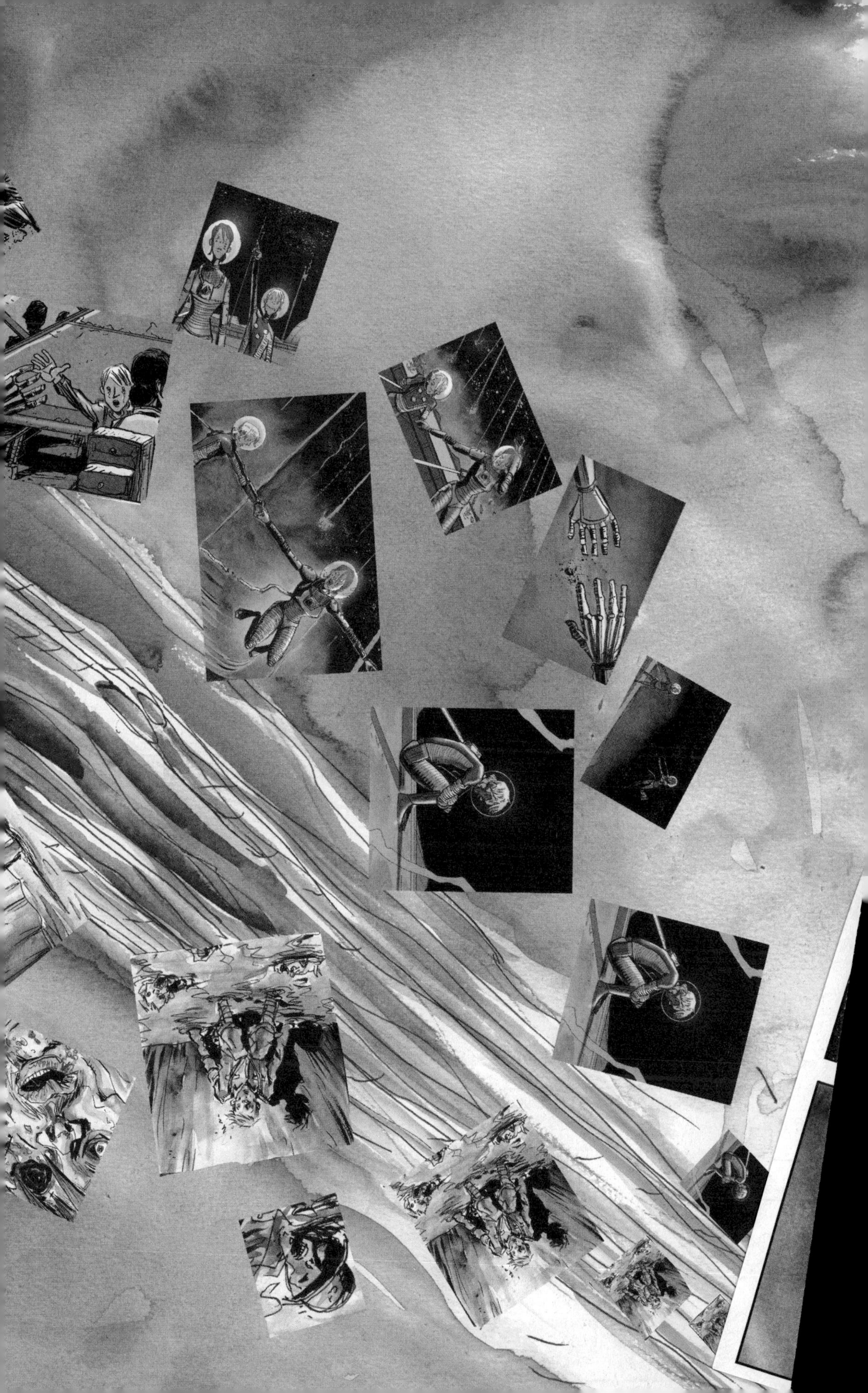

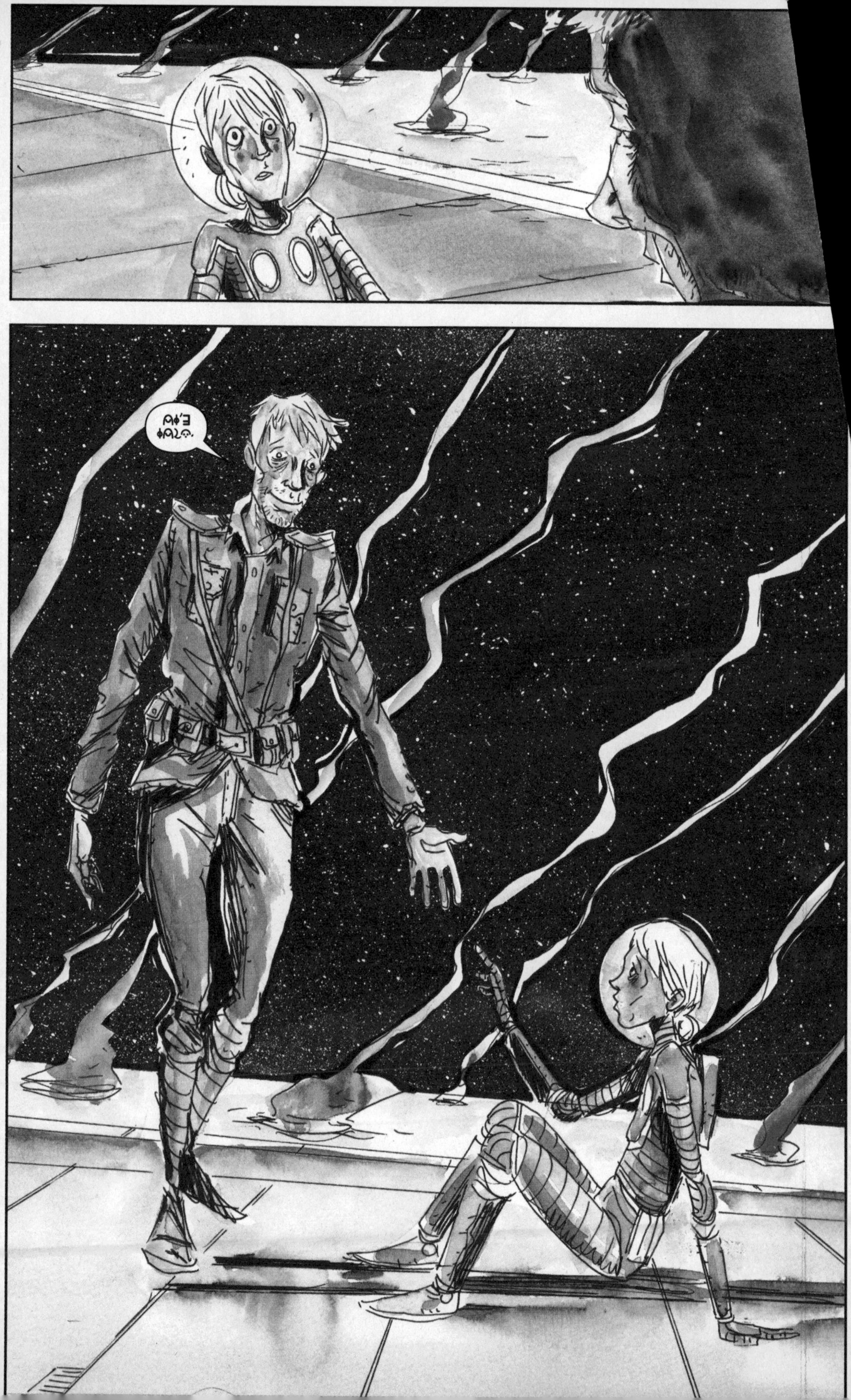

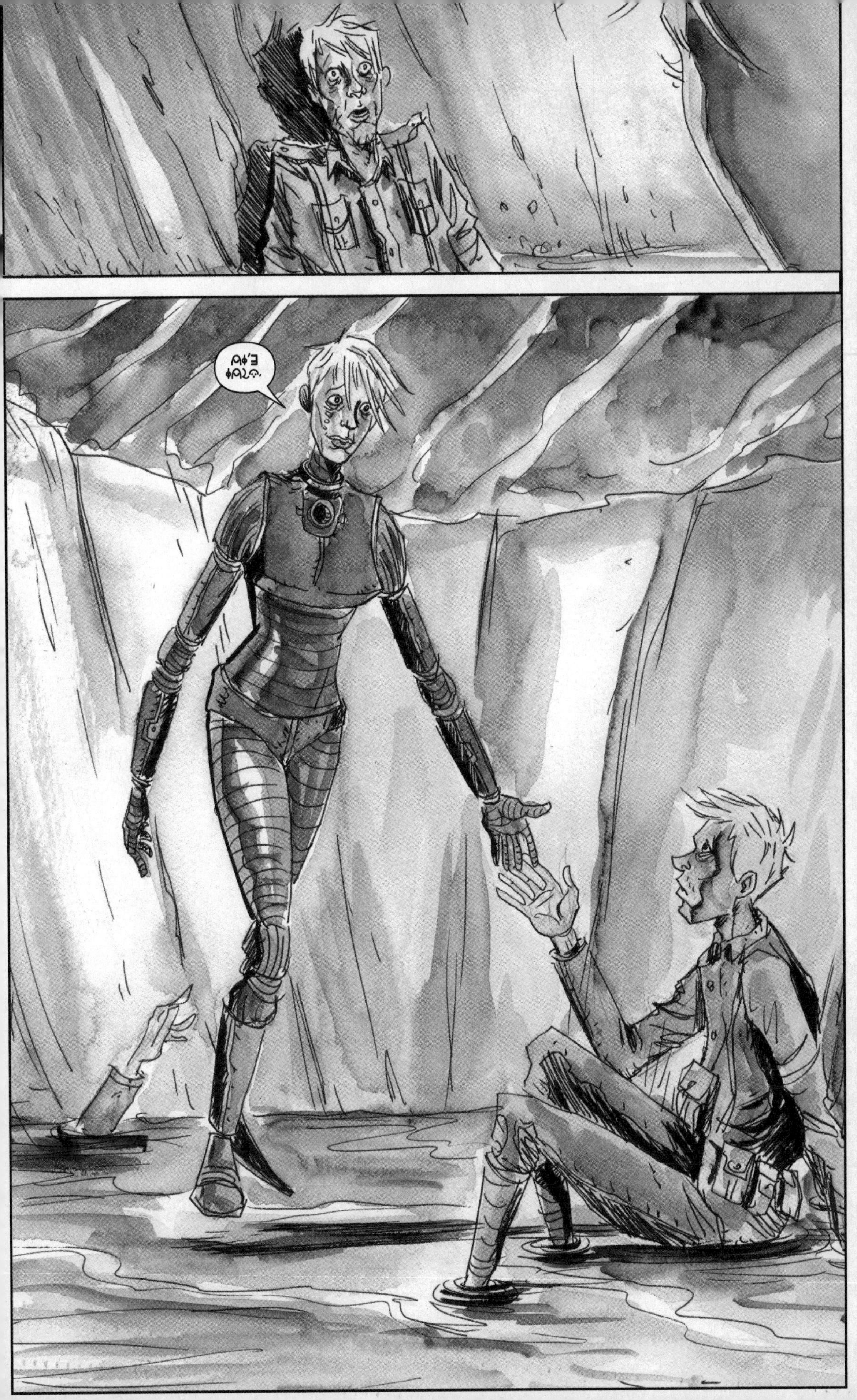

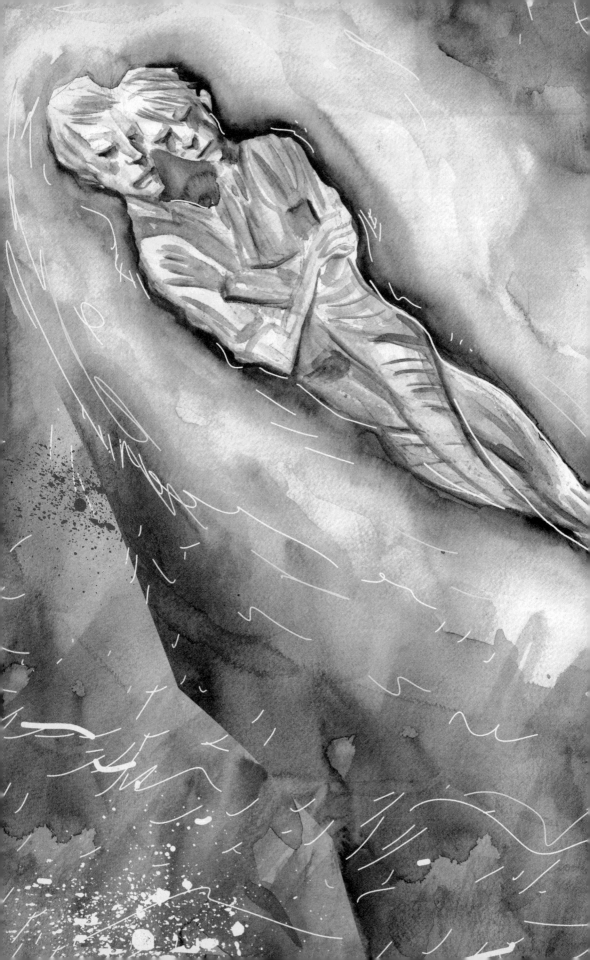

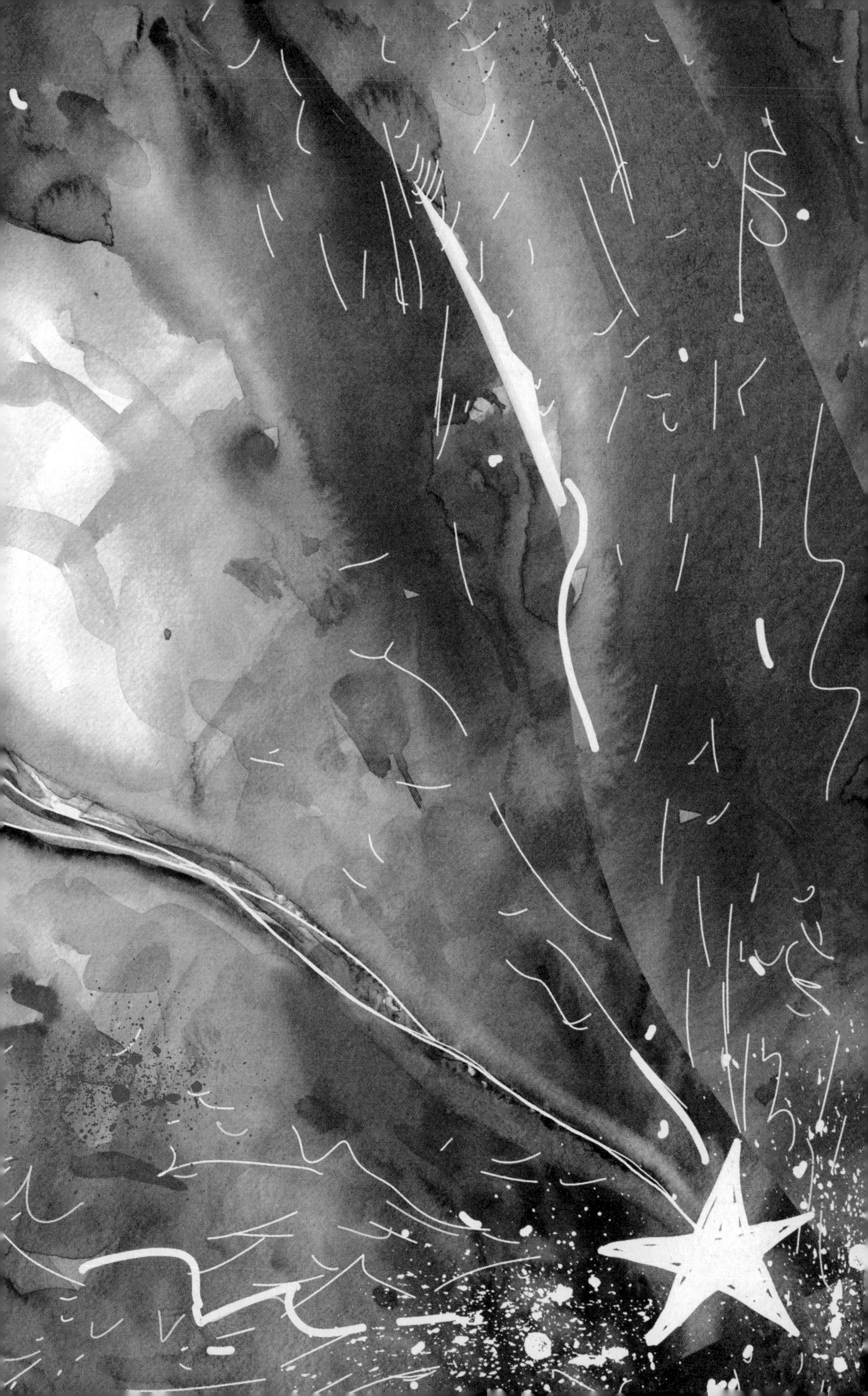

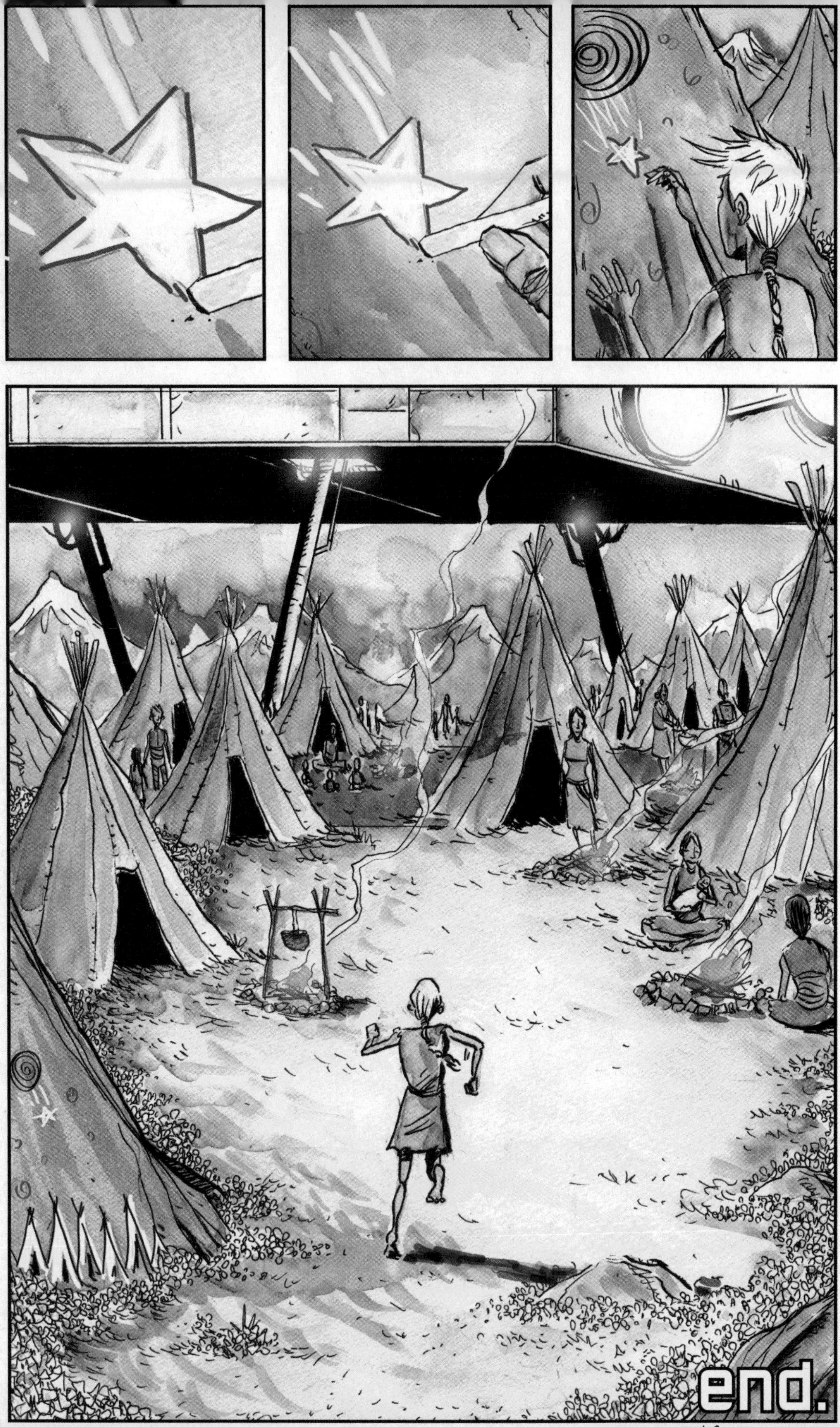
end.

TRILLIUM

Jeff Lemire

JEFF LEMIRE AND CHRIS ROSS ON THE ATABITHIAN FONT

"I wanted the language of the Atabithian alien race to be very visual. Less like letters or characters and more like glyphs. So, I enlisted a good friend of mine, Chris Ross, letterer and book designer, to take my drawings from the Atabithian wall and build a font. Chris did a fantastic job creating a really unique-looking design that became an essential part of not only the look of Trillium but the story as well."
--JEFF

"I had originally envisioned a 'stacking' language like Tibetan or Sanskrit that were components of a unified glyph, but Jeff wanted a letter-swap language so folks could decode and have fun with it more easily. Jeff also let me know that the Atabithians had three fingers, so I started out with their language being a base six numbering language. The numbering system I envisioned the Atabithians having was gestures, so the glyphs for their numbering reflects that. And like some cultures, their concept of zero would be representative of both "nothing" and "everything." There was a possibility of going down the Klingon-build-a-language-from-scratch rabbit hole, but I think Jeff's sense of making it accessible for folks to use or read was the best way to go."
--CHRIS

atabithian

--- A
--- B
--- C
--- D
--- E
--- F
--- G
--- H
--- I
--- J
--- K
--- L
--- M
--- N
--- O
--- P
--- Q
--- R
--- S
--- T
--- U
--- V
--- W
--- X
--- Y
--- Z

Find out more about building new worlds and languages by following Chris on Twitter @chrisross and checking out Jeff's blog, jefflemire.blogspot.com

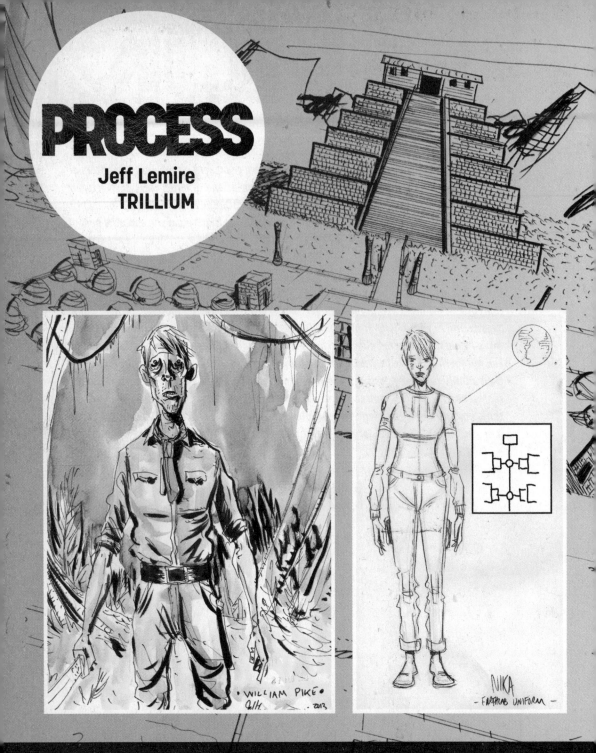

PROCESS

Jeff Lemire
TRILLIUM

WILLIAM PIKE 2013

NIKA
– EARTHLAB UNIFORM –

"World Building" is something I've never really had a chance to do. At least not as an artist. All of my creator-owned work to date has, for the most part, been very much grounded in reality and set in rural landscapes. Even SWEET TOOTH with all of its science-fiction elements was still very much set in the "real world." So one of the most exciting and rewarding aspects of working on TRILLIUM was the ability to step outside of the known world and quite literally design a new one.

I've been a fan of sci-fi since I was a kid, and getting the chance to make up my own spacesuits and space stations, design my own alien races, has been incredibly fun. Shown here are a few of my early designs for the futuristic world of TRILLIUM. I realized early on that as much as I wish I could, my art style just doesn't have the level of detail or "realism" that many other great sci-fi designers had. But I embraced that and I think the end result is something very

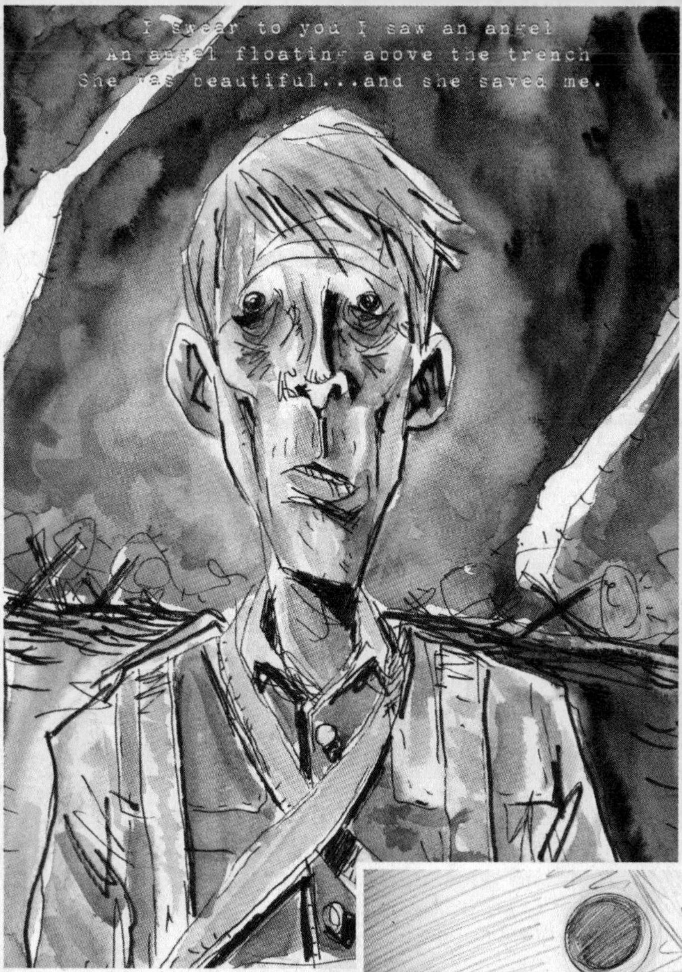
I swear to you I saw an angel
An angel floating above the trench
She was beautiful...and she saved me.

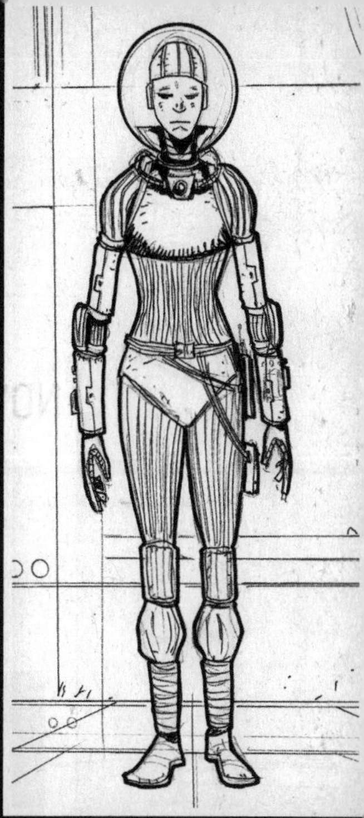

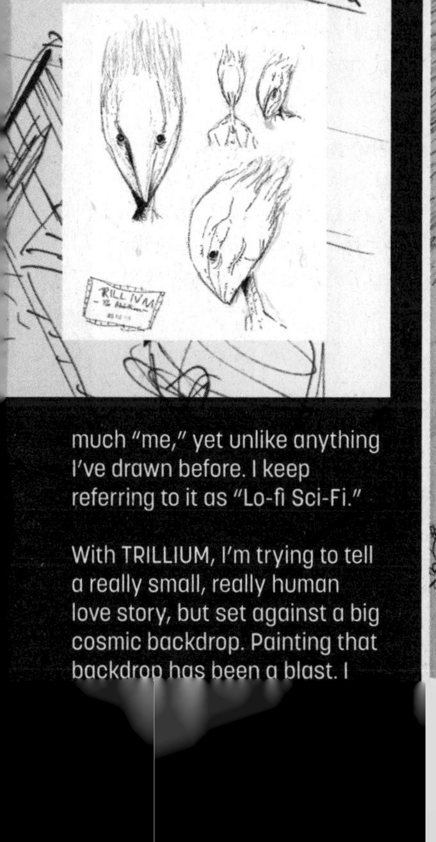

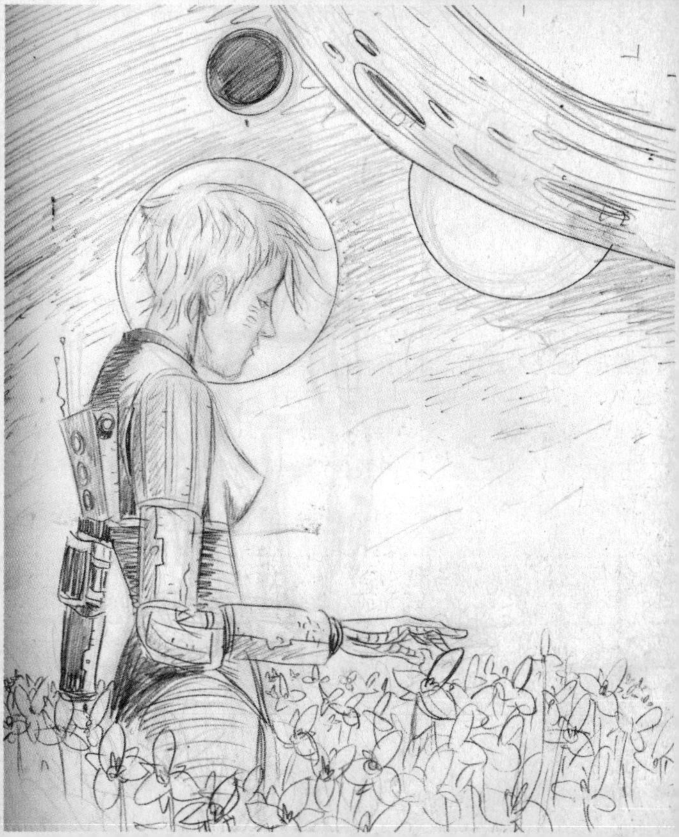

much "me," yet unlike anything I've drawn before. I keep referring to it as "Lo-fi Sci-Fi."

With TRILLIUM, I'm trying to tell a really small, really human love story, but set against a big cosmic backdrop. Painting that backdrop has been a blast. I

NOV 2 0 2014

New York Times Bestselling author Jeff Lemire is the creator of the acclaimed graphic novels SWEET TOOTH, *Essex County*, *The Underwater Welder* and the sci-fi love story, TRILLIUM.

His next original graphic novel will be *Roughneck* from Simon and Schuster.

Jeff is also a prominent writer for DC Comics where he currently writes the monthly adventures of GREEN ARROW and JUSTICE LEAGUE UNITED. He has also written the monthly adventures of ANIMAL MAN and SUPERBOY among many others.

In 2008 and in 2013, Jeff won the Schuster Award for Best Canadian Cartoonist. He has also received The Doug Wright Award for Best Emerging Talent and the American Library Association's prestigious Alex Award, recognizing books for adults with specific teen appeal. He has also been nominated for 8 Eisner awards, 7 Harvey Awards and 8 Shuster Awards.

In 2010, *Essex County* was named as one of the five [Essential Canadian Novels of the Decade.]

He currently lives and works in Toronto with his wife and son.